The Federal Interest in
Financing Schooling

List of Contributors

Stephen M. Barro
Paul Berman
Lawrence L. Brown
John J. Callahan
Stephen J. Carroll
Alan L. Ginsburg
Robert J. Goettel
Betsy Levin
Milbrey Wallin McLaughlin
Michael Timpane
Mary Vogel
William H. Wilken

A Rand Educational Policy Study

The Federal Interest in Financing Schooling

Edited by
Michael Timpane

Ballinger Publishing Company ● **Cambridge, Massachusetts**
A Subsidiary of Harper & Row, Publishers, Inc.

Copyright © 1978 by The Rand Corporation. All rights reserved. No part of this publication may be reproduced, stored in a retrieval system, or transmitted in any form or by any means, electronic mechanical photocopy, recording or otherwise, without the prior written consent of the publisher.

International Standard Book Number: 0-88410-184-3

Library of Congress Catalog Card Number: 78-5563

Printed in the United States of America

Library of Congress Cataloging in Publication Data

Symposium on the Federal Interest in Financing Schooling, Washington, D.C., 1976.
The Federal interest in financing schooling.

(A Rand educational policy study)
Sponsored by the Rand Corporation's Center for Educational Finance and Governance.
1. Federal aid to education—United States—Congresses. 2. Education—United States—Finance—Congresses. I. Timpane, P. Michael, 1934- II. Rand Corporation. Center for Educational Finance and Governance. III. Title. IV. Series: Rand educational policy study series.

LB2825.S9 1976   379'.121'0973   78-5563
ISBN 0-88410-184-3

Contents

List of Tables

Preface

The federal role in financing elementary and secondary education is perennially disputed among politicians and educators. It also appears that the debate will flourish at least for the remainder of the 1970s as Washington's education policymakers struggle to discover worthwhile revisions and additions to the federal Elementary and Secondary Education Act (ESEA). But what is so far missing from the debate is a comprehensive and systematic review by the scholars and policy analysts who have tried to discover the workings of the education system in all of its political, sociological, economic, and educational complexity.

This volume is an attempt at such a systematic review. Each chapter was originally presented at a symposium, The Federal Interest in Financing Schooling, which was sponsored by The Rand Corporation's Center for Educational Finance and Governance and held at Rand's Washington office on September 23-24, 1976. The symposium was attended by approximately thirty-five researchers and legislative aides and policy analysts deeply involved in the Washington education policy debate. The versions of the papers in this book include revisions that the authors have since made in light of two days of vigorous discussion at the symposium.

The work of the Center for Educational Finance and Governance is supported by the Office of the Assistant Secretary for Education, U.S. Department of Health, Education and Welfare, under Contract 300-76-0065. The views expressed herein do not, of course, reflect the views of the sponsoring agency.

Introduction and Summary

Michael Timpane
Mary Vogel

In the face of growing public concern about the quality and distribution of educational opportunities available to American youths in the 1960s, the federal government expanded its role in financing elementary and secondary education. This process of development has been encompassed mainly in the enactment and subsequent expansion and amendment of the Elementary and Secondary Education Act of 1965 (ESEA). Older federal programs for vocational education and for aid to areas impacted by federal activities have also been overhauled and expanded. During the past decade, federal expenditures for these educational purposes have increased roughly 100 percent, rising from $2 billion in fiscal year 1966 to a total of more than $4 billion in fiscal year 1976. Extensive changes in state and local practice—both educational and managerial—have stemmed from these federal efforts. These educational innovations have produced some widely proclaimed successes and failures, as well as some difficult lessons in the limits of federal influence and capacity.

For future policy development, the past experience raises a series of questions pertaining to definition and implementation of a meaningful federal role. Among the chief points raised are the following: What limits (if any) should be established for the federal involvement in education? Where should the federal government concentrate its financial support for education and how substantial should that funding be? What mix of regulatory standards and fiscal incentives should characterize the federal repertoire of policy instruments? How well are existing resource distribution and control provisions, contained in the categorical grant programs, complied with by states and local districts? Are existing grant control provisions necessary and sufficient to achieve federal resource allocation goals if these provision are strictly followed? How can the federal government tailor its assistance to provide effective support for the implementation of local projects? Can federal policy accommodate variation among the states in goals, management capability, and fiscal capacity? Can federal policy be integrated more successfully with state education efforts? How can federal policy respond more readily and systematically to changing education problems, to progress or decline in the capabilities of state agencies, and to shifts in federal program impacts as the federal programs themselves mature?

The main purpose of the Rand symposium, The Federal Interest in Financing Schooling,[a] was to review these issues systematically. The design and implementation of individual federal interventions has been inspected by much research, but relatively little has been done to synthesize this knowledge and to extract implications for the development of a more coherent and comprehensive federal role for the financing of schooling. The reauthorization of ESEA has been the chief topic on the congressional educational agenda for the past two years. Bills now passed by the House and Senate (in 1978) respond to many of the types of changes discussed here, but consideration of other changes has been deferred until the next reauthorization, a few years hence.

For the symposium, the Rand Corporation commissioned eight separate studies on selected aspects of the financing and management of federal education programs. The authors and symposium discussants were challenged to respond to three questions: First, given what you know about federal goals for education, how appropriate are the areas in which federal involvement is currently concentrated? Second, how effective are existing federal policy instruments in achieving those goals? Third, as we turn to the future, what changes in the federal role in financing schooling should we attempt to make?

In the first of the following papers, Timpane presents an overview of the goals, context, and problems of federal education policy since 1965—thereby providing a perspective and organization for subsequent discussion. He emphasizes the role that external factors, like demographic shifts, economic conditions, and public support for federal social policy, have had and will have upon the development of federal education policy. Levin examines the role of the courts as educational policymakers in their own right. She notes that court rulings constitute another major contextual element to be considered in the development and design of federal programs. Callahan and Wilken treat the topic of federal-state relations in education, note extensive changes in the patterns of state policymaking, and cite a pressing need for improved integration of federal and state activities. Carroll probes the limits of the federal role by exploring involvement in the labor market for teachers as one possible new

---

[a]The Rand Symposium, the Federal Interest in Financing Schooling, a two-day gathering of approximately thirty-five researchers, legislative aides, and policy analysts, was held in the Washington, D.C., office of The Rand Corporation in September 1976 under the auspices of the Rand Center on Educational Finance and Governance.

zone for federal intervention. Brown and Ginsburg press the boundary question still further with an examination of a potential role for the federal government in the disbursement of general purpose aid. Turning to implementation of the grant programs, both Goettel and Rand analysts Berman and McLaughlin scrutinize current patterns of state and local compliance with federal intent under the present categorical system of grants-in-aid. Goettel considers state compliance with respect to the allocation of ESEA Title I funds and finds considerable recent progress. Berman and McLaughlin address compliance at the level of the local district—arguing that even if funds are allocated in keeping with federal goals, local performance in the project implementation process effectively dominates programmatic outcomes and must be a topic of vital federal concern. Finally, Barro questions whether several of the existing resource control provisions in federal education programs are actually sufficient for the achievement of the federal goals; he suggests possibly broad implications for federal-state relations of the seemingly far-reaching intent of recent federal attempts to extend the allocative controls of federal education law.

In keeping with the mandate of the Rand Policy Center, the commissioned papers involve little original data collection;[b] instead, they attempt to organize and synthesize the results of previous research. The main ambition of the discussion that follows is to begin to create a framework for considering the future development of federal programs supporting elementary and secondary schooling. Much of the emphasis is on the allocation, distribution, and implementation of federal grants-in-aid. Other issues like educational and economic outcomes for students require separate attention.

The discussion that follows is a report on the proceedings of the symposium. It begins by describing the status of federal education activities today and goes on to address the main issues raised by the symposium that relate to definition of a federal role, developments in federal-state relations, and local performance of federal objectives.

THE FEDERAL ROLE IN ELEMENTARY AND SECONDARY EDUCATION

The expansion of the federal role in education signaled by the passage of the Elementary and Secondary Education Act of 1965 was achieved by an unusual convergence of interests and by the convergence at the same time of several crucial external forces. Among the external forces were swelling school enrollments caused by the entry of the postwar baby boom and by lower dropout rates, the economy's needs for an increased supply of highly skilled human capital, public demand for improved educational opportunities, and judicial

---

[b]The exception is Robert Goettel's paper, which contains preliminary findings drawn from original research-in-progress.

activism in the protection of equal rights and opportunities. With the exception of special education, for which new federal legislation has recently been passed, these exogenous forces presently seem to be working uniformly to limit, rather than expand, the federal role in education over the next few years.

Initial Definition of the Federal Role

A decade ago, the purposes underlying federal intervention were fairly clear and quite widely accepted. Michael Timpane lists five implicit purposes: (1) equal educational opportunity, (2) reform of state and local educational practices, (3) improving educational preparation for employment, (4) educational research, and (5) limited general support. Of these goals, equal educational opportunity has been the most important and is likely to remain so, given the continuing pressures on lower levels of government to balance the major concerns of basic levels of funding, on the one hand, and tax relief, on the other. To achieve equal opportunity, the main activity of the federal government has been to direct financial resources to specific disadvantaged groups. First and most important among these groups were the economically disadvantaged students who received aid under ESEA Title I. Successively, handicapped, non-English speaking, and Native American students have been added to the list of nationally important groups meriting a federal educational focus. The federal interest in educational reform and in innovation has mainly tried to expand the capability of local schools to incorporate improved educational practice. Support for this activity was provided orginally under ESEA Title III, but it now involves specifically directed efforts in such areas as desegregated schooling, reading, early childhood education, and career education. Educational research received most of its support under ESEA Title IV, later converted into the National Institute of Education. Training for employment was boosted by career and vocational education programs, while scattered general assistance was provided to states and localities under impacted areas aid and under various provisions for books, materials, and counseling services.

Recent Challenges and Defaults

In recent years, however, the focus of the federal role has grown somewhat less clear—partly at the hands of challengers and partly by default. Education programs have proliferated steadily over the decade, and now they promote such a wide spectrum of special interests (e.g., ethnic heritage, metric education, and environmental education) that the federal focus is difficult to pin down. In addition, conflict among federal, state, and local educational policymakers that was submerged during the early days of ESEA has resurfaced over such problems as the absence of cross-program coordination at the federal level, federal channeling of "pass through" money directly to localities, state-local allegations of excessive federal interference, unnecessary data and reporting requirements. Federal policymakers also counterclaim that many states and localities simply and consistently fail to carry out the intent of federal law. At the same time, the suspicion has grown among taxpayers and some educators that few of the federal policy interventions are capable of improving educational performance even under the best conditions. Many policy planners have de-emphasized grants-in-aid for education, as federal social policy tools, relative to income transfer and other individual support programs. All in all, there seem to be many reasons for fundamental reconsideration of the federal role in education by federal, state, and local officials.

Dynamic Nature of the Policy Context

Another problem for the development of federal education activities emerges from the changing nature of the American system of education and the interactions of federal policy with various components of that system. The nature of the federal involvement in education is affected not only by changes in external forces and political conditions, but also by changes over time in goals, program priorities, and administrative capacities of the states and local units of government.

Table I illustrates this dynamic problem. Relative to the federal government's goals and capacities, the status of the states differs, and the relationship changes continuously, state by state, as time goes by. Sometimes, for instance, a state or states share federal goals and surpass federal administrative capacity, while others resist federal priorities, some skillfully and some not. It has been and will be a difficult problem to keep the federal role effective in the face of these shifting patterns of state performance.

In addition, the "education problem" that a policy is designed to address is generally not a static situation, shifting, for example, from a teacher shortage and classroom overcrowding at one time to a teacher surplus and declining enrollments a few years later. Finally, the federal grant-in-aid programs

Table I. Goals and Capacities of the Fifty States Relative to the Federal Government[a]

	Goals				Capacity		
State	*Equal Opportunity*	*Reform and Education*	*Research*	*Job Preparation*	*General Aid*	*Policy Management*	*Resource Management*
State$_1$	+1	+2	+1	0	+3	+2	−3
.	.	.	.	.	.	.	.
.	.	.	.	.	.	.	.
.	.	.	.	.	.	.	.
State$_n$	0	+1	−2	0	+2	−1	0

[a]Scale ranges from −3 to +3.

themselves frequently undergo conspicuous modifications in practice as they mature, or they become embroiled in conflict and adapt. The process of program development resembles, in fact, a maturation process or a "life cycle."

John Callahan and William Wilken make the same point about school finance equalization reforms and categorical grants for educationally needy students. Ten years ago, the states were not engaged in either of these worthy pursuits, but today many states are; federal policies have not been able to adjust easily to complement these efforts.

The Role of the Courts as Policymakers

During the past twenty years, the federal courts have ruled frequently on fundamental issues of educational policy (e.g., desegregation, federal aid to church-related schools, and educational equity). The federal courts occupied this influential position within the policymaking arena during the same period that Congress and the executive agencies were attempting to reshape the legislative priorities of the country and to fashion programmatic activities in related areas, like education for the disadvantaged, the handicapped, and non-English speaking students.

The bulk of recent litigation in education has related to defense of individual freedoms and assurance of equal protection. The rulings have covered several specific areas: equal educational opportunity; school finance reform; aid to private schools; minimum educational requirements; student rights regarding privacy, freedom of expression and association, and appearance; and teachers' rights with respect to equal employment opportunity, freedom of speech and association, due process, certification, and collective bargaining.

The courts appear, however, to have entered most the the constitutionally significant areas of educational policy. Their activities in the future will concentrate on extending and perfecting their role in the previously defined areas. From their previous involvement, however, at least two major problems persist: devising effective remedies to secure constitutional rights and understanding the wide-ranging policy impacts and costs that extend far beyond the individual case under litigation. An individual court decision may have an impact on national political or budgetary priorities (even forcing tradeoffs among constitutional requirements!), or it may impose constraints on the education system that fundamentally affect the design, feasibility, or impact of educational grants-in-aid.

Possible Expansion of the Federal Role

Defining boundaries for the federal involvement in education is among the most difficult tasks in any discussion of the federal role. The absence from the Constitution of any explicit mention of the education function and its delegation of responsibility thereby to the states lends considerable flexibility to any effort to determine the appropriate federal domain in education. The major opportunity for an expanded federal role in education is contained in proposals for federal general purpose aid.

General purpose aid to local districts for education is a form of transfer of funds that has been periodically broached but never authorized by the federal government. Alan Ginsburg and Lawrence Brown depict three potential functions of general purpose aid programs: (1) helping states to equalize expenditures and wealth-based tax burdens within districts, (2) equalizing expenditures or burdens among the states, and (3) making the national school finance system more "adequate"; that is, helping states and localities to meet rising expenditure requirements that cannot be handled within existing revenue capacities. Ginsburg notes that, although general aid has never been authorized, existing federal categorical programs accomplish each of these objectives to a limited degree, and by almost every measure of resources delivered, educational quality has improved substantially during the past twenty years. Recent recession and inflation may be causing fiscal hardships that will not be permanent if the future consists of declining enrollments and a healthy economy. The cost of any general aid program that would contribute significantly to more "adequate" or equitable financing of schools is counted in billions. Ginsburg and Brown point out, however, that federal costs become more reasonable if some spending disparities are tolerated *or* a performance or service standard approach is used whereby limited awards of general purpose aid go to states that meet basic equalization criteria. Under this approach, which is similar to features of the Education for All Handicapped Students Act of 1975, there is no attempt to link individual grants-in-aid to specific uses or to preclude federal funds supplanting state and local contributions.

DEVELOPMENT AND MANAGEMENT OF FEDERAL PROGRAMS

After consideration of the federal role in elementary and secondary education, the second principal topic for symposium review was the performance, actual and potential, of the federal government in accomplishing its stated objectives through grants-in-aid.

Assessing the accomplishments of the federal categorical grant-in-aid programs serving education is more than a straightforward inventory of federal activity and its association with student performance over time. In fact, the impact of ESEA is fundamentally constrained by the extent to which state and local educators comply with the distributive and control provisions prescribed in the authorizing legislation. The federal government is rarely the actual provider of educational services. Rather, Stephen Barro observed, educational grant programs are more appropriately conceived of as intergovernmental transfers and the ability of the federal government to foster learning through instructional programs is constrained by state and local compliance. Thus, while evaluation of educational achievement is important, it is critical to know first whether the federal government has managed to channel resources to the intended groups of recipients and to ensure operation of specified types of programs in accordance with its objectives. Thus, the compliance question resolved into two issues: (1) compliance by the states and localities with respect to resource allocation and (2) proper implementation of individual projects by the local districts.

State and Local Compliance in Resource Allocation

Symposium discussion of state compliance in allocating federal resources centered on Title I, the largest and most well documented of the education grant programs. Robert Goettel[c] drew from his ongoing research on the Title I program to assert that state compliance with the distribution and resource control provisions of Title I has distinctly improved in recent years. Most basic program requirements, like concentration and comparability, are being adequately observed. Instances of noncompliance and nominal compliance are the exception rather than the rule. Improved compliance under Title I may indicate growing local acceptance of Title I goals and the growing experience and professionalism of federal, state, and local Title I staffs or both. Although Title I compliance patterns have improved, several major compliance issues remained to be solved:

- The relationship of compliance features like concentration and noncomingling to desegregation policies that dispersed many disadvantaged students
- Interstate variation in patterns of disadvantagement and in compliance actions
- The utility of compliance controls after states and localities improved their performance and compliance was routinely accomplished as well as the possible shift of management emphasis toward technical assistance

The thorniest problems for program management seemed to be the considerable variation among the states in goals, organizational infrastructure, management capability, and in the nature of the educational problems they face. The question was repeatedly raised: Can federal policymakers accommodate variance among the states by establishing federal expectations for each state in a more flexible and mature way—perhaps through development of a more individualized contractual relationship between the two parties (e.g., a state plan with "individualized" requirements)? This pressure for redesign was tempered, however, by a second judgment that program continuity contributes heavily to compliance, that is, the sustained presence of programmatic funding and regulations over time appear to operate through the climate of the education

---

[c]Goettel described his report as "a highly personal view" based on preliminary findings.

community to foster compliance.[d] The redesign of policy control instruments may be useful, but maintenance of continuity is crucial.

Implementation: The Preeminence of Localism

Once federal funds are properly allocated by the states and localities, local projects must still be installed and operated before the preconditions for affecting educational achievement are established; that is, the project must be implemented. Paul Berman and Milbrey McLaughlin emphasized this hard lesson. The ESEA program experience to date indicates, they said, that implementation activities mostly determine project success or failure and that the pattern of implementation is essentially determined by local factors and not by the level or kind of external resources. The implementation process has, moreover, several stages: (1) mobilization (generation of local support), (2) operationalization (adaptation of a new program to an individual site), and (3) institutionalization (routinization and permanence). The appropriate federal role may vary at each stage. It may start with a catalytic action at time of mobilization. During installation, however, a stage when success is particularly dependent on local personnel, the federal role may usefully be cut back to one of support and technical assistance, since a mutual adaptation between the federal program and local personnel appears to be vital to success. In the final stage of institutionalizing the federally sponsored change, local patterns of behavior are largely determined by events during the two preceding phases. Successful implementation has not occurred in the majority of federal projects, *but* the characteristics of "successful'" projects (e.g., local building planning, central office support) appear to be transferable. Thus, their effects can be duplicated.

Implications for Subsidies and Standards in the
Federal Policy Repertoire

The political and technical forces operating to limit expansion of federal involvement in education, the recent progress toward state and local compliance, and the importance of programmatic continuity and local support in effecting systemic change all suggest that at least some components of education grants-in-aid should be carefully reassessed. Control provisions embedded in the legislation may be neither necessary nor sufficient to accomplish federal objectives for resource allocation, *or* they may have become obsolete as assumed federal-state goal conflicts have dissolved or other dimensions of the policy context have changed. Or they may simply need to be enforced with greater selectivity, emphasizing, say, those programs where federal funding is substantial (in total expenditure and relative to the local contribution) and where the program's outcome is vital to the achievement of federal objectives. Simplification

---

[d]Discussants emphasized that programmatic continuity does not imply a static program, but instead a program in which elements such as objectives, staff, and some procedures are sustained as a program adapts or is reshaped.

of the existing categorical system could significantly reduce the backlash against excessive red tape and reduce calls for consolidations that offer no assurance that federal objectives would be met or that administrative procedures would be much diminished.

Finally, it seemed, from the provisions of the Education for All Handicapped Students Act, that the federal government might be moving toward a broader approach in its education grant compliance strategy; that is, asking from the recipient not just a guarantee of certain uses of federal funds but an entire federal-state-local program of specific dimensions.

Current Provisions for Resource Control

Stephen Barro provided a provocative study of the merits and drawbacks of several of the federal policy instruments to control the allocation of grant funds. Title I, for example, has two main resources control provisions: (1) designation of target schools and (2) comparability requirements. The rationale behind the target school provision was that a certain critical program mass may be necessary to ensure a visible and viable educational program, but its enforcement under limited appropriations entails a neglect of many disadvantaged children who do not live in areas with high concentrations of poverty. The comparability provisions were designed to ensure equal treatment of Title I schools in the municipal budget and to forestall federal funds supplanting local expenditures. Designed during a period when federal funds dominated the compensatory education efforts within virtually every state, comparability requirements may need to be adjusted to coordinate federal objectives with the compensatory education programs that several states have begun in recent years.

The program for vocational education has two other examples of resource control provisions, namely, a matching requirement and a maintenance of effort provision. At the time the matching provision was designed, state money constituted a miniscule proportion of vocational education expenditures in most areas with the federal government providing the bulk of the funding. The federal intention in using the matching requirement was to create an incentive for at least equal state expenditures for vocational education. In recent years, however, state efforts in this area have escalated until today states and localities match federal vocational education funds several times over. Thus, federal matching contributions no longer constitute an incentive for increased state spending at the margin, and the federal share is not fulfilling its stated purpose. Similarly, maintenance of effort provisions have had little meaning as inflationary increases in state budgets suffice to meet the requirements despite declining outlays in real terms.

Barro also suggested some logical bases for selective compliance procedures. Stringent federal controls and monitoring are most vital where programmatic objectives are critical, the federal contribution is large, and the federal-state goals are divergent. Conversely, strictures might be relaxed for small programs or for programs where the federal contribution is small relative to the state-local share and the intent of the program has low federal priority.

Grant Consolidation Versus Simplification

The costs and problems inherent in existing compliance procedures have led to calls for grant consolidation to reduce excessive federal red tape and to allow states and localities to diagnose their own educational needs and pre-scribe appropriate expenditures. However, there is an important distinction between grant consolidation and simplification: federal grant procedures may be streamlined in many ways short of a full-blown consolidation. As one example, Barro cited the nonsupplanting restrictions contained in many grants. They are virtually meaningless under many conditions anyway (with small amounts of money and inflation) and they may be one onerous requirement that might be discarded with minimal information loss.

In general, the reported shortcomings of the categorical grant system may be used with equal effectiveness to argue either for replacement with a consolidated system of block grants or for redesign and fortification of existing categorical requirements. The option selected should reflect educated estimates of the states' likely allocation criteria and management capability under alter-native grant systems, the technical and political feasibility of installing stronger control instruments in some components of the extant categorical structure, and the cost as well as the urgency of achieving the objectives contained in the categorical programs.

Resource Control and Program Change

A final conclusion was that federal grant programs are dynamic and progress through something akin to a "life cycle", that is, they tend to develop, mature, and grow obsolete unless treated to periodic renovation and overhaul. Most discussants agreed that many of the resource control provisions embedded in the various titles of ESEA were designed to work under limited conditions that may no longer exist and that thoroughgoing reassessment is needed. The development of federal grant programs may progress through stages, such as priority setting, resource distribution, full implementation, and achievement of educational outcomes. It may be proper to consider different policy instru-ments and different measures of success for use at various stages of the program maturation process.

Implications of a Universal Service Standard

The most dramatic change in control provisions would be a switch to a performance or service standard for state or local compliance. Essentially, the service standard requires that those states seeking federal subsidies achieve one or more goals or provide a certain educational service as the price for federal funding. The new Education for All Handicapped Children Act of 1975 takes this approach, mandating that the individual states provide a "free appropriate public education" for every handicapped student within their domain, not *with* but *in exchange for* federal funds.

Such a standard-setting approach combined with a subsidy is potentially a very strong tool for federal leverage. The service standard must relate to the main purpose of the grant, lawyers say, but virtually any regulatory mechanism might be employed. A service standard like that in the Education for All Handicapped Act also contains features that may make it attractive to the states, it allows the states to supplant their funds with federal resources if the service standard is met. In the absence of constraints on uses to be made of the funds, this provision would constitute something very close to general aid.

There are problems with standard setting, too: excess costs to the states in implementing the mandated standard, diversion of state and local funds from other important programs, and standards (e.g., mainstreaming) that prescribe specific educational techniques or processes. In implementation, a service standard may require a somewhat different, more individualized, and contractual type of approach to federal-state relations—a change likely to require a more flexible, discerning, and highly trained federal staff.

INTEGRATION OF FEDERAL AND STATE EFFORTS

Since the implementation of federal policy is inextricably bound to state and local performance, effective coordination among the three levels of government is vital. But confusion, duplication, and even conflicting regulations have sometimes been the order of the day. Two major developments in federal-state relations are called for, namely, specialization of a federal role that complements state education efforts and flexible and differentiated grant management to accommodate conspicious variation in management capability, especially among the states.

Specialization of Federal and State Functions

The current implicit division of labor between educators at the federal and state levels appears to assign to the federal level a main responsibility for equal educational opportunity, but there are federal programs addressing different aspects of this role and many federal programs with other aims altogether. There are many gray areas where the locus of responsibility is far from clear. Representatives of the states acknowledge that federal categorical programs often serve a legitimizing function, particularly for equity issues, and that this federal capacity is facilitated by the greater insulation of federal officials from the vagaries of local political life. Meanwhile, the states are pressed for aid to the disadvantaged, on the one hand, and tax relief and education for the "normal child," on the other. As John Callahan and William Wilken noted, these pressures lead to mixed results. In school finance reforms, for instance, states were trying to stem rising school taxes while increasing their capacity to meet "special needs." The result was relative but uneven improvement in intrastate expenditure disparities. The cross-pressures on states will increase, Callahan and Wilken suggest, with escalating demands for tax relief, continuing uncertainty about what constitutes a "right approach" to school finance equity, lack of legislative interest in school finance reform, the fiscal strain of decling enrollments, mounting education concern over state pension liabilities, and so on. The states feel that federal programs are of little help in addressing such problems. States and localities tend to view federal aid as supplemental money that cannot be integrated effectively into their own education efforts, even where the goals are similar.

Conflict between federal and state educational goals and policy instruments has prevailed to the exclusion of serious efforts to make federal and state operations complement each other. Moreover, despite significant and widening gaps among the states in such areas as compliance, management capability, progressive taxation, and fiscal capacity, there has been little development of flexible and differentiated federal strategies that would build capacity and enforce compliance where needed while relaxing requirements in instances where capacity and effective performance had been demonstrated.

NEED FOR ADAPTIVE FEDERAL POLICY MECHANISMS

In sum, federal education policy operates through an unwieldy system of grants-in-aid that have achieved some important outcomes but are overdue for reassessment. Federal grant programs are static in design, but they are forced to cope with continuously changing education problems in a dynamic context of state and local activity. Furthermore, federal programs themselves undergo substantial, albeit unplanned, change in practice as they age (e.g., accountability systems may be strengthened, and goal conflicts may be resolved).

Implicit in the notion of a dynamic education system and in symposium discussion is the theme that federal policymakers need to monitor program compliance, implementation, and performance systematically. They should modify and adapt their efforts on the basis of feedback indicating failure, success, obsolescence, irrelevance, and so forth. In the course of program "life cycles," programs may necessarily need reform or replacement, or their objectives may need redefinition. Programmatic continuity is vital if it combines continuity and adaptive capacity and is not mere perpetuity.

Among the initial obstacles to such an adaptive policymaking approach is the conceptual and practical difficulty of developing policies and programs amenable to adaptation, consolidation, or even termination, where appropriate. In general, federal programs should be designed with some built-in capacity for fine tuning without the agony of constant overhual.

Chapter One

Federal Aid to Education: Prologue and Prospects

Michael Timpane

The enactment of the Elementary and Secondary Education Act of 1965 (ESEA) has been hailed as a masterstroke of legislative art, combining concurrent national fervor for equal opportunity and for more education and overcoming the deeply rooted concerns of race, religion, and localism, which had long frustrated those who sought a significant federal role in elementary and secondary education. President Johnson, who signed the act, into law hoped that its passage would assure his standing in posterity as the "education President."

It seems as if the act was passed longer ago than 1965 because so much has happened to the federal education programs as a result of both internal and external developments. As is usually true, the moment of legislative triumph papered over quite profound differences in the goals and priorities preferred by various backers of federal aid. These differences were quick to reemerge and have persisted as the bases for arguments over program development and funding levels both in ESEA itself and in the additional federal educational programs that preceded it or have since been created. Similarly, the moment of legislative triumph marked the beginning of an extended and difficult period of program implementation, during which inexperienced and sometimes reluctant educational managers at every level of government committed most of the conceivable sins and mistakes, introducing federal resources into a dominantly local policy system.

FEDERAL ELEMENTARY AND SECONDARY EDUCATION PROGRAMS TODAY

In fiscal 1976, the federal government spent over $4 billion dollars on U.S. Office of Education (USOE) programs assisting elementary and secondary

Table 1-1.   Estimated Federal Expenditures for Elementary and Secondary Education Fiscal Year 1976

Programs	Expenditures ($ millions)
Aid to Target Groups (excluding set-asides)	
Disadvantaged (Title I and Follow Through)	2,109
Bilingual	99
Indian	57
Handicapped	326
	2,591
Other Grants to States and School Districts	
Support and innovation	185
Libraries and instructional equipment	147
Impacted areas aid	704
Vocational and adult education	617
Emergency school aid	272
Miscellaneous project grants	109
	2,034
Total	$4,625

Source: Education Division, "FY 1977 Labor-HEW Appropriations Bill," August 12, 1976.

education. This figure rose gradually from about $3 million in fiscal year 1972 and $2 million in fiscal year 1966. Of total national spending on elementary and secondary education, however, the federal contribution has remained a relatively constant 7-8 percent.

Except for impact areas aid and vocational education programs, these programs have begun since the mid-1960s (and both impact areas aid and vocational education have been altered a great deal during this time). Under each heading, one or several grants-in-aid go to state or local governments for some specified federal purpose. Federal policymaking is mostly concerned with the definitions of purpose and determination of grant provisions. Under these grant programs, the federal government operates no schools.

Until the 1960s, the federal government has had almost no policy-making role in elementary and secondary education in the United States. USOE collected statistics, a few hundred districts received payments to offset the financial impact of nearby federal installations, and very small amounts of money were distributed to the states to further vocational education. But in the year-to-year development of local school policies, the federal government had no role.

The reasons for this were more political than constitutional. The Constitution is silent on the topic of education—which was not even a public function at the time of its adoption. Later in the nineteenth century, when public elementary and secondary education began to develop, local government (joined gradually by the states) set all educational policy; the federal government showed little interest in playing a part.

During the past forty years, of course, the federal government has entered many new realms of social policymaking—in health, welfare, social insurance, employment and unemployment assistance, and in education. These developments were in response to the increasingly complex and interdependent nature of our society and economy, as well as to a growing national legislative and judicial commitment to concepts of equal opportunity and treatment. In education, specifically, the political and economic benefits of a well-educated citizenry became more manifest and more national in character, as geographical mobility increased and regional economic and social interests diminished. By the 1960s, Bailey and Mosher could describe the federal interest in education quite expansively:

> The federal government is logically concerned with education whenever questions arise about disparities in publicly supported educational opportunities and whenever it can be shown that educational activity bears significantly upon such issues of national value as unity, justice, domestic tranquility, the common defense, the general welfare, and the liberties of present and future generations.[1]

Nevertheless, elementary and secondary education was one of the last areas of federal involvement. For twenty years before the 1960s, proponents of federal involvement had been thwarted by three obstacles: localism and resistance to federal control of educational policymaking; divided opinion on aid to private, often church-related schools; and southern resistance to school desegregation requirements in postwar federal aid proposals.[2]

It took a remarkable conjunction of forces, mostly from outside the schools, to overcome these obstacles in 1965 and establish a distinct, if limited, federal role in elementary and secondary education. It is worth listing these conjoined forces since their persistence or transformation has been and will be important to federal educational policy. They were:

- A demographic explosion, pushing the numbers of school-age children from a relatively constant 28 million (a level that had persisted from 1930 to 1950) to 42 million in 1960.
- Dramatic increases in the quality and quantity of education demanded per child. Parents with more education themselves sought expensive educational improvements for their children (especially small classes and "modern" curricula), and society strove successfully to keep every student in school for more years. Between 1950 and 1960 alone, the average educational

attainment of the adult population climbed from 9.3 to 10.5 years of school-ing,[3] and total school spending tripled.[4]

- Equally dramatic increases in public support for civil rights and equal oppor-tunity programs.
- National economic policy that focused on the rewards of economic growth and the contribution thereunto of productive educated persons.
- Reportedly hopeful prospects for additional financial resources from existing federal taxes, compared to state and local revenue sources.[5]

In 1964 and 1965, President Johnson and his domestic policy ad-visors took three giant steps that ended with the enactment of ESEA in 1965.

- They enacted the Civil Rights Act of 1964, and in the process they wiped out the long-standing desegregation barrier to federal education aid.
- They inaugurated the War on Poverty with the Economic Opportunity Act of 1964, and in the process they provided a powerful new rationale for feder-al education aid to further equal educational opportunity.
- They pieced together a fragile coalition of education interest groups sup-porting a package of four specific grant programs—which provided limited benefits to each important group—states, localities, educational reformers, private schools, and disadvantaged children.

These events created the present federal role in elementary and secondary education. But federal education policymaking has not since ceased. Through extensive legislative activity (in 1966, 1967, 1968, 1970, and 1974), programs have been added, modified, consolidated, and occasionally dropped. Each year since 1967 education appropriations have been the topic of political contention, but the shape of the basic settlement has not changed. Federal education programs seem, by and large, to serve five distinct purposes:

1. Promoting equal educational opportunity. This ill-defined value is the most pervasive theme of federal education policy. Its most obvious expression is found in several grant-in-aid programs: each one designates a target group of students who are (by some yardstick) not adequately served by state and local programs. One or more categorical grants direct federal resources at each of them. Year in and year out, more than half of the federal elementary and secondary education dollars are devoted to this objective. ESEA Title I, deliver-ing grants to most local school districts for education programs aimed at several million low-income students, accounts for most of these resources—over $2 billion per year. Since 1965, Title I has been joined by smaller programs de-signed to direct educational resources for handicapped (1966), bilingual (1970), and American Indian (1972) students. These programs have not had the scope of Title I in terms of dollars spent, districts affected, or proportion of eligible

children served. But the Education for All Handicapped Children Act of 1975 calls for a federal commitment similar to that of Title I for this target group by 1980.

A more modest element of the equal educational opportunity program has focused on federal assistance for school districts undergoing racial desegregation of their schools. Such assistance began on a small scale under Title IV of the Civil Rights Act of 1964; since 1970, under emergency school assistance legislation, it has expanded to a quarter billion dollars per year in project grants.

2. Stimulating educational reforms. In the mid-1960s, American education was in the midst of a wave of educational reform. Most aspects of the curriculum, pedagogy, socialization functions, and management of American schools were coming under criticism, which was accompanied or swiftly followed by multiple proposals for change. Not surprisingly, federal education programs have reflected this process. Unhappily, the federal programs have also shared in the vicissitudes of these reform efforts—rapid shifts in their popularity and credibility, as the heydays of team teaching, individualization, new science curricula, behavior modification, management by objectives, inquiry learning, alternative schooling, aesthetic and moral education, career education, and basic skills swiftly come and often go.

Typically, working either through the state department of education or directly with the local school district or other educational institutions, the federal government funds a specific "innovative" local project for a limited period of time—the idea being either to foster locally selected improvements or to subsidize a local focus on particular nationally perceived problems. The first and largest of these programs was ESEA Title III, which left the districts free to choose the focus of the project and gave the states authority to approve them. In subsequent federal programs, the focus has been more on a specific federal substantive goal and specific federal approval for projects. The successive areas of federal interest have included:

- Teacher training projects (including Teacher Corps) in colleges and in school systems
- Extended nationwide development of projects in—
  Innovative compensatory education
  Exemplary vocational and career education
  Several new special education delivery strategies
  Reading improvement programs
- Skimpily funded special action projects in several areas: drug abuse, environmental education; women's equity; metric conversion; community use of schools; ethnic heritage studies; and so forth

All these programs account for a modest proportion of total federal education resources—usually less than $300 million per year.

For any given program, the federal resources subsidize a few or a few score of projects rationed among the thousands of eligible school districts according to geography, population, or relative need. The idea has been that each strategically placed demonstration will be observed and adopted by many school districts.

With their vague objectives and necessarily arbitrary criteria for selection and performance, these programs have suffered more than their share of management problems at each level of government. They have often only marginal connection to local educational operations (see below). The hoped for "demonstration effect" has rarely been observed.

Recently, some of these programs have been successfully tagged for consolidation (for example, ESEA Title III and several vocation education project grant programs) and even for elimination (as with teacher training grants under the Education Professions Development Act).

Related to these reform-minded project grants have been continuing federal efforts to improve state and local planning and management of education. Through ESEA Title V and through administrative set-asides in several grant programs, the federal government extensively subsidized state management of both federal and state programs (to the extent that half or more of the employees of many state agencies are today federally supported). Moreover, through the management strategies of several of the project grant programs, through the evaluation requirements in most federal educational legislation, and through sheer rhetorical persistence, the federal government has also played a major role in propagating the family of rational policy management reforms variously termed "needs assessment," "comprehensive planning," and "accountability."[6]

3. Supporting educational research. In education, as in many areas of national interest (like defense, medical science, agriculture), the federal government supports a large share of the nation's sponsored research. The federal government began its education program with the gathering of statistics in 1867; it began sponsoring educational research in the 1950s. The increasingly national character of many educational problems and the cost of modern scientific research have dictated a major federal responsibility for such research. This emerging responsibility was emphasized by the establishment of the National Institute of Education (NIE) in 1972. Smaller research programs concentrating on vocational education and special education also persist in USOE.

4. Promoting educational preparation for employment. The federal government has been especially responsible, since 1917, for the promotion of vocational education in the nation's schools. The schools' potential contribution to economic productivity was thus the first, and for a long time only, expressed national interest in education. Over the years, federal subsidies and regulations have established a veritable national subsystem of vocational education. From initially modest levels, federal appropriations have grown to over

$600 million per year. During the past decade, there have been substantial reforms in vocational education—including attempts to focus vocational programs on disadvantaged and handicapped students and to expand work-study and cooperative education programs. Lately, through the career education strategy, the federal government has also tried to infuse all aspects of elementary and secondary education with a vocational perspective.

5. Providing limited general support. The federal government has consistently declined to furnish general financial support for elementary and secondary schooling. In recent years, the push for such aid has been reinforced by the support of school finance reformers,[7] who have linked such aid to equal opportunity considerations, like those undergirding the state-local reform movement. To date, though, such proposals have not received serious legislative consideration. Federal action has been precluded (among other things) by the costs of significant levels of support (say, $20 billion for a one-third share), by the fear of federal control of education, by suspicions that massive federal dollars would inflate teacher salaries without purchasing extra services, and by concern that private and church school opposition to general aid (based on the fear that such aid to public schools would spell their demise) would cause the political basis for current federal education aid to become unstuck. So far, the federal interest in general purpose finance has been, in effect:

- The authorization of small planning grants to state-level school finance equalization reforms
- The continuation of impacted areas aid, which is general support to those school districts affected by the presence of federal installation or employees—*and* the reform of that aid to allow its incorporation into reformed state finance systems
- The consolidation of several subsidies for the purchase of school library and instructional equipment into a program of virtually unrestricted aid to local school districts

To be sure, the dividing line between general aid and restricted aid is often a hard one to draw. For example, Title I funds are intended, in part, to ease the financial distress of urban and rural school districts. To the extent that additional local expenditures to meet local needs are thereby foregone over the years, Title I is a specie of general financial assistance. Even by such generous definitions of general aid, though, the aggregation of federal financial assistance does not add up to anything close to the persistent dream of many educational interest groups that the federal government should furnish one-third of the general financial support for schooling.

Concealed in these neat distinctions is a considerable confusion about what the federal role is or should be. To some observers, the recent history of federal education policy is a dreary story of a succession of interest groups seeking "hunting licenses" (i.e., authorizing legislation) to bag federal resources; the dozens of programs represent no particular conception of the federal role, but are simply a scorecard in these appropriations sweepstakes.[8]

PERSISTENT ISSUES IN FEDERAL EDUCATION POLICY, 1965-1976

Even though the dimensions (if any) of the federal role have changed little in the past decade, federal educational policymaking has remained a spirited pastime. The outcome of an unchanged federal role resulted from extended discussion and analysis, and the development and operation of existing programs has involved the formulation and solution of numerous political and managerial problems that the original legislation had not foreseen. Most of the policy debate has concerned five issues: education's position in national social policy, priorities among federal education programs, recurring problems of race and religion, the management of federal education programs in the intergovernmental system, and the assessment of federal program effectiveness.

Education and Social Policy

The course of federal social policy can be traced in two obvious ways: legislation enacted and budgets approved. By both of these measures, elementary and secondary education has not enjoyed a high priority among federal social programs (even during a time when domestic expenditures in general were taking a consistently rising share of federal resources vis-à-vis defense spending).[9]

As noted earlier, only an unusual conjunction of forces allowed for the inauguration of a substantial federal aid program in the first place. ESEA was hardly enacted when this momentum began to fade. Along with the Office of Economic Opportunity, Model Cities, and manpower training (but unlike Medicare), ESEA was part of the antipoverty focus of the Great Society; it was hurt when the War on Poverty was displaced by the war in Vietnam. Even in the early years of ESEA (fiscal years 1967 and 1968), appropriations were unexpectedly lean as guns thinned out butter in Johnson Administration budgets. Moreover, the Coleman Report on Equal Educational Opportunity and the early evaluations of Head Start and Title I raised doubts among federal policy analysts about the effectiveness of educational interventions in general, and federal intervention in particular, for alleviating poverty and its effects. Among these social policy planners, attention soon shifted to the potential benefits of better income maintenance programs—where poverty could, it seemed, be more directly alleviated by federal action.

With the arrival of the Nixon Administration, the revised, lowered priority for federal education was reinforced. The new administration did not (as was feared) try to reopen the question of whether or not there ought to be federal aid to education. But is was openly skeptical about the effectiveness of the federal educational programs. It also wanted to limit federal social programs generally as well as the extent of central control over them. Its social policy proposals featured budget restraint and the New Federalism. Its domestic priorities were general revenue sharing and welfare reform. Its budgetary imperatives stemmed mainly from the swift growth and escalating costs of the federal obligation for income support and health financing. Targets for administrative improvement, decentralization, or demise were the Great Society grant-in-aid programs, which it believed were prolific, duplicative, and ineffective. Of these programs, elementary and secondary education programs were prime examples. Thus, education budget requests remained low, relative to legislative authority—usually at the nominal dollar levels of previous years. Few new programs were proposed; many of the existing programs were slated for consolidation and special revenue sharing with the states.

In Congress, the situation was a bit different. There were no serious attempts to enact large new elementary and secondary programs, but neither was there a willingness to shift priorities so quickly. Congress's impulse was to oversee and amend existing programs, to legislate small new programs without disturbing the contours of federal elementary and secondary education policy, and to keep aggregate funding levels at about the same real level of purchasing power, year to year.[a] But, like the Nixon Administration, its main priorities for new social programs and added federal resources lay elsewhere: improved Social Security benefits, expanded food stamp programs and Supplemental Security Income (SSI) for the elderly poor. Its most ambitious ventures into new education policy occurred in *higher* education, with the enactment of the Education Amendments of 1972, and in the development of successively more imaginative antibusing provisions (see below).

All in all, in the decade since 1965, elementary and secondary education programs have struggled to retain their modest but definite place in federal social policy. Indeed, during recent years, there has developed considerable sentiment for all levels of government to ratify this emerging division of social policy responsibilities: to agree that the federal government should

---

[a]In this annual process of trying to pull presidential budget requests moderately upward, the "education lobby" has had a limited but distinct effect. This lobby consists of several hundred specialized groups whose interests differ and whose Washington activities have historically been limited to small staffs with dominantly professional concerns. Their dealings with Congress were often hampered by fears of losing their nonprofit tax-exempt status.[10] They were pulled together, not by one of their own, but by the Johnson Administration, to support the passage of ESEA itself. In the Committee on Full Funding, several of the largest groups have, through "least common denominator" bargaining, joined together to secure modest congressional increases (8–10 percent per year) over administration budget requests in education. But they have not, in contrast, secured serious consideration, let along passage, for their long-standing request for larger scale general financial aid to schools.

shoulder the responsibility for economic stabilization, income security, and health insurance while state governments accept greater responsibility for the support of education.

Priorities in Federal Education Policy

Somewhat independent of the question of funding levels for the education budget is the question of what education programs are more important than others and deserve the greatest legislative and budgetary support.

In talking about program priorities, though, it is easy to over-simplify the objectives of the programs themselves. Many federal education programs have vague, multiple, and inconsistent objectives—sometimes intentionally so, to secure the widest possible basis for political support. But as time and program administration goes on, disputes emerge about the relative significance of various objectives for the same programs. For instance, the original goals of Title I included educational aid for poor and minority children, participation of the disadvantaged in educational decisionmaking, financial assistance for hard-pressed urban and rural school districts, and lubrication for local desegregation efforts, to name a few. In the minds of many recipient districts, these objectives were less significant, and less honored, in Title I spending than the objective of general financial aid. Federal program administrators quickly put their greatest emphasis on compensatory education objectives, but this view has not been shared by all interested parties. Consequently, in Title I and in many federal education programs, different persons may have different reasons for assigning the same relative program priority.

Nevertheless, there is one fairly simple choice that is repeatedly, if crudely, made in setting federal educational priorities: the relative emphasis that should go to the "new priority" programs enacted since the 1960s that stress educational opportunity and reform versus the "old established" programs like vocational education and impacted areas aid that support more established educational functions. In most USOE budgets, the argument has centered on executive-legislative disputes over whether or not to reduce the old established programs in the course of protecting the funding levels of the new priorities. In the decade after 1965 (and partly through the efforts of the Committee on Full Funding), the old established programs have at least held their own—enjoying rates of nominal growth as high as or higher than the new priorities. Only in the past two years (Fiscal year 1977, as supplemented by Carter administration request and Fiscal year 1978) have the large equal opportunity programs like Title I and the Education for all Handicapped grants begun to gain a noticeably larger share of budgetted resources. The least successful programs, in terms of budget levels, have been the research and demonstration programs.

The struggle also occurs, though less regularly, in the legislative authorization process. Here the action has most often involved the creation of additional new priorities (such as special education, bilingual education, Indian education, career education). To some, these legislative efforts represent the extension of federal attention to legitimate areas of national interest, but to others the continued authorization of uncoordinated, underfunded programs waters down earlier priorities or so proliferates priorities that none has any significance. Where the new programs are small, the potential damage is slight, but where they are large in intent and total federal resources remain scarce, they raise the specter of increased competition among needy target groups. At present, for example, this possibility clearly exists between disadvantaged students who need greater resources under Title I and handicapped students who have been promised greater federal and state resources under the Education for all Handicapped Children Act of 1975.

Race and Religion

Although the Civil Rights Act of 1964 removed desegregation requirements as a political barrier to federal aid, the federal response to constitutional requirements for desegregation has continued to be an important feature of federal educational policy. In the past few years, the most prominent example has been the various antibusing provisions that Congress has sought to attach to federal education legislation, intended to restrict federal efforts to foster or subsidize busing "for the purposes of achieving racial balance." But the basic policy problem is of longer standing and is more fundamental. It concerns the partial inconsistency between the objective of equal opportunity sought through school desegregation and the objective of equal opportunity sought through compensatory education benefits.

This issue first arose with respect to federal attempts to enforce the provisions of Title VI of the Civil Rights Act of 1964, which prohibited discrimination in the use of federal funds. The principal problem was that the sanction for the violation of Title VI was the withdrawal of federal funds. For local education agencies, this would have meant the withdrawal of Title I— funds that were intended precisely for the benefit of economically disadvantaged (often heavily minority) students. Thus, federal education program administrators who were not directly concerned with civil rights enforcement were from the outset ambivalent about it or, like their local counterparts, downright opposed.

In recent years, the nature of the dilemma has changed somewhat. After 1970 (and partly as an alternative to Title VI enforcement), the federal government supplied project grant assistance to local districts implementing desegregation plans. Now the inconsistency involved two federal grant-in-aid programs: one (ESAA) that fostered the dispersion among local schools of minority group students who were often disadvantaged, while another (Title I) sought to deliver compensatory education to high concentrations of these students in specific (and often virtually segregated) schools. During the past several years, there have been a number of halfhearted attempts to make the operations of those programs more complementary to one another, but no such plan has yet been adopted.

The issue of federal assistance to private, church-related schools has been less prominent than issues of racial discrimination in recent years, but it too has resisted any definite solutions. ESEA embodied an ingenious compromise on this issue, utilizing child benefit legal theory to skirt constitutional restrictions and furnish both services and equipment to private and parochial students. Unhappily, much of this promised aid was in the hands of state and local educational officials, who by local law or custom provided little or no aid to these private school students. Federal procedures to bypass these barriers were slow in developing. During the decade, moreover, parochial schools faced unusual cost increases, enrollment declines, and successively more stringent judicial restriction of access to public support.[11] Understandably, therefore, private school interests, disappointed in the performance of federal programs, were tempted by schemes for obtaining support through the remaining, arguably constitutional means of income tax credits and opposed to general aid plans that would not benefit them but would, rather, put them at a hopeless competitive disadvantage vis-à-vis the public schools.

One suspects, without being able to prove it, that this chronic susceptibility of education programs to politically hazardous disputes over issues of race and religion has the effect of dampening legislative enthusiasm for federal education programs.

Managing Federal Programs in the Intergovernmental System

In promoting ESEA, the federal government promised to remain a "junior partner" in education policy, and all federal legislation pays homage to local control, pledging that no provision of the legislation "should be construed to authorize any department, agency, office or employee of the United States to exercise any direction, supervision, or control over the curriculum, program of instruction, administration, or personnel of any education institution, school or school system."

Needless to say, reality has been more complicated than this. First of all, the federal government never decided to whom it should be a junior partner, the states or the local education agencies (LEAs). Sometimes a program was designed to deal primarily with one and sometimes with the other. Then, too, the same federal laws that abjured control sometimes required, for instance, parent involvement, acceptable instructional programs, or comparability of local expenditures as a condition for receiving federal aid. Moreover, the federal program managers developed additional guidelines for program management, elaborate program reporting requirements, and extensive program evaluations.

No one has been happy with the outcomes. Federal officials complain about a lack of state and local compliance with federal requirements.

States complain about senseless federal requirements. Local school officials complain about this, too, and also about senseless state requirements. In part, the argument is simply a matter of power and influence, where each successive level of government wants more resources and less direction from the ones above it. But there is also a legitimate question of program effectiveness. How will desired redistributions and reforms be best achieved, through careful federal direction of state and local effort or through state-local adaptation of federal priorities to local needs and practices.[12] Strengthened by federal resources (which sometimes supported state lobbying efforts in Washington!) and by evidence of increasing capacity for responsive governance (as in school finance reforms and state-level expansion of compensatory and special education programs), the states especially have persisted since 1965 in efforts to gain greater control of federal programs. They were successful right off the bat in 1967, capturing greater authority over Title III; recent proposals for revenue sharing and grant consolidation would enhance their authority much more. But most congressmen and target group leaders remain mindful that federal categorical programs were invented in the first place because state and local performance had been inadequate in the various areas of national concern. So far, the categorical structure of federal aid persists, especially with respect to programs aimed at national target groups. Modest consolidations have been achieved in grants to states for innovative and institutional support programs.

Lately, issues have been further complicated by the entry of state legislatures and executives into educational policymaking, especially school finance. These new actors want some control over federal programs, especially those programs that result in new demands on their fisc.

In the midst of this intergovernmental clatter, federal program officials must implement and manage the federal education programs, as they are legislated and occasionally modified by Congress. Constrained by federal-state-local rivalries, these officials must still be concerned with the distribution of federal financial resources, the implementation of federally supported activities, and ultimately with their program's effectiveness in improving educational processes and outcomes.

1. Distributive characteristics. Federal policymakers must be continually assured that federal funds flow to localities that have the specified programmatic need and that the funds are used to purchase appropriate services. This concern has been especially acute in Title I, where it has led to extensive provisions for maintenance of effort, for intradistrict comparability of expenditures to ensure that the federal aid is compensatory beyond the level of previous local efforts, and for requirements that the money be concentrated in schools having a relatively high proportion of disadvantaged students.

For the first several years after 1965, federal education programs were afflicted by chronically late annual appropriations, which left states and school districts uncertain of the timing, amount, and duration of federal aid. As a result, federal education dollars (especially for the newer programs) were perforce considered to be "soft money" to be used in such a way that the regular education programs would be unaffected by their absence (or as was unfortunately the case, their presence). In recent years, provisions for forward funding have alleviated this problem, but not before an unfortunate pattern of isolated federal project operations had been established in many school districts.

2. Program management concerns. Federal programs have used diverse management strategies, adapted to the particular program purposes and the structure of the relationships with the states. In general, these management strategies have concentrated on extensive planning and evaluation by state or local officials and upon various governance reforms like parent and community involvement, both in the planning and in the delivery of services. Sometimes, federal management has also extended to instructional priorities (notably with requirements under Title I that local services concentrate on instruction and basic skills). Federal program management always has a limited ability to enforce its will. Congress provides only limited staff and political support for enforcement and only the unrealistic option of funding cutoffs as a sanction for state and local noncompliance.

Federal program management has been challenged on all sides: for trying to control local operations too much, on the one hand, and for failing to produce substantial and effective local projects that reflect the federal intent, on the other; for bothering recipients with financial reporting requirements and for letting recipients misuse federal funds; and for proposing onerous evaluation requirements and for not knowing whether the federal programs work. As presently conceived, the job of federal program management is probably impossible. The federal managers cannot succeed until the contending powers in the educational system sit down and agree upon what functions they should and should not perform.

The Effectiveness of Federal Education Programs

Federal education programs have been unusually concerned with program effectiveness. Confronted at the outset with the need to overcome discouraging findings from the Coleman report about the effectiveness of new investments in schooling and with the evaluation requirements of federal law and modern planning theory, federal education programs have been more extensively evaluated than any public education programs in the previous history of the world. Moreover, federal education officials have tirelessly promoted evaluation among state and local officials.

It is probably impossible and certainly beyond the scope of this chapter to sum up the impact of federal elementary and secondary education programs.[13] As we have seen, the programs have multiple objectives, some distributive, others procedural, and some having to do with educational outcomes. In a too brief characterization, these several effects could be described as follows:

1. Distributive and financial effects. Federal funds are moderately progressive in their distribution among districts on the basis of wealth or income. Title I is quite progressive whereas other major programs are fairly neutral, but the total amount is small relative to total district expenditures.[14] Title I's comparability rule is, however, stimulating some equalization of expenditures among schools within school districts.[15]

2. Process and governance. Federal education programs have usually had too few employees and too many political and legislative constraints to manage local performance of federal priorities effectively. Federal program managers have relied on top-down planning and management strategies, which could not allow systemically for the diversity of state and local motivations and capacities and which have generated paperwork requirements that the state and local governments resent, resist, and sometimes subvert.

However, the indirect effects of federal management have been substantial. Even though they complain about federal requirements, many states and large school districts have followed the federal lead and accepted federal subsidies to develop comprehensive planning and evaluation systems of their own. Federal action has also stimulated staff diversification (e.g., paraprofessionals), specialization (e.g., reading specialists), and parent participation throughout the nation.[16]

3. Educational outcomes. Notwithstanding well-known problems of method and measurement, federal education programs have often been evaluated in terms of student achievement gains. Title I especially has been looked at this way. In the earliest studies, consistent educational gains were rarely found.[17] In recent studies, covering programs that have completed the turbulent implementation years, the results are less discouraging. There have been some achievement gains in well-implemented reading projects[18] and some September-to-June gains in average pupil achievement on statewide bases.[19] Most hopeful, perhaps, are recent indications from the National Assessment of Educational Program and other testing programs that nationwide average student achievement in the first four grades (where federal funds have been concentrated) is holding its own or going *up*, while other test results are going down.[20] But it stretches the evidence to conclude that federal compensatory programs can take the credit for this relative improvement.

In federal vocational education programs, better jobs and salaries are an important objective, but evaluations have not found strong positive effects of this kind.[21] For many other federal programs, evaluations have not sought to measure outcomes, but instead have centered on defining the state of program implementation.[22]

4. Other outcomes. The most interesting and profound effects of federal education programs may lie beyond the results of any particular study or program. They may lie in a murky realm called "leadership" or "opinion-making." It is often said that "federal money may be only 7 percent of the total, but federal influence has been much larger."[23] By such a reckoning, federal education programs have changed the entire policy system's priorities and behavior. The federal equal opportunity focus has some role in causing complementary state categorical programs (which have grown swiftly),[24] as well as state finance equalization reforms; similarly, federal preachments about accountability and career education have pushed state and local officials toward such programs.

EMERGING ISSUES IN FEDERAL EDUCATION POLICY

In recent years, the political intensity surrounding federal education issues has begun to subside. There are no longer serious arguments about whether or not there ought to be a federal role or about open-and-shut questions like whether federal programs are effective or ineffective. Budget levels for existing programs may be somewhat more generous; large, new program initiatives are less likely. Issues concerning the focus and quality of program and resource management dominate what policy debate there is and will probably continue to do so. What follows is merely a suggestion as to which such issues will be most prominent.

Some Trends and Forecasts

We have suggested previously that the overall significance and specific priorities of federal educational policy derived in part from national demographic and economic trends, legal requirements, and public attitudes toward education—noting that each of these factors pushed toward federal involvement in the 1960s. Which way are they likely to draw education policy in the late 1970s and 1980s?

1. Demography. Elementary and secondary school enrollments have dipped from 51 to 49 million between 1970 and 1975 and will decline by another 4 million (or roughly 8 percent) by 1980. After that, they will remain relatively stable. Throughout the decade, however, high school enrollments will continue to decline (by 15 percent between 1975 and 1985).[25] Moreover, average educational attainment levels (which are now almost identical for blacks and nonblacks under 30) will probably remain stable (i.e., 75–80 percent of each age cohort will complete high school). In probable consequence, local school districts will face serious problems in the "management of decline": utilization and consolidation of school buildings, personnel management in an era of fewer teachers and older collectively organized teachers, control of relatively fixed costs in administrative and support services, and retention of recently developed

special programs for needy students. The educational community will constitute a diminishing proportion of the taxpayers *and* of the service clientele in many jurisdictions. Many of the older urban school districts will continue to constitute a special case: fewer pupils, but more racially isolated, economically disadvantaged, and educationally needy; higher costs for both basic and special programs; and a stagnant tax base and fairly hostile state legislative majorities. At each level of government, relatively greater demand will exist for services (including, but not limited to, education) and subsidies benefiting the relatively larger numbers of adults.

2. National economic and budgetary conditions. If national economic recovery continues, without renewed inflation, then governmental revenues should once again be adequate for program maintenance—educational and otherwise. At the state level, funding levels for education support have increased to the present.[26] At the national level, even assuming economic recovery, there will be fiscal flexibility for only a few major initiatives over the next few years, once present obligations are met. By every current indication, programs of economic stimulus, welfare reform, and national health insurance will remain at the top of the list of likely initiatives. In the labor market, high school and college graduates as well as women reentering the labor market will continue to face fairly hard going in terms of jobs and salaries, at least until the labor market adjusts to the entry of recent large cohorts of youth.[27]

3. Costs of education. Slack demand will probably keep teachers' salary settlements at or below cost-of-living settlement levels. Stable or declining enrollments will keep aggregate cost increases (especially for capital expansion) down, but unit costs may still climb sharply because of fixed costs and inefficiency. Judicial or congressional mandates (e.g., for special education) are the most likely source of new cost pressures.

4. Attitudes toward support for schooling. It is unlikely that the majority of parents will return to earlier attitudes demanding expensive qualitative improvements in schooling. Social problems like school discipline and desegregation have for several years been as much on parents' minds as issues of school finance or educational quality.[28] Declining test scores, whatever their real meaning, are alarming to the public. Disillusionment with recent educational reforms seems to be growing, and some considerable skepticism and ideological hostility toward public institutions, including schools, may be a permanent side effect of a highly educated citizenry.

5. Interest group influence. Two groups among the sets of interest groups may increase their influence in federal education policy: (1) state legislators, governors, mayors, and other elected general government officials and especially (2) organized teachers in the National Education Association and American Federation of Teachers. The teachers, in particular, have played an unprecedented, positive political role in successful presidential and congressional campaigns. They may provide a new concentration of effective political influence

in Washington, even though they may remain at loggerheads with state and local bargaining adversaries and suspect in the eyes of some wary taxpayers.

If the future unfolds as described, educational policymaking will focus heavily on state level activity aimed at helping local education agencies to retrieve public confidence and manage decline. The relatively new state and local programs focusing on equity and innovation will do well to hold their own. Program expansion opportunities will be extremely limited, confined to a few still overlooked or underserved clienteles: preschoolers, handicapped students, and adults.

At the federal level, pressures for program expansion may concentrate on these same groups. Sentiment for large-scale general aid will remain moderate; progress here may depend greatly upon the political effectiveness of organized teachers. The federal government may be looked to even more than in the past to ensure equity for high-cost target groups, to assist financially pressed urban school districts, and to stimulate improved educational practice. In addition, organized teachers and other interest groups may press for national solutions to pervasive issues of indirect but substantial interest to education, like public employee bargaining rights and pension protections. On the other hand, state-local satisfaction of federal program priorities may become an increasingly difficult problem unless there is intergovernmental clarification of educational roles and missions and improved design and management of federal grant programs.

NOTES

1. Stephen K. Bailey and Edith K. Mosher, *ESEA: The Office of Educational Administers a Law* (Syracuse, N.Y., Syracuse University Press, 1968), pp. viii–ix.

2. John F. Jennings, "Federal General Aid—Likely or Illusory," *Journal of Law and Education*, 2 (January 1973), pp. 89 ff.

3. National Center for Education Statistics, *The Condition of Education* (Washington, D.C.: Government Printing Office, 1976), p. 8.

4. U.S. Department of Health, Education, and Welfare, *Digest of Educational Statistics, 1973* (Washington, D.C.: Government Printing Office, 1974), p. 35.

5. See, for example, Walter W. Heller, *New Dimensions of Political Economy* (Cambridge, Mass.: Harvard University Press, 1966), pp. 117 ff.

6. Michael Kirst and Gail Bass, *Accountability: What Is the Federal Role?* (Santa Monica, Calif.: The Rand Corporation, 1976).

7. See, for example, Joel Berke and Michael Kirst, *Federal Aid to Education: Who Benefits? Who Governs?* (Lexington, Mass.: Lexington Books, 1972).

8. See, for instance, Robert Andringa et al., *Perspectives on Federal Educational Policy: An Informal Colloquium* (Washington, D.C.: Institute for Educational Leadership, 1976), p. 1.

9. Edward R. Fried et al., *Setting National Priorities: The 1974 Budget* (Washington, D.C.: Brookings Institution, 1973).

10. Stephen K. Bailey, *Education Interest Groups in the Nation's Capital* (Washington, D.C.: American Council on Education, 1975).

11. See Robert D. Reischauer and Robert W. Hartman, *Reforming School Finance* (Washington, D.C.: Brookings Institution, 1973), pp. 95–146.

12. Harry L. Summerfield, *Power and Process* (Berkeley: McCutchan Publishing Corp., 1974).

13. A thorough summary of the results of evaluation studies is DHEW/OE/OPBE, *Annual Evaluation Report on Programs Administered by the U.S. Office of Education, FY 1975* (Washington, D.C.: Government Printing Office, 1975).

14. See Note 13.

15. See David Badger and Stephen Browning, *ESEA Title I Comparability: One Year Later* (Washington, D.C.: Lawyers Committee for Civil Rights Under Law, 1973).

16. Thomas C. Thomas and Meredith A. Larsen, *Educational Indicators and Educational Policy*, Occasional Paper of the Aspen Institute Program for Education in a Changing Society (Aspen, Colo.: Aspen Institute, 1976).

17. For a summary, see Michael T. Wargo et al., *ESEA Title I: A Reanalysis and Synthesis of Evaluation Data for Fiscal Year 1965 through 1970* (Palo Alto, Calif.: American Institutes of Research, 1972).

18. See USOE/OPBE, "A Study of Compensatory Reading Programs," A government executive summary, Xeroxed, September 1976.

19. Thomas C. Thomas and Sol H. Pelavin, *Patterns of ESEA Title I Reading Achievement* (Menlo Park, Calif: Stanford Research Institute, 1976).

20. *Education Daily*, September 1976.

21. See Michael Timpane et al., *Youth Policy in Transition* (Santa Monica, Calif.: The Rand Corporation, 1976), ch. 3.

22. See note 14.

23. See, for instance, Samuel Halperin, "ESEA:. . .The Positive Side," *Phi Delta Kappan*, 57 (November 1975), pp. 147–156.

24. Esther O. Tron comp., *Public School Finance Programs, 1975–76* (Washington, D.C.: Government Printing Office, 1976), pp. 16–17.

25. DHEW/NCES, *Projections of Educational Statistics to 1983–84* (Washington, D.C.: Government Printing Office, 1975), p. 21.

26. DHEW/NCES, *Condition of Education, 1976* (Washington, D.C.: Government Printing Office, 1976), p. 189.

27. Richard Freeman, "The Declining Economic Value of Higher Education and the American Social System," Aspen Institute Program for Education in a Changing Society (Aspen, Colo.: Aspen Institute, 1976).

28. DHEW/NCES, *Condition of Education, 1976* (Washington, D.C.: Government Printing Office, 1976), p. 52.

Chapter Two

The Federal Role in School Financing: A View from the States

John J. Callahan
William H. Wilken

While sometimes reluctant to admit it, most state education policymakers accept and encourage federal responsibility for funding a portion of public school costs. Federal dollars help them meet the needs of high-cost and disadvantaged children. Federal dollars sustain programs that would compete for state and local resources if federal funding were cut back or withdrawn. Federal dollars also sometimes give them the political leverage necessary to implement unpopular revisions in their own public school policies. Most state policymakers, however, are dissatisfied with federal education programs in their present form.[1] They want major changes in federal education laws and will press for them with mounting vigor.

A minority of them are motivated mainly by ideological considerations; they view existing programs as an undue infringement on state rights and Tenth Amendment guarantees; they want the federal government "to put the money on the stump and run." Most state policymakers, however, are driven by much more practical considerations. Some want reform because they believe federal programs often undercut the objective of providing all children an equal educational opportunity. Some want reform because they consider current federal programs insufficiently responsive to a new generation of educational problems. Some want change because stagnating state-local revenue collections make it increasingly difficult to meet the partially funded mandates of many federal programs.[2] Some want revision because they resent federal administrative requirements that encourage bureaucratic proliferation. In addition, a growing number want change because they feel that existing programs fail to provide a fair "balance of trade" between federal taxes paid and federal aid received.

The mounting demand for federal aid reform by state education policymakers involves governors, chief state school officers, legislators, state board of education members, and many lesser functionaries. Each of these officials, however, has tended to perceive the reform question and potential solutions from different vantage points. Governors and legislators have been interested primarily in the fiscal ramifications of federal programs. Chief state school officers and state education board members have worried mainly about the impact of federal programs on administrative practices and local school services. As a result, there have been state positions on many reform issues, but frequently not a unified state voice. Institutions like the Education Commission of the States, which represents all state education policymakers, often find it difficult to take a strong stance on federal legislation except on issues of the "least common denominator." Yet forces are now at work that are strengthening state policymakers' desire for federal aid reform and willingness to work more cooperatively to achieve it. Forces also are at work that may bring about important changes in Washington's posture toward the states. This paper examines these developments and their ramifications for revisions in federal education policy in the near future.

THE STATE SCHOOL FINANCE REFORM MOVEMENT

Nothing has had a greater impact on state attitudes toward federal education programs than the post-*Serrano* state school finance reform movement. Since 1971, more than 40 percent of the states have adopted new school finance laws that make children's educational opportunities directly dependent on state wealth, increasing their contribution to local school costs from about 39 percent of the total at the beginning of the decade to approximately 51 percent in 1975 (see Table 2-1). Several states have implemented new compensatory and bilingual education programs that are now funded at levels well in excess of the receipts from their federal counterparts. Many states have increased their spending on handicapped children by spectacular amounts, their special education aid amounting to more between 1972 and 1976 ($0.9 billion to $2.6 billion) than the growth of all federal aid to education between 1965 and 1969. Many states are also developing new educational assessment systems, some of which tie dollars to pupil performance.

The state school finance reform movement of the 1970s has been driven by three forces, two major and one minor. The most important influences have been court demands for equality of education opportunity and citizen demands for property tax relief. A significant but generally less important influence has been the demands of functionally specialized interest groups for improvements in specialized school services. Interest group activity is the only one of these pressures, however, that is well understood in Washington. The other two are of virtually no direct political consequence to any federal official. As a result, state and federal education decisionmaking in the 1970s has continued to move along separate courses much as in the past. The

Table 2-1. State Proportion of Total State-Local School Funding Pre- and Post-Reform Periods— Eighteen School Finance Reform States

State	Date of Reform	State Share of Total State-Local Expenditures in: Last Year Before Reform	First Year After Reform
Arizona	1974	42.0%	54.6%
California	1972	36.7	45.3
Colorado	1973	28.9	89.9
Connecticut	1975	24.2	No answer
Florida	1973	61.3	62.5
Illinois	1973	39.3	44.3
Indiana	1975	36.2	No answer
Iowa[a]	1971	32.5	36.3
Kansas	1973	29.8	47.7
Maine[b]	1973	38.6	38.5
Michigan	1973	49.4	52.9
Minnesota	1971	50.7	60.9
Montana	1973	27.5	43.8
New Mexico	1974	74.5	77.8
North Dakota	1973	32.2	46.1
Texas	1975	46.1	No answer
Utah	1973	58.4	61.9
Wisconsin	1973	31.8	39.0
18-state average		39.0	51.0 estimated

Source: National Education Association Research Division, *Estimates of School Statistics*, selected years and selected state data from the NCSL LEAP School Finance Data Base.

[a] Iowa's law has been phased in over several years. In 1975–76, the state share will exceed 50 percent.

[b] Reflects on $83,000,000 reported state appropriation rather than $100,000,000 as reported by the state commissioner of education.

school finance reform movement has changed the stakes of school politics within many states so substantially, however, that state-federal relations in the area of education policymaking cannot persist on a "business as usual" basis.[3]

The key concern of the state officials who have led the school finance reform campaign has been to preserve a delicate political balance between those seeking greater equity in school services and those wanting greater tax equity while keeping increases in school expenditures manageable. Reflecting this concern, most states have adopted the goal, not of equalizing education expenditures, but of providing for a better balance between school taxes and school expenditures while substantially lowering property taxes.[4]

This goal has been pursued in different ways from state to state, but virtually all states have relied on new fiscal controls. Several states have imposed limits on local school expenditures; others have established constraints on local school taxes. Even where controls have not been imposed, steps have been taken to assure a measure of property tax relief, Michigan's property tax circuit breaker law being a typical example.[5]

Most governors and legislators favor fiscal controls because they provide the public fairly visible evidence that efforts are being made to respond to its demands for tax relief. Moreover, many key state policymakers believe that fiscal controls may be the only politically acceptable basis for assuring that new state funding will reduce the historic service disparities between rich and poor school districts. It is becoming increasingly apparent, however, that fiscal controls have implications that extend well beyond the problems of property tax relief and school finance equalization.

Most importantly, fiscal controls are shifting the focus of responsibility for any increases in school taxes and spending from local officials to state officials. Fiscal controls, in short, are proving to be a double-edged sword. They allow state officials to claim credit for limiting school budget growth but also make them more responsible for any growth that eventually takes place.

Fiscal controls notwithstanding, property tax loads are continuing to rise in a number of reform states because of the failure of income growth to keep pace with rapidly inflating real estate value growth in the last few years. Moreover, several states are just now going through property assessment reforms that may markedly raise residential assessments and property taxes.[6] Thus, school property tax relief and school spending and taxing controls will be the continuing hallmark of new school finance reform in the years to come.

The excessive concentration of school tax relief and reform poses a variety of fiscal problems for state decisionmakers that they are now just beginning to tackle. In several states with finance reforms that emphasize property tax and not school expenditure equity, analysis has revealed that there has been relatively little closing of expenditure gaps between property-rich and property-poor districts (see Table 2-2.). Poor districts still spend low, and rich districts still spend high.[7] Presumably, educational offerings in these two types of districts

Table 2-2. Expenditure, Wealth, and State Aid Data of Kansas School Districts by Wealth Decile, 1973-74 and 1974-75

Wealth Decile	Wealth per Pupil	1973-74 General Fund Budget per Pupil	State Air per Pupil	Wealth per Pupil	1974-75 General Fund Budget per Pupil	State Aid per Pupil
1	$14,904	$ 700	$429	$16,120	$ 784	$501
2	20,243	780	420	23,206	868	501
3	23,283	674	375	27,198	870	440
4	26,310	839	384	31,087	923	409
5	29,604	864	351	34,972	983	389
6	32,577	943	330	39,171	1,007	342
7	37,013	992	301	42,250	1,101	281
8	43,475	1,092	236	52,796	1,186	174
9	52,002	1,155	66	64,339	1,299	42
10	75,705	1,460	0	89,476	1,549	0

(Total Districts = 310)

Source: NCSL computations from school finance data supplied by the Kansas Department of Education.

remain widely disparate..Reflecting concern about this problem, moves are afoot in Michigan and Colorado, for example, to bring about greater expenditure equality among local districts while some states that have briefly experimented with power equalization plans have either dropped them or kept them as a relatively minor part of their finance reform, since they feel that richer districts tend to exert more school tax effort than poorer ones and hence receive more state school aid.

Though basic aid reform has generally emphasized school property tax relief and fiscal controls on school spending, state officials have also placed additional aid behind high-cost pupils and high-cost areas (see Table 2-3). Pupil-weighting systems in several states and the development of major categorical programs for compensatory, special, and bilingual education have given more state school aid to special needs children. Several urban states give additional aid to urban areas as a result of their high noneducational tax burdens, their high concentrations of hard to educate pupils, or their relatively high living costs. Moreover, this new emphasis on additional urban aid is now serving as important precedent in court suits that are seeking greater recognition of urban education needs in New York and Ohio.[8]

In summary, the terrain of the state school finance battleground will remain fairly constant in the next few years to come. Demands for school tax relief and school tax equalization will continue unabated. States will continue to place various fiscal controls on their local school districts to see that these ends are met. At the same time, good government and good education groups will continue to press for greater expenditure equalization than is now contained in most state school finance plans. This battle will focus on the selected educational needs of special types of pupils and specific types of school districts.

NEW STATE INITIATIVES CHANGE DECISIONMAKERS' VIEWS OF FEDERAL PROGRAMS

Prior to recent school finance of reforms, many state officials took a somewhat *laissez-faire* attitude toward federal education programs. The post-*Serrano* reforms, however, have changed this situation dramatically. Like it or not, state officials are now much more responsible for educational funding. The state share of public school costs in many reform states has increased dramatically. State elected officials are now much more directly and visibly responsible for local property taxes because of the education tax focus of recent reforms. State officials have also become more clearly identified with school costs as organized professionals have begun to key their salary and benefit demands to state funding decisions.

As their stake in school funding has mounted, state education decisionmakers rather naturally have developed a great sensitivity to any federal education programs that may be damaging to their own policies and programs. In a recent survey aimed at legislators who chair state education committees,

Table 2-3. Summary of Special Needs Addressed in Selected State School Finance Systems, 1975

States[a]	State Compensatory Education Program	State Bilingual Education Program	Basic Aid Formula Adjustments					District Wealth Definition		
			Disadvantaged Pupils	Concentration of Disadvantaged Pupils	Density or District Size	Noneducational Tax Overburden	Education Price Differences	Includes Income	Per AFCD Pupils	Per Capita
Arizona	X	X								
California	X	X								
Colorado		X								
Connecticut	X				(X)[b]			X		X
Florida										
Hawaii	X						X			
Illinois		X	X	X						
Kansas								(X)[c]	X	
Louisiana		X						X		
Maryland										
Massachusetts						X				
Michigan	X				X					
Minnesota		X	X	X						
Missouri		X	X							
Nebraska			?							
New Jersey		X								
New Mexico		X							?	
New York		X	X	X						
Ohio	X			X,						
Oregon	X									
Pennsylvania	X		X	X	X					
Rhode Island	X							X		
Texas	X	X								
Utah		X								
Virginia	X									
Washington	X							(X)[c]		X
Wisconsin	X									
Totals	13	12	5–6	4	2	1	1	3	1–2	2

Source: CSL, *School Finance Reform: A Legislator's Handbook* (Washington, D.C.: NCSL, 1976), p. 40.

[a] Delaware, Indiana, and Nevada, the remaining "urban states," have no urban adjustments whatsoever.
[b] (X) Not operative in 1974–95.
[c] (X) Does not benefit central city districts.

Table 2-4. NCSL Survey of State Education Committee Chairmen, August 1976—Question on Title I Consolidation

Congress will consider renewal of the ESEA Title I (compensatory education) program during 1977. What should Congress do?

	Percent of Education Committee Chairmen Who say:			
Region	*"Leave in Present Form"*	*"Completely Overhaul"*	*"Consolidate into Block Grant Program"*	*"Eliminate Program"*
U.S. Total	27.7%	6.4%	61.7%	4.3%
Northeast	37.5	.0	62.5	.0
South	23.1	7.7	69.2	.0
Midwest	31.3	12.5	56.3	.0
West	20.0	.0	60.0	20.0

Source: NCSL, *Press Release on State Education Chairmen Survey on School Finance* (Washington, D.C.: NCSL, 1976).

one question asked how Congress should act on the renewal of the Elementary and Secondary Education Act (ESEA) Title I program during 1977.[9] Chairmen from most states with new school finance reform laws, many from the South or West, indicated overwhelmingly that Congress should either make the Title I program part of a federal education block grant or abolish the program altogether. Chairmen from states primarily in the Northeast, which have been slow in acting on reform, in contrast, tended to give more support to keeping the Title I exactly in its present form (see Table 2-4).

States Want Programs That Are Wealth Equalizing. State policymakers who have been active in the school finance reform movement want federal education programs revised for several reasons. Most important perhaps, they want the federal government to eliminate elements of its education aid programs that complicate their efforts to deal with the fiscal equilization problem. This concern has surfaced most visibly in state protests about the anti-equalizing features of the impact aid program and the new federal aid program for handicapped children.

Impact Aid. Following adoption of their new school finance programs in the early 1970s, Kansas, North Dakota, Maine, and New Mexico sought permission from Congress to take steps that would permit them to supplant state school aid with federal impact aid. While some have interpreted this move as an effort to cut state education costs, the primary objective was to reduce fiscally disequalizing impact aid windfalls. Responding to state pressure, Congress first authorized this option under the so-called Dole Amendment to the 1972 school lunch bill and then reapproved it under Section 5(d) (3) of Public Law 93-380, the Education Amendments of 1974. Implementation of Section 5(d) (3), however, depends on approval of regulations defining the characteristics of an equalizing school funding system.

The current Section 5(d) (3) regulations illustrate the problems that can be encountered in meshing federal programs with state equalization efforts. After considerable debate over congressional intent, the U.S. Office of Education (USOE) promulgated proposed regulations in 1975 defining an equalizing school funding system as one with less than a 20 percent difference between the per pupil spending level of its fifth and ninety-fifth percentile school systems. This standard, however, failed to consider three important facets of state equalization efforts: (1) that state reform legislation has not been designed to bring all expenditures to a uniform standard, but to ensure that local wealth does not determine expenditure levels; (2) that state reform legislation is being phased in over several years and would be hindered by any standard that failed to take account of ensuing incremental equalization; and (3) that many states have widely divergent local school expenditures that do not reflect inequities nearly so much as wide-ranging differences in operating costs imposed by extremes in population, sparsity, density, and local education agency size. Accordingly, only Florida, Iowa, and New Mexico would have been classified as having equalizing school finance systems.

Recognizing this, several states pressed USOE to reconsider its equalization standard, one pointing out that it could respond to federal inflexibility with actions that would compel the federal government to deny impact aid to all local education agencies. USOE then finally published rules that judge state equalization efforts on the basis of "fiscal neutrality."

Federal Aid for Handicapped Children. Public Law 94-142, the new federal program for handicapped children, has been another source of debate on the disequalizing properties of federal education funding. Few elected officials at the state level quarrel with the intention of the federal handicapped legislation. Some are even enthusiastic about it because they believe it will reinforce their own efforts to aid handicapped children, efforts which in the last four years have yielded an increase in state special education aid of about $1.7 billion[10] (see Table 2-5). Policymakers in several states are worried, however, that Public Law 94-142 (PL 94-142) may have a substantial disequalizing impact if anticipated annual appropriations of over $1 billion are permitted to flow out through the current distribution formula, which gives no consideration to local wealth and bases aid entitlements on the number of pupils receiving special education and related services.

The substate distribution formula of PL 94-142 is no accident. Under previous federal handicapped legislation, ESEA VI-B in particular, funding was distributed to localities on a "project basis." Local education agencies had no predetermined aid entitlement; they could receive funds only if they developed and operated a service package meeting the approval of the state

Table 2-5. Special Education Revenue from State Sources for the Education of School-Aged Handicapped Children in Local Education Agencies, Fiscal Year 1972 to Fiscal Year 1976

States	Special Education Revenue from State Sources				
	Fiscal Year 1972[a]	Fiscal Year 1975[b]	Fiscal Year 1976[b]	% Increase Fiscal Year 1972-1975	% Increase Fiscal Year 1975-1976
U.S. Total	$910,067,207	$2,038,038,111	$2,467,000,000 est.	123.9	21.1
Alabama	9,843,722	28,350,000	34,630,000	188.0	22.2
Alaska	4,094,460	9,390,432	N.R.	129.3	--
Arizona	3,209,234	16,635,465	20,500,000	418.4	23.2
Arkansas	485,000	6,743,150	8,959,000	1290.3	32.9
California	154,009,596	207,303,962	230,658,900	34.6	11.3
Colorado	6,750,000	22,665,000	24,600,000	235.8	8.5
Connecticut	15,705,684	51,119,000	60,280,000	325.5	17.9
Delaware	8,300,000	16,900,000	19,900,000	92.0	17.8
Florida	42,842,415	113,514,605	137,000,000	165.0	20.7
Georgia	18,178,026	43,138,645	62,964,000	137.3	43.9
Hawaii	6,636,652	8,534,358	9,227,038	28.6	8.1
Idaho	1,900,510	9,311,000	11,623,000	389.9	24.8
Illinois	59,575,000	115,066,000	135,950,000	93.0	--
Indiana	3,756,908	16,500,000	22,010,000	339.0	33.4
Iowa	3,700,000	10,765,000	38,650,142	190.9	259.0
Kansas	3,841,000	9,476,000	12,108,000	146.7	27.3
Kentucky	11,665,552	20,427,000	33,436,000	75.1	58.8
Louisiana	1,675,280	31,450,273	44,474,484	1777.3	41.4
Maine	1,352,615	4,350,000	5,500,000	221.6	26.4
Maryland	27,066,000	40,977,000	53,653,000	31.4	34.9
Massachusetts	18,120,250	93,000,000	132,900,000	413.2	--
Michigan	55,000,000	90,050,000	123,800,000	63.7	37.6
Minnesota	18,633,000	28,500,000	38,500,000	53.0	35.1
Mississippi	240,000	8,199,119	11,108,744	3316.3	35.5
Missouri	14,005,208	28,229,434	32,304,044	101.6	14.4
Montana	5,676,340	13,457,275	19,200,486	137.1	42.7
Nebraska	3,472,000	10,326,357	12,336,840	197.4	19.5
Nevada	3,565,950	6,293,000	8,096,000	76.5	28.7
New Hampshire	336,117	1,304,851	N.R.	47.2	--
New Jersey	32,655,944	61,540,794	67,710,000	88.5	10.0
New Mexico	4,500,000	12,661,000	15,442,000	181.5	22.0
New York	0	196,559,631	227,241,650	--	15.6
North Carolina	22,555,864	40,821,227	47,000,000	81.0	15.1
North Dakota	670,548	1,591,746	3,500,000	137.3	119.9
Ohio	66,245,825	103,046,563	121,438,568	55.6	17.8
Oklahoma	1,250,000	7,624,585	9,365,000	510.0	22.8
Oregon	3,962,496	5,273,196	N.R.	33.1	--
Pennsylvania	81,403,000	168,000,000	190,000,000	106.4	7.1
Rhode Island	13,500,000	16,500,000	N.R.	22.2	--
South Carolina	10,073,473	19,029,489	31,845,556	88.9	67.3
South Dakota	350,000	350,000	850,000	0	142.9
Tennessee	13,459,033	33,513,923	38,498,000	149.0	14.9
Texas	74,186,400	190,805,000	209,885,000	157.2	10.0
Utah	10,057,320	13,573,252	19,214,982	35.0	41.6
Vermont	2,069,576	3,173,000	3,549,000	53.3	11.7
Virginia	11,107,000	21,328,675	N.R.	92.0	--
Washington	24,383,645	33,283,263	38,400,000	36.5	15.4
West Virginia	2,004,208	4,633,525	N.R.	31.2	--
Wisconsin	22,282,238	37,752,286	47,400,000	69.4	25.6
Wyoming	743,815	5,000,000	N.R.	572.2	--

[a]Source: U.S. Bureau of Education for the Handicapped.

[b]ESEA Title VI-B State Plan Amendments, U.S. Bureau of Education for the Handicapped, fiscal year 1976.

education agency. This plan allowed state officials discretion to direct available federal funds to areas of greatest need. Awards, however, often went less to the areas of greatest need than to communities with the greatest "political pull," to areas with the strongest "grantsmen," or to the localities most likely to operate projects sufficiently successful to confirm the wisdom of the grantors.[11] Under mounting pressure from the "losers," Congress attempted to eliminate this sort of problem in the future by limiting state discretion over the distribution of handicapped program funds to 25 percent of the total.

This arrangement, unfortunately, represents only a limited solution to the equity problem. Some communities, undeniably, will be treated more fairly than in the past. The value of this gain is questionable, however, for three reasons. First, a disproportionate share of available funds will flow in the same direction as in the past—to affluent suburbs with well-established special education services. Second, the communities with the greatest unmet special education needs—typically large cities and poor rural areas—will receive so little additional revenue that it is unlikely to provide much of a fiscal incentive for them to correct their past service differences. Third, state education agencies will be required to invest large amounts of time and effort in overseeing local aid payments that in many cases will be less than $10,000. The federal government, however, refuses to pay for any administration costs greater than $250,000 or 5 percent of a state's PL 94-142 aid entitlement.

FEDERAL PROGRAMS IGNORE NEW PROBLEMS

State policymakers are increasingly disenchanted with federal education programs not just because of their adverse impact on equalization, but also because of their failure to provide assistance that can be applied against a new generation of educational problems. Most current federal programs were implemented or experienced their greatest growth during the 1960s when the most troublesome problems facing the public schools were related to growth—providing supplementary services for the disadvantaged, responding to educational demands generated by the technological breakthroughs of the Soviet Union, and adding new classrooms. The most urgent problems facing the public schools today, however, are not by-products of growth, but of decline—declining enrollments, declining pupil achievement, declining public interest in school spending, and declining ability to meet old obligations, especially the unfunded debt of pension systems.

The problems of the 1960s, to be sure, are still with us in many respects. Disadvantaged children still lag well behind in educational achievement; gifted children who achieved so much attention in the wake of Sputnik are a resource that often receives little special attention; and "sunbelt" states continue to face the problems of swelling enrollment and capital construction. The new generation of problems, however, presses so hard in many areas that it seriously undermines state and local ability to respond to these needs, and federal aid provides no direct relief.

Declining Enrollment. Probably the most onerous problem facing state school finance reform is declining enrollment. It is a policy problem that state and local officials cannot control. Yet its fiscal and educational ramifications will be a continuing headache for years to come.

The most troublesome aspect of declining enrollment is the fact that school costs frequently cannot be cut back at a rate parallel to the loss of children.[12] Per pupil education costs continue to rise as children leave school. Often equally important, labor-management relations in many school districts are rent asunder as teachers, often younger and better trained, are laid off while administrator ratios remain constant or increase and as the professional quality of many school faculties becomes disjointed. Moreover, enrollment decline raises the issue of school consolidation at a time when the emotional attachment to local control of schools remains high.

Making matters worse, enrollment decline seems to have had an adverse impact on the gains made in state school finance reform. State officials have been under great pressure to provide declining enrollment bonuses, aid to ease the pains of change. As a result, bonuses often flow to rich and small districts that already have advantaged positions in their state school finance systems[13] (see Table 2-6). Bonuses do nothing to promote consolidation or to encourage greater local participation in intermediate districts that can provide services on a more cost-efficient basis.

Debate over Declining Productivity. Conflict over educational productivity is still another problem affecting the course of state school finance reform. In the wake of the Coleman report and Jencks' research,[14] a growing share of the public has concluded that dollars have little impact on educational quality. This is reflected in decreasing public concern about school finance problems and rising concern with school discipline and educational curriculum reform. It also heightens the idea that school tax reform is far more important than school expenditure equalization.

The lack of prominently publicized educational research that can isolate those school resources that make a difference in educational outcomes seriously blunts state school finance reform at this point.[15] Indeed, much of the existing research on educational productivity seems to point to several phenomena that will make it difficult to replicate past state school finance reforms.

First, productivity research seems to indicate that schools are simply not well organized or staffed sufficiently to raise educational outcomes. The lack of a well-established science of pedagogy also seriously hampers efforts at improving education productivity.[16] The particular structure of the teaching profession, with its relatively low pay in professional terms, its inability to

Table 2-6. Percent Change in Iowa School District K to 12 Headcount Enrollment September 1971 to January 1975, Within Deciles of Average School District Net Assessed Valuation per Formula Pupil, Fiscal Year 1976ᵃ

Decile	Average Net Assessed Valuation per Formula Pupil Fiscal Year 1976	Percent Change in School District K to 12 Headcount Enrollment, September 1971 to January 1975			Variation Indexᵇ
		Average	Minimum	Maximum	
Total	$17,003	− 5.3%	5.9%	55.0%	147.2%
1	8,956	− 0.8	−14.5	26.7	1137.5
2	11,182	− 2.0	−12.0	16.0	320.0
3	12,610	− 4.9	9.0	−19.6	116.3
4	13,856	− 4.1	14.5	−19.6	143.9
5	15,053	− 5.0	−17.1	22.2	148.0
6	16,636	− 6.2	5.9	−16.4	83.9
7	18,275	− 6.2	8.3	−17.6	98.4
8	20,222	− 5.6	−22.8	55.0	208.9
9	28,574	− 8.0	8.2	−20.7	86.3
10	29,664	−10.1	17.7	−28.9	78.2

ᵃNCSL calculations based on data from Iowa Department of Public Instruction and Iowa Comptroller's Office. All averages are unweighted means.

ᵇCoefficient of variation.

recruit the best academic talent at the elementary and postsecondary levels, and the fact that many poorly trained and ill-prepared teachers remain in the educational systems in need of greatest improvement, leads many distinguished commentators to doubt the utility of adding any more funds for state school finance reform. Add to this popular research that indicates expensive schooling is simply not a prerequisite to economic success in later life, and the public willingness to raise more funds for finance reform seems weak indeed.[17]

Moreover, rising public concern about levels of educational achievement seems to have spurred a resurgency of concern about local school governance policies. School decentralization is a main feature of urban school politics. Alternative schools are beginning to flourish within many public school systems where there is public support for revising school discipline and curriculum policies in favor of a return to the "basics." Parental involvement in schooling decisions is increasingly promised in federal Title I programs and in newly established state special education programs, and the public remains hostile to school consolidation that may dilute their control of local school policies. Finally, in many cases, local voters are prepared to administer harsh fiscal discipline in their local schools if the case merits it—as witnessed by the declining public support of local school tax and bond referenda in the past several years.[18]

Pensions. The last complicating factor in state school finance reform has been the increasing state preoccupation with the fiscal stability of teacher and other state employee retirement systems, which are often inadequately funded to meet future liabilities. Benefits have been increasing at a rate considerably greater than contributory funding, and the pressure is on state decisionmakers to revise the fiscal features of these retirement systems to avoid future fiscal crises of the New York variety.[19] State decisionmakers also are gradually beginning to reassess the relationship of their retirement systems to the federal Social Security System, to deal with the possible federal takeover or wholesale regulation of state-local public employee systems and to assess the impact that retirement policies are having on teacher mobility and teacher retention during a period of declining enrollment. As state policies in these teacher retirement matters begin to crystallize, there may be fewer funds to meet the demands of conventional school finance reform.

In summary, the new policy demands on the state decisionmakers—declining enrollments, educational productivity, and teacher retirement policies—may be diverting their interest from conventional school finance reform policies. If they do so, there will be less interest in providing additional funds for reform, and state officials may also become less concerned about seeking revisions in federal education policy.

Other Problems. State demands for reform in federal education problems are driven by much more than their impact on equalization or their

**Table 2-7. NCSL Survey of State Education Committee
Chairmen, August 1976-Question on State Budget Conditions**

What is likely to be the general condition of your
state's budget by the beginning of 1977?

	Percent of Education Committee Chairmen Who Say:			
Region	*"Strong Surplus"*	*"Limited Surplus"*	*"Balanced"*	*"Taxes Must Increase or Expenditures Must be Cut"*
U.S. Total	25.5%	37.3%	27.5%	9.8%
Northeast	.0	50.0	37.5	12.5
South	20.0	40.0	26.7	13.3
Midwest	26.7	33.3	26.7	13.3
West	46.2	30.8	23.1	.0

Source: See Table 2-4.

failure to provide help for new school problems. Other factors that influence the state position are tight budgets and aggravation over federal accountability requirements.

Tight Budgets. During the heyday of their school finance reform efforts—two, three, and four years ago—state policymakers were blessed by one of the most bountiful periods of state revenue collection ever experienced. State treasuries nationwide ran surpluses of a sort that had not been seen in years. Like the federal government, states were the beneficiaries of a national economic boom. But when the boom collapsed in 1974, state revenue collections fell back sharply while expenditure demands continued to mount.

State revenue collections, fortunately, are now beginning to pick up. State budget officers and legislative leaders in most states report that their budgets should experience modest growth throughout 1976[20] (see Table 2-7). It is clear, however, that the growth is not going to be sufficient in many states to support any sweeping school finance reform initiatives of the variety adopted in the wake of *Serrano*. Major school finance reforms are still under consideration in several states, but no one expects quick legislative action. Rather, most states will concentrate their efforts on maintaining funding levels of past reforms or on making marginal improvements in a variety of categorical programs, especially programs designed for handicapped and vocational students.

Hemmed in by tight budgets, many state educational policymakers are becoming agitated about provisions of federal programs that require outlays that reduce their decisionmaking leeway. The greatest source of irritation in this respect is the imposition of mandates that require the provision of services, but which do not provide the funding needed to cover a large share of the associated costs. Currently, for example, many state policymakers are doubtful

Table 2-8. NCSL Survey of State Education Committee Chairmen,
August 1976—Question on Federal Special Education Mandates

As you may know, the federal Education for All Handicapped Children
Act of 1975 (PL 94-142) requires states to provide appropriate
special education services for all handicapped children by fiscal
1979. Will your state be able to meet this goal?

	Percent of Education Committee Chairment Who Say:		
Region	Yes	Probably	No
U.S. total	26.5%	61.2%	12.2%
Northeast	62.5	25.0	12.5
South	28.6	42.9	28.6
Midwest	13.3	80.0	6.7
West	16.7	83.3	.0

Source: See Table 2-4.

that they will be able to raise the funds needed to meet the service mandates of
PL 94-142 (see Table 2-8). Recent estimates by state education agencies suggest
that the cost of meeting the requirements of PL 94-142 may total about $9
billion. By contrast, some estimate that the aggregate surplus of all state budgets
is unlikely to be more than about $3.0 billion a year between now and 1980.[21]
    One of the ironies of PL 94-142 is that it raises serious initial
funding problems for many states but does contain a feature that would provide significant relief to state and local special education costs in the not too
distant future. Unlike almost every other federal program of consequence. PL
94-142 allows state and local governments to use federal funds to supplant
revenues from state or local sources once the point of providing full educational
opportunity for all handicapped children is reached. Many groups organized on
behalf of handicapped children are very concerned about this feature, however,
and its future may depend to a great degree on the discretion exhibited in its
use.
    Mounting dislike of federally imposed costs is reflected not only
in policymakers' attitudes toward program mandates, but also in their rising
anger with educational professionals who use federal dollars to initiate activities
that have been deemed inappropriate in the state policymaking process. While
federal dollars may impose no burden on state or local government initially,
they almost always create costs in the long run because they develop a constituency that presses for supplementary state or local funding, especially if
federal funding dries up. State officials are more and more cognizant of this
problem and are railing against it with increasing frequency. As one leading
state education policymaker stated recently: "Federal involvement can create
an artificial economic boom that will cause communities to forget, when federal

dollars begin to disappear, the initial purpose of the program or for whom it was designed. It is common for the number of jobs that will be eliminated to become the major factor used. . .to continue a program, without regard to whether the children who made it all possible received any benefit."[22]

State policymakers are actively attempting to control the fiscally stimulative effects of federal programs. Several state legislatures are now insisting that no federal funds may be spent unless they are specifically appropriated in the legislative process. Part of this legislative initiative, however, involves concern about limiting the political discretion of state executives as much as interest in holding down the stimulative impact of federal programs. Reflecting this dual motivation, the Pennsylvania General Assembly justified its recent decision to bar expenditure of all federal funds without state legislative approval in the following statement:

> There has been increasing concern among legislators at instances in which the executive branch has used federal funds to avoid legislative intent. In some cases, the executive has used such funds as "foot-in-the-door" tactics to start a new program.
> When the federal funds expire, the pressure to continue the program is then aimed at legislators, who bear the brunt of financial difficulties without ever having participated in the decision to start the program.[23]

Unreasonable Accountability Costs. Another objection to many federal programs shared by many state decisionmakers is their often excessive accountability costs. While few state policymakers expect the federal government to provide education dollars without strings attached, most feel that existing federal accountability requirements are unreasonably expensive and time-consuming. Some chief state school officers claim that they currently must allocate at least 40 percent of their administrative work load to meeting federal paperback requirements even though federal funds generally provide no more than 7 percent of state-local education revenues. Studies now underway by the federal "paperwork commission" may soon provide independent corroboration of this claim, or at the very least, they may help to place it in proper perspective.

HOW CAN FEDERAL-STATE EDUCATION POLICY BE MADE MORE COOPERATIVE?

The divergent political interests of federal and state decisionmakers must be better coordinated if both levels of government are to commit themselves to fiscal policies that will serve the educational interests of both majority and minority groups at the state and national levels. This requires considerably more federal understanding of the fiscal and educational advances many states have made in the post-*Serrano* era; yet it will also require state acknowledgment of the long-standing and well-entrenched nature of federal concern for the educational and fiscal programs of selected special interest groups. A more cooperative federal-state relationship in education finance might be based on several new policies initiated at the federal level that will support and enhance the more positive fiscal and educational advances that states have made in the last few years.

Support for the Basic Fiscal Equity of State Funding Programs. Outside of impact aid, the federal government does not provide any unconditional aid for the support of state-local education finance systems. General revenue-sharing proceeds may be earmarked for education but only at the state level.[24] Independent school districts are not direct recipients of revenue-sharing funds, and general purpose local governments are prohibited from earmarking any of their receipts for education. Indeed, the only support for the fiscal equity of state-local school finance systems lies with the relatively modest funds that are now authorized for school finance planning under Section 842 of Public Law 93–380. This aid program, moreover, has the same drawbacks of earlier federal support of state education department personnel; it can lead state decision-makers to conclude that finance reforms are more inspired by federally influenced state bureaucrats than by any genuine, broad-based political desire for school finance change.

The federal government could pursue a selected number of policies to offer more broad-based support of the fiscal equity of state school funding systems. First, it could support impact aid reforms where needed. It could provide for more realistic regulations that would give more states the option of counting impact aid in their basic aid allotments where they desire to do so. PL 93–380 also could be further amended to prevent poor districts from losing needed impact aid, as they do now, in comparison to rich districts once a state makes the decision to count impact aid in its basic aid formula.

On a much more significant scale, however, the federal government could accept one or more major policies committing greater national support for state school finance equity. First, it could provide that school districts share in expanded revenue-sharing proceeds according to the same general aid formula now in use for general local governments. Or it could adopt a smaller scale and better directed general aid program for school districts in a state that was adjudged to be in need of greater general aid. These districts might be the low-spending school districts in a state that need such extra funds to upgrade their educational offerings or districts that simply are unable to make any additional fiscal effort in support of higher local school taxes. In most cases, these districts would be low-spending rural jurisdictions or urban school districts that are facing rising tax pressures on local budgets. Another but more indirect way of aiding state school finance reform might be to underwrite properly structured state property tax relief programs. In many cases, these programs serve to take the "sting" out of local school taxes. Federal support of these programs might provide states with the opportunity of either widening the income eligibility of these programs or of offering even greater tax relief for low-income families and individuals for whom the property tax is still the most onerous tax.[25] Federal advances on any of these fronts would convince many state decisionmakers that federal officials both understand and support fiscal advances that many states have made in reforming their school finance systems.

Continued Categorical Grant Reform. Another way in which federal decisionmakers could support state school finance policies is to press ahead with many of the categorical grants reforms that have been enacted in the last few years along with a more deliberate consideration of recent education block grant proposals.

State decisionmakers now are beginning to understand that federal legislators are, in some measure, slowing down the proliferation of education categorical grants. Grant consolidation of the variety that occurred in PL 93-380 and that is now contained in PL 94-482 in vocational education indicates that federal decisionmakers are concerned that too great a number of discrete categorical grants will hamper the effective management of federal education funds and dilute the aggregate amount of education funding that can be directed for selected minorities of concern to national decisionmakers. State decisionmakers welcome this trend, which makes their oversight and control of such funds a more manageable proposition.

Along the same lines, state legislators and other state interest groups have been actively seeking a way by which Congress will give more active deliberation to large-scale education block grants. In this matter, there was broad-based state government support for the recent administration block grant proposal (HR 12196) though several state groups felt that such a block grant should be better funded than the administration initially proposed and that there should be some more specific ground rules about the funding competition between Title I and handicapped children.

In the same vein, several states have expressed an interest in the optional block grant proposal of Senators Domenici and Bellmon. While the bill contains the potential for federal-state conflict over block grant eligibility standards, interest is especially high in those states that have engaged in comprehensive consolidation of their own aid formulas—Maine, New Mexico, and Florida stand out in particular—and that desire to have the greatest coordination of federal and state education aid programs. All these developments suggest that state decisionmakers will continue to be enthusiastic about the idea of large-scale block grants once funding problems can be solved.

State support for sweeping education block grants is also an indication of growing state oppositon of several facets of existing and newly enacted federal education legislation. First, states contend that the local funding pass-throughs provided in the special education law may compromise future state plans to direct both federal and state funds to districts with extraordinary special education needs—poorer districts that do not always make an adequate effort to mount a high-quality special education program. A related interest is being shown by states that have their own state-funded compensatory education programs and that wish to relate more explicitly the funding flows of federal and state programs in this area.[26]

Similarly, it appears that states will be more active in opposing or reshaping the educational mandates that come hard on the heels of new funding programs. Concern with regulations now being developed pursuant to Section 504 of the Vocational Rehabilitation Act as well as the various substantive mandates contained in PL 94-142 has led one state, Minnesota, to pass a new law prohibiting state and local agencies from funding any of the excess administrative costs associated with the law. Even more states are now questioning some of the service mandates that may be implied in providing a "free and appropriate" education for all handicapped children, even those children that are so severely handicapped as to be virtually uneducable. For the federal government to pass a law with such staggering fiscal implications and simply not identify or pay this greater share of the costs so mandated dilutes state support for new federal initiatives in this and other special interest areas.

The quid pro quo for continued federal commitment to categorical and block grant reform, however, will undoubtedly demand some new state school finance policies as well. The federal government, for example, may encourage more state involvement in compensatory education funding as the price of nationwide or optional block grants. Increased federal support for grant consolidation or block grants might come with the price tag of having states develop targeted categorical programs to meet the special needs of urban and rural areas or having states drop those disequalizing features of present aid programs such as save-harmless or flat grants. In short, if states are to be given more control over the flow of federal funding, they should be prepared to demonstrate that their own funding systems are geared to meet the fiscal needs of special pupils and high-cost areas.

More Positive Federal Involvement in Education Research and Labor-Management Issues. The last area where the federal government can play a more positive role in federal-state education policy is by placing greater emphasis on setting national educational research and management policies. It is probably safe to say that the nationally funded education research beginning with the Coleman report has done a great deal to undermine the popular faith in investing more dollars in education. Further national research involvement with educational vouchers has hampered national research community relations with the teaching profession. Conflicting educational research has made it difficult for most lay decisionmakers to design productive ways for education to be improved at the state and local levels. All this occurs as more states develop educational testing and minimal competency programs designed to identify the skills being imparted to children in their educational settings. The public demand seems clear—get back to the basics of developing fundamental elementary cognitive skills for our children and make sure that they have attained these skills at adequate levels throughout their educational careers. At the same time, the educational community remains in an intellectual and moral quandary as to how these skills are produced and how schools should be run to produce such skills. While it is beyond the scope of this chapter to suggest ways in which this complex task can be approached, the national government must do more to develop and disseminate understandable research into ways in which educational productivity might be improved. In turn, state and local governments have to identify the influences that hamper educational productivity—whether it is the inability of districts to hire adequate new teaching staff in times of declining enrollment or local inability to revise teaching salary schedules to attract better qualified teachers to urban and rural districts where education is more difficult to provide. A joint federal-state responsibility for identifying and implementing programs to increase educational productivity is necessary in the years to come.

A related issue concerns federal-state relations in labor-management relations. While the recent *N.L.C.* v. *Usery* desicision may foreclose the passage of a national public employee collective bargaining law, many states are still concerned about undue federal encroachments on their public policy prerogatives in these areas. Most state decisionmakers have to contend with active teacher lobbies that are continuing to press for increases in teacher pay and fringe benefits along with continuingly tighter restrictions regarding teacher tenure and job specifications. Recent revisions in some state labor-management relation laws have contributed to fairer and more stable labor-management relations in many cases, especially where the terms and conditions of public employee bargaining have been better delineated, where impasse procedures for bargaining have been more explicitly structured, and where bargaining units have been more specifically defined. Thus, while several states still have no or relatively unsophisticated bargaining laws, many states, in the judgment of impartial observers, have laws with features far superior to those contained in recent proposed federal collective bargaining bills. Federal preemptive legislation would deny the positive experimentation that many states are exhibiting in this area.[27]

However, this is not to deny the continuing need for more stable labor-management relations in many states. Declining enrollments will begin to cause more teacher layoffs in the future; more disputes about seniority rights and tenure conditions are bound to arise at the state and local levels. States without a variety of impasse procedures may find themselves coping with illegal strikes since there may be little effective means of following through legitimate grievances for teacher groups. School management in states with more rigid labor relation laws may find it difficult to promote necessary personnel and fiscal economies during periods of enrollment decline.

Closely related to this personnel issue is the wholesale revision of retirement systems that have increasingly become prevalent as teachers bargain more for deferred income items and less for current salary increases. As pension overhauls occur, the fiscal strain on state budgets will become more pronounced, especially when they are not making adequate payments to keep their pension funds actuarially sound or when they have to consider early retirement policies to induce some positive job mobility within a relatively static teacher force.

The federal government would be wise to play a supportive rather than preemptive role in assisting states in dealing with these school management problems. More explicit studies of the ways in which state pension systems and Social Security should be coordinated are needed; more technical assistance for smaller states in developing better actuarial estimates of pension funding plans and greater incentives for pension portability would be valuable assets in pension reform. In labor relations, similar assistance would be productive. More study of the effectiveness of various impasse procedures, more scrutiny of the quality of labor management practices in states where the terms and conditions of employee bargaining are either broad or narrow, and more explicit studies of the impact of various types of labor-management policies on educational budget setting would be a positive role for the federal government to play. Of course states must expect that insofar as varied state practices do lead to unnecessary turmoil in pension or labor-management policies, the demand for federal intervention and standardization of labor-management and pension policies will increase.

CONCLUSION

This chapter has noted the main areas of state-federal conflict in educational finance. In brief, the federal government must understand that recent and forthcoming state school finance policies are grounded in the need to serve majority political interests in education. Property tax relief, expanded educational opportunities for regular day-school children, enhanced educational productivity, and more stable labor-management and pension policies seem to be the primary concerns of state policymakers. They are not unmindful of the needs of high-cost students; indeed, their new funding policies reflect renewed and vigorous concerns for the needs of these groups. At the same time, the concerns for these groups cannot deflect from their need to solve the major school finance and management problems alluded to above. If federal school aid policies compromise state decisionmakers' abilities to deal with these problems effectively, the federal influence in education, barring massive new funding of education by the national government, will continue to be minimal.

At the same time, state governments should work to see that the federal commitment to high-cost or special needs children is not diluted. But they also must seek ways in which a more positive federal-state partnership in dealing with minority and special interest concerns can be fashioned. The states must respect the fact that the federal government can make a substantial contribution to the funding of programs for special needs children that cannot always be accommodated in new or future state school finance reforms.

This mutual understanding for a more cooperative federal-state role in educational finance can materialize if the following policies are pursued:

- Federal decisionmakers recognize state constitutional mandates in education and balance their concerns for educational minorities with support for the main tax and expenditure policies contained in recent state school finance reforms.
- Federal decisionmakers fashion a federal-state relationship in education that preserves the fiscal and programmatic policies of state that have "reformed" their education finance systems while encouraging other states to adopt these state-based, rather than federally mandated, reform policies.
- Federal decisionmakers focus their overriding policy concerns on four or five major educational grant programs and stop trying to act like a national school board in a variety of areas. This, of course, will mean the diminution of the power of selective national interest groups in some cases.
- States take a more aggressive and forthright stance about the adverse effects of federal intrusion into their educational programs and refrain from the usual politics of trying to merely dilute the effects of fundamentally unsound federal education policies.
- States develop more explicit fiscal and programmatic concern about the needs of the educationally and economically disadvantaged in their school finance programs and erase the picture of state governments as being hostile or apathetic to the concerns of these minority interests.
- States recognize that there is a legitimate but focused federal interest in educational policy areas such as (1) support for additional programs for the disadvantaged, (2) high-quality educational research, and (3) support of well-planned and well-thought-out innovations that can improve educational productivity and stabilize educational labor-management relations at the state and local levels.

NOTES

1. National Conference of State Legislatures (NCSL), *Press Release on State Education Committee Chairman Survey About School Finance* (Washington, D.C.: NCSL, 1976), Question 3.

2. Ibid., Question 4.

3. See Joel S. Berke et al., "Federal Aid and State School Finance: Present Patterns and Future Alternatives," in John J. Callahan and William H. Wilken, eds., *School Finance Reform: A Legislators' Handbook* (Washington, D.C.: NCSL, 1976), pp. 94–104.

4. John J. Callahan and William H. Wilken, op. cit., Chapter 1, pp. 1–12.

5. For a description of Michigan's property tax relief program as well as that of many other states, see Abt Associates, *Property Tax Relief Programs for the Elderly: A Compendium Report* (Cambridge, Mass.: Abt Associates, 1976).

6. Governor's Advisory Panel of Consultants, *Educational Finance and the New York State Real Property Tax: The Inescapable Relationships* (Albany, N.Y.: The Governor's Panel, 1976).

7. John J. Callahan and William H. Wilken, op. cit., Chapter 1.

8. The New York court suit is being brought by the four largest cities in the state; the Ohio litigaton is being brought by the city of Cincinnati.

9. NCSL, op. cit., Question 7.

10. William H. Wilken and David O. Porter, "State Aid for Special Education; Who Benefits?" (Washington, D.C.: National Institute of Education Grant NIE-G-74-0021), ch. 1.

11. This still occurs even in newly reformed state special education programs. See Wilken, ibid., ch. 3.

12. Illinois Task Force on Declining Enrollments in the Public Schools, *Final Report* (Springfield, Ill., December 1975).

13. National Conference of State Legislatures, *An Assessment of the Tax and Expenditure Equity of Iowa's School Finance System* (Washington, D.C.: NCSL, 1976), ch. 4.

14. Christopher Jencks, *Inequality* (New York: Basic Books, 1973).

15. Anita Summers and Barbara L. Wolfe, "Which School Resources Help Learning? Efficiency and Equity in Philadelphia Public Schools," *Federal Reserve Bank of Philadelphia Business Review* (February 1975).

16. F. Raymond McKenna, "Piaget's Complaint-And Mine: Why is There no Science of Education?" *Phi Delta Kappan* (February 1976), pp. 405–409.

17. For a contrary review, see C. Russell Hill, *Education and Earnings—A Review of the Evidence* (Washington, D.C.: The Education Planning Staff, Office of Assistant Secretary for Planning and Evaluation, Department of Health, Education, and Welfare, May 1976).

18. The recent special levy defeats in the State of Washington, for example, have caused the Washington legislature to appropriate nearly $65 million in special levy relief ostensibly to be directed to school districts whose voters refused to vote additional school tax millage.

19. Bernard W. Jump, Jr., *State and Local Employee Pension Plans: Watching for Problems* (Columbus, Ohio: Academy for Contemporary Problems, 1976).

20. National Governors' Conference, *Fiscal Profile of the States Survey No. 2* (Washington, D.C.: National Governors' Conference, 1976).

21. David J. Ott et al., *State-Local Finances in the Last Half of the 1970's* (Washington, D.C.: American Interprise Institute, 1975).

22. Harry Wulgalter, "Straight Talk," *Compact,* 10 (Summer 1976), p. 30.

23. "Shapp, Pa. Legislature Locked in Conflict Over Power to Appropriate Federal Funds," *The Bond Buyer* (September 7, 1976), p. 9.

24. See various revenue-sharing use reports published by the U.S. Office of Revenue Sharing.

25. See Alan Odden et al., *Final Report of the Educational Finance Committee of the Missouri Governor's Conference on Education* (Denver, Colo.: Education Commission of the States, 1976), p. 97.

26. See the recent report of Mr. Charles Blaschke on Michigan's state-funded compensatory education program.

27. See Institute of Educational Leadership, *Collective Bargaining and the Role of State Departments of Education* (Washington, D.C.: Institute of Educational Leadership, 1975). This document contains the proceedings of the Second Conference on the Prospects for Federal Collective Bargaining Legislation in the Participating States.

Chapter Three

The Courts as Educational Policymakers and Their Impact on Federal Programs

Betsy Levin

Educational policymaking traditionally has been the sole prerogative of state and local public school authorities. There is no express constitutional basis for the federal government's involvement in what is principally a state function, although Congress has the power under the Constitution's "taxing and spending clause"[1] to provide funds for education to states and localities and to require that certain conditions be met to qualify for or retain these funds.[2] While the importance of education has been recognized by the federal government from the beginning,[3] it was not until the late fifties that efforts to expand the federal role in education were initiated,[4] culminating in the passage of the Elementary and Secondary Education Act in 1965 (ESEA).[5] Thus, what was once considered exclusively a state and local responsibility came to be shared with the federal government.

From one perspective, however, the federal government still plays only a relatively minor role in education. Of $67.9 billion spent annually for public elementary and secondary education, the federal share is only $5.3 billion or 7.8 percent.[6] But the federal money has a larger impact than the proportion of total educational dollars it constitutes suggests. Federal aid, rather than being in the form of general aid to education, is directed at specific national priorities such as greater equity for certain target groups[7] or educational reform and innovation.[8] The federal government is seen as the more appropriate level both for attaining greater equity for minority interests and for stimulating education reform that state or local governments, which respond to the pressures of a parochial majority. Thus, although primary responsibility for education remains with the states, the use of categorical funds has given the federal government the leverage to play a significant role in educational policy, particularly in equity and reform. This focus is evident from the fact that categorical aid to various

47

target groups now amounts to more than half of all federal aid to elementary and secondary education.[9] Among the remaining federal aid programs, most—such as the demonstration and innovation projects of ESEA Title III or the grants for the improvement of state and local planning—are directed at educational reform. Although in the past there has been considerable pressure for a substantial increase in general federal support, it is unlikely that this will occur in the near future.[10]

Federal leverage over educational policy is achieved through the use of incentives or through the use of sanctions if states and localities fail to meet the conditions prescribed by Congress. The federal government's enforcement mechanisms are quite limited, however—the principal sanction being the termination of funds. Because the only real sanction is so draconian in nature, often injuring most those the legislation was designed to help, the enforcement mechanisms are seldom invoked. Clearly, this is a major reason why minorities and other aggrieved groups or individuals have turned to the courts in seeking the twin objectives of educational equity and reform. Thus, the courts can be seen as another instrument of federal policy.

The Scope of Educational Policymaking by the Judiciary. The federal courts began to assume a significant policymaking role in the field of education at about the same time that the legislative and executive branches of the federal government were expanding their involvement in education. The intrusion of the courts into educational policy in the last two decades has been unprecedented, and it has much more directly challenged the primacy of the educational bureaucracy than the actions of the executive and legislative branches. The opening wedge was *Brown* v. *Board of Education*,[11] and for the remainder of the fifties the courts were primarily concerned with implementing the constitutional requirement that no student be denied an equal educational opportunity because of his race. While the courts' involvement in the dismantling of dual school systems has continued unabated,[12] the courts have also become involved in other areas that long had been the prerogative of school authorities.

Since 1968, the United States Supreme Court has reviewed cases involving nearly every major area of educational policy: school curriculum questions,[13] student rights of free expression and of nondisruptive protest,[14] exemptions from state compulsory school attendance laws,[15] school finance reform,[16] school desegregation,[17] bilingual or English-language instruction for those with limited English skills,[18] school personnel policies,[19] student discipline,[20] and liability of school officials for violating the civil rights of students.[21] The involvement of the lower federal courts and of state courts in the education sector has been even more pervasive. Among the equal educational opportunity issues litigated in these courts, beginning in the late sixties, are unequal resources for poor school districts[22] and poor school children,[23] the failure to provide appropriate education for the handicapped,[24] discrimination in admission to schools[25] or to particular programs on the basis of sex,[26] and the tracking and classification of students.[27] Courts have also become involved in accountability questions—whether a school system that fails to provide an average child with the basic reading, writing, and computational skills should be considered guilty of educational malpractice and held liable for damages.[28]

The constitutional rights of teachers also expanded during the sixties and early seventies—encompassing such diverse areas as free speech,[29] mandatory maternity leave,[30] and the ways in which teachers are certified.[31] The growth in power of teachers' organizations, manifested by the substantial number of states that have recently adopted laws permitting collective bargaining, was also a development of the sixties. As teachers increasingly move toward unionization, new questions in education involve not only the right to bargain collectively and the right to strike or to apply other sanctions, but also the right to bargain about various aspects of educational policy. This brings into focus the broader question of the legal rights of various competing groups and individuals to control public education decisionmaking—including school boards, school administrators, municipal officials, teachers, parents, students, community leaders, federal and state agencies, and courts.

Limitations on the Judicial Process in Education. Although the involvement of the courts in certain areas of educational policy has been criticized by some as an inappropriate usurpation of the policymaking functions of school authorities, it should be recalled that where violations of the Fourteenth Amendment's equal protection or due process clause or the First Amendment's establishment of religion or its freedom of speech clause are alleged, the courts cannot refrain from entering the area and deciding the specific case before them.

Moreover, litigation often does not initiate an issue but reflects movements and trends in society. The students' rights movement, which peaked at the height of the hostility to the war in Vietnam, has subsided so that cases concerned with the suppression of student protests and the hair length regulation cases have declined as cases involving disciplinary measures have increased. The rapid increase in the organization of teachers and the increase in the jurisdictions that collectively bargain with them has led to more frequent litigation. The plethora of government regulations, partly in response to Congress's failure to eliminate what are all too frequently deliberate ambiguities in the law, also provokes litigation until the ambiguities in congressional intent are clarified.

To the extent that the political system ultimately resolves claims of inequities by adopting legislation responsive to the judicially declared constitutional standards, the role of the courts is to draw attention to these inequities after those pressing such claims had been unable to obtain the attention of the political system. Thus, the federal courts in many respects should be seen as but another instrument of national policy—with all three branches of government working toward those policies that will best attain the objectives of greater equity and fairness for various groups neglected by society.

This is not to imply that there are no problems stemming from judicial involvement in education. In many cases the impact of such involvement extends far beyond the immediate case and the litigants before the court in ways that are often not apparent to the court. In other cases, the information available is not complete or easily analyzed by an inexpert judge and thus does not lead to the development of the most effective remedies. Whether the legally mandated reforms resulted in benefits for the particular parties before the court or the classes they represented is beyond the scope of this chapter. The possible impact of the recent spate of education decisions on other groups not immediately before the court will be considered, however—the most obvious impact being on the budget. Education must compete for a limited number of taxpayer dollars with other public services such as criminal justice, welfare, and environmental protection. Various interests within education must also compete: the proponents of bilingual education with those of special education for the handicapped; the vocational or career education advocates with those seeking greater emphasis on the college preparatory curriculum; and those backing compensatory education with those reasserting a demand for education for the gifted.

When a court orders a particular remedy, it does not have before it either information as to the total amount of resources available or information about the competing claims for those resources. Moreover, even if the court had this information, there is no appropriate mechanism by which it could establish a system of priorities among the competing claims because that is a function of the political process. Thus, the judicial process is limited in the extent to which it can resolve such issues. On the other hand, federal funding decisions by Congress and the executive branch may have an impact on the allocation of resources mandated by the courts under the Constitution. Such decisions by the political branches of the federal government may distort state legislative and administrative allocations made in compliance with court orders.

The recent legal developments in education are described and their relevance for federal policies and programs discussed in the remainder of this chapter. The tensions stemming from the increasing involvement of the courts in educational issues once left to state and local governments are outlined briefly. How the legislative and executive branches can best facilitate rather than impede the states' compliance with court mandates is also discussed.

EQUAL EDUCATIONAL OPPORTUNITY

School Finance Reform

Interdistrict Disparities. The first major legal breakthrough in school finance reform occurred in 1971 when the California Supreme Court, in

Serrano v. *Priest,*[32] adopted the so-called principle of "fiscal neutrality," which means that education is a fundamental right that cannot be conditioned on the wealth of a child's parents or neighbors. The court had found that the state system of financing education, with its heavy reliance on the local property tax, even with state subventions, resulted in substantial disparities among school districts in per pupil revenues because of the variation in taxable property wealth. Thus, the school finance system discriminated against those who lived in districts with low property wealth and was held to violate the equal protection clause.

Following the *Serrano* victory, fifty-two actions were filed in thirty-one states, with federal court decisions in three states[33] and state court decisions in six more.[34] With little variation, these courts—with the exception of those of New York and Maryland—followed the legal analysis articulated by the *Serrano* court. In one of the federal court cases, *San Antonio Independent School District* v. *Rodriguez,* the state of Texas appealed to the Supreme Court, and on March 21, 1973, a five-to-four decision was handed down, holding that the Texas system of financing schools, while in need of reform, did not violate the Fourteenth Amendment.[35] The Court held that the school finance system did not discriminate against any definable class of poor persons and that education was not a "fundamental right"[36] since it was neither explicitly nor implicitly guaranteed by the Constitution. The Supreme Court found that there is no "interference with fundamental rights where only relative differences in spending levels are involved,"[37] thus rejecting the educational "input" measure of equality of educational opportunity (e.g., dollars, physical facilities, and teacher-pupil ratios). Instead, a "minimum adequacy" standard was taken as the appropriate measure of equal educational opportunity. The Court found that there was no evidence that the Texas system did not provide "an adequate minimum educational offering in every school in the state."[38]

This decision halted the first phase of the school finance reform movement—that based on the Fourteenth Amendment of the Constitution. But the school finance reform movement did not come to a total halt. The *Serrano* case and its progeny had exposed the inequalities in school finance systems, and it was difficult to sweep the situation back under the rug. State courts were still an available forum, and state constitutional provisions could be the basis for a legal challenge.[39] Less than a month after the *Rodriguez* decision, the New Jersey Supreme Court held that New Jersey's school finance statutes violated the New Jersey constitution, which commands the legislature to provide a "thorough and efficient system of free public schools."[40] Suits were soon brought in various state courts around the country alleging that the state systems of financing education were in violation of the *education clauses* of their state constitutions.[41] In some states, the state *equal protection clause* rather than (or in addition to) the education clause was relied on by the plaintiffs in their challenge to the financing system, since unlike the federal constitution, nearly every state constitution contains an explicit educational provision.

Reforms. As a result of the post-*Serrano* litigation, a number of states significantly reformed their school finance systems. Many of these reform measures were enacted in the 1972-73 period before the Supreme Court's decision in *Rodriguez* and during a period in which many state treasuries had an unanticipated surplus.[42] After the first round of school finance litigation, it had become apparent that many of the proposed reforms were too simplistic, however. The fiscal neutrality or wealth-free standard, devised in response to a system in which low property values correlate with low per pupil expenditures, fails to recognize the fiscal problems of central city schools, which stem not from low property values but from higher costs for both education and other public services.[43] The four largest cities in New York State (New York City, Rochester, Buffalo, and Syracuse), intervening in *Board of Education of Levittown* v. *Nyquist,*[44] are now raising these issues.

The Current Situation. To equalize per pupil expenditures within a state, it is necessary to add save-harmless clauses for wealthier districts and to "level up" the poorer districts to make the reform politically palatable, thus requiring the state to spend much more for education than in all likelihood is currently being spent. One effect, then, of the *Serrano* decision is to force a reordering of priorities at the state level. The state is not given "credit" toward compliance with the *Serrano* mandate if, for example, it fully assumes the cost of teacher retirement, formerly an expense of the districts. Nor does state categorical aid for handicapped or gifted programs, bilingual education, driver training, or remedial reading count toward compliance with the decision since categorical aid does not "equalize" expenditures. To be in compliance with the court decree, the state will have to put more of its tax dollars into general aid than it otherwise might have, potentially shortchanging various groups such as the handicapped or educationally disadvantaged. This, then, is an illustration of the tension that can be created by a court order in response to one type of complaint, compliance with which has an effect on a wholly different group not party to the litigation.

As is evident from the foregoing, the cost of implementing new finance systems is massive. At the same time, however, the state treasury surpluses have shrunk. With less money available, legislators have become concerned about spending money where it will have the most impact. The debate over whether "dollars make a difference"—that is, whether education will be improved when the finance system is reformed—continues and is now going on in the courts as well as legislatures. While the courts have reached no definitive conclusions, they have pointed in directions that directly affect the outcome of the debate for legislators.[45]

The Federal Role. To date, the federal government has played almost no direct role in stimulating school finance reform or in assisting states that are attempting to enact reforms. Indeed, some federal programs can indirectly work *against* state efforts to equalize per pupil expenditures. With the exception of Title I aid,[46] most federal programs are disequalizing.[47] The provision of the federally impacted areas aid statute,[48] which prohibits states from treating such aid as local revenue for purposes of the state distribution formula, particularly distorts state equalizing formulas. It was recently amended, however, to allow a state to consider a local district's impacted areas aid payments as local revenue in allocating funds if the state has an "equitable" school finance formula already in effect.[49] The regulations define an "equitable" system as one that the state court has not held invalid and where the disparity among districts in per pupil revenues is 20 percent or less, excluding capital outlay.[50] The principal difficulty with the disparity standard is that very few states can qualify. Many states have begun to reform their school finance systems, however, and the inability to coordinate these reforms with federal aid programs such as impact aid can undermine the new laws.

Even if federal aid programs were equalizing rather than antiequalizing, the federal share of education funds in any state is too small to affect the present inequitable revenue distribution pattern across school districts. A number of proposals were made in the post-*Serrano*-pre-*Rodriguez* period, therefore, that called for an increased federal share to be used specifically to reduce expenditure disparities or tax inequalities among districts within a state.[51] Most of these proposals provided for a federal incentive program for equalizing interdistrict expenditure disparities. The only such program to be enacted, however—and yet to be fully funded—is that provided under § 842 of the Education Amendments of 1974.[52] This law provides that a state may be reimbursed for the cost of developing or implementing a school finance plan. With only very sketchy legislative guidelines—stating that the plan be "consistent with such standards as may be required by the fourteenth article of amendment to the Constitution" and have as its primary purpose achievement "of equality of educational opportunity for all children"—the Department of Health, Education and Welfare (HEW) adopted regulations for an acceptable plan.[53] The lack of clarity of these guidelines and the fact that the courts are not in agreement as to what the Fourteenth Amendment requires means that almost any plan submitted can receive approval. Moreover, the total amount of money authorized is far too small to offset the massive amounts really needed for reforming state school finance systems.

One difficulty with any program of federal aid for school finance reform, manifest even in this minor planning grant program, lies with the setting of a federal equalization standard by which reform is to be measured. There is little agreement as to whether equal educational opportunity means tax relief (the equalization of tax burdens), education resource equity (the equalization of per pupil expenditures), or even minimally adequate education rather than equal education. The courts will continue to deal with the special problems, such as urban cost differences and municipal overburden, raised by the *Levittown* v. *Nyquist* suit. In addition, there are new problems, such as declining enrollments and increased pension liability, that differ among states and districts within states. Finally, federal standard setting is bound to involve significant additional costs that will not be offset by a program involving only small amounts of federal revenue, and thus these costs would have to be borne by the states. Some states also have already enacted progressive reform measures while other states still maintain systems that result in gross disparities among school districts. One program, therefore, would not deal adequately with both kinds of states unless different standards were established, allowing the more progressive states greater leeway after certain criteria were met.

Federal Alternatives. In sum, where courts—either state or federal—have ordered state authorities to develop a nondiscriminatory financing system, there are several ways in which the political branches of the federal government can work with and not against the judiciary and state legislatures:

1. Since the state treasury surpluses of many states have diminished and politically feasible reforms require a substantial input of money, the federal government could provide much larger scale assistance to equalize per pupil exependitures than is now available under Section 842. Perhaps a law similar to the Emergency School Aid Act (for desegregating school *districts*) could be enacted, which would provide funds to assist *states* in adopting and carrying out school finance reforms—whether court ordered or voluntary. Federal "equalization standards" must be sufficiently flexible and varied so as not to penalize those progressive states that have already considerably reformed their school finance laws. There can be no single national equalization standard as school finance reform must be tailored to the characteristics of each individual state.
2. Federal aid programs such as impacted areas aid should be evaluated to determine whether they are antiequalizing or otherwise impede state reform efforts, and they should be revised accordingly.
3. The federal government could assist states by undertaking research to seek more sophisticated formulas and disseminating the results. Research should include investigation into cost differentials for the same level of education, the cost of programs for pupils with higher needs, and factors such as size of the school district that might produce diseconomies of scale.

Intradistrict Disparities. There are only two intradistrict disparity cases of significance—one decided before *Rodriguez* was handed down and the other after. In *Hobson* v. *Hansen*,[54] substantial differences in the per pupil expenditures for teachers' salaries and benefits were found to exist between schools attended by the wealthier, predominantly white students in Washington, D.C., and schools in the low-income, minority sections of the city. Since the school board was unable to advance a compelling state interest justifying this unequal treatment, the court found it to be a violation of the equal protection clause and ordered per pupil expenditures for teachers from the regular budget to be equalized within 5 percent in all of the city's elementary schools.[55]

Brown v. *Board of Education of the City of Chicago*[56] is the only significant post-*Rodriguez* case involving intradistrict disparities in school expenditures, and in the absence of a racial classification, the court would *not* distinguish the intradistrict suit from *Rodriguez*. The court, noting that the disparities, which were primarily due to the school board's teacher assignment policies, could be due to "administrative convenience, sudden unexpected demographic changes, and response to the special education need of certain neighborhoods," applied the weaker, rational relationship test and held that such disparities were not irrational. The concentration of higher salaried teachers in certain schools was attributed to the city's voluntary teacher transfer policy, which enabled the more experienced teachers to transfer to the more "desirable" schools. The court endorsed this policy since it "presumably helps keeps these teachers in the Chicago school system, which upgrades the skill level of the system as a whole."[57]

What is the impact on the school system of a court decree ordering the elimination of intradistrict disparities and what is the relationship of the court decree to federal program requirements? The Washington, D.C., school system is now under court order to equalize expenditures, including longevity pay, for classroom teachers within a 5 percent range of the average per pupil expenditures for *all* schools in the system, or it will risk having the school board and the superintendent held in contempt of court. The school system is also required by the Title I guidelines to equalize expenditures for all instructional staff, *not* including longevity pay, within a 5 percent range of the average per pupil expenditures of the system's *non-Title I* schools,[58] or it will risk losing millions of federal dollars for compensatory programs. The school system claims that it cannot comply with the court order and with the federal guidelines at the same time, and there has been no coordination by the federal government between the Title I requirements and the court decree. It is clear that coordination of federal legislative and judicial requirements, now lacking in Washington, D.C., is essential.

Title I and Aid to Private Schools

Recent decision of the Supreme Court appear to have sharply curtailed the circumstances under which public aid can be given to nonpublic schools without violating the establishment clause of the First Amendment. These decisions may have an impact on Title I of the Elementary and Secondary Education Act of 1965 (ESEA), which provides funds to disadvantaged children regardless of whether they attend public or private schools,[59] as well as on any federally financed voucher program that includes nonpublic schools.

In *Meek* v. *Pittenger*,[60] the Supreme Court reviewed a Pennsylvania statute that required auxiliary programs such as guidance counseling, health services, speech and hearing services, and remedial reading and arithmetic to be provided to nonpublic school children on the premises of nonpublic schools by public school teachers, counselors, and other public school personnel. The Court held the statute unconstitutional because the state, in order to ensure that such teachers would remain nonideological, would necessarily become entangled with the church.

The Title I guidelines for such auxiliary services as remedial reading and arithmetic are quite similar to the provisions of the Pennsylvania statute.[61] Consequently, with the seeming exception of programs providing bus transportation, school lunches, and public health facilities,[62] it appears that public school personnel funded under Title I could not be used to provide auxiliary, remedial services to educationally deprived children on parochial school premises since teachers are not "self-policing" items like books. Yet remedial services are the heart of the Title I program.

If the establishment clause bars the use of publicly employed remedial teachers funded under Title I in parochial schools, the impact may not only be felt by those schools but by the public schools as well. In an earlier case,[63] the Supreme Court had held that under Title I state education officials must provide services to parochial school children that are "comparable in quality, scope, and opportunity for participation" to those provided children in the public schools.[64] If the state cannot provide "comparable" services without using public school teachers on private school premises, then it must eliminate the use of on-the-premises instruction in *public* schools and use "other means, such as neutral sites" for both public and private school students.[65]

Thus, dual enrollment or neutral site instruction may be the only available option to preserve the heart of the Title I program.[66] However, there are some states, Missouri being the most notable example,[67] where such programs are prohibited by state law. In that situation, according to the Supreme Court, the state has the option of nonparticipation in the Title I program altogether.

Federal Alternatives. Because of the possibility that the long-established formula—which permitted the advocates of public aid to parochial schools and those who opposed such aid for political and constitutional reasons to join forces—may collapse, alternative approaches to distributing Title I aid should be considered. If transportation, school lunches, or health facilities are the only services permitted in parochial schools, Title I programs in *public* schools may have to be reduced to comply with federal law unless the "comparable services" requirement is changed.

The Exclusion of the Handicapped from Public Education

The first legal breakthrough for the handicapped came in a pre-*Rodriguez* case, *Pennsylvania Association for Retarded Children (PARC)* v.

Pennsylvania.[68] In that state, retarded children could be excluded from the public schools if they had been certified as "uneducable and untrainable" or had not attained the mental age of a normal five-year-old child. The plaintiffs introduced evidence that *all* mentally retarded persons are capable of benefiting from a program of education and training. Without deciding whether education was a fundamental right, the court concluded that the policy of providing education to normal children while denying it entirely to a substantial number of children with mental handicaps "established a colorable constitutional claim even under the less stringent rational basis test."[69] The parties entered into a consent agreement whereby the state recognized its "obligation to place each mentally retarded child in a free, public program of education and training appropriate to the child's capacity. . . ."[70]

Impact of *Rodriguez*. Although *Rodriguez* failed to find that education was a fundamental right because it was neither explicitly nor implicitly guaranteed by the Constitution, the case did distinguish the interdistrict financing inequities, which produced relative differences in the quality of education, from a state "financing system [that] occasioned an absolute denial of educational opportunities to any of its children."[71] Arguably, then, excluding a class of children such as the mentally retarded from the public schools would violate the equal protection clause of the Fourteenth Amendment on the ground that some minimum quantum of education is a fundamental right.

Cuyohoga County Association for Retarded Children and Adults v. *Essex,*[72] which was decided in 1976, seems to be at odds with the *PARC* case. In *PARC*, however, the plaintiffs had introduced uncontradicted testimony by four expert witnesses who convinced the court that "all mentally retarded persons are capable of benefiting from a program of education and training. . . ,"[73] whereas the Ohio court heard no evidence and had only a "limited record" before it. The Ohio court thus expressly limited its decision "to matters of facial constitutionality" and, relying on *Rodriguez*, used the more lenient rational basis standard of equal protection to uphold Ohio's statute as constitutional.

Even if a minimum quantum of education is not a fundamental right under the Constitution and even if the Supreme Court refuses to recognize the existence of any new suspect classifications such as the handicapped, *Rodriguez* may nonetheless not significantly impede litigation in nonschool finance areas if the cases are brought in state courts since education is explicitly referred to in almost every state constitution. Thus, education may be construed as a fundamental right under the state's equal protection clause.

Educators have debated whether it is better to place educable mentally retarded students in special classes with teachers specifically trained to deal with their handicaps or to "mainstream" them—that is place them in regular classrooms with supplemental and supportive services. Although by no means has the debate been resolved,[74] the courts,[75] and now the recently enacted federal law,[76] have unequivocally come down on the side of "mainstreaming" the handicapped. One difficulty in moving from the theory of mainstreaming the handicapped to practice, however, is the lack of funds and trained treachers to provide the support necessary to enable the handicapped child to function in the regular classroom.[77]

Costs. What are the likely costs of these legally mandated reforms? What will the necessary tradeoffs with other programs be? Unless additional money is appropriated, either at the state or federal levels, to meet the costs implicit in the court orders, the funds available for educating the ordinary student or the sufficiency of funds allocated to equalizing the state education finance formula may be affected.[78] Without additional funds, the setting of group against group may occur.

Pursuant to the consent order of 1972 in *PARC*, the State of Pennsylvania sought to locate and identify all excluded youngsters. By April 1973, 15,000 retarded children were located, 7,398 of whom had been totally excluded from any educational program.[79] While the consent order's ultimate price tag is still unclear, there is little doubt that the cost of implementation is high. In addition to locating and identifying all excluded youngsters, the state must conduct medical and psychological evaluations of those mentally retarded children it feels are unfit for regular classroom instruction and reevaluate any child excluded from regular classroom instruction every two years as well as any time a change in his program is contemplated.[80] In addition, the state must establish a hearing mechanism whereby dissatisfied parents may contest the school district's placement recommendation. The cost of providing "due process," also required by recent federal legislation, is discussed below.

There are other, nondollar costs that must be kept in mind. As noted above, placing a child in a regular classroom without providing additional services may be more detrimental to the child and to the other students in the class than leaving this child in a special education class. Yet without additional funds and trained personnel, this is likely to be the situation in the aftermath of a court order. On the other hand, the harm that can result from misclassification of a student by leaving the student in a class for the educable mentally retarded is extremely serious.

Labeling. There have been several court cases concerned with the "mislabeling" of students. In both *Larry P.* v. *Riles*[81] in California and *Hobson* v. *Hansen*[82] in Washington, D.C., the plaintiff students contended that their erroneous placement in special classes for the retarded or for the slow learner was a denial of equal protection. Neither court denied the authority of the state to label children as exceptional and to segregate them according to those labels.

However, since a disproportionate number of minority children were classified and placed in the lower ability groups or tracks, the strict standard of equal protection review could be used.[83]

The Federal Role. The federal role with regard to the handicapped is significantly enlarged by the passage of the Education for All Handicapped Children Act,[84] which provides funds that are to reach the level of $3 billion by 1981—more than the federal government now spends on Title I and impact aid combined.[85] The act also mandates stringent and costly procedural safeguards.[86] Whenever the educational agency proposes to *initiate* or *change* the identification or placement of a child or *refuses* to take such action, written notice in the parents' own language must be provided. Parents are entitled to a hearing (upon their initiative), and it may not be conducted by an employee of the state or local education agency. At the hearing, parents may have counsel and may present evidence and confront and cross-examine witnesses. The possible impact of these requirements can be determined from the estimates made by school authorities in Pennsylvania after the consent order in the *PARC* case, where they found they were spending approximately $500 on each hearing—about half the amount that is spent on the education of the normal or average student for the entire school year.[87]

Clearly, then, the impact of a court decision ordering those mentally and physically handicapped children who have been *totally* excluded from any public schooling to be given a public education will be substantial in both man-hours and dollars expended. Without additional federal or state appropriations, the court order may cut into other priorities of the school system.

Federal Alternatives. What could the federal government do that it is not now doing? One approach might be to enact a law similar to the Emergency School Aid Act that would provide federal funds to districts that, either under court order or voluntarily, are attempting to meet the needs of handicapped children. Under such a law, districts could get funds and technical assistance—including counsel and special experts—to establish appropriate hearing mechanisms and to develop better systems of identification of the handicapped than, as is so often done today, resorting to the opinions of the inexpert classroom teachers.

Equal Educational Opportunity for Pupils with Varying Educational Needs

Does equality of educational opportunity mean that school districts are constitutionally required to provide "compensatory" education according to the needs of educationally disadvantaged children? No case has held that such children are constitutionally entitled to compensatory education, but this issue is implicit in a number of cases involving both the physically and mentally handicapped and the "linguistically handicapped."

Physically and Mentally Handicapped Students. Several of the handicapped cases go beyond the situation of the totally excluded child and seek education "appropriate to the needs" of the handicapped child. In a recent case, residents of a New York institution for the mentally retarded alleged they had not been provided an adequate public education. The federal district court, citing *Rodriguez*, declared that there was no constitutional requirement to provide the mentally retarded with a certain level of special education.[88]

In a case in Philadelphia, involving children with "specific learning disabilities," the plaintiffs alleged that they were "deprived of an education appropriate to their specialized needs" even though they were afforded access to the same curriculum as normal children.[89] They argued that they cannot derive *any* educational benefit from the normal curriculum without special instruction aimed at their learning handicaps. Thus, they are "constructively excluded from public educational services, because—for them—the instruction offered is virtually useless, if not positively harmful." The court indicated that since *Rodriguez* "left open the possibility that the denial of a minimally adequate educational opportunity may trench upon a fundamental interest, if the state has undertaken to provide a free public education," the plaintiffs might be entitled to the strict scrutiny standard of review "because a classification has functionally excluded them from a minimally adequate education."

Linguistically Different Students. Some education reformers argue that the "linguistically handicapped" are in the same position as the mentally and physically handicapped children who are excluded from public schooling. Students of limited English-speaking ability receiving an education intended for typical English-speaking pupils are being deprived of their fundamental right to a minimum quantum of education when they are compelled to sit in a classroom in which they cannot communicate. The result, in effect, is their constructive exclusion from the classroom and thus a violation of the equal protection clause.[90]

When this question reached the Supreme Court in *Lau* v. *Nichols,*[91] however, the Court avoided the constitutional issue. The decision relied solely on § 601 of the Civil Rights Act of 1964, which states that "no person. . .shall, on the ground of. . .national origin, . . .be denied the benefits of. . .any program or activity receiving federal financial assistance."[92] The Court held that this statutory provision and its regulations required a school district receiving federal funds to provide assistance to students with English language deficiencies.

The Federal Role. In 1974 Congress adopted statutory language resembling the regulations promulgated by HEW to implement § 601,[93] which clearly established the principle that the state must affirmatively overcome the language deficiencies of non-English-speaking students.

The Bilingual Education Act was passed in 1968 as an amendment to

ESEA.[94] In order to qualify for benefits under this act, the student must be of "limited English-speaking ability."[95] Though the estimated "need" was five million children[96] in 1975, federal funds reached less than 270,000 children.[97] Thus, if courts continue to hold that federal statutes mandate that the states affirmatively overcome the language deficiencies of students of limited English-speaking ability or if courts find that not to do so will violate the equal protection clause of the Constitution, the states and localities will have to bear the bulk of the fiscal burden entailed in complying with such court orders.

Federal Alternatives. An additional approach that the federal government might take in the case of students of limited English-speaking ability is similar to that suggested for handicapped children. If, under Section 601 of the Civil Rights Act and its implementing regulations, children may not be handicapped in receiving an education because of their limited English-language ability, then a law similar to the Emergency School Aid Act may be appropriate. Under the Emergency School Aid Act, bilingual education assistance is now available for an area undergoing desegregation, but funds and technical assistance are also needed for *any* area impacted by non-English-speaking students. Since the current estimate is that federal funds under the Bilingual Education Act reach less than 5.4 percent of the total "need," states and localities now must bear the bulk of the burden of complying with Section 601's requirements.

The Right to a Minimum Level of Education

Another category of students functionally denied a suitable education is illustrated by *Peter Doe* v. *San Francisco Unified School District.*[98] Peter, who graduated from high school after having been enrolled in the district's schools for 12 years, brought an "educational malpractice" suit against the school district for "negligently and carelessly" allowing him to graduate from high school although he could only read at the fifth-grade level. Tests showed Peter to be of average intelligence, his attendance record was average, and he was never a disciplinary problem. Although teachers and administrators assured his mother that he was achieving at his grade level, when he graduated from high school, his skills in reading, writing, and computation were only at the fifth-grade level. He sought damages for lost wages due to his restricted occupational opportunities and additional compensation for the cost of private tutoring.

The court held that, in view of what it called "public policy considerations," the school district as a matter of law does not owe the plaintiff a "duty of care" such that it would be liable for its breach.

Similar cases are being brought elsewhere. If such suits are ultimately successful in obtaining a ruling that a school system is legally accountable for the adequacy of the education a student gets—that is, for the output rather than the inputs—it could have a significant but mixed impact on educational institutions. While it might deter "teacher-caused educational deficiencies,"[99] a successful educational malpractice suit might also deter people from teaching altogether, discourage innovative and experimental ways of teaching disadvantaged children, and, as the *Doe* court points out, reduce funds available for the classroom.

Equal Educational Opportunity and Race

The Student's Right to a Desegregated Education. School desegregation was the first major area of education in which the courts became actively involved, beginning with *Brown* v. *Board of Education.* That involvement continues today in what has become an ever more complex situation with the primary focus on what are appropriate remedies and what are their limits. The Supreme Court has declared that the objective of all school desegregation remedies is "to eliminate from the public schools all vestiges of state-imposed segregation."[100] To achieve this objective, an "[a]wareness of the racial composition of the whole school system is likely to be a useful starting point in shaping a remedy to correct past constitutional violations." Thus, "the very limited use. . .of mathematical ratios [is] within the equitable remedial discretion of the District Court."[101] Nevertheless, "[t]he constitutional command to desegregate schools does not mean that every school in every community must always reflect the racial composition of the school system as a whole."[102] The pairing or clustering of schools, the altering of attendance zones, and majority-minority transfer plans are permissible remedial tools.[103] Busing is also a permissible tool to achieve the objective of eliminating "state-imposed segregation," but it is limited by time and distance contraints in accordance with the age of the students involved.[104] While the Supreme Court has not addressed the question directly, circuit courts have generally held that the possibility of substantial "white flight" *cannot* be a consideration in formulating a remedy.[105] A metropolitanwide or interdistrict remedy can be implemented only where it can be shown that segregation in one school district *resulted from* discriminatory actions by officials in other school districts or by state officials.[106] Finally, once a school district has established a racially neutral system of student assignment, it need not annually readjust the attendance zones when the "normal pattern of human migration" results in changes in the racial makeup of some of the schools.[107]

Through such "second-generation problems" as ability grouping and the selective use of disciplinary measures, minority children may continue to be denied equal educational opportunity even though the school system has been "desegregated." The courts, therefore, have held that when a formerly dual, segregated school system is in the process of being dismantled, pupil assignment by standardized achievement or IQ test scores is unconstitutional where the intended result is the perpetuation of the dual system.[108]

Where it is not clear that ability grouping is racially motivated or has a racially discriminatory effect,[109] it would seem to be constitutionally permissible to utilize such a practice. The unresolved controversy over whether heterogeneous or homogeneous grouping is a better educational practice[110] makes it difficult for courts to adjudicate issues surrounding the use of these practices except where they are blatantly racially motivated or are suspect by first being implemented during a desegregation suit.

Suspensions, expulsions, and other disciplinary measures can also bring about the resegregation of schools.[111] One recent survey has shown that black students are suspended three times as often as whites in elementary school and twice as often in secondary school.[112] These practices have been attacked in the courts with only limited success.[113] However, the due process requirements for the imposition of such sanctions as suspensions and expulsions, articulated recently by the Court in *Goss* v. *Lopez*,[114] may slow down the use of such practices on disproportionate numbers of minority students.

Costs. The impact that court-ordered desegregation has on a local school district is well known by now. In addition to busing costs, there are costs attributable to teacher retraining, curriculum development, and remodeling of buildings necessitated by the pairing of schools.[115] Federal funds are too restricted, both in terms of the timing and the nature of the expenditures, to provide much assistance to states and localities. Expenditures necessitated by the desegregation process no doubt constitute the largest diversion of funds that would otherwise have been budgeted for different school purposes. This is not to say that these dollars would otherwise have been spent for better education; it has been shown that the process of desegregation can bring about significant educational reforms for the entire system that otherwise would not have been attained.[116]

The Federal Role. There are several federal programs that have an impact on the desegregation process, not all of them favorably. One commentator has pointed out that even those federal programs that are designed to *aid* desegregation, such as the Emergency School Aid Act, are targeted on the wrong part of the process.[117] The time for such assistance is *after* the immediate transition period when everything is in flux, because the real process of planning, curriculum development, and the restructuring of classroom operations often is just beginning when federal funds are withdrawn. The predominant federal response to the constitutional requirement of desegregation has been negative—enacting legislation that either is specifically designed to impede the process or acts to undercut the process. Representative of the first type of legislative response are the antibusing laws.[118] The legislative prohibition on the use of federal funds for busing has been upheld by the courts.[119]

The requirement in ESEA Title I that there be a concentration of Title I eligible students before compensatory education funds will be allocated to school districts or schools undercuts the dispersal of low-income students in the urban areas who are predominantly minority students. Several other measures that failed to pass—such as the Quality School Assistance Act—were designed to concentrate resources in the cities with large low-income populations and thus would have had a similar effect on efforts to disperse the minority student population from core urban areas.

Federal Alternative. In no way can the courts be expected to retreat from their position on school segregation. The Supreme Court's command that school districts desegregate *now* must be taken as a given. The focus of attention should be on what is the most effective way to make school desegregation work and what institutions or mechanisms can support or supplement the involvement of courts in drawing school desegregation plans. Courts also might consider whether there are areas of educational policy that are inappropriate for judicial intervention. One such area for a "hands-off" policy by the judiciary might be ability grouping, which would be left to the educators unless it is shown that its use is racially motivated. Discipline may be another such area as long as the requisite procedural safeguards are provided.

Equal Employment Opportunity for Teachers. The *Singleton* principles for the desegregation of faculty, articulated by the Fifth Circuit Court in 1969, continue to be applied by the courts.[120] *Singleton* requires that, when a school district is under court-ordered desegregation and there is an anticipated reduction in faculty resulting from the implementation of the order to disestablish the dual school system and create a unitary system, objective criteria must be developed to evaluate teachers who might be dismissed or demoted. In the absence of these objective, nondiscriminatory criteria, teachers may not be discharged even for professional inability. Claims of discrimination in public school employment on the basis of race are not based solely on the Constitution's equal protection clause; they are often based on Title VII of the Civil Rights Act of 1964—extended to cover school employees in 1972.[121]

Certification and Credentialling of Teachers. The use by school authorities of test scores as the basis for certifying teachers or for hiring or promoting one teacher or administrator in preference to another has been challenged on the ground that it has a disproportionate adverse effect on minorities and denies them access to employment in the system. Both the Graduate Record Examination (GRE) and the National Teachers' Examination (NTE) have been so used, despite the fact that the Educational Testing Service (ETS), which developed these tests, has said that the tests are not appropriate for measuring qualification to teach or the level of teacher competency. If the use of such tests to determine that minority teachers are unqualified to be hired or promoted is challenged on constitutional grounds, *Washington* v. *Davis*[122] requires that racially discriminatory *intent* must be shown, which is a difficult burden for plaintiffs;

if challenged under Title VII, however, only a disproportionate racial *effect* need be shown. If any criterion for evaluating and rewarding teachers results in a disproportionate number of minority teachers being adversely affected, to survive a Title VII suit, it would have to be "validated" before being used.

In a recent South Carolina case, summarily affirmed by the Supreme Court, the use of scores on the National Teachers' Examination for hiring and for salary payments, although having a highly disproportionate impact on black teachers, was held not to deny equal protection of the laws on the ground that there was no intent on the part of the state to discriminate. The use of the NTE was also held to meet the requirements of Title VII because a state study demonstrated that the content of the NTE matched the content of the teacher training programs in the state. Thus the state met its burden under Title VII of showing the validity of the test.[123]

Equal Educational Opportunity and Sex

The constitutional issues about sex discrimination are much less settled than are those of race. In determining whether sex-based legislation violates the equal protection clause of the Fourteenth Amendment, the Supreme Court has been divided as to the standard to be applied. A majority of the Court does seem to think that a minimum rationality test is no longer appropriate, but while sex discrimination has been elevated to a higher level of constitutional protection than most other forms of discrimination, the Court has not treated sex as race—that is, as a suspect class triggering the strict scrutiny standard of review.[124] With the passage of Title IX of the Education Amendments of 1972, the federal government has also indicated its concern with the differential treatment of students based solely on sex.[125] Title IX also extends to sex-based discrimination in employment in the public schools,[126] as do the Equal Pay Act[127] and Title VII of the Civil Rights Act of 1964.[128]

The Student's Right to An Education Without Discrimination Based on Sex

Admission to Special Schools. Academically elite public high schools exist in a number of school districts and have often discriminated on the basis of sex—either by total exclusion of students of one sex or by requiring higher entrance requirements for women applicants. The Third Circuit Court of Appeals recently held that neither the Equal Educational Opportunities Act nor the Fourteenth Amendment to the Constitution prohibited the exclusion of a female student solely on the basis of sex from an all-male college-preparatory public high school where there was an all-female academic high school of comparable quality that the plaintiff could have attended.[129] The dissenting judge termed this decision a return to the "separate but equal" doctrine, but the majority pointed out that only where women have been deprived of benefits rather than being offered them on the same basis as the opposite sex has the Supreme Court held laws that discriminate on the basis of sex unconstitutional.[130] Title IX would not have been of any greater help than the Constitution to the plaintiff in obtaining admission to an all-male school as long as there is another school with comparable courses, services, and facilities available to her.[131]

The Ninth Circuit Court of Appeals, using a "strict rationality" test, held the differential admissions standards of an elite academic high school in San Francisco to be an unconstitutional violation of the equal protection clause.[132] Title IX regulations also prohibit the use of such differential admissions criteria. A student may not be excluded on the basis of sex from admission to a school unless comparable courses, services, and facilities are otherwise made available "pursuant to the same policies and criteria of admissions."[133]

Pregnancy. School districts frequently suspend or expel pregnant students or unwed mothers. The federal courts, however, generally prohibit such actions without a showing that the presence of the particular plaintiff will present a danger to her physical or mental health or will have an adverse effect on the education of her classmates.[134] Rules that completely exclude pregnant students or unwed mothers from the public schools can probably be challenged successfully under the equal protection clause. The *Rodriguez* decision should not be a bar since such exclusion absolutely deprives a child of education, and thus the strict scrutiny standard of equal protection would apply. One court, however, has relied on *Rodriguez* to uphold school board policy denying readmission of a 15-year-old unwed mother to high school since she could complete her education by attending night school.[135] Title IX regulations, which prohibit the exclusion of pregnant students or students who are parents from *any* education program or activity unless the student *chooses* to participate in a separate portion of the program or activity, clearly would cover this situation today.[136]

Federal Role. Title IX regulations all but blanket the area of sex discrimination in the schools. Thus, the pressures for equality on the basis of sex, which had barely begun in the courts, quickly shifted to Congress. Enforcement mechanisms, however, are either weak or so draconian that they are not likely to be frequently used. School systems that are not in compliance can have their current funds revoked, or they can be barred from eligibility for future awards.[137] In addition, HEW may refer a case to the Department of Justice with a recommendation that appropriate proceedings be brought.[138] The Seventh Circuit Court of Appeals, however, has recently held that while Title IX is designed to encourage voluntary compliance with the ban against sex discrimination and provides for an *administrative* hearing, Congress did not envision "the rather drastic remedy of individual lawsuits."[139] Thus, the law created no right of private, individual action when a student has been denied admission to a school or a course solely on the basis of gender.

The sanctions provided in Title IX—termination of or refusal to grant assistance—are expressly limited by the act to the particular entity that fails to comply with the act and additionally to the particular *program* or *activity* in which the discrimination occurs.[140] Title VI has an analogous restriction, but in the majority of cases involving elementary and secondary schools, this restriction has not caused any great difficulty since racial discrimination has tended to be systemwide.[141] By contrast, sex discrimination is often limited to particular educational programs or activities—such as athletics—that may receive no federal funds even though the school system as a whole is receiving federal assistance under various federal acts. Title IX, however, has been construed broadly by HEW to reach any area of sex discrimination in educational institutions receiving federal assistance even though the particular program or activity in question receives no federal aid directly.

Costs. Title IX requires affirmative action by school systems. Complying with the regulations should significantly alter many of the educational programs now offered in the public schools, and it will also have a substantial budgetary impact. For example, the amount of money now spent on athletic programs for male students far exceeds that typically allocated to women's athletics. While the regulations do not require *equal* expenditures for males and females, among the factors examined to determine whether equal opportunitites are available are the provision of equipment and supplies, travel allowances, and facilities.[142] The cost of upgrading these areas for women is bound to be high. Similarly, the amount of money allocated to vocational courses formerly only for males (because of lower pupil-teacher ratios and the use of expensive equipment) frequently exceeds that spent on courses that teach secretarial and homemaking skills to female students. Again, the expenditure of substantial sums—or the elmination of a number of courses—will necessarily be required. At present, the federal government does not provide financial assistance to school districts struggling with compliance.

Equal Employment Opportunity for Teachers.[143] In 1974 the Supreme Court, in *LaFleur,* held that a school board policy requiring pregnant teachers to take mandatory leaves far in advance of their expected delivery dates violated the due process clause of the Fourteenth Amendment.[144] The cutoff dates had no valid relationship to a legitimate state interest but rather created an irrebuttable presumption that every teacher who reached this date was physically incapable of continuing her duties.

Title VII of the Civil Right Act and the Equal Employment Opportunity Commission (EEOC) guidelines promulgated pursuant to that act[145] have also been the basis for overturning mandatory maternity leave rules and policies excluding pregnancy-related disabilities from the school district's coverage of disability benefits. The Supreme Court, however, has held that neither the Fourteenth Amendment[146] nor Title VII[147] are violated by a disability plan that excludes pregnancy.

PROTECTION OF INDIVIDUAL RIGHTS OF STUDENTS AND TEACHERS

Since *Tinker* v. *Des Moines Independent Community School District*[148] and *Pickering* v. *Board of Education,*[149] the courts have attempted to strike a balance between the freedom of the individual—whether teacher or student—and the necessity for order and stability of the educational enterprise. In some respects, the legal rights of teachers are indistinguishable from those of students. Certainly the teacher is neither more nor less able to disrupt the educational process or to challenge the rules and regulations of school administrators that govern personal appearance, speech, and association.[150] The close relationship between the nature of the teacher's job and "academic freedom," however, affects the judicial approach to constraints on the teacher's conduct and speech in different ways from that of students. Although children are not yet accorded the full panoply of constitutional rights,[151] teachers are adults and are entitled to the same constitutional rights as other adults, subject to whatever constraints are dictated by the special nature of public educational institutions.[152] In some respects, however, the teacher's rights are *more* restricted than the student's because of certain distinctions between student and teacher: the student is required by compulsory attendance laws to attend school; the teacher is there voluntarily and is free to seek employment elsewhere. In addition, since teachers are viewed as role models for student behavior, they have been dismissed for their activities out of school as well as in school.

The results of judicial activity in this area have little direct impact on federal policies, but the constraints that may be imposed on the educational enterprise with respect to its students and employees may produce an indirect effect of which federal educational policymakers should be informed.

Right of Privacy and Related Rights

The Supreme Court has held that "a right of personal privacy," or a guarantee of certain areas or "zones of privacy,"[153] is constitutionally protected. A significant proportion of the "privacy" cases have been concerned with the aspect of privacy relating to personal autonomy. This right has been raised in some of the cases challenging regulations about hair length and dress. Another important aspect of privacy concerns the right not to have personal information about a person disclosed to others. There are few cases, however, holding that this aspect of privacy is protected. Thus, it is Congress rather than the courts that has stressed the need for protection from the government's intrusive acquisition of information or dissemination of personally identifiable information.[154]

Access to Student Records. The question of who has access to a student's permanent file (e.g., other teachers, potential employers, or the FBI) and what can go into the file (e.g., disciplinary records, psychiatric reports, IQ scores, and unverified and unchallenged reports that the student is a "trouble-maker" or "disrespectful") have been the subject of much discussion, but there are few court cases. A few states, either by law or school board regulation, allow parents and students access to the full school record.[155] Generally, however, students and parents have been denied access to the student's own records even though others outside the school system have been allowed to see them.

Federal Role. In 1974 the Family Educational Rights and Privacy Act (commonly known as the "Buckley Amendment")[156] was enacted, establishing comprehensive guidelines to ensure students and their parents access to their school records and to prevent invasions into familial and student privacy occasioned by the release of school records to third persons without prior student or parental consent. The Buckley Amendment provides that federal funds are either to be terminated or refused to any educational agency that violates its provisions. There has been little judicial activity in this area. State legislatures have been more active, and now more than twenty-five states have laws or regulations governing access to student records. Only four states, however, permit parents or students to challenge material in the record.[157] The Buckley Amendment and not judicial decisions will substantially change the policies of a significant number of states.

Search of Students and Their Lockers. A major controversy surrounds the question of whether students are constitutionally protected against searches of their person or property. The issue has come up with increasing frequency as the use of drugs and violence on school grounds has increased. The Fourth Amendment prohibits "unreasonable" searches and seizures conducted by police officials. Since the Supreme Court has recognized that students in school as well as out of school are "persons" under the Constitution who possess certain constitutional rights that the state must respect,[158] police officers are governed by the Fourth Amendment in their treatment of students both on and off school property. Thus, any evidence obtained by the police through an "unreasonable" (and therefore unconstitutional) search and seizure of a student, on or off school grounds, is inadmissible in a state or federal criminal prosecution. Whether or not such evidence must also be excluded from school disciplinary proceedings is an open question.

Some cases have questioned whether the Fourth Amendment applies to searches and seizures by school officials. Some courts have held that parental authority over a student is delegated to school administrators and teachers, and when disciplining students, they are therefore subject only to the same standard of reasonableness that applies to parents in disciplining their children.[159] Thus, in many jurisdictions, school officials are permitted to search and submit the fruits of such search as evidence in delinquency and criminal proceedings.[160]

In sum, there is little protection for students against searches of their person or property, although if the students clearly do not consent to the search, there is a possibility in some jurisdictions that any evidence found will be barred from use in court and even in school disciplinary proceedings. The Supreme Court has not yet clarified whether or not the Fourth Amendment applies to students while on the school premises.

Right of Privacy. A somewhat different aspect of the right of privacy was raised in a suit seeking to enjoin school officials from implementing a program designed to identify potential drug abusers among the junior high school population in a Pennsylvania school district.[161] The program sought through subjective and highly personal questionnaires to identify the students possessing personality traits similar to those of actual drug abusers, inquiring into family religion, race, and whether or not one or both parents "hugged me good night when I was small," "tell me how much they love me," or "make me feel unloved."[162]

The plaintiffs contended that the program was an invasion of their constitutionally protected right of privacy. The court treated the right of privacy solely within the context of family relationships and child rearing.[163] Consequently, it is not entirely clear whether the Constitution protects the privacy rights of the parent, of the student as a member of the family, or of the family as a unit.[164] The court enjoined the school officials from administering the program on the ground that there was not a sufficiently informed *parental* consent necessary for the waiver of constitutional rights, and in the absence of such consent, the public interest in coping with the problem of youthful drug abusers was outweighed by the individual's right of privacy in the family setting.[165]

The extent to which tests—including psychological tests and assessments and evaluations that incorporate questions eliciting data to determine the socioeconomic status of students—are being administered to students by the schools is rapidly increasing. A potential conflict exists between the need for such data to improve or evaluate the effectiveness of educational programs and the desire to focus on the noncognitive aspects of education and the student's (or his family's) right to privacy. Such tests, whether administered by federal, state, or private researchers and evaluators or by local school officials, will continue to be scrutinized by the courts. Even for those tests that survive such scrutiny, it is likely that a sufficiently informed consent by parents and by students will be required by the courts.

First Amendment Rights of Free Association and Privacy Rights of Teachers. The private lives of teachers have more of an effect on their job security than is true of most professions because of the frequently stated belief that the teacher is a role model responsible for shaping young minds. In one recent case, a teacher was dismissed for living with a male who was not her husband.[166] The teacher argued that the dismissal violated her constitutional rights of privacy and freedom of association. The court, however, declared that "the state is entitled to require teachers to maintain a properly moral scholastic environment" in view of its independent "interest in the well-being of youth" as well as its interest "in preserving the right of parents to control the upbringing of their children."[167]

Other Substantive Constitutional Rights of Students and Teachers

Freedom of Expression and Association. The recent court decisions concerned with substantive constitutional rights of students such as freedom of expression and association do not have a direct impact on federal policies. However, the constraints within which school officials must act and the costs that these court decisions may impose on the system are factors of which federal policymakers should be aware.

Tinker v. *Des Moines Independent Community School District*,[168] the leading case on the First Amendment rights of public school students, held that the wearing of an armband (symbolically to protest the war in Vietnam) was a form of pure speech, and therefore entitled to protection under the First Amendment even though it was exercised by students on school premises. The Court held that, in the absence of any showing that the conduct would "materially and substantially interfere" with the operation of the school, the conduct could not be prohibited. The Court did not, however, articulate any standards for determining what showing is required in order to find "material and substantial interference." Thus, the lower courts have developed varying standards as they have applied the *Tinker* principles to cases involving newspapers, leaflets, buttons, and after-school political clubs or organizations.

First Amendment Rights of Free Speech for Teachers. If the school board has dismissed, transferred, demoted, or disciplined its employees for constitutionally impermissible reasons or has failed to provide the constitutionally required procedural safeguards, its actions can be overturned. In the absence of evidence of these grounds, the employee has the very heavy burden of proving that the board's actions are an abuse of discretion or arbitrary, capricious, or malicious, or not based on substantial evidence—a burden the employee can meet only rarely. Even where school board actions are challenged by teachers on the ground that they involve unconstitutional infringements upon their rights to freedom of speech, association, and privacy, the initial burden is upon the teacher to establish that the school board's action was in fact based on constitutionally impermissible reasons.[169]

In *Pickering* v. *Board of Education*,[170] the Supreme Court indicated that the government has legitimate interests as an employer that differ from its interests in regulating the speech of the general public. The problem, therefore, is to arrive at a balance between the interest of the teacher, as a citizen, in commenting upon matters of public concern and the interest of the state, as an employer, in promoting the efficiency of the public services it performs through its employees.[171] The Court suggested that the state's interests might outweigh those of the teacher where either discipline by immediate superiors or harmony among co-workers was in issue,[172] and lower courts have often seized upon this to rule against teachers who have claimed that they were being penalized for exercising their right of free speech.

Personal Appearance Regulations

Regulating Hair Length. The basic question with regard to school board regulation of personal appearance is whether a student has a federal constitutional right to govern his own appearance. Among the constitutional protections that have been asserted are the First Amendment's freedom of symbolic expression, the Ninth Amendment's "unenumerated rights," the Fourteenth Amendment's due process and equal protection, or the penumbras of the First, Fourth, Fifth, and Fourteenth Amendments. The issue of whether a male student attending a public school has a constitutionally protected right to wear his hair in any manner that he pleases has thoroughly divided the federal circuit courts. The Supreme Court has contributed substantially to this stalemate by its repeated refusals to review such cases.[173]

Dress Codes. Some courts that have held that hair length regulations impinged upon a constitutionally protected right have suggested that a dress code might *not* be unconstitutional because clothes, unlike hair length, can be changed after school.[174] Other jurisdictions have struck down dress codes as infringing upon a personal liberty protected by the Fourteenth Amendment unless there is an outweighing state interest to justify the restriction.[175]

As with some of the other areas of students' rights, the greatest impact of the hair length and dress code cases on school systems stems from the frequency of litigation and its concomitant costs, although the number of cases seems to have dropped off recently. Because of the conflicting decisions, it is difficult to predict the outcome of such suits in advance.

Student Discipline and Procedural Due Process

Corporal Punishment. The principal sanctions used by school officials for student violations of rules and regulations are corporal punishment, suspension, and expulsion. The issue of corporal punishment has recently been challenged on substantive constitutional grounds as well as on procedural due process grounds—that is, the use of corporal punishment violates the Eighth Amendment's prohibition against cruel and unusual punishment. The lower courts have been divided on this point, some holding that, depending on the severity of the punishment, the age of the student, and other circumstances, corporal punishment may violate the Eighth Amendment.[176] By contrast, some courts have flatly held that the Eighth Amendment does *not* apply in a civil context,[177] noting that, if the punishment is excessive, the student has a remedy in a tort or criminal action, not federal constitutional law.

In addition to whether there is a *substantive* constitutional right to be free from corporal punishment, the issue of whether, without *procedural* safeguards, the use of corporal punishment by school authorities would be an unconstitutional deprivation of the student's Fourteenth Amendment right not to be deprived of liberty without due process of law has been litigated. A three-judge district court in North Carolina held that there is a constitutionally protected liberty interest of "personal security," and thus corporal punishment could not be inflicted arbitrarily.[178] The Fifth Circuit Court of Appeals, however, in a case arising in Florida, held that there are no constitutionally mandated procedural standards "for an activity which is not substantial enough, on a constitutional level, to justify the time and effort which would have to be expended."[179] The Supreme Court, in *Ingraham* v. *Wright*, affirmed the Fifth Circuit's opinion, holding that the use of corporal punishment did not violate the Eighth Amendment and that the failure to provide due process was not a violation of the Fourteenth Amendment.

Suspensions and Expulsions. *Goss* v. *Lopez*,[180] decided by the Supreme Court in 1975, was concerned with whether school authorities in removing a student from school, either temporarily or permanently, are constitutionally obligated to provide some kind of "due process of law." If a student does have a constitutional entitlement to procedural due process, how much process is due? The *Goss* Court's response to these questions established the following: (1) a state that chooses to provide public education may not withdraw the right to an education "absent fundamentally fair procedures"; (2) a student's property interest or right in education is such that a ten-day deprivation resulting from the student's suspension from school is not *de minimis*; (3) for a ten-day suspension, procedural due process requires "that the student be given oral or written notice of the charges made against him and, if he denies them, an explanation of the evidence the authorities have and an opportunity to present his side of the story"; and (4) notice and hearing should "as a general rule" *precede* removal from school. The majority went on to state what was *not* invariably required: "the opportunity to secure counsel, to confront and cross-examine witnesses supporting the charge, or to call. . .witnesses to verify his [the student's] version of the incident." In other words, "truncated trial-type procedures" are not required in most cases involving brief disciplinary suspensions.

The *Goss* majority found a liberty as well as a property interest entitled to Fourteenth Amendment protection. This liberty interest of which students may not be deprived "without due process of law" concerns the students' reputation, i.e., the students' interest in keeping their names free from any stigma. According to the Court, the infringement is the potential damage to the students' standing with their fellow pupils and teachers and the interference with their future employment and higher education opportunities by the notation of the disciplinary action on the students' records.

Precisely what kind of notice and hearing are mandated by *Goss*? How much more process is due for a suspension of *over* ten days or for an expulsion? The most the Court says on this point is that "[l]onger suspensions or expulsions for the remainder of the school term, or permanently, may require more formal procedures."[181] Moreover, the Court suggests that in certain "unusual" circumstances, even in the case of a short suspension, more procedures than are outlined in *Goss* may be required.

Costs. The costs of due process hearings—in dollars, man-hours, and other more intangible aspects[182]—may be considerable. One of the principal questions raised by *Goss* is from where are the funds to be diverted to pay for the court-mandated due process hearings? What programs might be affected? What impact will the requirement of due process hearings have on the demands on staff time? Or will school officials find the cost of removing disruptive children to be so great that they will let them remain as a disruptive influence in the classroom? On the other hand, school administrators may undercut any impact of the decision by adhering to the form rather than the substance of the quite minimal procedural requirements of *Goss* or by resorting to sanctions other than suspension and expulsion in order to avoid the *Goss* requirements.

Federal Role. The sum of all the due process requirements imposed on school systems by recent court decisions and by federal legislation—for example, the assignment to classes for slow or retarded students or the imposition of certain sanctions—may soon engulf the institution of education unless state or federal government help is provided both in the form of technical assistance (e.g., counsel) and financial assistance.

Procedural Due Process Rights of Teachers

If tenured teachers are dismissed from their positions, their due process rights entitle them to notice, a hearing, and an explanation of the reasons for their loss of employment. Nontenured, probationary teachers are generally not entitled to such procedural safeguards prior to dismissal, the theory being that they have no property right in continued employment that is protected by the due process clause of the Constitution. Only if a nontenured teacher is able to establish either a "property" interest in the teaching position or that his or her "liberty" has been curtailed as a result of dismissal, would the teacher be entitled to procedural safeguards upon termination of employment. The Supreme Court, in *Board of Regents* v. *Roth*, defined a *property interest* as a "legitimate claim of entitlement" created either by state law or "existing rules *and understandings.*"[183] *Perry* v. *Sindermann*[184] indicated that such a claim could even be derived by implication from an employer's words and conduct in light of the past employment practices of the school district and the circumstances surrounding the particular employment situation. All this meant, however, was that the nontenured teacher who was able to show that the circumstances surrounding his or her appointment "vested" in him or her a "property right" was entitled to *notice* of the nonrenewal of the appointment and a hearing.

In 1976, however, in *Bishop* v. *Wood*[185] the Supreme Court indicated that it will not readily imply a property interest sufficient to require procedural due process. In this case (which involved a policeman), the Court stressed the necessity of examining state law to determine whether the particular circumstances of an employment situation give rise to a constitutionally protected property interest and whether the "procedures" provided in the state law are all the "process" that is due under the Constitution when the employee is deprived of his or her "property."[186]

A nontenured teacher may also be able to challenge dismissal as infringing upon a "liberty interest" in his or her reputation in the community. A teacher's *liberty* is curtailed when dismissal is based on a charge that might "seriously damage his standing and associations in his community" by jeopardizing his or her "good name, reputation, honor, or integrity."[187] Mere dismissal does not infringe upon that liberty interest so as to require due process procedures. A deprivation of liberty occurs only where the dismissal or nonretention of a teacher so stigmatizes the teacher as to foreclose future employment opportunities or to damage substantially his or her standing in the community.

Impact on Federal Policies. Even where the courts have held that certain procedural safeguards—such as notice and a hearing—are constitutionally required before a teacher or administrator can be dismissed, the impact on school systems in costs and manpower still will not be nearly as great as that attributable to the due process hearings accorded students either under the Constitution[188] or statutes.[189]

Liability of School Officials

The impact of many of the judicial decisions concerning various constitutionally protected rights of students will depend in large part on the willingness of lower courts to find school officials liable in damages for failing to accord students their constitutional rights. The Supreme Court, in *Wood* v. *Strickland*,[190] held that a school board member (and presumably other school officials) "is not immune from liability for damages. . .if he knew or reasonably should have known that the action he took within his sphere of official responsibility would violate the constitutional rights of the student affected" and, in so doing, acted in "disregard of the student's *clearly established* constitutional rights."[191] Only violations of "clearly established rights" or of "settled, indisputable law"[192] are grounds for damage actions. Exactly when a constitutional right is "clearly established" was left unanswered. The major question, then, is to what extent the burden is on school authorities to know what the state of the law is and to seek out legal advice before they act. The only guidance from the Supreme Court is that, while school officials must be aware of the "clearly established" constitutional rights of their students, they are not "charged with predicting the future course of constitutional law."[193]

Taking the Court's requirement in *Goss* v. *Lopez* that due process be afforded students before they are suspended or expelled together with the *Wood* v. *Strickland* decision, what will the probable impact on the school system be? The *Goss* majority states that "we have imposed requirements which are, if anything, less than a fair-minded school principal would impose upon himself in order to avoid unfair suspensions,"[194] implying that the decision will have very little impact in terms of time or money. We already know, however, that the introduction of due process hearings in certain circumstances has been quite costly, and the "brooding omnipresence" of *Wood* v. *Strickland* may make administrators actually give more process than is due to avoid possible liability. Moreover, while the Court said that some kind of notice and some kind of hearing is to be afforded students facing a less than ten-day suspension, the Court also said that "more formal procedures" may be required for longer suspensions.

The dissent sees the likely impact of the *Wood* decision somewhat differently. Elected or appointed citizens without legal expertise who provide unpaid, voluntary service on boards of education are unlikely to seek out such positions in the future to the detriment of the school system. According to the dissenting opinion, school officials will have to have a "unique competency in divining the law."[195] Concern has recently been expressed about the possible refusal of insurance companies to write liability policies to cover school board members.[196] If this is true, then this fact, coupled with the *Wood* decision, may mean people will be less enthusiastic about running for a school board seat in the future. Again, no *direct* impact on federal policies will result from *Wood* v. *Strickland* and its progeny. Instead the impact is at most indirect, stemming from the constraints that may be placed on local school systems, particularly with regard to discipline.[197]

COLLECTIVE BARGAINING

In the last few years, there has been a substantial increase in state legislation and in court decisions affecting public employee collective bargaining. Most jurisdictions that have enacted statutes that authorize collective bargaining require that the school board (or other public agency) negotiate with an exclusive bargaining representative. This sets up a conflict—one that does not occur in the private sector—between the government agency's statutory duty to conduct business openly and to hear the views of the public, on the one hand, and, on the other hand, the principles of labor law that require private negotiations by bargaining representatives. In *City of Madison Joint School District No. 8 v. W.E.R.C.,*[198] the Madison school board, in accordance with local law, held a public meeting at which a representative of a minority group of teachers presented arguments in opposition to an agency shop agreement then under negotiation. The state supreme court held that, by hearing the arguments, the board violated its duty to bargain with the exclusive agent. The First Amendment interests in the freedoms of speech and petition of the individual school teachers, who are also citizens speaking at a public meeting, had to give way to the labor law principle of exclusive representation in bargaining. The Supreme Court of the United States reversed the decision, holding that the circumstances of the particular case—in which a nonunion teacher was not seeking to bargain and was not authorized to enter into an agreement on behalf of any teachers—were not such that curtailing the teacher's speech was justified.[199]

There are two principal issues in the collective bargaining area: the extent to which school boards can legally "bargain" or "negotiate" with teachers' organizations, or what are managerial prerogatives and hence nonmandatory subjects of bargaining; and the extent to which school employees may resort to the strike as a weapon. The courts are in utter disarray as to what are negotiable items[200] and what must be reserved to the discretion of school boards.[201] With regard to the strike weapon, only four states have statutes expressly permitting strikes by teachers or other public employees.[202] Even in these states, courts have sharply limited the circumstances under which strikes can take place.[203]

Federal Role. Despite the substantial variations among states, the general trend seems to be toward developing procedures to deal with public employees that are comparable to those in the private sector. As an extension of this movement toward eliminating the differences in the treatment of public and private sector employees, a bill to amend the National Labor Relations Act to extend collective bargaining rights to state and local employees was introduced. Passage of such a bill, however, may now be precluded by the Supreme Court's decision in *National League of Cities* v. *Usery.*[204] This case attacked the constitutionality of the 1974 amendments to the Fair Labor Standards Act that extended the minimum wage and maximum hour requirements to nearly all public sector employees. The majority found that to determine the wages to be paid employees retained to carry out governmental functions, the hours those employees are to work, and the compensation to be paid for overtime work is to engage in "functions essential to [the] separate and independent existence" of the states, and held that Congress cannot abrogate the state's plenary authority to make such determinations. Thus, *National League of Cities* indicates that the "state sovereignty" doctrine (which includes the "states' abilities to structure employer-employee relationships") could be superseded by congressional action under the authority of the commerce clause only in an emergency or exceptional circumstances.

There are two possible grounds for distinguishing a federal law allowing public sector employees to organize and bargain collectively from the law held unconstitutional in *National League*. Neither of these grounds is particularly strong. First, a so-called "process" law might not be affected by the *National League* decision inasmuch as a law merely requiring states to bargain collectively with their public employees does not force the relinquishment of some state and local governmental activities to comply with federal dictates. The concern in *National League* was that the minimum wage-overtime compensation law would distort state and local spending priorities and hence policy choices, while a law simply requiring states to engage in the process of collective bargaining under federal jurisdiction does not. However, the concern expressed with the 1974 amendments is that they would "significantly alter or displace the states' abilities to *structure* employer-employee relationships." Congress may not withdraw from the states "the authority to make those fundamental employment decisions" involved in discharging their function of furnishing public services. It is difficult to believe that the Court, which struck down the federal minimum wage law on the ground that it forced states to alter policies relating to "those fundamental employment decisions," would uphold a law, grounded in the commerce clause, that would require states and municipalities to recognize unions, provide for the collection of union dues, impose compulsory arbitration and so on.

The majority opinion in *National League* suggested another possible basis for distinguishing a federal collective bargaining law applied to public sector employees from a federal minimum wage law. The Court noted that reserved for future decision was whether a federal law affecting "integral operations of state governments," enacted under Congress's power under Article I, Section 8, clause 1 (the spending power), would be constitutional.[205] Thus, a federal law that conditions the granting of federal funds (e.g., revenue-sharing money) upon compliance with public employee collective bargaining provisions might be constitutional. Even if the relation between such a condition and revenue-sharing funds is too diffuse, there are other programs where such a condition would have a more direct relationship; for example, the granting of Title I ESEA money to a state could be conditioned on the state's accepting the jurisdiction of the National Labor Relations Board over its public school employees. The argument would be that in this case a state has a "choice" that it does not have when Congress imposes a minimum wage under its commerce clause power—that is, it could forego federal funds rather than accept public employee collective bargaining. Is that enough of a distinction, however, to make it an *un*constitutional interference with "state sovereignty" when collective bargaining is forced on the states under Congress's commerce power but constitutional when it is the condition for receiving federal funds? On the other hand, should the Court find Congress's spending power to be limited in the same way as the commerce clause power, the impact on federal educational policy would be staggering. Since education is a government service "which the states and their political subdivisions have traditionally afforded their citizens," Congress's power to attach some presently used conditions to exercises of the spending power could be sharply restricted. It seem unlikely, however, that the Court meant to apply the *National League of Cities* principle so broadly.

In sum, whether or not *National League* will prevent the federal government from attempting to develop more uniform and more effective collective bargaining procedures remains to be seen. It is likely that, because of this doubt, efforts to pass such legislation in the near future may diminish while efforts intensify at the state level.

SUMMARY AND CONCLUSIONS

The two major objectives of federal involvement in education have been to achieve greater educational equity for certain groups neglected by society and to stimulate educational reform and innovation. While the amount of federal money appropriated for elementary and secondary education is quite small in proportion to the total expended annually by state and local governments, the impact is far larger than the dollar amount would indicate because the funds are concentrated on these priorities. Congress has the constitutional authority to mandate certain policies as the condition for receiving federal funds. The federal government's enforcement mechanisms are quite limited, however, being either so weak as to be useless or so draconian as to be employed only rarely. Some districts still refuse to accept any federal money, and in those districts the federal government has very limited leverage to accomplish its equity or reform objectives. One reason why minorities and other aggrieved groups have turned to the courts is to attain the educational equity the executive and legislative branches are unable to bring about. Thus, in this sense, federal courts are only a part of the arsenal used to implement federal policies.

What limits should there be to the areas in which the courts intervene and on the ways in which they intervene?

1. When courts enter the field of education in determining the appropriate remedy, they often are required to examine social science data. Courts need assistance in coping with the data litigants provide, and they need to know what other data, which *not* provided by the litigants, are relevant to ascertain the long-range impact of the remedy. Judges at times have resorted to masters,

experts, and commissions to assist them in acquiring data and information not provided by the parties. This has not always produced the "best" results because of the biases of the "experts." Even a panel of "neutral" social scientists might not be helpful in some situations, such as when there is no agreement among social scientists as to either the research findings or the conclusions to be drawn from those findings. Yet the court cannot wait until the controversies are resolved; it must act on its own "common sense approach" to settle the dispute before it.

2. When the parties before the court frame the issues or even when the court relies upon its own experts or masters, the full impact of the suit may not be realized. Courts need assistance in assessing the *broader* impacts of their remedies, perhaps to ascertain which is the remedy with the least adverse impact on those groups *not* party to the litigation, but still a remedy that achieves the just result for the plaintiffs whose constitutional rights have been adjudged violated. A panel of social scientists and other appropriate persons might provide a "judicial impact statement" on alternative remedies and their effects. Such an "impact statement," for example, might attempt to estimate the cost of providing an education "appropriate to [each handicapped child's] needs"—the cost, the educational impact, the effect on other programs, the availability of supporting services, and so on—as well as the impact of alternative remedies.

3. Courts need to know what they *cannot* do. For example, educators do not now know how to equalize educational outcomes. For this reason, courts, even with the assistance of "experts," are not in a position to do any better. Educators are divided over the efficacy of ability grouping. Should the courts, then, get involved once it is determined that ability grouping is not simply a subterfuge for resegregation? Neither heterogeneous nor homogeneous grouping should be elevated to a constitutional principle on the basis of our present knowledge, nor should the decision as to whether "mainstreaming" or special education classes is the best *educational* approach for the mentally handicapped.

Certain reforms in education must come from the legislature and not the courts—for example, voucher plans, performance contracting, or school site budgeting and management. The judiciary can, however, provide a more generalized standard or guideline within which voucher plans would be one attempt to attain that standard.

In sum, courts must continue to redress specific inequities as, for example, the suspension or expulsion of students for exercising their First Amendment right of free speech or the deliberate use of testing and tracking to bring about a resegregated school system. But the judicial branch is not the only federal institution that seeks educational equity for minorities and the disadvantaged. Congress also enacts programs to aid certain groups who are confronted with barriers to equal educational opportunity and who are overlooked or not deemed of high priority by state and local governments. In such a case,

Congress works *with* the courts to achieve greater educational equity. Congress could also enact programs that provide incentives to states to correct inequities themselves, such as disparities in resources among their school districts, or it could make adjustments in current federal programs that tend to undercut state attempts to correct inequities. Here Congress would be assisting states to act *before* the courts have acted—or if the courts have acted, Congress would assist the states in achieving compliance with court orders more effectively and efficiently than the states could on their own. This chapter has shown some of the restrictions that the courts have imposed on the ways in which federal legislation, aided by executive regulations, has addressed or is likely to address certain education issues. A few programs—by no stretch of the imagination an exhaustive list—have been suggested as alternative methods by which Congress and the executive branch could begin to work with the courts to accomplish the objectives of greater educational equity and reform.

NOTES

1. "The Congress shall have the power (1) to lay and collect taxes, duties, imposts, and excises, to pay the debts and provide for the common defense and general welfare of the United States. . . ," *U.S. Constitution,* Art. I, § 8. Congress also has the power, under § 5 of the Fourteenth Amendment and under the Commerce Clause, to enforce various antidiscrimination requirements even without the "carrot" of federal funding.

2. *See* Oklahoma v. United States Civil Service Commission, 330 U.S. 127 (1947).

3. *See* S. Rep., No. 146, 89th Congress, 1st Session (1965), Elementary and Secondary Education Act of 1965. As the report points out, education was singled out for special attention in the Northwest Ordinance of 1787, id. at 4.

4. The enactment of the National Defense Education Act, 20 U.S.C. §§ 401 et seq. (1970), was triggered by the successful launching of Sputnik in 1957 by the Russians. The only major federal aid to education program prior to 1958 was the federally impacted areas aid, first enacted in 1950, and renewed repeatedly since then. 20 U.S.C. §§ 236 et seq. (1970), *as amended* (Supp. IV, 1974).

5. 20 U.S.C. §§ 241 et seq. (1970).

6. Based on 1975–76 estimated expenditures for public elementary and secondary education, taken from *National Center for Educational Statistics, The Condition of Education,* 189, Table 1–21 (1976).

7. *See,* e.g., Title I of the Elementary and Secondary Education Act of 1965, 20 U.S.C. §§ 241(a) et seq. (1970); Education for All Handicapped Children Act of 1975, 20 U.S.C.A. §§ 1405 et seq. (Supp. 1976), amending 20 U.S.C.A. §§ 1401 et seq. (1974); Bilingual Education Act, 20 U.S.C.A. §§ 880b to 880b–13 (Supp. 1976).

8. *See,* e.g., Title III of ESEA, 20 U.S.C. §§ 841 et seq. (1974);

Education Professions Development Act (the Teacher Corps), 20 U.S.C. §§ 1091 et seq. (1974); Title V of ESEA (grants to improve state and local planning), 20 U.S.C. §§ 861 et seq. (1974).

9. *See The Budget of the United States Government Fiscal Year 1977*, Appendix 344–52. (1976).

Aid for Target Groups	1975 Expenditures (Millions of Dollars)	
Grants for disadvantaged children (primarily Title I ESEA and Followthrough)	$1,929	
Grants for bilingual education	93	
Indian education	42	
Education for the handicapped	200	
Grants for vocational education for students with special needs	20	
	$2,284	
Emergency School Aid (for desegregating districts)—includes civil rights advisory service	133	
	$2,417	Total for Target Groups
Grants for Innovation and Reform		
Grants for innovation (e.g., strengthening state education departments, dropout prevention)	$ 160	
Right to Read	12	
Grants for innovation and reform of vocational education	35	
	$ 207	Total for Innovation
School Assistance in Federally Affected Areas	$ 656	
Other		
Library and instructional resources, drug abuse and envirnomental education, basic vocational education, and so on	$ 642	
	$1,298	
	$3,922	Total for "General Aid"

The new Education for All Handicapped Children Act, 20 U.S.C.A. §§ 1405 et seq. (Supp. 1976), *amending* 20 U.S.C.A. §§ 1401 et seq. (1974), will raise the funding level from $226 million to $3 billion over the next six years.

10. *See* Timpane, *Federal Aid to Schools: Its Limited Future,* 38 *Law and Contemporary Problems,* No. 3, 493 (1974).

11. 347 U.S. 483 (1954).

12. The principal Supreme Court decisions in school desegregation start in 1954 with Brown v. Board of Education (*Brown I*), 347 U.S. 483 (1954); and Brown v. Board of Eduation (*Brown II*), 349 U.S. 294 (1955); and include Greene v. County School Board, 391 U.S. 430 (1968); Alexander v. Holmes County Board of Education, 396 U.S. 19 (1969); Swann v. Charlotte-Mecklenburg County Board of Education, 402 U.S. 1 (1971); Wright v. Council of the City of Emporia, 407 U.S. 451 (1972); United States v. Scotland Neck City Board of Education, 407 U.S. 484 (1972); Keyes v. School District No. 1, 413 U.S. 189 (1973); Milliken v. Bradley, 418 U.S. 717 (1974); Pasadena City Board of Education v. Spangler, 96 S. Ct. 2697 (1976); and Dayton Board of Education v. Brinkman, 97 S. Ct. 2766 (1977).

13. Epperson v. Arkansas, 393 U.S. 97 (1968).

14. Tinker v. Des Moines Independent Community School District, 393 U.S. 503 (1969).

15. Wisconsin v. Yoder, 406 U.S. 205 (1972).

16. San Antonio Independent School District v. Rodriguez, 411 U.S. 1 (1973).

17. Milliken v. Bradley, 418 U.S. 717 (1974) and Keyes v. School District No. 1, 413 U.S. 189 (1973).

18. Lau v. Nichols, 414 U.S. 563 (1974).

19. Cleveland Board of Education v. LaFleur, 414 U.S. 632 (1974).

20. Goss v. Lopez, 419 U.S. 567 (1975) (suspensions) and Ingraham v. Wright, 97 S. Ct. 1401 (1977) (corporal punishment).

21. Wood v. Strickland, 420 U.S. 308 (1975).

22. Serrano v. Priest, 5 Cal.3d 584, 487 P.2d 1241, 96 Cal. Rptr. 601 (1971).

23. Hobson v. Hansen, 327 F. Supp. 844 (D.D.C. 1971).

24. Pennsylvania Association for Retarded Children v. Pennsylvania, 343 F. Supp. 279 (E.D. Pa. 1972) and Mills v. Board of Education, 348 F. Supp. 866 (D.D.C. 1972).

25. Vorchheimer v. School District of Philadelphia, 532 F.2d 880 (3rd Cir. 1976), *aff'd by an equally divided Court,* 430 U.S. 703 (1977); Berkelman v. San Francisco Unified School District, 501 F.2d 1264 (9th Cir. 1974).

26. Ritacco v. Norwin School District, 361 F. Supp. 930 (W.D. Pa. 1973) (athletics) and Della Casa v. Gaffney, Civ. Action No. 171673 (San Mateo Super. Ct., stipulated judgment filed April 11, 1973) (auto shop).

27. Larry P. v. Riles, 502 F.2d 963 (9th Cir. 1974) and Hobson v. Hansen, 269 F. Supp. 401 (D.D.C. 1967), *aff'd sub nom.* Smuck v. Hobson, 408 F.2d 175 (D.C. Cir. 1969) (en banc).

28. Peter Doe v. San Francisco Unified School District, Civ. No. 36851 (Cal. Ct. App., August 6, 1976) (slip opinion).

29. Pickering v. Board of Education, 391 U.S. 563 (1968).

30. Cleveland Board of Education v. LaFleur, 414 U.S. 632 (1974).

31. National Education Ass'n. v. South Carolina, 15 FEP Cases 1196 (1977), *aff'd mem.* 98 S. Ct. 756 (1978); United States v. North Carolina, 400 F. Supp. 343 (E.D.N.C. 1975).

32. 5 Cal.3d 584, 487 P.2d 1241, 96 Cal. Rptr. 601 (1971).

33. Van Dusartz v. Hatfield, 334 F. Supp. 870 (D. Minn. 1971); Rodriguez v. San Antonio Independent School District, 337 F. Supp. 280 (W.D. Tex. 1971), *rev'd*, 411 U.S. 1 (1973); and Parker v. Mandel, 344 F. Supp. 1068 (D. Md. 1972).

34. Robinson v. Cahill, 118 N.J. Super. 223, 287 A.2d 187 (1972), *supplemented* in 119 N.J. Super. 40, 289 A.2d 569 (1972), *aff'd as modified,* 62 N.J. 473, 303 A.2d 273 (1973); Hollins v. Shofstall, Civ. No. C–253652 (Ariz. Super. Ct., June 1, 1972), *rev'd*, 110 Ariz. 88, 515 P.2d 590 (1973); Sweetwater County Planning Commission v. Hinkle, 491 P.2d 1234 (Wyo. 1971), *juris. relinquished*, 493 P.2d 1050 (Wyo. 1972); Caldwell v. Kansas, Civ. No. 50616 (Dist. Ct. August 30, 1972); Milliken v. Green, 389 Mich. 1, 203 N.W.2d 457 (1972), *vacated*, 390 Mich. 389, 212 N.W.2d 711 (1973); and Spano v. Board of Education of Lakeland Central School District No. 1, 68 Misc.2d 804, 328 N.Y.S.2d 229 (Super. Ct. 1972).

35. San Antonio Independent School District v. Rodriguez, 411 U.S. 1 (1973).

36. In reviewing legislation that has been attacked as violating the equal protection clause of the Fourteenth Amendment of the federal constitution, the traditional equal protection standard of review is the minimal rationality standard. All that need be shown to uphold the legislation as constitutional is that the legislation's objective is a legitimate goal of the state and that there is a rational relationship between the goal sought and the legislative classification. This test presumes the law under attack to be valid, thrusting the burden on the *plaintiff* to show that the legislation is arbitrary or irrational. Legislation is subjected to a stricter standard of review, a more rigid scrutiny, if it classifies on the basis of a "suspect" trait (such as race or nationality) or if "fundamental" interests (such as the right to vote or free speech) are involved. Under this test, the burden is on the *defendent state* to show a *compelling* state justification for this particular legislative scheme and that the legitimate objectives of the legislation could be accomplished by no less onerous, less discriminatory means.

37. 411 U.S. at 37.

38. Id. at 45.

39. Justice Marshall suggested this course of action in his dissenting opinion in *Rodriguez*. "[N]othing in the Court's decision today should inhibit further review of state education funding schemes under state constitutional provisions." 411 U.S. at 133, n. 100.

40. Robinson v. Cahill, 62 N.J. 473, 509, 303 A.2d 273, 292 (1973).

41. *Cases plaintiffs lost*: Thompson v. Engelking, 96 Idaho 793, 537 P.2d 635 (1975) (plaintiffs relied on state equal protection clause as well as education clause); Northshore School District v. Kinnear, 84 Wash.2d 685, 530 P.2d 176 (1974); Olsen v. Oregon (Super. Ct. Ore., September 3, 1976) (slip opinion) (plaintiffs relied on state equal protection clause as well as education clause). *Cases still pending*: Horton v. Meskill, 31 Conn. Supp. 377, 332

A.2d 113 (Hartford County Super. Ct. 1974) (plaintiffs won in trial court, appeal pending) (plaintiffs relied on state equal protection clause as well as education clause); Board of Education of Levittown v. Nyquist, No. 8208/74 (Super. Ct., Nassau County, N.Y.); Pauley v. Kelly (Cir. Ct., Kanawha County, W. Va.).

42. Levin, *School Finance Reform in a Post-Rodriguez World, National Organization on Legal Problems in Education , Contemporary Legal Problems in Education,* 156, 172 (1974); see also J. Callahan and W. Wilken, *School Finance Reform: A Legislator's Handbook,* 8–9 (1976).

43. B. Levin, T. Muller, and C. Sandoval, *The High Cost of Education in Cities,* 2 (1973).

44. No. 8208/74 (Super. Ct., Nassau County, N.Y.). A decision has recently been handed down in Seattle, Washington, which was also being tried on an "urban differential" theory. A similar lawsuit was successfully brought in Cincinnati, Ohio. Board of Education of Cincinnati v. Walter, No. A7662725 (Hamilton County C.P. Ct., Ohio, Nov. 28, 1977).

45. The New Jersey and California courts set seemingly different standards as to the equal educational opportunity that the legislature is required to provide under their state constitutions. For the California court, expenditure differences reflect the degree of opportunity provided by the educational system. Its standard is based on inputs (the disparities must be reduced to "amounts considerably less than $100 per pupil"). The state must "provide for uniformity and equality of treatment to all pupils of the state," meaning that "the state may not. . .permit. . .significant disparities in expenditures, between school districts. . . ." Serrano v. Priest, Civ. No. 938,254 (Cal. Super. Ct., April 10, 1974) (slip opinion) at 51. No relationship between inputs and outcomes need be shown.

The New Jersey Supreme Court, however, does not require that the remedy be equalization of expenditures. *Robinson* v. *Cahill,* in holding that the state legislature is constitutionally compelled to provide a "thorough and efficient" education, requires the state to provide a minimally adequate education to all districts—a standard not unlike that suggested by the Supreme Court in *Rodriguez.* According to the New Jersey court, the "thorough and efficient" education guaranteed by the state constitution is "that educational opportunity which is needed in the contemporary setting to equip a child for his role as a citizen, and as a competitor in the labor market." Robinson v. Cahill, 62 N.J. 473, 515, 303 A.2d 273, 295 (1973). The problem is that neither the New Jersey court nor the majority in *Rodriguez* has provided a way to determine what minimum level of expenditure would produce an adequate education. In sharp contrast, the *Serrano* trial court indicates that the adequacy of the educational program is constitutionally irrelevant; it is the "quality" of the educational program *relative to* other districts that is the issue.

46. Title I of the Elementary and Secondary Education Act of 1965, 20 U.S.C.A. §§ 241(a) et seq. (1974), *as amended* (Supp. 1976).

47. See Berke, Sacks, Bailey, Campbell, *Federal Aid to Public Education: Who Benefits?* in *Federal Aid to Education* (J. Berke and M. Kirst, eds., 1972). *See also* J. Berke, *Answers to Inequity,* 127–61 (1974).

48. Educational Agencies Financial Aid Act, 20 U.S.C.A. §§ 236 et seq. (1974), *as amended* (Supp. 1976).

49. 20 U.S.C. § 240(d) (2) (A) (Supp. IV, 1974).

50. 85 Fed. Reg. 19116 (§ 115.62 [b] [1]). The 20 percent disparity requirement may be waived by the U.S. Commissioner of Education when he finds that there are "exceptional circumstances" in the state in question, if expenditures in the state will be no less equalized if impact aid is taken into account than if it is not, if the amount of revenue available to a local school district in the state is not predominantly a function of its own wealth, if the state aid program recognizes the higher need of certain target group pupils and the higher costs due to cost of living differences, or sparsity or density factors, and if the state program is one in which a substantial proportion of funds comes from state rather than local revenues. 85 Fed. Reg. 19116 (§ 115.62 [c]).

51. *See*, e.g., S. 1817, National Education Act of 1973 (introduced by Sen. Humphrey) (to reduce tax inequalities); S. 2414, Elementary and Secondary Education Assistance Act of 1973 (introduced by Sen. Mondale) (to reduce expenditure disparities).

52. Education Amendments of 1974, 20 U.S.C.A. § 246 (Supp. 1975).

53. 45 C.F.R. §§ 156.1 et seq. (1975).

54. 327 F. Supp. 844 (D.D.C. 1971).

55. Although *Hobson* predated the *Rodriguez* decision, the plaintiffs might have succeeded in spite of *Rodriguez*. First, the wealth involved is not district wealth but personal wealth. Thus, the system discriminates against a definable group of poor people, *see* San Antonio Independent School District v. Rodriguez, 411 U.S. 1, 22 (1973), and may therefore create a "suspect classification," triggering the stricter equal protection standard. Even if the weaker standard is utilized, however, it could be argued that there is no rational basis for a system that maintains disparities in educational expenditures among schools within a single district. In *Rodriguez,* the Court found that to encourage local autonomy by permitting districts to decide how much to spend on education by selecting their tax rates was a legitimate state purpose even if the result was substantial disparities among districts. Discrimination among schools within a single district, however, could not possibly serve such a purpose since it is the central board that decides how much is to be spent in each school, not the individual school.

56. Brown v. Board of Education of the City of Chicago, 386 F. Supp. 110 (N.D. Ill. 1974).

57. Id. at 123.

58. 45 C.F.R. § 116.26 (1975).

59. Title I of the Elementary and Secondary Education Act of 1965, 20 U.S.C. §§ 241(a) et seq. (1970), *as amended* (Supp. IV 1974).

60. 421 U.S. 349 (1975).

61. 45 C.F.R. § 116.19(e) (1975).

62. *Meek,* 421 U.S. at 364.

63. Wheeler v. Barrera, 417 U.S. 402 (1974).

64. *United States Office of Education Program Guide No. 44,* §

4.5 (1968), reproduced in *Title I ESEA, Participation of Private School Children—A Handbook for State and Local School Officials,* U.S. HEW Pub. No. (OE) 72–62, at 41–42 (1971).

65. *Wheeler,* 417 U.S. at 425.

66. Dual enrollment has been used as a means of carrying out joint instructional programs for public and nonpublic school students. Under this system, children who are enrolled in nonpublic schools are released by their schools several times a week to attend special classes in the public schools or in libraries or recreation centers nearby.

67. See Wheeler v. Barrera, 417 U.S. 402 (1974). See also Special District v. Wheeler, 408 S.W.2d 60 (Mo. 1966).

68. 343 F. Supp. 279 (E.D. Pa. 1972) (consent decree).

69. Id. at 283, n. 8.

70. Id. at 307. *See also* Mills v. Board of Education, 348 F. Supp. 866 (D.D.C. 1972).

71. 411 U.S. at 37.

72. 411 F. Supp. 46 (N.D. Ohio 1976).

73. 343 F. Supp. at 296.

74. *Compare* Dunn, *Special Education for the Mentally Retarded— Is Much of It Justified?,* 35 *Exceptional Children,* 5 (1968) *with* MacMillan, *Special Education for the Mildly Retarded: Servant or Savant?,* 2 *Focus on Exceptional Children,* No. 9, at 1 (1971). A summary of some of the arguments for and against special classes for the retarded is provided in Fink and Glass, *Contemporary Issues in the Education of the Behaviorally Disordered,* in *The First Review of Special Education,* 137 (L. Mann and D. Sabatino, eds., 1973).

75. In PARC, the consent order, affirmed by the court, provided that "placement in a regular public school class is preferable to placement in a special public school class. . . ." 334 F. Supp. 1257, 1260 (E.D. Pa. 1971). See also Lebanks v. Spears, 60 F.R.D. 135 (E.D. La. 1973); and Mills v. Board of Education, 348 F. Supp. 866 (D.D.C. 1972).

76. The Education for All Handicapped Children Act, 20 U.S.C.A. § 1412(5) (Supp. 1976), establishes a system of priorities, including the requirement that handicapped children be educated in normal settings "to the maximum extent appropriate" and that they be educated in the "least restrictive environment."

77. One commentator has noted that as a result of a court decision in California and the state legislature's enactment of a law shortly thereafter, thousands of EMR children have been returned to regular classrooms. The commentator points out the problems, however.

[A] closer look at the situation presents a dismal picture. Children being returned to the regular classes are provided little of the necessary additional support, enrichment, and remedial services which will redress the effects of their prior educational experiences and permit them to function at the level of other students in the regular classes. Apparently, they are not expected to do well, and many will not. It seems certain that the blame for their failure will be placed on the children, rather than on a system that will not modify itself and its resources to meet their particular needs.

Cohen and DeYoung, *The Role of Litigation in the Improvement of Programming for the Handicapped*, in *The First Review of Special Education*, 270 (L. Mann and D. Sabatino, eds., 1973).

78. An idea of the level of funds involved can be gleaned from Mills v. Board of Education, 348 F. Supp. 866 (D.D.C. 1972), and its aftermath. At the time the suit was brought, there was no accurate count of the number of children who would be affected as the District of Columbia school system had not conducted the census required by statute. The plaintiffs speculated that as many as 18,000 of the District's estimated 22,000 handicapped children were *not* receiving special education when the suit was brought. A Board of Education study showed that prior to the suit, there were approximately 3,800 handicapped children receiving some publicly supported special education, 348 F. Supp. at 868, and according to some rough figures made available by the District of Columbia school system, the special education budget for the 1971-72 year was approximately $7 million. Letter from Doris A. Woodson, Assistant Superintendent, Department of Special Education, Public Schools of the District of Columbia, July 8, 1976. The budgeted amount is for direct education, supervision, and administration of public school special education programs; it does not reflect such services as transportation, building maintenance, utilities, psychological evaluation, social services, and therapy. Id. When *Mills* was decided, the number of students served increased to 11,047 while the budget increased to over $10 million. During the 1976 school year, the number of students served was 14,536, requiring a budget of nearly $12 million.

79. Kirp, Buss, and Kuriloff, *Legal Reform of Special Education: Empirical Studies and Procedural Proposals*, 62 *Calif. L. Rev.* 40, 63 (1974).

80. Over 60,000 evaluations had to be conducted in Pennsylvania. An elaborate evaluation is said to take from four-and-one-half to five hours. Id.

81. 343 F. Supp. 1306 (N.D. Cal. 1972), *aff'd*, 502 F.2d 963 (9th Cir. 1974).

82. 269 F. Supp. 401 (D.D.C. 1967), *aff'd sub nom.* Smuck v. Hobson, 408 F.2d 175 (D.C. Cir. 1969) (en banc).

83. The recent Supreme Court case of *Washington* v. *Davis*, 96 S. Ct. 2040 (1976), however, may affect the extent to which the stricter standard may be relied upon to overturn the use of standardized tests to label minority children. In *Davis*, the use of a standardized aptitude test resulted in the rejection of a disproportionate number of minority applicants to the police force. The Supreme Court held that disproportionate impact alone does not make a prima facie case of impermissible discrimination and does not trigger a stricter standard of review. If *Davis* is followed in this area, either deliberate, purposeful discrimination will have to be shown, or the use of IQ or other tests must be shown to be wholly irrational for sorting children.

In some school systems, Spanish-speaking children have been tested in English and then classified as mentally retarded. *See*, e.g., Diana v. State

Board of Education, Civ. No. C–70–37–RFR (N.D. Cal. June 18, 1973) (case terminated by stipulated settlement). Arguably, the use of such tests to classify these children is wholly irrational and hence would be invalid even under the traditional equal protection standard.

Labeling has been successfully challenged in a somewhat different context in a recent Pennsylvania case. Merriken v. Cressman, 364 F. Supp. 913 (E.D. Pa. 1973). In that case, students were subjected to personality testing purportedly to identify potential drug abusers. Both the personal nature of the questions asked during the testing and the potential for dissemination of the data acquired were held to be unconstitutional violations of privacy. The court treated privacy as a fundamental right, violated by the use of stigmatizing labels unless the state had a compelling interest to be served by the testing.

84. 20 U.S.C.A. §§ 1405 et seq. (Supp. 1976), *amending* 20 U.S.C.A. §§ 1401 et seq. (1974).

85. According to estimates for 1974, $1.8 billion was spent under Title I and $0.5 billion under impacted areas aid for a total of $2.3 billion. *National Center for Education Statistics, HEW, Digest for Educational Statistics, 1974 Edition,* 131, Table 142 (1975).

86. 20 U.S.C.A. § 1415(a) (Supp. 1976).

87. Kirp, Buss, and Kuriloff, *Legal Reform of Special Education: Empirical Studies and Procedural Proposals,* 62 *Calif. L. Rev.* 40, 81, n. 146 (1974).

88. New York State Association for Retarded Children, Inc. v. Rockefeller, 357 F. Supp. 752, 763 (E.D.N.Y. 1973).

89. Frederick L. v. Thomas, 408 F. Supp. 832 (E.D. Pa. 1976).

90. Ross, *The Potential Impact of Rodriguez on Other School Reform Litigation,* 38 *Law and Contemporary Problems,* 566, 573 (1974).

91. 414 U.S. 563 (1974).

92. 42 U.S.C. § 200d (1970).

93.
No state shall deny equal education opportunity to an individual on account of his or her. . .national origin, by. . .(b) the failure by an educational agency to take appropriate action to overcome language barriers that impeded equal participation by its students in its instructional programs.

Equal Educational Opportunity Act of 1974, 20 U.S.C. § 1703(f)(Supp. IV 1974).

94. Bilingual Education Act, 20 U.S.C. §§ et seq. (Supp. IV 1974).

95. 45 C.F.R. § 123.01 (1975).

96. Based on estimates of USOE, HEW, of children in need of special language programs. The National Center for Education Statistics estimates that 4,200,000 children between the ages of 4 to 18 speak a language other than English. Information supplied by J. Rendley, Office of Bilingual Education, HEW, telephone conversation, August 10, 1976.

97. Information supplied by J. Rendley, supra.

98. Civ. No. 36851 (Cal. Ct. App., August 6, 1976) (slip opinion).

99. Comment, *Educational Malpractice,* 124 *U. Pa. L. Rev.* 755, 758 (1976).

100. Swann v. Charlotte-Mecklenberg Board of Education, 402 U.S. 1, 15 (1971).

101. Id. at 25.

102. Id. at 24.

103. Id. at 27–29.

104. Id. at 31.

105. *See*, e.g., United States v. Board of School Commissioners, 503 F.2d 68, 80 (7th Cir. 1974), *cert. denied*, 421 U.S. 929 (1975).

106. Milliken v. Bradley, 418 U.S. 717 (1974). Four post-*Milliken* cases where such actions have been found and an interdistrict remedy ordered are Newburg Area Council v. Board of Education, 510 F.2d 1358 (6th Cir. 1974), *cert. denied*, 421 U.S. 931 (1975); United States v. Missouri, 388 F. Supp. 1058 (E.D. Mo. 1975), *aff'd in part and rev'd in part*, 515 F.2d 1365 (8th Cir. 1975); United States v. Board of School Commissioners, 368 F. Supp. 1191 (S.D. Ind. 1973), *aff'd in part and rev'd in part*, 503 F.2d 68 (7th Cir. 1974), *cert. denied*, 421 U.S. 929 (1975); and Evans v. Buchanan, 393 F. Supp. 428 (D. Del. 1975), *aff'd mem.*, 423 U.S. 963 (1976).

107. Pasadena City Board of Education v. Spangler, 96 S. Ct. 2697 (1976).

108. *See*, e.g., Moses v. Washington Parish School Board, 456 F.2d 1285 (5th Cir.), *cert. denied*, 409 U.S. 1013 (1972) and Lemon v. Bossier Parish School Board, 444 F.2d 1400 (5th Cir. 1971).

109. Washington v. Davis, 96 S. Ct. 2040 (1976), may have eliminated the racially discriminatory impact test, so that challengers of ability grouping would be confined to proving racial motivation to obtain redress.

110. The arguments that have been made, both for and against ability grouping, are summarized in *National Education Association, Ability Grouping*, 8–10 (Research Summary No. 1968–S3).

111. *See Children's Defense Fund, Children Out of School in America*, 130–34 (1974).

112. *Children's Defense Fund, School Suspensions: Are They Helping Children?*, 61 (1975).

113. *See*, e.g., Rhyne v. Childs, 359 F. Supp. 1085 (N.D. Fla. 1973), *aff'd sub nom.*, Sweet v. Childs, 507 F.2d 675 (5th Cir. 1975) and Tillman v. Dade County School Board, 327 F. Supp. 930 (S.D. Fla. 1971). *But see* Hawkins v. Coleman, 376 F. Supp. 1330 (N.D. Tex. 1974).

114. Goss v. Lopez, 419 U.S. 565 (1975).

115. The State of Michigan sought to delay implementation of the Sixth Circuit order to expand desegregation in Detroit because the state was unable to pay $5.8 million to the Detroit school system, which is required by the order. The district court had required certain "educational components" (e.g., programs for reading, testing, in-service training, counseling) to be included in the desegregation plan and directed the State of Michigan to pay 50 percent of the cost of the new programs. This money, the state argued, would have to come out of the funds appropriated for other state departments or would require the state to assume an unconstitutional deficit. The Sixth Circuit, however, upheld the requirement, stating that it was "within the equitable powers of the court

to require the State of Michigan to pay a reasonable part of the cost of correcting the effects of de jure segregation which state officials, including the Legislature, have helped .to create." Bradley v. Milliken, 540 F.2d 229, 245 (6th Cir. 1976). The court of appeals also affirmed the district court's order that the state bear 75 percent of the cost of additional buses. This decision was affirmed by The Supreme Court. Milliken v. Bradley, 97 S. Ct. 2757 (1977).

    116. Orfield, *How to Make Desegregation Work: The Adaptation of Schools to Their Newly-Integrated Student Bodies,* 39 *Law and Contemporary Problems* at 315 (1975).

    117. Id. at 339.

    118. *See,* e.g., 20 U.S.C. § 1651 and § 1656 (Supp. IV, 1974) and most of §§ 1701 et seq. (Supp. IV 1974).

    119. 20 U.S.C. § 1652(a) (Supp. III, 1973), 20 U.S.C. § 1228 (Supp. IV, 1974). *See* Carroll v. HEW, 410 F. Supp. 234 (W.D. Ky. 1976).

    120. Singleton v. Jackson Municipal Separate School District, 419 F.2d 1211 (5th Cir. 1969), *rev'd in part,* 396 U.S. 290 (1970).

    121. 42 U.S.C. §§ 2000e et seq. (Supp. II, 1972), *amending* 42 U.S.C. §§ 2000e et seq. (1970).

    Since coverage was extended to teachers only in 1972, there are few Title VII cases in which a teacher has alleged that the school system's actions toward him or her have been racially discriminatory. The Supreme Court has held that in order to meet the initial burden of establishing a prima facie case of racial discrimination, the teacher plaintiff must show

> (i) that he belongs to a racial minority; (ii) that he applied and was qualified for a job for which the employer was seeking applicants; (iii) that, despite his qualifications, he was rejected; and (iv) that, after his rejection, the position remained open and the employer continued to seek applicants from persons of complainant's qualifications. McDonnel Douglas Corporation v. Green, 411 U.S. 792, 802 (1973).

    The burden then shifts "to the employer to articulate some legitimate, nondiscriminatory reason for the employee's rejection," but "the inquiry must not end there" because the employee must "be afforded a fair opportunity to show that. . .[the employer's] stated reason for. . .[the employees] rejection was in fact pretext." Id. at 8-2, 804.

    Of Title VII sex discrimination cases against public school systems, a significant majority are concerned with mandatory pregnancy leave or exclusion of pregnancy-related disabilities from the school system's disability benefits coverage. Most of the nonpregnancy cases concern faculty appointment and tenure decisions at institutions of higher education.

    122. 96 S. Ct. 2040 (1976).

    123. National Education Association v. South Carolina, 15 FEP Cases 1196 (D. S.C. 1977), *aff'd mem.,* 98 S. Ct. 756 (1978).

    124. *See* Craig v. Boren, 45 *U.S.L.W.* 4057 (December 21, 1976). A number of lower courts, however, have treated sex-based classifications as

suspect. *See*, e.g., Held v. Missouri Pacific Railroad, 373 F. Supp. 996 (S.D. Tex. 1974); Daugherty v. Daley, 370 F. Suppl. 338 (N.D. Ill. 1974); Wisenfeld v. Secretary of HEW, 367 F. Supp. 981 (D. N.J. 1973), *aff'd*, 420 U.S. 636 (1974); and Ballard v. Laird, 360 F. Supp. 643 (S.D. Cal. 1973), *rev'd*, 419 U.S. 498 (1974).

125. Title IX of the Education Amendments of 1972, 20 U.S.C. §§ 1681 et seq. (Supp. IV 1974). *See* 45 C.F.R. § 86.1 et seq. (1975).

126. 20 U.S.C. §§ 1681 et seq. (Supp. IV 1974), *as amended*, 20 U.S.C.A. § 1681 (Supp. 1976). *See* C.F.R. §§ 86.51 et seq. (1975).

127. 29 U.S.C. § 206 (1970), *as amended*, 29 U.S.C. § 206 (Supp. III, 1973).

128. 42 U.S.C. §§ 2000e et seq. (Supp. II 1972), *amending* 42 U.S.C. §§ 2000e et seq. (1970).

129. Vorchheimer v. School District of Philadelphia, 532 F.2d 880 (3rd Cir. 1976).

130. Because of a four-four split, there is no Supreme Court opinion and the Third Circuit's decision stands. 430 U.S. 703 (1977).

131. 45 C.F.R. § 86.35 (1975).

132. Berkelman v. San Francisco Unified School District, 501 F.2d 1264 (9th Cir. 1974). *See also* Bray v. Lee, 337 F. Supp. 934 (D. Mass. 1972).

133. 45 C.F.R. § 86.35(b) (1975). Another regulation prohibits schools from "giv[ing] preference to one person over another on the basis of sex, by ranking applicants separately," by "apply[ing] numerical limitations upon the number or proportion of persons of either sex who may be admitted," or "otherwise treat[ing] one individual differently from another on the basis of sex." Id. § 86.21.

134. *See*, e.g., Shull v. Columbus Municipal Separate School District, 338 F. Supp. 1376 (N.D. Miss. 1972); Ordway v. Hargraves, 323 F. Supp. 1155 (D. Mass. 1971); and Perry v. Grenada Municipal Separate School District, 300 F. Supp. 748 (N.D. Miss. 1969).

135. Houston v. Prosser, 361 F. Supp. 295 (N.D. Ga. 1973).

136. 45 C.F.R. § 86.40(b) (1975).

137. "Compliance. . .may be effected (1) by the termination or refusal to grant or to continue assistance. . . ." 20 U.S.C. § 1682 (Supp. II 1972). The substantially identical language of Title VI (for race) is found in 42 U.S.C. § 2000d–1 (1970).

138. "Compliance may be effected. . .(2) by any other means authorized by Law. . . ." 20 U.S.C. § 1682 (Supp. II 1972). 45 C.F.R. §§ 86.71, 80.8(a) (1975).

139. Cannon v. University of Chicago, 559 F.2d 1063 (7th Cir. 1976).

140. In the words of the statute, termination of federal assistance for failure to comply "shall be limited in its effect to the particular program, or part thereof, in which. . .noncompliance has been. . .found. . . ." 20 U.S.C. § 1682 (Supp. II 1972).

141. *But see* Stewart v. New York University, No. 74, Civ. 4126 (S.D. N.Y., March 16, 1976).

142. 45 C.F.R. § 86.41(c) (1975).

143. In addition to cases concerned with discrimination in employment on the basis of race or sex, there are a number of cases alleging unconstitutional discrimination on the basis of age. Most of these cases involve state statutes or school board policies that require teachers to retire at a certain age. The Supreme Court's recent decision in *Massachusetts Board of Retirement* v. *Murgia*, 96 S. Ct. 2562 (1976), in which a statute mandating the retirement of state police officers at age 50 was upheld as not violative of the equal protection clause, suggests that such constitutional challenges will be unsuccessful in the future. The Age Discrimination in Employment Act, 29 U.S.C.A. §§ 621 et seq. (1975), only applied to individuals between the ages of 40 and 65. Moreover, an employer is permitted to "observe the terms of a bona fide employee benefit plan such as a retirement, pension, or insurance plan. . . ." and pursuant to such a plan, an employee may be involuntarily retired irrespective of age. 29 C.F.R. § 860.110 (1975). Thus, a statutory attack on a fixed retirement age for teachers is likely to be no more successful than a constitutional attack.

144. Cleveland Board of Education v. LaFleur, 414 U.S. 632 (1974).

145. 29 C.F.R. § 1604.10(b) (1975).

146. Geduldig v. Aiello, 417 U.S. 484 (1974).

147. General Electric Co. v. Gilbert, 45 *U.S.L.W.* 4031 (December 7, 1976).

148. 393 U.S. 503 (1969).

149. 391 U.S. 563 (1968).

150.
First Amendment rights, applied in light of the special characteristics of the school environment, are available to teachers and students. It can hardly be argued that either students or teachers shed their constitutional rights to freedom of speech or expression at the schoolhouse gate.

Tinker v. Des Moines Independent Community School District, 393 U.S. 503, 506 (1969).

151. [T]he power of the State to control the conduct of children reaches beyond the scope of its authority over adults. Prince v. Massachusetts, 321 U.S. 158, 170 (1944). *See also* Ginsberg v. New York, 390 U.S. 629 (1968).

152. Pickering v. Board of Education, 391 U.S. 563, 568 (1968).

153. Roe v. Wade, 410 U.S. 113 (1973).

154. *See*, e.g., The Privacy Act of 1974, 5 U.S.C. § 552a (Supp. IV 1974) and Family Educational Rights and Privacy Act of 1974, 20 U.S.C. § 1232g (Supp. IV, 1974).

155. *See*, e.g., *Ore. Rev. Stat.* § 336.195 (1971).

156. Family Educational Rights and Privacy Act of 1974, 20 U.S.C. § 1232g (Supp. IV 1974).

157. Note, *The Buckley Amendment: Opening School Files for Students and Parental Review*, 24 *Catholic U.L. Rev.* 588, 593-94 (1975). The Buckley Amendment provides a right to challenge and correct inaccurate data

contained in student records. 20 U.S.C. § 1232g(a) (2) (Supp. IV 1974).

158. Tinker v. Des Moines Independent Community School District, 393 U.S. 503 (1969); *In re* Gault, 387 U.S. 1 (1967).

159. *See*, e.g., Mercer v. State, 450 S.W.2d 715 (Tex. Civ. App. 1970); *In re* Donaldson, 269 Cal. App.2d 509, 75 Cal. Rptr. 220 (1969).

160. One court has held that school officials have a right even to use moderate force in obtaining obedience by a student in search of his locker, where the primary purpose of the search is not to obtain criminal convictions but to secure evidence of student misconduct. *In re* Donaldson, 269 Cal. App.2d 509, 75 Cal. Rptr. 220 (1969).

161. Merriken v. Cressman, 364 F. Supp. 913 (E.D. Pa. 1973).

162. Id. at 916.

163. 364 F. Supp. at 918. The court cited Griswold v. Connecticut, 381 U.S. 479 (1965) and Roe v. Wade, 410 U.S. 113 (1973) as sources of the privacy right.

164. *See*, e.g., Comment, *Protecting the Privacy of School Children and Their Families Through the Family Educational Rights and Privacy Act of 1974*, 14 *J. Family Law* 255, 259 (1975); Note, *Constitutional Law–Right of Privacy–Personality Test Used by School to Identify Potential Drug Abusers Without Informed Consent of Parents Violates Students' and Parents' Right of Privacy*. 27 *Vand. L. Rev.* 372 (1974).

165.

> The Court, in balancing the right of an individual to privacy and the right of the government to invade that privacy for the sake of public interest, strikes the balance in favor of the individual in the circumstances shown in this case. In short, the reasons for this are that the test itself and the surrounding results of that test are not sufficiently presented to both the child and the parents, as well as the Court, as to its authenticity and credibility in fighting the drug problem in this country. There is too much of a chance that the wrong people for the wrong reasons will be singled out and counselled in the wrong manner. 364 F. Supp. at 921.

166. Sullivan v. Meade Independent School District, 530 F.2d 799 (6th Cir. 1976).

167. Id. at 804. *But cf.* Andrews v. Drew Municipal Separate School District, 507 F.2d 611 (5th Cir. 1975), *cert. dismissed as improvidently granted*, 96 S. Ct. 1752 (1976).

168. Even if the teacher satisfied the burden of showing that his conduct was constitutionally protected and was a motivating factor in the school board's decision not to rehire him, if the school board can show by a preponderance of the evidence that it would have reached the same decision even in the absence of the protected statements made by the teacher, the school board will prevail. Mt. Healthy City School District Board of Education v. Doyle, 429 U.S. 274 (1976).

169. 393 U.S. 503 (1969).

170. 391 U.S. 563 (1968).

171. Id. at 568.

172. Id. at 570, n. 3.

173. The Supreme Court, however, has decided a hair regulation case concerning policemen. The plaintiff in that case alleged that the maximum hair length regulation violated his First Amendment right of freedom of expression and his Fourteenth Amendment guarantees of due process and equal protection. The Supreme Court held that the hair regulation must be "considered in the context of the county's chosen mode of organization for its police force." Kelly v. Johnson, 96 S. Ct. 1440, 1445 (1976). The burden was on the plaintiff to show that the regulation was irrational and arbitrary and therefore a deprivation of his liberty. The majority found that either a "desire to make police officers readily recognizable to members of the public, or a desire for the *esprit de corps* which such similarity is felt to inculcate within the police force itself," is a rational justification. Id. at 1446. Whether this rationale will be applied in the context of the school system is not yet clear.

174. *See,* e.g., Richard v. Thurston, 424 F.2d 1281, 1285 (1st Cir. 1970); Copeland v. Hawkins, 352 F. Supp. 1022, 1025 (E.D. Ill. 1973); and Dunham v. Pulsifer, 312 F. Supp. 411, 419 (D. Vt. 1970).

175. Bannister v. Paradis, 316 F. Supp. 185 (D. N.H. 1970) (male student wearing dungarees).

176. *See* Baker v. Owen, 395 F. Supp. 294 (M.D. N.C.), *aff'd mem.,* 423 U.S. 907 (1975).

177. Ingraham v. Wright, 525 F.2nd 909 (5th Cir.) (en banc).

178. Baker v. Owen, 395 F. Supp. 294 (M.D. N.C.) (1975).

179. Ingraham v. Wright, 525 F.2d 909, 919 (5th Cir. 1976), 97 S. Ct. 1401 (1977).

180. Goss v. Lopez, 419 U.S. 565 (1975).

181. 419 U.S. at 584.

182. One commentator has summed up the possible intangible impacts of *Goss.* Kirp, *Proceduralism and Bureaucracy: Due Process in the School Setting, 28 Stan. L. Rev.* 841, 851–64 (1976). *See also* 419 U.S. 565, 589-90, 593 (1975) (Powell, J., dissenting).

183. 408 U.S. 564 (1972) (emphasis added).

184. 408 U.S. 593 (1972).

185. 96 S. Ct. 2074 (1976).

186. *See* Van Alstyne, *Cracks in "The New Property": Adjudicative Due Process in the Administrative State, 62 Cornell L. Rev.* 445 (1977).

187. Board of Regents v. Roth, 408 U.S. 564, 573 (1972).

188. *See* e.g., Goss v. Lopez, 419 U.S. 565 (1975).

189. *See* § 615 of the Education for All Handicapped Children Act of 1975, 20 U.S.C.A. § 1415 (Supp. 1976).

190. 420 U.S. 308 (1975).

191. Id. at 322 (emphasis added). If he acted with "malicious intention to cause a deprivation of constitutional rights or other injury to the student," he would also be liable. Id.

192. Id. at 321.

193. 420 U.S. at 322, *quoting* Pierson v. Ray, 386 U.S. 557 (1967).

194. 419 U.S. at 583.

195. 420 U.S. at 331 (Powell, J., concurring in part and dissenting in part).

196. *Education Daily,* July 21, 1977.

197. The Supreme Court has recently held that students who were unconstitutionally suspended because school authorities failed to provide the requisite procedural safeguards, were nevertheless not entitled to substantial damages absent proof of actual injury caused by the deprivation of constitutional rights. The burden is on the plaintiffs to show actual injury. If they are unable to do so, they are entitled to recover only nominal damages for the denial of procedural due process. Carey v. Piphus, 46 *U.S.L.W.* 4224 (U.S. March 21, 1978).

198. 69 Wis. 2d 200, 231 N.W.2d 206 (1975), *rev'd,* 45 *U.S.L.W.* 4043 (U.S. December 8, 1976).

199. In Abood v. Detroit Board of Education, 431 U.S. 209 (1977), the Supreme Court held that it was not violative of the First Amendment to compel nonunion employees in the public sector to pay "a service fee equal in amount to union dues" for union expenditures directly related to collective bargaining. (The payment was compelled pursuant to an agency shop agreement between a school board and a union.) The Court did, however, hold that that portion of the compulsory service fee spent for purposes *not* directly related to collective bargaining could not be required of the nonunion plaintiffs. The Court held that the First Amendment right to "refus[e] to associate" prevented compelling any of the nonunion challengers "to contribute to the support of an ideological cause he may oppose as a condition of holding a job as a public school teacher." Id. at 235.

200. *See, e.g.,* Red Bank Board of Education v. Warrington, 138 N.J. Super. 564, 351 A. 2d 778 (1976) (classroom preparation time); West Hartford Education Association v. DeCourcy, 162 Conn. 566, 295 A. 2d 526 (1972) (class size); and Joint School District No. 8 v. Wisconsin Employment Relations Board, 37 Wis.2d 483, 155 N.W.2d 78 (1967) (school calendar).

201. *See,* e.g., Pennsylvania Labor Relations Board v. Mars Area School District, ____ Pa. Cmwlth ____ , 344 A.2d 384 (1975) (teachers' aides); Board of Education, South Stickney School Dist. III v. Johnson, 21 Ill. App.3d 482, 315 N.E.2d 634 (1974) (teacher assignments); West Hartford Education Association v. DeCourcy, 162 Conn. 566, 295 A.2d 526 (1972) (school calendar); and Seward Education Association v. School District, 188 Neb. 772, 199 N.W.2d 752 (1972) (teacher assignments, class size).

202. *Hawaii Rev. Stat.* § 89–12 (1972); *Ore. Rev. Stat.* § 243.726 (1973); *Pa. Stat. Ann.* tit. 43, § 1101.1003 (1975); and *Vt. Stat. Ann.* tit. 21 § 1730 (1975).

203. *See* Hawaii Public Employees Relations Board v. Hawaii State Teachers Association, 54 Hawaii 531, 511 P.2d 1080 (1973); Bristol Township Education Association v. School District of Bristol Township, 14 Pa. Cmwlth 463, 311 A.2d 767 (1974); and Philadelphia Federation of Teachers v. Ross, 8 Pa. Cmwlth 204, 301 A.2d 405 (1973).

204. 96 S. Ct. 2465 (1976).

205. 96 S. Ct. at 2474, n. 17. The Court also suggested that a law based on § 5 of the Fourteenth Amendment might be upheld as constitutional. A case recently decided by a federal district court in Iowa provides an indication of the type of law that would withstand a challenge to its constitutionality when grounded in § 5 of the Fourteenth Amendment. There, the Equal Pay provisions of the Fair Labor Standards Act, 29 U.S.C. § 206(d) (1963), were upheld on the ground that even though these provisions—like the minimum wage/maximum hour provisions—were based on Congress' Commerce Clause Power, the intent of the Equal Pay Act was to bar discrimination on the basis of sex, and "[d]iscrimination in pay on the basis of sex is not an attribute of sovereignty within the contemplation of the Tenth Amendment. . . ." Usery v. Bettendorf Community School District, 45 *U.S.L.W.* 2187, 2188 (S.D. Iowa, September 1, 1976). *See also* Usery v. Salt Lake City Board of Education, 45 *U.S.L.W.* 2155 (D. Utah, August 31, 1976) (alternate ground for upholding Age Discrimination in Employment Act as applied to state employees is § 5 of the Fourteenth Amendment). *Cf.* Oklahoma v. United States Civil Service Commission, 330 U.S. 127 (1947).

Chapter Four

The Federal Influence on the Production and Employment of Teachers

Stephen J. Carroll

In the twenty years following the end of World War II, the United States experienced a great upsurge in the demand for teachers. A combination of demographic, social, political, and institutional forces accelerated this demand. The most obvious factor was the postwar baby boom, which inundated the elementary schools and later on the secondary schools and colleges. The launching of Sputnik drew national attention to the quality of American education, the numbers of people educated, and the numbers of teachers we were producing. Federal and state governments intervened to encourage more education among young people at all age levels, to enlarge educational opportunities for the disadvantaged, and to reduce the dropout rate.

These forces worked so effectively that a surplus of teachers emerged in the late 1960s. Although all markets are imperfect, the operations of a relatively free market can ordinarily be expected to rectify imbalances between supply and demand. Partly because of institutional constraints, however—notably, a rigid salary structure, strict policies or hiring and promotion, and reverance for the teacher-student ratio—the labor market for teachers is sluggishly responsive at best to the laws of supply and demand. Furthermore, in spite of the teacher surplus and the baby bust that began around 1966 and is now leaving empty classrooms and idle teachers in its wake, the colleges continued to produce large numbers of new teachers. The surplus of the late 1960s surged onward to become a superabundance in the 1970s. Many of the newer teachers are perforce unemployed today or have gone into occupations unrelated to teaching.

To end this "waste" of good teachers, some observers of the educational scene believe that government intervention is again needed. For several reasons, the following analysis of the market for teachers concludes that such a recourse would be unwise and could be harmful. There are clear indications that, if the market is left to itself, its internal processes will cause the surplus to peak in the near future, then gradually decline and end sometime in the mid-1980s, to be followed by a teacher shortage soon thereafter. Because there is always a lag, sometimes a prolonged one, between the adoption of a government policy on education and its ultimate effects, those effects may materialize long after the need for the policy has passed, and it may bring undesirable consequences. Belated attempts to reduce the teacher surplus in the late 1970s and early 1980s may end up by worsening the teacher shortage of the later 1980s.

The current teacher surplus is a serious problem, of course, but government actions to adjust supply and demand would probably amount to mere tinkering with symptoms of the fundamental problem. It would be far more productive for both government and the educational system to turn their attention to the institutional factors that impede the market adjustment process. The analysis presented here is offered as a starting point for that endeavor.

We begin with a brief summary of the demographic and educational policy context within which the market functions. We then discuss the institutional factors that explain the market's resistance to the laws of supply and demand. We briefly consider what these factors portend for the likely future performance of the market. We conclude with a discussion of the major alternatives available to the policymaker who is concerned with the market's future performance and the possible effects of policy choices.

THE CONTEXT OF THE MARKET

The labor market for elementary and secondary teachers operates in a context fashioned by demographic trends and patterns and by education policies. The central feature of the demographic context is the roller coaster curve of the birth rate over the past half century. Birth rates declined sharply at the onset of the Great Depression and stayed low throughout the 1930s and the war years. Annual numbers of births over this fifteen-year period were approximately 2.5 million. A baby boom followed hard on the heels of World War II. Births increased to annual levels of 3.6 to 4.3 million between 1947 and 1966. Thereafter, fertility measures began to decline sharply, signaling the onset of a baby bust. By the early 1970s, births numbered 3.1 to 3.2 million annually. This absolute decline was especially surprising in view of the rapidly increasing number of potential mothers in the population—members of the baby boom cohorts who were well into the years of childbearing by the late 1960s. For example, although there were close to 900,000 more women of chiildbearing age in 1972 than in 1971, there were 300,000 fewer births.

Peristalsis—the spasmodic process by which a python swallows a pig—is an apt metaphor for how the United States has been absorbing the sequence of baby bust/boom/bust. The salient feature of the population's age distribution is the baby boom bulge (persons aged ten to twenty-eight in 1975) moving through successive age boundaries. The leading edge of this bulge (persons now in their late twenties) began to enter elementary schools in the early 1950s, moved on to the secondary schools in the early 1960s, and then to colleges and universities in the mid-1960s. Recently plummeting birth rates have left a relative dearth of children under about ten years of age. For every 100 children under five years old in 1965, there were only 78 in 1975. This shrinkage began to affect elementary schools in the late 1960s and the secondary schools in the mid-1970s. Beginning in the early 1980s, the numbers of persons in the traditional college-age range (eighteen to twenty-one) will diminish and continue to shrink through the mid-1990s.

The 1950s and 1960s also saw a proliferation of educational policies aimed at increasing the enrollment rates of persons among the secondary and post-secondary school ages. A variety of programs aimed at reducing dropout rates among secondary school students was introduced in the 1950s and early 1960s. By the mid-1960s, attention turned to the enrollment rates of students in the college-age ranges. Federal and state governments profoundly affected the possibilities (and aspirations) for higher education by rapidly expanding student financial aid and subsidized public higher education. At the same time, efforts to increase enrollment rates among kindergarten-age children were expanded.

The confluence of rapid growth in both the numbers and enrollment rates of school-age children jammed elementary schools in the 1950s and then secondary schools in the early 1960s. Although substantial numbers of children entered private schools, the large majority had to be accommodated in the public schools (see Table 4-1).

Improving enrollment rates was not the only educational policy objective of the 1950s and 1960s. In the years following the Korean War, there was widespread pressure for improving the quality of education, further intensified by the Soviet Union's launching of Sputnik. A few years later, the War on Poverty formalized the drive for equality of educational opportunity as a national objective. To most people, that meant improving the quality of the educational services provided to the poor and the disadvantaged.

The nation wanted better schools and was willing to pay the price. State and local support of the public schools doubled between 1945 and 1955, doubled again in the next decade, and doubled again by 1970.[1] Federal support grew from less than 1 billion dollars in 1964 to about 4 billion dollars in 1970. Part of this growth was eaten up by inflation, and part reflected the need to increase spending proportional to increases in enrollments. Nonetheless, there was substantial growth in the real financial resources made available for each student (see Table 4-2).

Educators (and most other people as well) have traditionally viewed class size as the primary indicator of educational quality. Consequently, the size

Table 4-1. Enrollment by Level: Alternate Years, 1950–1974

Year	Elementary[a]			Secondary		
	Total	Public	Private	Total	Public	Private
1950	22.0	19.4	2.6	6.4	5.7	0.7
1952	23.6	20.7	2.9	6.6	5.9	0.7
1954	25.8	22.5	3.3	7.0	6.3	0.7
1956	27.9	24.3	3.6	7.7	6.9	0.8
1958	29.6	25.7	3.9	7.9	7.9	0.9
1960	31.9	27.6	4.3	9.5	8.5	1.0
1962	33.2	28.6	4.3	10.7	9.6	1.1
1964	34.1	29.3	4.8	12.2	10.9	1.3
1966	35.3	30.6	4.8	12.9	11.6	1.3
1968	36.9	32.3	4.6	13.9	12.5	1.4
1970	36.7	32.6	4.1	14.4	13.0	1.4
1972	35.5	31.8	3.7	15.1	13.9	1.2
1974	34.2	30.7	3.5	15.5	14.3	1.2

Source: Bureau of the Census, *Historical Statistics of the United States; Colonial Times to 1970* (Washington, D.C.: Government Printing Office, 1975), p. 368. Bureau of the Census, *Statistical Abstract 1975* (Washington, D.C.: Government Printing Office, 1975), p. 114.

[a]Includes kindergarten.

Table 4-2. Public Elementary and Secondary School Expenditures: Alternate Years, 1950–1974

	Current Expenditures			
	Total (in billions)		Per Pupil ADA	
Year	Current Dollars	Constant (1970) Dollars	Current Dollars	Constant (1970) Dollars
1950	4.7	7.5	209	333
1952	5.7	8.2	244	351
1954	6.8	9.5	265	372
1956	8.3	11.7	294	413
1958	10.3	13.6	341	451
1960	12.3	15.8	375	482
1962	14.7	18.5	419	526
1964	17.2	21.1	460	563
1966	21.1	25.0	537	636
1968	26.9	29.9	658	731
1970	34.2	34.2	816	816
1972	41.8	38.4	990	909
1974	48.1	39.0	1147	929

Source: Bureau of the Census, *Historical Statistics of the United States; Colonial Times to 1970* (Washington, D.C.: Government Printing Office, 1975), p. 89.

of the teacher force had to at least keep pace with enrollments, and the demand for greater quality gave impetus to a drive for reductions in pupil-teacher ratios. Schools wanted and could afford more and more teachers. But the booming demand was more than the nation's teacher training institutions could handle. Their enrollments were modest, the product of the relatively small cohorts of the depression and World War II years and the relatively low postsecondary enrollment rates of the 1950s. Postsecondary enrollments grew slowly throughout the 1950s, and the production of new college graduates lagged even further behind.

At the same time, the demand for college graduates in all fields was skyrocketing. The 1950s and early 1960s saw rapid growth in the professions and in such industries as finance, insurance, chemicals, petroleum, electronics, and aircraft, whose work forces had traditionally absorbed a disproportionately large share of college graduates. The public sector's demand for college-educated workers expanded with equal vigor.[2] Moreover, the expansion of the higher educational system, which began in the late 1950s, demanded more college faculty, thereby stimulating expansion of postgraduate education. During most of the 1960s, so many college graduates entered postgraduate schools that the proportion of college graduates among all new labor-force entrants actually declined. Attractive job opportunities beckoned college graduates in all sectors of the economy; education was hard pressed to compete.

Small cohorts of college-age persons, low rates of postsecondary enrollment, and intense competition for college graduates combined to keep the rate of new teacher production well below the demand. In the 1950s and early 1960s, the nation's stock of trained teachers was growing fast enough to keep up with the growth in enrollments, but the public schools' attempts to reduce class sizes were largely frustrated by the lack of teachers. Despite an increase of 27 percent in the real resources available per pupil between 1956 and 1964, the schools could accomplish only a decrease of 6 percent in the pupil-teacher ratio at the elementary level and had to accept a slight increase in the ratio at the secondary level. Even so, they had to fill many teaching positions with persons lacking full certification.

By the mid-1960s, the large baby-boom cohorts were reaching college age, and state and federal programs aimed at spurring postsecondary enrollment rates were well under way. Enrollments in colleges and universities soared. By the late 1960s, colleges and universities were annually producing two or three times the number of new teachers they had been turning out in the 1950s. But the first waves of the baby boom had passed through the elementary and secondary schools by then. Although large numbers of children were entering school for the first time each year, nearly as many were completing secondary school. Enrollment growth rates began to slack off, and schools were finally able to recruit enough teachers to bring down class sizes.

After a brief period of catching up, the labor market for teachers came into balance toward the end of the 1960s. But the forces that ended the teacher shortage continued to operate. By the early 1970s, elementary and secondary enrollments leveled off though not the production of teachers, and the nation found itself with a full-blown teacher surplus.

THE LABOR MARKET FOR TEACHERS

We have noted how demographic factors influence the market for teachers; now let us consider why.

The Market Process

The mechanism by which human resources are allocated among productive activities is the occupational labor market, which, like any market, is an abstraction of bargaining interactions between buyers (employers) and sellers (potential employees). In theory, an unfettered market automatically balances the supply of an demand for any commodity, including labor, through continuous price adjustments. If an item becomes scarce—that is, if the supply falls short of demand, buyers bid against each other for the available items and prices go up. New suppliers are encouraged to enter the market. Suppliers have an incentive to produce more and buyers to buy less until the shortage "clears." The reverse occurs when supply exceeds demand. Thus, the participants in a market automatically strive toward that price at which the quantities demanded and supplied are in equilibrium—that is, where sellers are provided exactly the amount that buyers want to acquire.

In reality, markets do not operate that precisely, but unfettered markets tend to function according to these principles, and imbalances—shortages and surpluses—tend to be averted or, at worst, restricted in magnitude and duration.

Theoretically, then, the early waves of the baby boom should have triggered a series of wage adjustments, precluding the teacher shortages that plagued the educational system in the 1950s and early 1960s. Teachers' salaries should have grown rapidly relative to salaries in other occupations, inducing more and more people to seek teaching positions and simultaneously pressuring schools to hold down the numbers of newly hired teachers. Similarly, the falloff in the rate of enrollment growth that followed the baby bust should have set off declines in teachers' salaries, leading would-be teachers to seek employment in other occupations and making it easier for schools to afford more teachers.

Teachers' salaries did grow more rapidly than salaries in other occupations from the mid-1950s through the early 1960s. The average teacher's salary in 1964 was 32 percent larger than in 1956. By comparison, between 1956 and 1964 the average income of males twenty-five years old and over, with four or more years of college, grew 23 percent, and the average earnings of full-time workers (a measure of economywide wage trends) increased 27 percent. However, the teacher shortage persisted in spite of the higher salaries, and higher salaries have persisted since then in spite of the teacher surplus. Teachers' salaries grew by 44 percent over the 1968–1974 period, while the earnings of male college graduates and of wage and salary workers in general grew by 33 percent and 46 percent, respectively.[a]

The explanation for the ostensible immunity to the laws of supply and demand in the market for teachers lies in several interrelated institutional factors. Chief among these are an inability to develop rational measures of output, inflexibility in determining measures of input, an inflexible compensation system, and, underlying these factors, the fact that education is almost exclusively a public sector enterprise. The participation patterns in the labor force of women, who account for the large majority of elementary and secondary teachers, also inhibit the market adjustment process.

Measures of Output

For centuries, wise minds and dull have failed to uncover measurable, reproducible relationships between what is brought to the education process (inputs) and what emerges from it (outputs). But because the "value" of education is largely unquestioned, administrators proceed with a missionary's reverence for revealed truth. Lacking objective criteria for determining the quality of its output, education has turned to a preoccupation with inputs. In this process, it relies on criteria molded in historical practice, the most hoary of which is the number of teachers needed for a given number of students.

In 1960 the largest and oldest teachers' association in the United States, the National Education Association (NEA), opined that

> . . .class size must be adjusted to the capacities of the very best teachers obtainable in large numbers. And the vast weight of experience places this need in the range of one teacher for 25 elementary school children. . . ."[3]

That estimate was scarcely an innovation; it represented no improvement on the opinion of the Hebrew sage Rava, expressed 1600 years earlier:

> The number of pupils to be assigned to each teacher is twenty-five. If there are fifty, we appoint two teachers. If there are forty, we appoint an assistant, at the expense of the town.[4]

(Since 1971, the NEA has used twenty-four as its ideal elementary class size,[5] in apparent willingness to defy the vast weight of experience by a reduction of one.)

---

[a]Teachers' salaries have declined in real terms since 1970, but so have the wages and salaries of workers in general and college graduates in particular.

One important effect of the sanctity of the pupil-teacher ratio as a criterion of quality has been to make the demand for teachers relatively inelastic. In periods of teacher shortage, for example, school districts are extremely reluctant to increase class sizes; to preserve their desired ratio they will go so far as to hire teachers who are unqualified or underqualified according to their own standards.

Measures of Input

The criteria for determining who *is* qualified to teach are as arbitrary and inflexible as the teacher-pupil ratio. Again, because the characteristics that make a competent teacher are not measurable, the necessary qualifications have been arrived at through the professional judgment of educators, and they derive primarily from the teacher's own education. Some years ago certification required completion of a two-year teacher preparation course; today it requires four years, and some state are moving to a five-year certificate. This increase is purported to increase teachers' "professionalism"; it is not based on any demonstrated improvement in educational results. Once in the profession, teachers can enhance their qualifications by acquiring further educational credits regardless of their relevance to the teacher's assignment. Experience on the job also counts, but in terms of years of service, not in terms of demonstrated competence.

Certification requirements impede market adjustments in two ways. First, as with other professions, entry into teaching requires a long training program conducted in institutions that are separate from, and independent of, the ultimate employer. In occupations where job training is relatively brief and under the control of employers, it is possible to achieve a reasonably fast response to changes in the demand for labor. But in teaching, as in law or medicine, shifts in supply lag behind shifts in demand not only by the time period required for training but also by delays arising from the communication gap between training and using institutions. Schools of education, for example, do not base their enrollment goals on projections of school district demand, nor do school districts adjust their demand for teachers to the number of students enrolled in schools of education.

Second, and perhaps more important, is the fact that, as the profession is defined, only certified teachers can be hired on a permanent basis. Since the art of "good" teaching cannot be (or has not been convincingly) anatomized, it is considered indivisible and the possession of certified teachers alone. Consequently, whereas other employers may respond to market conditions by varying the mix of inputs or restructuring their processes to use fewer people with expensive skills, the schools are loath to hire anyone but a certified teacher for every position whatever the cost.

Inflexible Wages

The compensation system used almost universally in teaching is the uniform salary schedule, under which within a given district all teachers with the same formal qualifications are paid the same salary rate regardless of the type of skills they have (elementary teaching, secondary biology teaching, etc.) or their relative abilities. Salary systems in professions other than teaching recognize differences between individuals in both the nature of their skills and their ability to practice those skills effectively. Salary differences among the teachers with a district, however, depend solely on differences in educational credits and years of experience.

The uniform salary schedule arises from the same traditions as pupil-teacher ratios and teacher certification requirements; it exacerbates the rigidities imposed by them and imposes further rigidities of its own. It severely limits a school district's ability to alter its salary levels in response to market conditions. Districts can attempt to attract qualified teachers who have entered other occupations by offering them higher salaries only if the whole schedule is revised upward, that is, only if all other teachers receive commensurate raises. The cost of such an adjustment is prohibitive.[b] Conversely, districts are barred by contractual agreements from lowering salaries, and since they must pay everyone according to the same schedule, they cannot offer lower salaries to prospective employees who in times of surplus would be happy to accept them.

In recent years, militant action by teachers' unions to preserve the salary gains won during the past decades of teacher shortage have further restricted market processes. Normally, in a period of manpower surplus, one would expect salaries to level off or even fall; however, although teacher salaries did not keep pace with inflation in the mid-1970s, they kept pace with salaries in most other occupations *despite* the growing teacher surplus.

A Public Sector Enterprise

These impediments to market processes escape serious challenge because education is a public sector activity; it is not marketed to customers at a price. In the private sector, the competition for customers imposes performance constraints, a continuing search for determinants of quality, and some flexibility in setting wages and prices. This is true throughout business and industry and even in professions whose "product" is as difficult to measure as education's. Doctors and lawyers, for example, must satisfy their clients or lose them. The public schools, in contrast, have virtually no competition and therefore scant incentive to rationalize their practices. Most of their customers cannot afford to take their business elsewhere and thus penalize an inferior "product."

---

[b]Suppose, for example, that a district employing 1,000 teachers is unable to fill ten more positions at its starting salary of, say, $8,000 per year. It might be able to obtain nine more teachers if it could offer them $9,000 and might be willing to made do with them, leaving one position vacant. But to increase the starting salary by $1,000, the district would have to raise the entire salary schedule by that amount (or more, if it had to maintain the relative salaries of various levels on the schedule). The cost of those nine teachers would be $1,081,000, or about $120,000 apiece. The district is more likely to accept the shortage of ten teachers. A district unable to meet its needs for teachers having certain skills is in a similar position even if teachers lacking those skills are readily available.

Even the customers who can afford private schools must continue to pay school taxes, and thus they cannot penalize the public schools by denying them "income."[c]

Similarly, the publicly supported institutions that train teachers have little incentive to anticipate the demand for their product; their budgets are based on the amount of "raw material" they have on hand, not on their "sales." Most businessmen confronted with a rapid buildup of unsold inventory would be quick to lay off workers, shut down facilities, and embark on a market survey. But the responsibility for anticipating changes in the demand for teachers does not lie with teacher-training institutions, nor indeed with any part of the education system.

The Reserve Pool of Teachers

Women account for about two-thirds of all elementary and secondary school teachers, and their labor force participation patterns strongly influence the labor market. A predominant characteristic of the teaching profession, as well as of other occupations that employ a high proportion of women, is the existence of a "reserve pool" of qualified teachers who have left (or never entered) the profession to raise families. These reserve teachers often return to the market after their own children have entered school. At any time, then, there is a substantial number of trained teachers who are not participating in the labor force but who may at some future date attempt to reenter the teaching profession.

The size of the reserve pool and, consequently, its contribution to the supply of teachers is unknown. The NEA estimates that in 1960 the reserve pool included over 300,000 teachers, of whom about 18.3 percent (about 55,000 persons) sought teaching positions.[6] Today's reserve pool, swelled by the large cohorts of college graduates trained to teach during the 1960s and early 1970s, is certainly much larger. One study suggests that there were over 1.4 million reserve teachers in 1970.[7] If 18.3 percent of them attempted to enter classrooms in 1970, something like a quarter of a million reserve teachers would have sought teaching positions that year. By comparison, the total number of new college graduates qualified to teach that year was about 300,000, of whom roughly a quarter are likely to have voluntarily pursued some occupation (including homemaking) other than teaching.[d] Thus, in 1970 reserve teachers may have made up half of the total supply of teachers.

---

[c]Educational voucher systems, if introduced on a large scale, may remedy this problem. Few such systems have been implemented, however, and the schools remain isolated from the "discipline of the market."

[d]The NEA reports that in the 1950s and the early through mid-1960s, roughly 70 to 75 percent of the new graduates qualified to teach entered teaching positions each year. As teaching jobs were readily available throughout that period, we can assume that roughly a quarter of new graduates qualified to teach opted out of education, at least temporarily. See the NEA's annual reports, *Teacher Supply and Demand in the Public Schools*, Washington, D.C.

Moreover, it is likely that the proportion of reserve teachers actively participating in the teacher labor market today is larger than was the corresponding proportion in 1960. Then few teachers involuntarily entered the reserve pool; teaching positions were generally available, and the teachers in the reserve pool were there because they chose to enter other occupations. Today the reserve pool includes large numbers of teachers who want to teach but cannot because not enough teaching positions are open. The unemployed or underemployed teacher is much more likely to seek a teaching position than is the teacher who opted for a different occupation. We can speculate that the reserve supply accounts for as much as 20 to 30 percent of a pool comprising 1.5 to 2 million persons.

A teacher reentering the labor force from the reserve pool is likely to have been out of the labor force for several years and to have had at most only a few years of work experience, and that in teaching, before withdrawal. For most reserve teachers, then, the alternative to teaching is to accept relatively low-paid jobs in the secretarial, clerical, and sales occupations. The possible need to reassume full-time responsibilities in the home during the summer months when their own children are out of school must also be considered. Thus, the reentry patterns of many reserve teachers do not reflect a response to conditions in the labor market for teachers. Instead, exogenous factors (e.g., past patterns of family formation) largely determine the numbers of reserve teachers who will attempt to enter teaching positions in any given year.

There are, to be sure, significant numbers of trained teachers engaged in other labor market activities; they, too, are members of the reserve pool.[e] For these people, the decision to seek a teaching position represents a choice between one form of labor market activity and another—a choice presumably influenced by conditions in the labor market for teachers. But the use of uniform salary schedules limits the responsiveness of this component of the reserve pool. Because teachers are paid according to their education and teaching experience, the experience and skills they gain in other labor market activities do not count. Teachers who have entered alternative occupations that offer advancement with experience would begin at the bottom of a district's salary schedule were they to accept a teaching position. Only teachers who find themselves in jobs offering little chance for advancement (and such jobs tend to be low paying as well) are likely to consider teaching an attractive alternative.

In sum, the reserve supply of teachers is highly inelastic. For the most part, it consists of teachers returning to the labor market after discharging family responsibilities and teachers who had been forced into less attractive occupations by the teacher surplus. People in either situation are likely to consider a teaching position far superior to their alternatives. The numbers of such persons seeking teaching positions at any time is thus largely insensitive to current conditions in

---

[e]In view of past patterns of labor force participation, it would appear that this component of the reserve pool is disproportionately male.

the labor market for teachers; the numbers are determined instead by the choices made by students entering colleges over the preceding twenty or thirty years (which affect the size of the pool), past patterns of family formation (which affect teachers' current family responsibilities), and the surplus (which built up a backlog of teachers awaiting an opportunity to enter a teaching position).

The Effect of Rigidities in the Market

That the market for teachers has attained equilibrium in perhaps two years out of the last thirty reflects collisions between sharp demographic changes and the iconic traditions of the education industry. Each year from the early 1950s until the mid-1960s tidal waves of baby boom children were inundating the schools while mere rivulets of depression babies were trickling out of teacher preparation programs—and large proportions of those rivulets were withdrawing from the labor force to form their own families. The number of pupils to be taught far outran the number of teachers being produced. In dealing with this unprecedented situation, the schools invoked their traditional values and in many ways worsened matters.

First, the hallowed pupil-teacher ratio drove them to translate enrollment growth into demand for more teachers. In turn, the demand drove the salary schedule upward.

Second, the equation between certification and competence meant that even when this ever-increasing demand for staff was partly met by employing underqualified people, the shortage of *qualified* teachers was not eased.

Third, had it not been for the strictures of the uniform salary schedule, salaries could have risen until the shortage disappeared. This is not to say that every school district would have satisfied every conceivable need for a teacher and everyone who was eligible to teach would have been employed. Reaching equilibrium means simply and specifically that all positions are filled that can be filled *at that salary offered* and all teachers who would accept teaching jobs *at that salary* are employed. Even at the height of the shortage, there were fair numbers of qualified teachers who could have been lured from other pursuits if the schools had been able to pay their price without simultaneously increasing the salaries of the entire teacher force.

The current surplus in the market for teachers is, ironically, a product of the same baby boom that created the shortage. A generation later, the baby boom children are emerging from college in huge numbers, many of them trained as teachers, only to find declining school enrollments because of the baby bust of the late 1960s. But the use of uniform salary schedules precludes sufficient declines in salaries to bring about their employment. The result is that many more qualified teachers are seeking jobs in teaching than there are jobs for them.

In summary, shortages and surpluses of teachers are not symptoms of market malfunction; they are artifacts of imposing the educational systems' values on the marketplace. If teachers' salaries could be freely adjusted, market forces would produce equilibrium between supply and demand. As matters stand, fixed salaries generate disequilibrium between supply and demand, and the penalty is teacher shortages or surpluses. Unless education is willing to alter its values, that penalty will be levied alternately on society in the form of undermanned classrooms or on teachers in the form of gross unemployment.

THE DYNAMICS OF THE MARKET AND PROSPECT FOR THE FUTURE

Despite market rigidites, an adjustment process of sorts is operating. In the absence of a freely adjusting salary structure, unemployment and underemployment among teachers is growing, and enrollment in schools of education is dwindling in response. Over the 1964-1973 period, which saw a transition from general shortage to general surplus, the rate at which college graduates were preparing to teach dropped 25 percent (see Table 4-3).

A data base developed by the American Council on Education (ACE) offers further insight into what is likely to happen to teacher production rates in the future. In an annual national survey, the ACE obtains data on the career plans and intentions of entering college freshmen. Table 4-4 summarizes

Table 4-3. Teacher Production Rates: 1966-1973

Year	Number of Bachelor's Degrees Granted (in thousands)	Number of Bachelor's Degre Recipients Qualified to Teach (in thousands)	Teacher Production Rate (percent)
1960	368	130	35.3
1961	369	129	35.0
1962	388	142	36.6
1963	416	154	37.0
1964	466	174	37.4
1965	501	190	38.0
1966	520	171	33.0
1967	558	183	32.9
1968	632	203	32.1
1969	728	230	31.5
1970	792	244	30.7
1971	840	266	31.6
1972	887	264	29.8
1973	922	255[a]	27.6[a]

Source: Department of Health, Education, and Welfare, *The Condition of Education 1976* (Washington, D.C.: Government Printing Office, 1976), p. 197. National Educational Association, *Teacher Supply and Demand in the Public Schools* (Washington, D.C.: Annual Report).

[a]Estimated.

Table 4-4. Estimated Percentages of Entering Freshmen Intending to Pursue a Teaching Career: 1966-1975

Year	*Proportion Intending to Pursue a Teaching Career*		
	Male	*Female*	*Total*
1966	11.3	34.1	21.7
1967	11.2	36.4	22.4
1968	12.7	37.5	23.5
1969	10.9	36.5	22.1
1970	9.6	31.0	19.3
1971	7.5	24.8	15.4
1972	5.7	19.5	12.1
1973	4.1	14.1	8.8
1974	3.8	11.9	7.7
1975	3.2	10.3	6.5

Source: American Council on Education, *The American Freshman: National Norms* (Washington, D.C.: Annual Report).

some of the results. The trends in the data are obvious. Between 1968 and 1975, the proportion of entering college freshmen who intended to enter elementary and secondary teaching dropped by two-thirds.

It seems reasonable to expect this trend to continue as long as the surplus persists. If it does, the annual supply of new teachers, which is already dropping, must eventually fall below the annual demand. At that point, schools will have to begin to tap the reserve pool, thus reducing its size. The teacher surplus will then begin to evaporate, but it will take some years for it to vanish entirely. In short, the market is operating to restore balance between supply and demand.

The end of the surplus is not at all the end of the story, however. The same lagging forces that end the surplus will automatically engender a subsequent teacher shortage. Teacher production in any given year depends on the career choices made by students who entered college four or more years earlier. The size of the reserve pool, given the demand for teachers, depends upon the career choices made by college entrants throughout the previous two or three decades. Its size will change from one year to the next only to the extent that current teacher production differs from the sum of the current change in the demand for teachers and teacher production ten, twenty, and thirty years ago. Assuming a roughly constant demand for teachers, the surplus will continue as long as the supply of eligible new graduates plus the reserve supply exceeds the net demand. Even if teacher production declines sharply, the surplus will persist until the reserve pool is substantially reduced. That will occur only after a series of years in which the number of teachers proudced falls substantially below the numbers produced decades earlier.

The important point is that this inertia works in the opposite direction as well. Suppose that the surplus ends in, say, 1985. The situation in that year will be approximate equality between net demand and the sum of reserve supply and new supply. But that balance will have been achieved through declines in both components of supply, and those declines will continue for a while at least. The students who entered college in the preceding two or three years will have made curriculum choices during a period of teacher surplus, and presumably, only a small proportion of them will have elected teacher training. The annual numbers of new teachers will continue to decline; the reserve pool will contract yet further; and the supply of teachers will grow yet smaller. After three or four years, the college students who entered after the end of the surplus will begin to graduate, teacher production will begin to grow, and annual supplies of new teachers will begin to grow. But the reserve pool and, consequently, the supply of reserve teachers will continue to contract until new teacher production climbs to levels higher than they were decades earlier. Since the surplus is not likely to end until teacher production has fallen well below the earlier levels, this climb will require some time. In sum, it appears that if and when the surplus ends, lacking some prior policy intervention, the inertia in the system will lead to the almost immediate onset of a substantial and prolonged teacher shortage.

Despite uncertainty about the precise future dimensions of the supply of teachers, federal and state policies toward elementary and secondary education, and other factors that influence the market, the foreseeable interplay of ongoing demographic trends with adaptive behavior on the supply side of the market is likely to engender continuing inbalances in the market. We can expect the current teacher surplus to continue, though diminishing in severity, through the 1970s. We can expect it to end in the mid-1980s. We can also expect a teacher shortage to emerge almost immediately thereafter.

Depending on the element of timing, several other demographic forces may deepen or prolong the shortage. First, by the mid-1980s, the initial large cohorts of teachers produced in the mid-1950s will be reaching advanced ages[f] increasing numbers of active teachers will retire, and persons not actively engaged in teaching are likely to begin withdrawing from the reserve pool. Second, school enrollment, which were previously level, will start to rise 2 to 3 percent annually in 1985, assuming a continuation of current (Census Series E) fertility levels. This growth will accelerate substantially if the fertility rate increases. Third, the number of persons turning twenty-two years old (roughly the age at which newly qualified teachers emerge from college) will begin to decline about 4 percent annually starting in 1986. There will be a pause in the decline between 1989 and 1992, followed by a more precipitous decline of about 16 percent in the following three years (echoing the post-1970 decline in births).

---

[f]For example, 22 percent of all teachers active in 1971 were fifty years old or older and are therefore certain to retire by the mid-1980s. An additional 18 percent were forty through forty-nine, the majority of whom are likely to retire by the end of the 1980s.

POLICY IMPLICATIONS

Debate on the question of whether and how policy should respond to the teacher surplus has tended to focus on the "waste" of trained teachers unable to obtain teaching positions and on the "waste" of the resources used to train them. The several policy proposals that have been put forward are directed to the "problem" of reducing the current teacher surplus; they would attempt to reduce the supply of teachers, increase the demand, or both. It has been suggested that schools of education should tighten up their admissions criteria or otherwise limit their enrollments, states and the federal government should eliminate programs that encourage students to enter teaching and increase their support of education so that more teachers can be hired, certification authorities should impose more stringent credentialling requirements, teacher retirement systems should develop incentives for early retirement, and so forth.

Our analysis suggests that the policy debate has been shortsighted and somewhat misdirected. It has largely ignored the underlying market processes that caused the surplus and has paid little attention to the institutional structure of the teacher labor market and the ways in which it affects the market process. No diagnostician has inquired whether the teacher surplus is the malady or merely a symptom of the malady.

Education is a vast, decentralized system with no single locus for decisionmaking. Fifty state education agencies and a host of accreditation and certification bodies decide who may train teachers and what that training shall comprise. The 1,200 colleges and universities with approved programs decide how many and which students will be trained. The number of applicants for training programs depends on the decisions of the nearly two million students entering higher education each year. The number of applicants for teaching positions depends on the decisions of the perhaps two million reserve teachers and the 300,000 new teachers who graduate each year. Hiring decisions rest with 16,000 independent school districts throughout the country. The amount of money available to the system, either directly through local taxes or indirectly through federal and state subsidies, depends on how citizens and their government officials view society's public and private needs.

The interests of the many decisionmakers in this system are diverse and often conflicting. There are no mechanisms, aside from the market, for reconciling the decisions emanating from the various segments of the system. Even if decisionmakers were willing to subordinate their own or their institutions' interests to achieve a larger goal, there are no means whereby they can coordinate their actions. Responses to the surplus thus far are indicative of these problems. Some schools of education began to limit their enrollments soon after the surplus appeared; however, most did not, and the decline in the numbers of students choosing teacher education programs has led some schools to actively encourage students to enter such programs. Some states have eliminated incentives to students who enter teacher preparation programs; others have not, and so on. All in all, except for the sharp drops in the numbers of students opting for teacher preparation, responses to the surplus have been sporadic, piecemeal, fragmented, and, from the perspective of the market as a whole, ineffectual. In the absence of means for the coordination and control of the system, it is difficult to see how the situation could be improved.

Moreover, the inertia in the teacher labor market implies that, except for truly massive interventions, there is likely to be a substantial lage between the implementation of a policy and the time when it begins to have any significant effect on the market. For example, teachers entering the market from the reserve pool might account for as much as half the current supply of teachers. Limitations on enrollments will have only small effects on the supply of teachers until the reserve pool is drained. Similarly, if reserve teachers' certifications are protected by grandfather clauses, the introduction of more stringent credentialling requirements will have only a small effect on the supply of teachers in the near term.

There is a real possibility, then, that policies aimed at reducing the supply of teachers or increasing the demand will begin to take effect only after the need for them is past. If our analysis of the dynamics of the teacher labor market is correct, processes are already at work that will bring an end to the surplus, probably within the next decade. We also foresee that a teacher shortage will follow hard on the heels of the end of the surplus. It can be as difficult and time-consuming to reverse a policy as it was to implement it in the first place. We may well find ourselves effectively restricting the supply of teachers or increasing the demand just when we need programs that have the opposite effect.

The alternative is to develop greater flexibility in the teacher labor market. If that can be accomplished, the automatic processes of the marketplace can assume a larger role in reconciling the diverse interests that impinge on the teacher manpower situation, thereby reducing or averting imbalances between supply and demand.

For example, teacher-training institutions have little or no incentive to cut back on their enrollments during a surplus. On the contrary, enrollment limitations would probably require them to reduce their budgets, lay off faculty or lose them by attrition, and accept a less important place in the higher educational scheme. They would also face the problem of retaining the capacity to step up teacher production if the need arose (as it may within a decade). But the core of the difficulty is that their primary function is universally held to be the preparation of new teachers for elementary and secondary schools. (Many schools of education offer courses for teachers who wish to upgrade their skills or qualify for a higher salary level, but these courses are usually adjuncts to the main curriculum.) Consequently, they justify their existence by perpetually adding to the supply of teachers regardless of the demand.

Schools of education could break out of that role, however, and assume new functions. For example, they could work with school districts to deivse programs for retraining district teachers, perhaps in innovative teaching methods that have proven their worth in experimental projects. (The movement toward teachers' centers is a step in this direction.) One can even envision schools of education offering training in pedagogical skills for people who have use for them in occupations other than teaching in an elementary or secondary school. Such a strategy would allow a school of education to maintain its capacity during a surplus without adding unduly to the supply of teachers, and by shifting its emphasis, it could increase teacher production during a shortage.

The time may also have come for the educational community to allow greater flexibility in the uniform salary schedule. Suppose, for example, that a district, perhaps in consultation with teachers' representatives, were free to "place" a newly hired teacher at any experience step in its salary schedule. Thereafter, the teacher would move up the schedule in the normal way. This procedure would allow the district to offer a lower salary in hiring a teacher who had previous experience or a higher salary to a potential teacher who lacked teaching experience. The former option would be useful during a surplus; the latter would allow the district to attract reserve teachers with skills that are in short supply without simultaneously raising the salaries of its entire staff. The use of concepts such as merit pay, incentive pay, and "hazardous duty" pay may afford further flexibility.

The notion of awarding degree credits to college students for experience outside formal educational settings is gaining acceptance. It may be possible to extend the same notion to the teacher certification process.

These are but a few of the possibilities; there are many others, including frontal attacks on the institutional barriers to the market adjustment process. A full exploration of those possibilities is beyond the scope of this chapter. Our purpose here is to point out the directions in which policy must move if chronic educational manpower problems are to be alleviated. Above all, policymakers should shun the temptation to apply "quick fixes" to superficial symptoms and strive instead to resolve the underlying problems of adjustment in the teacher labor market.

NOTES

1. Department of Health, Education, and Welfare, *Digest of Educational Statistics 1975* (Washington, D.C.: Government Printing Office, 1976), p. 60.

2. For further details see Richard Freeman, "The Declining Economic Value of Higher Education and the American Social System." Paper presented at a conference, Education in a Changing Society, Aspen Institute for Humanistic Studies, July 1975.

3. National Education Association, *Teacher Supply and Demand in Public School 1971*, NEA Research Memo, Washington, D.C., 1972, p. 25.

4. B.T. Baba Bathra 21 a.

5. National Education Association, *Teacher Supply and Demand in Public Schools 1971,* NEA Research Memo, Washington, D.C. 1972, p. 25.

6. National Educational Association, *Teacher Supply and Demand in Public Schools 1974,* NEA Research Memo, Washington, D.C., May 1975, p. 3.

7. Edward Rattner, Burton Dean, and Arnold Reisman, "Supply and Demand of Teachers and Supply and Demand of Ph.D.s," unpublished paper, Case Western Reserve University, Cleveland, Ohio, June 1971, p. 44.

Chapter Five

A Federal Role in the General
Program of School Finance

Lawrence L. Brown, III
Alan L. Ginsburg

The federal government finances less than 10 percent of elementary and secondary education. Rather than spreading its effort thinly across programs for all children, it derives maximum impact from its funds by directing them to particular categories of educational activities. Interest at the federal level in the expansion of its policies into general education finance is not now high, given current deficits in the federal budget and the Supreme Court's failure in *Rodriguez* to uphold lower court rulings on the unconstitutionality of wealth-related disparities in school district spending levels. The obvious question is why examine the issue of a broadened national involvement in general education finance at all?

It would be incorrect to gauge the likelihood of federal participation in general education policies over the long run by the ebb and flow of political interest at the national level. Passage of a federal general support program was nearly a reality almost a decade ago before it was overtaken by events and the passage of the more reform-oriented Elementary and Secondary Education Act of 1965.[a] Only a few year ago, interest peaked again when the Nixon Administration proposed a multibillion dollar program of general purpose school aid focusing on school property tax relief.[1] The debate over a broader federal role will continue to confront policymakers. This is especially so given the continuing and building state concern with eliminating inequalities in general purpose school revenues. Undoubtedly, in developing federal education programs and policies, officials at the national level will find it increasingly difficult to ignore state school finance reform efforts and will find it necessary to take a closer look at the federal role in the general program of education finance.

---

[a]One of the initial obstacles preventing the effective use of federal compensatory education funds under Title I, ESEA was a misguided belief by some school officials that Title I was actually a general support program.

This discussion considers possible federal roles in the general program of education finance, whereby "general program of education finance" we mean programs that allocate resources that are untied as to specific expenditure purpose. The only current instance of federal involvement in such programs is impact aid assistance, which compensates districts for the presence of children from families who work and reside on federal property. Although important to particular districts, nationally its funds are less than 1 percent of all school revenues.

Given this limited current effort, any movement by the federal sector into general education finance needs to be undertaken with caution and with due regard for the way such actions will affect the operation of the nation's educational system at all levels of government. This chapter attempts to lay the groundwork for future discussions in this area. Subsequent sections examine reasons for extending the federal role to the general program of school finance, explore different kinds of federal strategies in this area, and assess the implications of these strategies for federal policies.

REASONS FOR FEDERAL INVOLVEMENT

Several different kinds of problems are frequently cited as justification for broadening federal involvement in general education finance. In school equalization, federal policies are now directed primarily at special need populations such as the economically disadvantaged or educationally handicapped. This drive to equalize has recently been broadened to include a concern over reducing disparities in educational spending that are related to variations in wealth base across geographic areas. Interest is evidenced at the federal level by a number of congressional bills that propose legislation to reduce disparities in available resources across school districts within states. Other bills propose to reduce these disparities across states. Finally, those who perceive the educational finance system as being plagued by resource inadequacies are also proponents of a general support policy.

Interdistrict Equity. In recent years, the problem of inequality of educational opportunity to children who attend school districts deficient in taxable wealth base has received considerable attention from state courts and legislators. A number of states have implemented major reforms of their finance systems to reduce the association between per pupil expenditures and local fiscal capacity.[2] In many other states, however, unequalized systems have not been restructured, and in many of the reform states it is still not clear that the remodeled systems will achieve "adequate" equalization levels. These uncertainties, coupled with the unpredictable pace of the reform movement in the future, could generate strong pressure for federal government involvement.

Evidence of inequality of educational opportunity across school districts is based specifically on the strong association between a district's educational opportunities and its average fiscal capacity. The first state court cases, beginning with the landmark *Serrano* decision, were based on measures of disparities that reflected the prevailing notions of school district needs.[3] Revenues (or expenditures) per pupil as the measure of educational opportunity were related to property valuation per pupil, the indicator of fiscal capacity. The strong direct association observed between the two within a state was sufficient to demonstrate to the courts the failure of state aid systems to neutralize the advantages of high-wealth districts.

These disparities are illustrated by comparing the patterns of association between revenues and property valuation for school districts within five states (Table 5-1). These states, chosen to reflect different regions of the country and varying degrees of urbanization, are the two urban states of New York and Ohio and the three more agricultural states of Arkansas, Nebraska, and Oklahoma.[b] The relative level of local revenues is strongly associated with the relative wealth of school districts in all five states. For example, the local per pupil revenues of Arkansas districts in the bottom quartile of wealth amount to only 62 percent of the state average. By contrast, districts in the top quartile of wealth generate 145 percent of the statewide average, or nearly two and a half times that of low-wealth districts. Similar patterns are observed in the other four states.[c]

The lower spending levels of low-wealth districts cannot be attributed to a below-average tax effort for education. In four of the five states, these districts are exerting an above-average tax effort, ranging from 111 to 124 percent of the state averages. This is shown in the last column of Table 5-1, where the ratio of local school revenues to the property tax base is employed as an implicit measure of local school tax effort.

State aid in these five states partly reduces the revenue advantages of the high property wealth districts, but in all instances it fails to overcome these local revenue advantages entirely (Table 5-1, columns 2 and 3).[d]

Similarly, federal aid does little to reduce these local property wealth-based advantages. This is partly because the federal share of total revenues is small and partly because federal programs tend to be directed toward

---

[b]These five states are also the states that have not implemented major reforms of their school finance systems since 1970. For purposes of analysis, the 1970 data should, therefore, provide a sufficiently accurate picture of the current school finance picture in these states.

[c]Table 5A-1 in the appendix presents this information for all states. Since it was not necessary to discuss all of the states in order to illustrate the broad policy issues addressed by this study, we have simplified our presentation by limiting our examination to five states. Persons who wish to examine a more detailed set of data may refer to the appendix.

[d]Revenues were selected over expenditures because only revenues could be broken out with our data base into local, state, and federal sources.

Table 5-1. Revenue per Pupil by Local, State and Federal Sources and Local Revenue Effort by District Wealth: For Five States (Relative to State Average)—1970

Districts Classified by Relative Property Wealth by State[b]	Revenue per Pupil[a]					
	Local (1)	State (2)	Local + State (3)	Federal (4)	Local + State + Federal + (5)	Local Revenue Property Value (6)
Arkansas						
Low (25%)	0.62	1.10	0.86	1.15	0.91	0.96
Middle (50%)	0.96	1.02	0.99	1.05	1.00	1.02
High (25%)	1.45	0.87	1.15	0.75	1.09	1.00
Nebraska						
Low (24%)	0.76	1.03	0.82	1.58	0.87	1.24
Middle (50%)	0.99	1.02	1.00	0.88	0.99	1.00
High (25%)	1.25	0.92	1.18	0.65	1.15	0.76
New York						
Low (25%)	0.58	1.28	0.93	0.38	0.91	1.17
Middle (50%)	1.00	0.93	0.97	0.90	0.97	1.00
High (25%)	1.41	0.85	1.13	1.82	1.16	0.83
Ohio						
Low (25%)	0.66	1.29	0.84	0.73	0.83	1.11
Middle (50%)	0.98	0.96	0.97	0.96	0.97	0.97
High (25%)	1.37	0.79	1.21	1.36	1.22	0.95
Oklahoma						
Low (25%)	0.61	1.21	0.90	1.81	0.99	1.18
Middle (50%)	0.74	0.98	0.86	0.80	0.85	0.81
High (25%)	1.92	0.82	1.38	0.58	1.31	1.22

Source: The data base for the analysis is the combined 1970 Census and ELSEGIS file that was structured to provide information representative of the states. The data base has been supplemented by a special survey of school district property valuations that have been equalized to adjust for differences between true market and assessed valuations within a state.

[a]Pupils are measured by average daily attendance. Average pupil revenues are shown normed to the state average.

[b]The district groups are defined as low—those districts of lowest property valuation per pupil within each state containing 25 percent of the children; middle—those districts next lowest in relative property value that contain 50 percent of the children; and high—the remaining districts and 25 percent of the children.

low-income areas rather than areas of low property wealth. Hence, although federal aid is directed heavily to low property wealth districts in those states where low property wealth and low income occur simultaneously, in urban states like New York and Ohio it is directed away from such areas. This is because the primary beneficiaries of federal programs, low-income populations, are concentrated in the cities where property wealth is generally high relative to the state average (Table 5-1, column 4).

In summary, it would appear that local resources dominate the overall pattern of total revenues across districts because state and federal aid in combination is neither large enough nor sufficiently well directed to affect this dominance significantly (Table 5-1, column 5). These results are typical of the evidence that prompted the courts to find that many school finance systems were in violation of their state's guarantees of an equal educational opportunity to all children regardless of their district's wealth base.

Interstate Equity. Inequalities of educational opportunities do not stop at state borders. Individual states differ widely in their spending and revenue levels for education, and these differences are closely related to their fiscal capacity. Only the federal government is in a position to reduce disparities of this kind to acceptable levels.

Disparities across states in nonfederal education revenues per pupil are quite large (Table 5-2, column 2).[e] The range is from a high of 172 percent of the national average in Alaska to a low of 60 percent of the national average in Mississippi—a disparity ratio of nearly three to one. This range in nonfederal revenues across states is larger than the corresponding disparity ratios across districts in about half the states.[4] Furthermore, revenue comparisons per pupil across states show a strong positive association with income per pupil, one useful interstate measure of fiscal capacity.[f] Nonfederal revenue effort, the ratio of a state's nonfederal revenues to its personal income, is *not* associated to any significant degree with the relative level of a state's income, and this is not a primary reason for the lower revenue levels of poor states (Table 5-2, column 5).

In general, federal aid is concentrated on the very lowest income states and certain higher income states with high costs and large concentrations of special need children (Table 5-2, column 3). On balance, these federal aid allocations moderately reduce revenue disparities across states. For instance,

---

[e]The figures in Table 5-2 represent the most current statistics for revenue (1970) and income (1974). Property valuations per pupil, the indicator of school district fiscal capacity displayed in Table 5-1, are unavailable across states. Property wealth may be less appropriate than personal income, in any event, since the state governments, which finance over half of nonfederal school revenues nationally, rely heavily on income-based taxes. Additionally, pupils are defined by enrollment since average daily attendance is not uniformly available on a statewide basis from published statistics.

[f]The correlation is 0.76 between per pupil income and nonfederal revenues while the disparity ratio of nonfederal revenues between highest and lowest income quartiles is 1.67 : 1.

Table 5-2. Income and Revenues per Pupil by Source and Nonfederal Revenue Effort for States Relative to the National Average

State (Ranked by Income per Pupil)	Income per Pupil (1)	Nonfederal Revenue per Pupil (2)	Federal Revenue per Pupil (3)	Total Revenues per Pupil (4)	Nonfederal Revenue as a Percent of Personal Income (Col 2 ÷ Col 1) (5)
U.S. Average	$24,307.	$1,291.	$132.	$1,423.	5.31%
			Index (U.S. Average = 100)		
DISTRICT OF COLUMBIA	161.2	132.0	279.5	145.6	81.9
NEW YORK	134.9	164.5	78.2	156.6	122.0
NEW JERSEY	129.2	137.7	57.2	130.2	106.6
ILLINOIS	125.8	137.7	89.0	133.2	109.6
CONNECTICUT	125.7	116.9	48.9	110.6	93.1
HAWAII	119.0	116.4	89.1	113.8	97.8
PENNSYLVANIA	118.1	126.2	117.4	125.4	107.0
CALIFORNIA	117.4	108.7	108.1	108.6	82.6
RHODE ISLAND	116.8	119.3	100.6	117.6	102.3
DELAWARE	116.6	122.5	104.1	120.8	105.1
FLORIDA	116.2	98.2	63.7	95.0	84.6
KANSAS	114.6	113.5	145.6	116.5	99.1
MASSACHUSETTS	114.6	122.4	50.6	115.8	106.9
MARYLAND	113.6	124.3	73.1	119.5	109.5
NORTH DAKOTA	111.4	92.5	77.9	91.2	83.1
ALASKA	109.7	171.5	298.4	183.2	156.5
OHIO	106.3	94.8	58.5	91.5	89.3
MICHIGAN	106.2	98.6	38.4	93.0	92.9
NEBRASKA	106.1	87.1	70.1	85.5	82.1
WASHINGTON	104.0	108.5	96.0	107.3	104.4
OREGON	103.1	89.2	66.7	87.1	86.5
MISSOURI	102.5	87.4	91.1	86.8	85.3
WISCONSIN	102.2	115.2	91.3	113.0	112.8
NEVADA	101.5	98.6	55.9	94.7	97.3

IOWA	101.3	125.8	59.6	119.7	124.3
COLORADO	99.5	111.6	79.9	108.6	112.2
MINNESOTA	99.3	117.9	68.1	113.3	118.9
VIRGINIA	97.7	88.5	106.7	90.2	90.7
NEW HAMPSHIRE	94.1	87.8	55.0	84.8	93.4
INDIANA	92.7	89.0	52.5	85.7	96.1
ARIZONA	92.1	106.8	123.7	108.4	116.0
WYOMING	90.5	74.3	70.1	73.9	82.2
OKLAHOMA	90.4	82.9	107.4	85.2	91.8
KENTUCKY	88.7	72.1	97.0	76.7	82.5
TENNESSEE	88.1	70.9	86.3	72.3	50.8
GEORGIA	87.5	72.1	97.0	74.4	82.5
TEXAS	87.3	91.4	103.7	92.5	104.8
MONTANA	87.2	96.9	66.2	94.1	111.2
SOUTH DAKOTA	86.9	80.3	134.5	83.3	92.2
NORTH CAROLINA	86.9	82.6	121.7	86.2	95.2
VERMONT	83.6	115.4	72.2	111.4	138.2
IDAHO	82.2	76.6	94.8	78.3	93.3
ALABAMA	81.7	73.5	138.1	79.5	90.0
LOUISIANA	80.3	71.0	147.6	78.1	88.6
WEST VIRGINIA	79.7	78.2	107.5	80.9	98.2
MAINE	78.8	84.0	72.5	82.9	106.6
SOUTH CAROLINA	78.4	70.5	119.2	75.0	89.9
ARKANSAS	78.0	67.7	121.8	72.7	86.9
MISSISSIPPI	71.0	59.9	157.5	69.0	84.5
UTAH	69.7	85.4	66.5	83.6	122.6
NEW MEXICO	69.5	82.8	210.2	94.6	119.1
			Interquartile Rankings[a]		
1	124.8	132.2	93.2	128.6	105.5
2	110.7	105.4	63.6	101.5	95.1
3	98.1	98.2	84.1	96.9	100.0
4	83.2	79.4	113.6	82.6	95.4

Source: See footnote and source notes at end of chapter.

[a]States are grouped into quartiles on the basis of income (Column 1)

Mississippi's relative education revenues rise from 60 percent of the national average for nonfederal revenues to 69 percent with federal revenues included. However, even with federal revenues added, the maximum to minimum disparity ratio in total revenues across all states continues to be high—revenues in Alaska are reduced from 2.9 to 2.7 times those in Mississippi. Federal aid has an equalizing tendency across states ranked by their per pupil incomes, but it is neither sufficiently large nor directed perfectly enough to low-income states to reduce disparities significantly.

Fiscal Adequacy.[g] There have been calls recently to increase the federal portion of total expenditures for elementary and secondary education on grounds that federal funds are needed to ensure adequate total expenditure levels. Typically, proponents of this position support their claims by citing examples of specific local areas that have turned down bond issues, closed schools before completion of the school year, or shortened school days. These are isolated examples, however, and, as the following evidence suggests, do not appear to be representative of the condition of education in most school districts.

One indirect measure of adequacy is the trend in expenditures, as an upward trend indicates the continuing availability of funds. On this score the record is positive. In the past two decades, spending for elementary and secondary education increased dramatically. In the first decade it doubled (from $11 billion in 1953-1954 to $22 billion in 1963-1964), and in the second decade it almost tripled (expenditures were almost $60 billion by 1973-1974). However, federal aid still represents only 9 percent of the total, a share that many representatives of the education community find to be seriously low.

Total dollar expenditure trends, however, are not the best measures of growth in the real level of educational services. A better perspective is provided by examining per pupil expenditures, which rose from $313 in 1951-1952 to $1,182 in 1972-1973. This increase might be viewed as reflecting a combination of increases in both the services provided and the prices of education resources. If these figures are adjusted according to changes in the Consumer Price Index (CPI), three-fourths of the increase might be attributed to real increases in services and one-fourth to inflation. But because teacher salaries have increased much more sharply than the CPI—207 percent compared with 67 percent—changes in the CPI probably understate the increased cost of educational resources.

Indeed, if expenditure increases over the period are adjusted using an index of teachers' salaries, only 20 percent of the increase in spending is attributable to real increases in services. On the other hand, there is evidence to suggest that qualifications of teachers have improved in recent years (the proportion of teachers with masters degrees grew from 23 percent of all elementary

---

[g]National trend data summarized in this section are shown in Table 5A-2 in the appendix.

and secondary teachers in 1966-1967 to 33 percent in 1973-1974), and it seems reasonable to assume that considerably more than 20 percent of the increase in spending reflects real increases in teacher quality and educational services. This conclusion is supported by other evidence showing pupil-teacher ratios declining nationally from 24.2 in 1951-1952 to 20.2 in 1972-1973.

The large cities have shared in the expenditure and service increases. Table 5-3, showing enrollments, pupil-teacher ratios, and expenditures for fifteen districts serving large city areas over an eight-year period, indicates that these cities have not had to serve a growing student population. Moreover, pupil-teacher ratios generally decreased over the period. Per pupil expenditures rose substantially during this time, consistent with the national trends already reviewed.

In general, evidence supporting the existence of a fiscal inadequacy in the financing of the general education program is not compelling. Given the overall upward trend in real educational expenditures that has been observed, it would be difficult to justify greater federal intervention on this basis alone.

NEW FEDERAL DIRECTIONS

The preceding review suggests that intrastate and interstate inequalities in educational resources may justify federal intervention in the general program of education finance. Although the potential benefits from federal intervention into the general program of education finance are many, the risks and potential costs of such involvement are high. Many federal policymakers may not wish to take such risks or make such commitments. Since the federal policy role we are discussing is a new one, it is unlikely that it either should or could be implemented without careful assessment of its consequences over the long run. The following discussion looks at several ways the federal government can enter the area of general education finance and assesses them as to how well each achieves its stated objectives, how much each is likely to cost, and how well each balances with accepted federal education concerns. Two federal strategies are examined: establishment of performance standards for interdistrict equalization and creation of separate interstate equalization mechanisms. As discussed previously, because evidence supporting the existence of a fiscal crisis in education is not compelling, we have chosen not to address issues relating to the creation of broad federal support strategies for remedying such difficulties. We do, however, discuss an apparent inequity in current federal general support mechanisms—the failure to extend direct participation in federal general revenue sharing to school districts.

Interdistrict Equalization Standards

Although historically the federal government has been loath to play a major role in equalizing state school finance systems, pressures that may increase the federal effort in this area are building. For example, recent legislation

Table 5-3. Trends in Pupils, Current Expenditures per Pupil, and Pupil-Teacher Ratios for Selected Large City School Systems, 1965–1972

City	Pupils				Current Expenditures per Pupil				Pupil-Teacher Ratio			
	1965-1966	1970-1971	1971-1972	1972-1973	1965-1966	1970-1971	1971-1972	1972-1973	1965-1966	1970-1971	1971-1971	1972-1973
Baltimore	169,777	166,409	163,800	160,549	$ 520	$ 973	$ 948	$1,034	23.8	19.5	20.1	20.9
Boston	83,902	83,000	95,000	83,000	549	1,036	1,011	1,217	20.7	20.2	20.8	17.0
Chicago	498,398	480,000	483,016	470,000	500	1,124	1,240	1,322	23.9	17.4	22.0	20.1
Cleveland	142,275	136,460	135,000	133,000	492	950	1,056	1,232	26.7	24.0	23.7	25.6
Dallas	138,564	151,108	146,527	144,449	384	650	762	791	25.7	25.6	23.4	22.7
Detroit	267,462	—	267,225	258,209	524	—	1,155	1,360	26.1	—	25.8	25.6
Houston	209,581	215,000	208,086	201,646	353	623	717	718	25.5	23.8	22.9	23.2
Los Angeles	618,705	630,795	621,185	619,608	540	869	932	998	27.3	22.1	21.8	22.4
Milwaukee	116,952	119,805	117,734	112,970	518	901	1,063	1,304	24.9	20.2	22.0	20.4
New Orleans	95,116	95,000	94,020	90,200	348	779	822	965	25.1	20.9	20.7	18.5
New York	950,149	963,000	931,660	942,000	903[a]	1,461	1,607	1,724	20.1	15.6	15.8	15.5
Philadelphia	240,358	247,658	234,098	243,600	558	1,247	1,553	1,509	22.7	20.4	17.1	20.4
St. Louis	99,283	93,995	94,024	90,000	524	986	897	1,000	25.8	22.6	23.9	19.0
San Francisco	—	85,098	78,100	75,140	—	1,125	1,575	1,512	—	18.1	16.9	16.5
Washington, D.C.	—	135,505	131,260	126,485	578	1,046	1,063[a]	1,327	23.5	18.1	20.1[a]	19.3

Source: National Center for Education Statistics, USOE, "Statistics of Public Elementary and Secondary Day Schools," 1965, 1970, 1971, 1972.

[a]Estimated by USOE.

has established a low-level appropriation of $13 million for planning grants to assist states in reforming their finance structures. In addition, the impact aid program added a new provision recently that requires the federal government to establish criteria for assessing school finance structures in impact aid states. The provision permits states that meet these standards to reduce thier own state aid payments to impact aid districts by a portion of the amount these districts receive from the federal government. Although both provisions are relatively modest departures from past federal policy, together they do reflect an increasing concern in Congress and elsewhere that the federal government play a more active role in promoting general school finance reform.

Given the new impact aid provisions as a point of departure, the most logical way for the federal government to promote reform is for it to refine that program's standards and apply them universally to all state systems. In effect, under this approach the federal government would assume an active standard-setting role by creating and enforcing generalized criteria for judging whether a state has in place a school finance system that adequately equalizes educational opportunities across its school districts.

Creating and applying such standards is by no means an easy or straightforward task. For example, one particularly difficult design problem confronting federal policymakers is the need to develop standards that strike a proper balance between control and flexibility. On the one hand, standards must be specified with enough precision to permit their use in identifying or eliminating unwanted and questionable practices. On the other hand, they must be flexible enough to treat the many different but equally valid state aid formulas in a neutral, evenhanded manner.

Stringent standards based wholly on traditional notions of school finance reform are probably unwarranted at the federal level.[5] Revenue and expenditure disparities can arise for many reasons other than educational inequality. Hence, federal standards should have the ability to distinguish between excesses brought about by resource inequities and high spending made necessary by special local circumstances such as high education costs or extreme concentrations of handicapped, language-limited, or poor children. Alternatively, if the federal government does not have the know-how to adjust for these circumstances, state governments should not be penalized for making the adjustments themselves.

The importance of this last design consideration is suggested by the data for cities in Table 5-4. The fact that center city revenues and property valuations per pupil are at or above their respective state averages in four of five states strongly suggests that cities and the states in which these cities are located would be heavy losers under any traditional test of fiscal performance that examined only the relationship between property wealth and revenues per pupil (Table 5-4, columns 1 and 2). On the other hand, flexible federal standards that permit states to establish finance systems that explicitly recognize and

Table 5-4. Selected Measures of District Need and Capacity by Metro Class for Five States, 1970 (All Measures Shown Relative to State Averages)

Urban Class[a]	Revenue per Pupil[b] (1)	Property per Pupil[c] (2)	Property per Capita[d] (3)	Teacher Salary[e] (4)	Percent Disadvantaged[f] (5)
Arkansas					
Center City	1.09	1.44	1.23	1.06	0.73
Largest	1.16	1.73	1.43	1.12	0.72
Suburban	0.92	0.73	0.92	0.97	1.01
Non-Metro	1.00	0.96	0.97	0.99	1.06
Nebraska					
Center City	1.00	0.91	0.72	1.09	0.92
Largest	0.95	0.95	0.75	1.08	1.05
Suburban	0.98	0.82	0.97	1.01	0.61
Non-Metro	1.01	1.10	1.18	0.93	1.15
New York					
Center City	1.08	1.39	0.89	1.00	1.67
Largest	1.13	1.47	0.91	1.00	1.78
Suburban	0.97	0.83	1.13	1.03	0.61
Non-Metro	0.91	0.66	0.82	0.90	0.74
Ohio					
Center City	1.15	1.18	0.99	1.18	1.55
Largest	1.37	1.31	1.07	1.31	2.19
Surburban	1.03	1.01	1.07	0.98	0.76
Non-Metro	0.81	0.81	0.91	0.88	0.86
Oklahoma					
Center City	0.94	1.23	1.13	1.06	0.94
Largest	1.34	1.49	1.40	1.06	0.81
Suburban	0.97	0.82	0.95	0.96	0.68
Non-Metro	1.06	0.96	0.94	1.00	1.23

Source: 1970 supplemented U.S. Census and ELSEGIS Data Base.

[a]Table uses 1970 U.S. Census definitions of metro class.

[b]Nonfederal revenue per pupil in average daily attendance (ADA).

[c]Property valuation (adjusted to market value) per pupil (ADA).

[d]Property valuation (adjusted to market value) per capita.

[e]Average salary of instructional staff.

[f]Orshansky Poverty Population of school-age (5-17) children plus 35 percent of the estimated number of school-age children from families with non-English language mother tongue.

adjust for special circumstances will treat these areas in a much more equitable manner.

For example, although cities are places of high relative revenues and property wealth per pupil, a number of circumstances reduce these apparent advantages. In particular, cities have relatively high nonschool tax burdens resulting from the large number of noneducational services they must provide to all their residents. These other obligations can drain available tax capacity for education.

The magnitude and importance of these nonschool burdens is partially suggested by what happens to the cities' relative wealth position when per capita property value—a measure of fiscal capacity that reflects the tax burden resulting from all public service requirements—is substituted for property value per pupil (Table 5-4, column 3).

The center city is uniformly lower across all states on the measure per capita fiscal capacity than on the corresponding measure per pupil. This reflects the greater concentration of nonpublic school populations within the cities. The cities' higher proportions of private school attendees, dropouts, families without children, and elderly persons also contribute to this result. Not surprisingly, suburban districts in all states and nonmetropolitan districts in some appear wealthier on a per capita property measure.

Other evidence showing that cities have high relative instructional staff costs and, in urban states, extremely large concentrations of high-cost special need children underscores the fact that the cities' advantages are more apparent than real (Table 5-4, columns 4 and 5).[h] The results suggest strongly that federal performance standards based on overly simplistic notions of interdistrict equity would serve the nation poorly. By failing to adjust or by discouraging state adjustments for special local circumstances such as those just reviewed, overly stringent standards would cause more harm than good and could conceivably increase inequalities in educational opportunity.

Another major consideration in designing federal school finance standards concerns the problem of achieving a reasonable balance between the degree of equalization that is desired and the added costs engendered by requiring adherence to the standards. Most states will find it difficult to achieve

---

[h]The special need population was estimated by summing the number of children from poor families (using the official federal poverty standard) and the number of children of limited English-speaking ability (LESA). Although it has been posited that there are more uncorrected handicapping conditions among the poor, documentation for this notion is not available. We have, therefore, omitted any adjustment to reflect a greater than average concentration of poor handicapped children.

LESA children were estimated from information obtained from an informal telephone survey of officials responsible for federal Title VII bilingual programs in four states with heavy concentrations of Spanish-surnamed persons. This survey indicated that about 35 percent of the Spanish-surnamed children are limited to English-speaking ability (i.e., about 1.8 million children nationally). This estimate does not include those children who may need no bilingual assistance but who could benefit from bicultural activities.

compliance by reducing revenues in high-spending districts; consequently, they will be compelled to level up revenues in resource-deficient districts. The simple inescapable fact for state governments is that in the absence of federal aid (for which there is currently little support), equalization requires new school spending and becomes increasingly costly as disparities in per pupil revenues (or expenditures) are reduced to narrower limits. Then the problem for the federal government is to establish realistic standards that achieve a reasonable degree of equalization at a price most states can afford.

Table 5-5 is instructive in this respect. The first row of the table presents the aggregate costs in 1970 to level up to alternative percentiles of per pupil revenues within each state. For example, the cost to raise all districts within each state up to the per pupil revenue level of the median revenue district is $1.7 billion. It is $3.1 billion to level up to the seventieth percentile and $9.7 billion to level to the ninety-fifth percentile.

These costs would understate the costs prevailing now if they grew in relation to the 8.8 percent growth in total spending that has occurred between 1970 and 1975, but they would overstate them to the degree that recent reforms lessened the magnitude of revenue disparities within states.

The table also shows the national average disparity between the ninety-fifth percentile district and all other districts that results when low-revenue districts are leveled up to designated revenue percentiles. For instance, leveling up all districts to the median district (fiftieth percentile) within each state would yield average nonfederal revenues in the ninety-fifth percentile district that are 138 percent of the average revenues in the rest of the districts. Leveling to the seventieth percentile would reduce the difference to 123 percent, while leveling to the ninetieth percentile would yield a difference of 106 percent.

These cost results confirm our earlier conclusions and caution against a federal standard that seeks to do too much. A federal goal to reduce real wealth-based expenditure or revenue disparities to less than 30 or 40 percent

Table 5-5. Disparity Ratio and Costs of Equalizing all Lower Revenue Districts to Specified Within-State Percentiles.

| | *Percentile* | | | | | |
	50	*60*	*70*	*80*	*90*	*95*
Cost (billions)	$1.7	$2.3	$3.1	$4.3	$6.9	$9.7
Disparity ratios[a]	1.38	1.31	1.23	1.15	1.06	1.0

Source: 1970 supplemented U.S. Census and ELSEGIS data base.

[a]Disparity ratios are between the ninety-fifth percentile district and average revenues in all other districts when revenues are leveled up to designated revenue percentiles. Revenues are state and local revenues per pupil in average daily attendance (ADA).

is probably unrealistic given the high costs that states would have to absorb to achieve it. On the other hand, a federal goal to eliminate the most extreme disparities is probably realistic and could be accomplished by spending between $1.7 and $2.3 billion.

Choice of a Federal Standard. The form of most proposed federal standards has generally varied according to what kinds of disparities are to be controlled. Some standards have been proposed that reduce variations in services by controlling spending (expenditure disparity standards), while others have sought to control variations in district proportions of unequalized revenues (fiscal neutrality standards).

An *expenditure standard* generally establishes limits on the amount of variation in per pupil current operating expenditure permissible across districts. Capital expenditures are excluded from consideration because the services derived from such spending accrue to a district over a period of succeeding years.

An expenditure standard can be put into operation in a variety of ways. For example, one can establish a minimum level of acceptable spending (e.g., 90 percent of the state median), but leave the maximum unspecified. Alternatively, one can establish limits on the ratio of maximum to minimum spending; or a test can be devised to limit the average expenditure variation across districts within states. Among these three alternatives, the second is most discussed, probably because it achieves the greatest potential for control.

One drawback of expenditure standards is that they have little ability to discriminate between excessive spending based on wealth differences and high spending resulting from special needs (the higher price of education and heavy concentrations of disadvantaged that burden many cities, for example). Thus, although they can eliminate spending disparities, they can also create greater inequities by depriving high-need areas of appropriate services. Given the present limited state of knowledge, it would be very difficult for the federal government to specify an expenditure standard that adjusts for these special local circumstances.[6]

A related although more basic criticism of expenditure standards and disparity ratio tests is that they are not neutral with respect to the different, but equally effective, capacity equalization plans adopted throughout the nation. Critics note, for example, that expenditure disparity tests discriminate against states that have adopted equal revenue yield formulas. If the federal government must establish standards, it is argued, the standards should at least allow spending to vary with special local circumstances and preferences for schooling. The fiscal neutrality standard is proposed as a possible alternative for dealing with these difficulties.

A *fiscal neutrality standard* sets a minimum on the proportion of total educational revenues in a state or district raised in a fiscally neutral way—

that is, financed from the wealth of the state as a whole rather than from a local tax base. This standard is aimed principally at lessening the dependence of expenditures on available local fiscal capacity to support education.

The standard is based on a test that classifies all revenues from state and local sources as equalized, if they fall into either of two categories:

1. State and local resources generated by a program that guarantees all districts within the state equal revenue per pupil per unit of local tax effort (as defined by the state)
2. A program that distributes state aid on the basis of some objective measure of pupil or district need within the state

Funds flowing through a state equalization program are covered under the first set of conditions. For instance, a pure power equalization formula meets the test by definition, and a pure foundation formula also meets the first set of conditions since all districts exert the same tax effort to raise the foundation program amount.[i]

The second set of conditions counts nonmatching state aid as equalized if it is allocated proportionately throughout the state according to some objective basis of pupil or district need. For example, states provide school resources through grants not tied to a local tax effort requirement, such as categorical grants for special need pupils. Such grants fail the first set of conditions (local tax effort is zero) despite the fact that they are raised from the wealth of the state as a whole and are distributed on the basis of pupil need. These funds do, however, qualify as equalized under the second criterion.

State aid systems are exceedingly complex financing mechanisms, emerging out of the compromises necessary to achieve both equity and political acceptability. The breakout of a state's school budget into its equalized and unequalized portions can pose some judgemental and technical problems. The treatment of flat grants, hold-harmless provisions, and state tax rebates returned to the district of origin are only several examples of the problems complicating this division. However, a recent study conducted by the National Conference of State Legislatures (NCSL) demonstrates that, although data collection difficulties exist and judgement calls must be made, a fiscal neutrality test is a feasible alternative to the expenditure disparity test, at least for the ten states in which the study was conducted.[7]

The choice between expenditure equalization and fiscal neutrality standards should emerge from considerations of both equity of opportunity

---

[i]A foundation program guarantees each district a minimum per pupil expenditure provided that its tax effort is at or above some minimum level specified by the state. A power equalization program equalizes over a range of tax efforts. It guarantees all districts making the same tax effort an equivalent revenue per pupil. In either type of program, guaranteed revenue per pupil can also be adjusted for other district circumstances, such as district size or cost of education.

and the proper federal role in educational finance. The expenditure disparity standard sets rigid limits on per pupil expenditure variations and is preferred by advocates of a strong equalization policy who would not allow the quality of a child's education to vary at all with parent or community preferences. The fiscal neutrality standard allows resources to vary with local priorities as reflected in relative tax effort, but not with local wealth. Those who prefer it argue that federal interference is excessive when it controls parent or community choice over spending levels financed on an equalized wealth basis and that it is self-defeating because it encourages flight from public to private schools, thereby reducing the support and quality of public education. Moreover, the uncertainty over the effect on revenues and expenditures of special pupil needs, educational costs, and other special circumstances argues for maximum local flexibility over educational fiscal decisions, even if the price is less federal control over equalization.

While we prefer the fiscal neutrality standard because it offers the most flexible approach, a basic standard that offers states a choice between both options is a feasible mechanism for federal control of interdistrict disparities. The problem remains to establish reasonable cutoffs for both tests. Our preference is to allow the maximum flexibility that is consistent with achieving equity within state equalization goals—that is, around 30 to 40 percent variation on the disparity ratio test; for the fiscal neutrality test, a similar 30 to 40 percent maximum could be applied on the percentage of unequalized funds in any single district within a state.

Interstate Equalization Mechanisms

If the federal government sees fit to involve itself in the local financing of general education programs by establishing and enforcing interdistrict equalization performance standards, is it not reasonable that, at the very least, it do something itself about the interstate variations that exist in capacity to support education? After all, even if every state had an acceptable equalization program, there would still be educational inequities because some states are poorer than others. Presumably, these states would be at a considerable disadvantage because they would have to exert relatively greater tax efforts to achieve parity with wealthier states. Although it can be argued that interdistrict reform ought to be financed by state governments because the inequities giving rise to the need for reform are generated by the states, the burden of financing interstate reforms is much more clearly a concern for the federal government. How the federal government might assume this responsibility is the subject of the following discussion.

Perhaps the most frequently discussed mechanism for achieving some measure of interstate equalization is the discretionary education block grant. This mechanism would distribute federal funds that states or school districts could spend for any valid educational purpose. A grant designed to achieve interstate equalization would allocate proportionately greater funds to resource-deficient states to equalize up their effective fiscal capacities available to support education. For example, the national government might distribute aid in accordance with the difference between the revenues per pupil a state raises at its current levels of effort and capacity and the amount of revenue per pupil it would raise if its current effort were applied to some other guaranteed level of capacity.

Such a proposal could be implemented in several different ways depending on how the federal government decided to define fiscal capacity and on the level of fiscal capacity it chose to guarantee. Four hypothetical programs have been selected to illustrate the importance of choosing between different measures of capacity and different guarantee levels and to describe the cost and coverage implications of interstate equalization programs in general.

The first two programs employ a money income measure of fiscal capacity (i.e., personal money income per pupil). The first program allocates federal aid so as to make up the difference between the per pupil revenues a state currently raises and those it would raise if its present tax effort were applied to the national average income base. The second program guarantees a higher level of fiscal capacity by making up the difference between what a state currently raises and what it would raise if it had fiscal capacity equal to that of the District of Columbia, the highest capacity state.

The third and fourth programs employ a different measure of fiscal capacity than the first two—a measure based on the Advisory Commission on Intergovernmental Relations (ACIR) estimate of total public financing capability (i.e., ACIR revenue capacity per pupil).[8] The ACIR measure was chosen because it is commonly considered to be a more comprehensive index of a state's fiscal capacity as it takes into consideration all the principal sources of revenue available to a state.[9] Note, for example, how the potential revenues from amusements in Nevada and mining in Wyoming push those states far higher on the ACIR index than on the income-based capacity measure (Table 5-6, columns 1 and 2).[j]

Like the first programs, these last two differ from one another in the level of capacity guarantee each provides. That is, the third program guarantees each state an average capacity base, while the fourth makes up the difference between what a state raises on its own and what it would raise if it had the resources of the highest capacity state. The general characteristics of each of these four programs, as well as their costs and scope of coverage, are summarized

---

[j]When the ACIR state-by-state results for 1966–1967 were expressed in relative terms per capita and compared with measures of relative income per capita, the two figures were found to be within 10 percent of one another in about half of the states. Compared with the broader measurement, income per capita appeared to underindicate the fiscal capacity of seventeen states by 10 percent or more and to overindicate the capacity of six states and the District of Columbia by 10 percent or more.

in Table 5-7. State-by-state allocations under the various plans are shown in Table 5-6 (columns 7 to 10).

The cost to the federal government of a program that guarantees national average capacity is $2.6 billion when fiscal capacity is measured by income and about $4.1 billion when the ACIR capacity measure is used. Both programs direct their aid to the low-capacity states, although the ACIR-based program achieves somewhat broader coverage than the income-based program. Equalization grants range from $479 per pupil (Utah) to $7 per pupil (Colorado) when income is used and from $472 (Utah) to $12 per pupil (Massachusetts) when the ACIR measure is employed. Many large urban states (e.g., New York, New Jersey, and Illinois) are ineligible for assistance under either program.

The guarantees of maximum state per pupil capacity spread funds more broadly across the states, but both programs have astronomical costs, which make them practically and politically unfeasible. Quite clearly, programs that guarantee more than national average fiscal capacity will provide better coverage than those that do not, but they will do so at costs that are prohibitively high.

There are additional problems associated with all of these proposals. One is the difficulty in determining which states are truly resource deficient. Differences in fiscal capacity, however measured, are only one source of disparities in educational opportunity across states. For example, those states with higher fiscal capacity under either measure are also states that tend to have higher educational expenses, as indicated by cost proxies like the index of teachers salaries (Table 5-6, column 3). Moreover, although higher capacity states do tend to retain some advantage in real services, as indicated by their lower pupil-teacher ratios (Table 5-6, column 4), the advantage they gain is not nearly as great as one might expect from their higher revenue levels.[k]

Another source of disparity in educational opportunity that must be accounted for is the greater concentration of high-need pupils in particular states. The greatest concentrations of children with special educational needs (e.g., low-income and limited English-speaking children) are in the low-income-revenue-capacity states (Table 5-6, column 5). These children are

---

[k]These results across states are subject to the same qualifications that applied to our interdistrict analysis—that is, instructional staff salaries and pupil-to-teacher ratios cannot be taken at face value since they have not been adjusted for differences in instructional staff quality. Another indicator of differences in education costs across geographic areas is the annual budget for a four-person family calculated by the Bureau of Labor Statistics (BLS) in selected Standard Metropolitan Areas. It is reasonable to expect that school systems in high cost of living areas have to provide their instructional staff with proportionately greater salaries than staff of equivalent quality receive in low-cost areas, all other factors being equal. The 1973 annual BLS budget for a four-person family at an intermediate level of living shows a range of from $10,959 in Austin, Texas, to $16,520 in Anchorage, Alaska. This differential of over 50% is further evidence of the need for incorporating an interstate cost of education adjustment in any interstate equalization formula.

Table 5-6.   Selected Measures of State Need, Capacity, and Cost for Alternative Interstate Equalization Plans

States (Ranked by Income per Pupil)	Selected Measures of State Need, Capacity, and Cost						Capacity Equalization Plans			
	Income per Pupil (1)	ACIR Rev. Capacity per Pupil (2)	Average Teachers Salaries (3)	Pupil Teachers Ratios (4)	Percent Disadvantaged Children (5)	Title I Rev per Pupil (6)	National Average Capacity Guarantee Entitlement per Pupil		Maximum Capacity Guarantee Entitlement per Pupil	
							Plan I: $2,676 B (7)	Plan III: $4,075 B (8)	Plan II: $31,555 B (9)	Plan IV: $30,133 B (10)
U.S. Average	$24,307	$2,767.1	$11,777	119.0	24.9	$40				
		Index (U.S. Average = 1.00)								
District of Columbia	161.2	139.6	129.9	93.4	159.3	240.1	$ 0	$ 0	$ 0	$ 120
New York	134.9	129.4	135.4	88.8	144.5	143.7	0	0	414	328
New Jersey	129.2	112.5	113.6	86.8	86.6	96.9	0	0	440	562
Illinois	125.8	109.2	NA	97.1	100.8	99.8	0	0	501	655
Connecticut	125.7	110.0	100.0	87.8	88.3	73.9	0	0	427	540
Hawaii	119.0	115.6	129.1	107.4	111.1	82.5	0	0	532	438
Pennsylvania	118.1	97.0	104.9	96.6	97.0	100.0	0	51	595	801
California	117.4	119.8	129.1	108.6	98.5	86.3	0	0	524	346
Rhode Island	116.8	96.7	113.6	96.5	121.3	101.0	0	52	586	839
Delaware	116.6	107.2	106.5	98.4	73.9	108.4	0	0	605	623
Florida	116.2	120.3	89.1	100.2	96.9	107.3	0	0	491	306
Kansas	114.6	113.3	90.9	85.8	76.9	79.5	0	0	596	466
Massachusetts	114.6	99.2	101.0	85.2	91.1	76.2	0	12	643	799
Maryland	113.6	98.1	116.4	103.2	73.2	88.4	0	31	672	838
North Dakota	111.4	110.6	84.0	87.7	136.8	107.4	0	0	534	419
Alaska	109.7	137.2	164.0	96.3	90.0	61.9	0	0	1,041	195
Ohio	106.3	95.1	96.8	106.5	69.6	61.9	0	63	632	698
Michigan	106.2	92.0	132.0	112.1	85.4	99.6	0	110	660	793
Nebraska	106.1	109.4	85.1	90.5	85.2	73.0	0	0	583	411
Washington	104.0	106.3	115.6	113.3	68.9	79.7	0	0	772	568

Oregon	103.1	105.8	105.3	97.7	68.6	91.3	0	0	648	474
Missouri	102.5	96.1	89.1	95.8	86.2	83.4	0	45	646	624
Wisconsin	102.2	90.1	108.8	92.7	90.1	78.2	0	163	659	979
Nevada	101.5	149.4	108.0	119.5	48.1	44.7	0	0	750	0
Iowa	101.3	94.7	98.2	92.5	72.6	65.9	0	90	961	937
Colorado	99.5	99.0	101.9	100.7	78.4	74.8	7	13	894	732
Minnesota	99.3	93.8	104.1	97.0	87.1	76.3	11	100	960	901
Virginia	97.7	90.3	96.0	99.6	86.8	93.0	27	123	743	748
New Hampshire	94.1	96.9	89.2	94.3	70.1	51.5	71	37	828	615
Indiana	92.7	83.4	94.6	116.5	55.1	51.3	91	230	850	910
Arizona	92.1	98.2	105.2	104.6	101.4	84.5	118	26	1,035	719
Wyoming	90.5	126.7	94.3	85.2	19.5	78.1	101	0	750	172
Oklahoma	90.4	105.4	81.5	95.7	95.8	93.1	114	0	839	447
Kentucky	88.5	82.0	83.0	106.0	125.6	121.5	119	204	762	766
Tennessee	88.1	80.0	87.5	108.9	115.3	113.7	123	229	759	793
Georgia	87.8	80.4	90.2	112.7	112.0	109.0	133	227	784	799
Texas	87.3	91.2	96.6	98.0	119.2	110.6	172	114	1,000	752
Montana	87.2	93.4	93.4	93.7	81.0	91.5	183	88	1,061	749
South Dakota	86.9	89.5	79.1	94.0	127.2	99.9	158	122	886	694
North Carolina	86.9	77.7	94.8	110.6	100.4	114.6	161	307	913	785
Vermont	83.6	80.2	84.7	78.1	82.0	96.0	292	368	1,384	1,285
Idaho	82.2	78.7	86.7	109.6	60.7	77.1	214	267	951	858
Alabama	81.7	73.7	90.0	100.9	146.9	143.0	213	339	924	975
Louisiana	80.3	95.8	85.7	102.3	178.3	150.2	226	41	925	513
West Virginia	79.7	70.9	89.0	103.0	112.2	109.0	257	414	1,033	1,117
Maine	78.8	69.8	90.2	94.3	87.7	72.1	292	469	1,134	1,235
South Carolina	78.4	66.1	84.1	105.0	133.8	136.5	250	466	961	1,145
Arkansas	74.0	74.7	81.9	107.4	137.5	147.4	240	297	932	875
Mississippi	71.0	70.3	79.1	105.6	208.2	205.7	317	327	964	870
Utah	69.7	70.0	95.5	122.8	56.0	49.3	479	472	1,468	1,250
New Mexico	69.5	90.5	93.4	104.2	175.6	140.3	468	113	1,409	696

Source: See notes at end of chapter for data sources.

Table 5-7   General Characteristics of Four Alternatives Interstate Equalization Plans

Program	Capacity Measure	Guarantee Level	Total Cost (Billions)	Coverage
1	Income per pupil	National average income per pupil ($24,367)	$ 2.676	26 states
2	Income per pupil	Income per pupil in highest state (DC— $39,186)	$31.555	All states, but not D.C.
3	ACIR revenue capacity per pupil	National average revenue capacity per pupil ($2,767)	$ 4.075	33 states
4	ACIR revenue capacity per pupil	Revenue capacity per pupil in highest state (Nevada— $4,133)	$30.133	All states except Nevada

present in all states to some degree, however, and certain of the wealthier states, such as New York and Rhode Island, are also places with above-average concentrations of disadvantaged. These wealthier states are not likely to be helped by either one of the two programs that guarantee a fiscal capacity at least equal to the national average—the only programs discussed so far that can be given serious consideration.

A politically acceptable equalization program would have to take all of the preceding factors into account and, at a minimum, would have to assure some federal aid to everyone. This would raise substantially the cost of even the least expensive program. For example, if in addition to its capacity equalization grant, each state were to receive a minimum grant of $50 per pupil, price tag on the minimum cost program (the first program discussed) would rise by $2 billion to about $4.6 billion. This is a high price to pay to provide equalization grants of $2.6 billion.

An additional difficulty with all of these interstate equalization proposals is that one of the principal impacts of an educational block grant would likely be the substitution of federal revenues for those raised currently from nonfederal sources. Revenue substitution possibilities reduce the likelihood that a discretionary education block grant would result in a significant improvement in school quality. This is especially true if substitution of federal for nonfederal revenues is high in the lower capacity states. While rates of substitution are not precisely calculable, estimates based on past experience with other programs range as high as two-thirds of each federal aid dollar.[10] Although substitution rates can be controlled by conditioning the receipt of federal funds on

the exertion of a specified minimum revenue or expenditure effort for education, instituting such controls would run counter to other efforts aimed at improving educational productivity. Indeed, such controls may only aggravate this
problem by pushing expenditures to unacceptable and unnecessarily high levels.

In view of these difficulties, other mechanisms for achieving interstate equalization goals besides an education block grant merit exploration.
Because funding allocations under existing federal education programs have been
shown to have an equalizing tendency across states ranked by their relative
per pupil incomes, they represent an alternative to a new interstate equalization block grant. The program most closely associated with a policy of aid to
lower capacity areas is compensatory education assistance under Title I of the
Elementary and Secondary Education Act. Title I funds are allocated at their
highest per pupil levels in the low-income states and certain higher income
states with concentrations of low-income children (Table 6-6, column 6).
An increased Title I allocation would go a long way toward addressing interstate
capacity equalization objectives and has the added advantages of working within
an existing federal support mechanism and concentrating assistance where it is
needed most—on high-cost special need populations in all states. It is noteworthy that Title I is currently funded at only 40 percent of its authorized level,
so that good reason exists for its expansion.

Extending General Revenue Sharing to Education

The federal general revenue sharing program is another mechanism
already in place that can potentially contribute to some of the same ends sought
through education block grants. Structural changes in the program would be
required for education's present modest level of participation to be expanded—
changes that could raise difficult philosophical, technical, and political problems.

General revenue sharing distributes about $6 billion annually to over
38,000 units of government. Distribution of entitlements is made on the basis of
a complex formula that takes into account a government's service burden (population), economic capacity (relative inverse per capita income), and tax effort
(tax-to-income ratio). At present, states, counties, townships, municipalities,
and Indian tribes receive funds from the program. School districts are not permitted to participate directly in the program, and until recently, local governments were not allowed to use their shared revenues for educational purposes
(other than capital improvements, which constitute only about 1 percent of
local government usage). What additional shared revenues education has received
have been obtained directly from state government allotments (state governments have never been prohibited from spending on education) or indirectly,
because other functions' claims on nonfederal revenues are less than they would
have been without revenue sharing (i.e., through revenue substitution). At
present, state governments receive about one-third of each year's revenue-
sharing entitlement and, on the average, pass on to education a little over half

of this amount (about $1 billion annually). This state pass-through of revenue-sharing money has undoubtedly resulted in direct benefits for education. In particular, at least one major state has identified these funds as the principal source of financing for its interdistrict equalization plan.[11] The indirect benefit to education resulting from substitution is generally considered undeterminable.[12]

Several arguments have been made in favor of expanding education's participation in revenue sharing—either through new arrangements that permit direct allocations to school districts or by strengthening those provisions that generate indirect benefits to education. The principal argument favoring some such expansion points to the present program's failure to treat all public functions and governments neutrally. If one of the program's original purposes was to provide some minimum level of support to help financially pressed governments provide critical public services, it is difficult to understand how school districts and education were so poorly provided for. Although it cannot be demonstrated that the education sector is experiencing a fiscal crisis that makes it more needy than others, neither is there reason to believe that education and education agencies are less needy than those governments and services that participate more directly in the program's benefits.

Several other related arguments have been made in favor of expanding education's participation in federal general revenue sharing. For example, Reischauer notes that education absorbs some 40 percent of the resources of state and local governments and is obviously a major functional responsibility of these units. It is therefore only reasonable, he argues, that revenue sharing—the major program through which the federal government helps states and localities meet their responsibilities—should define a more active role for this function. Moreover, since the tax effort term in the interstate distribution formula includes taxes levied for education purposes, it would seem logical to include school districts in the list of eligible recipients. This is an especially compelling argument when one considers that, even though the local government tax term in the distribution formula excludes education tax revenues, localities in states with high relative education tax efforts nevertheless benefit proportionately from the higher state entitlement resulting from the way tax effort is treated in the interstate formula.[13]

Reischauer has noted another reason for making school districts eligible jurisdictions:

> During the past few years several federal aid programs have evolved in the direction of block grants. The new manpower (CETA), community development, mass transit and Law Enforcement Assistance programs and, of course, revenue sharing are manifestations of this trend. Block grant distributions are determined by a fixed formula and benefits are generally spread among a great many units of government. They offer federal policymakers natural vehicles by which to transmit assistance to state and local governments during

national economic crises. Already there are several indications of this happening. The sudden downturn of the economy in late 1974 prompted Congress to pump additional resources into the CETA program for public service employment; a second example, suggested in the 1976 budget, is to augment the General Revenue Sharing Program by $2 billion to compensate state and local governments for the increased energy costs that would result from the President's energy proposals. As long as school districts are not direct beneficiaries from these broad block grant programs, they will be bypassed by emergency supplements to federal aid. For example, school districts stand to gain little from the two proposals mentioned above although they are, by any standard, major employers and major energy users.[14]

Undoubtedly, this line of reasoning will have especially strong appeal for proponents of the fiscal crisis argument.

The principal federal response to these and similar arguments in favor of increased participation for education in general revenue sharing is contained in the *Fiscal Assistance Amendments of 1976,* which extended the law for federal revenue sharing through September 30, 1980, and dropped the list of priority uses that has barred local governments from putting revenue-sharing money into education.

While technically putting school districts on an equal footing with other agencies in competing for local funds, the measure stops short of proposals that would have made school districts direct participants. Proponents of direct school district participation, such as the National School Boards Association, contend that, although the act makes school districts legally eligible to receive money, in practice the funds will probably continue to flow elsewhere. The problem involved in getting any of the revenue-sharing money for education is complicated by ". . .questions like the powers delegated to local governments under state charters, the nature of intergovernmental cooperation agreements in states that have them, noncontiguous boundaries under which school districts might have to deal with more than one unit of local government, and finally, the possibility of taxpayer suits if a local government tried to use revenue-sharing funds for eduation to make up, for example, for defeated tax levies."[15]

States differ widely in their laws about transferring funds between units of government. In thirteen states both government agencies have to have the same "authority" before any transfer can take place at all. Other states call for an agency to have "prime responsibility" in at least two areas of services. State attorneys general have interpreted intergovernmental cooperation agreements in a variety of ways, and their rulings would affect the local government-local education agency revenue sharing picture. The effect of these problems, suggest some observers, is that the new amendments will make next to no difference at all to the districts.[16]

Opponents of direct school district participation in revenue sharing cite several reasons why such a modification to the present program would not be feasible. Opponents argue that there are *philosophical difficulties* connected with including school districts in general revenue sharing because the program is intended to provide financial assistance to general purpose, multifunction governments. Since these units are the major providers of services to citizens, they are the most burdened governments and therefore are most deserving of general federal assistance.

Critics of this argument would note that about 40 percent of state and local government expenditures are for education and that much of this amount is attributable to school district functioning. They would also argue that some general purpose governments, townships in particular, have been revenue-sharing recipients in good standing over the first years of the program even though many of them can hardly be characterized as multipurpose governments.[17] Though new provisions would eliminate some of the less active general purpose governments from the program, it is difficult to understand how school districts can continue to be excluded on a "services to citizens" criterion.

Equity problems are also often cited. Opponents note that if school districts are allowed to participate, a similar "courtesy" will have to be extended to other special purpose units of government.

A countering argument suggests that education is in a somewhat unique situation. Not only are school districts excluded from the competition for funds, but also barriers to local government revenue-sharing spending on education are greater than barriers to such local government spending on functions of other special districts. Even granting that some improvements will result from the new provisions, these constraints are not markedly affected, and education continues at a disadvantage.

Technical problems may also arise if school districts are added to the local competition, but these difficulties can generally be overcome. School districts could compete in the same way as counties, townships, and other local governments for funds. Dependent school districts that are part of other general purpose governments could either be included in the school district competition directly or, alternatively, could be accounted for by permitting parent government competition on the basis of total rather than adjusted taxes.

The allocation formula in the school competition might deviate from that used by general purpose governments. For example, to reflect school district needs, pupil-based measures could be substituted for per capita ones. Additionally, the school district tax base (generally property per pupil) could replace the present per capita income capacity index. Tax effort, of course, would be based on educational taxes raised by the district or parent government as appropriate.

Program cost and dilution fears are no doubt at the heart of most of the arguments against a more direct revenue-sharing role for education.

Without additional funding, large amounts of money would be diverted away from general purpose governments—a politically unacceptable consequence.[18]

One solution to the dilution problem is obvious; that is, increase the total annual entitlement so as to hold present recipients harmless at current or near current funding levels while ensuring a large measure of direct participation for school districts on a basis equivalent to that permitted other recipient jurisdictions. Additional annual costs for such a proposal would vary depending on how school districts were allowed to participate, but they have been estimated to range as high as $4 billion.

A somewhat less direct way to include education in the program would be to create a separate state-level education set-aside of revenue-sharing funds with pass-through provisions for subsequent redistribution to local education agencies. Costs for this proposal would be kept to around $1.2 billion if the set-aside were created from the local governments' revenue-sharing pot and apportioned to states on the basis of relative local revenues raised for elementary and secondary education. For example, if the approximately $4 billion appropriated to local governments for revenue sharing in 1974 had been divided into education and noneducation portions based on local revenue effort for education of about 30 percent, about $1.2 billion would have been set aside for LEA use and an equivalent amount would have been required to hold present recipients harmless.[19]

If neither of the preceding direct participation strategies are politically or economically feasible, an alternative might be to facilitate greater indirect educational benefits through less drastic, lower cost modifications to the present program. As has been noted, on the average, state governments currently use about one-half of their one-third share of annual revenue-sharing money to support education. One way to facilitate increases in the amount of revenue-sharing money available to education might therefore be to encourage a more equitable division of entitlements between state governments and local governments. For example, if the state-local division of entitlements were allowed to vary in proportion to the actual share of total public service expenditures (or revenues), the national split between state governments and local areas would be about half-and-half rather than one-third–two-thirds.[20] Assuming that state governments continued their current spending patterns, this aggregate increase in state government entitlements could be expected to yield a total additional indirect revenue-sharing benefit to the educational sector of about $500 million per year.[1]

The cost of this alternative would vary depending on whether one

---

[1]An arrangement that would allow intrastate entitlements to vary based on relative expenditures but which would limit total interstate variation to the current one-third–two-thirds arrangement is also possible. This alternative could be implemented at no extra cost and considerable benefit to selected high-spending state governments (and presumably to their school districts and education systems).

wished to hold local governments harmless at current entitlement levels. If a full hold-harmless clause were desired, added costs would be a relatively modest $1 billion. Without a hold-harmless clause, program costs would not rise at all.

Though cost-dilution arguments against participation are persuasive, the equity and neutrality arguments in favor of taking part are equally compelling. Moreover, there may be a flaw in the dilution argument that needs to be addressed. In particular, although direct "discretionary" payments to general purpose governments would in most instances decline as a result of education's participation in revenue sharing, the aggregate amounts available to service residents of these jurisdictions would increase, or if no additional funding were provided for the program, they would stay about the same. When viewed from a resident population perspective, the local impact of education's participation is the sum of the funds received by general purpose governments and education agencies. Although some resident areas may lose funds (in particular, the center cities in which education is a smaller share of the budget), the cost-dilution objections to an expanded participation by education seem less well founded than generally believed.

The two direct participation proposals that have been discussed do pose one special requirement that cannot be overlooked by educators; that is, direct school district participation in revenue sharing, however accomplished should be implemented so as to be consistent with state equalization programs, or federal equalization standards if these are adopted. This requirement could be handled quite easily by establishing provisions permitting state governments with acceptable equalization plans to count all or a portion of the school district revenue-sharing aid as their own aid. As we have noted, this is a technique already used with some success by the present Impact Aid program. Its implementation here would thus be consistent with established policy; it would have the added advantage of providing at least a portion of the incentive that is needed to gain acceptance of a national equalization standard.

In summary, we think a plan for extending the present guarantees of the program for general revenue sharing to education can be devised at relatively modest additional funding (between $1 and $2 billion). Such an extension makes sense because it would eliminate the unwarranted impediments to the application of revenue-sharing grants for educational purposes and could provide some of the leverage needed to gain acceptance for a national interdistrict equalization standard.

CONCLUSION

A persuasive case can be made in support of a federal role in certain aspects of the general program of education finance. Federal involvement in other areas appears to be unnecessary, costly, or inefficient. Our principal findings with respect to specific federal strategies in the general program area are:

- Interdistrict disparities in educational opportunity remain only by state fiat and their reduction is an integral part of any overall national strategy for the equalization of educational opportunities. The development of a basic interdistrict equalization standard that includes both fiscal neutrality and disparity ratio tests is feasible and would not excessively raise state costs.

- An education block grant to achieve interstate equalization has serious difficulties. Politically acceptable plans fail to direct funds efficiently to low-capacity states, are quite costly, and raise serious technical problems. The Title I program offers an existing mechanism through which to channel additional funding and achieve some of the interstate equalization objectives by helping states shoulder the burden created by their neediest and most costly students. Current Title I spending is over $2 billion below the costs of full funding.

- The creation of a broad federal support strategy for the general educational program was rejected because the evidence supporting a fiscal inadequacy in total education spending is not compelling. However, expansion of education's participation in the general revenue sharing program merits consideration. This proposal would give rise to a general purpose federal funding mechanism that is far more neutral with respect to expenditure purpose than the current program. The revenue-sharing funds are also available to act as an "incentive" on which to condition compliance with interdistrict equalization standards.

Although the above proposals warrant assessment on their individual merits, a federal role in the general program of educational finance can also be viewed within a new framework of federal-state relations in education. Recently, there has been considerable interest at the national level in proposals to consolidate federal authority and restructure the typical federal to local administrative network so as to strengthen federal-state and state-local relationships. The proposed policies of statewide equalization performance standards and general revenue sharing for education represent a shift in this direction and away from federal concern with local categorical controls and funding. Although this chapter has not dealt with federal categorical policies, per se, further analyses are warranted to determine the feasibility of developing similar performance standards and new funding mechanisms in this program activity to accomplish a totally integrated federal-state-local system for the provision of educational services.

NOTES

1. See January 1972 State of the Union Address in which President Nixon first proposed massive federal general purpose support conditioned upon states providing local property tax relief.

2. The structure of state school finance systems in effect in each state for 1975–1976 is described in Esther O. Tron, "Public School Finance Programs, 1975–1976" (Washington, D.C.: Office of Education, Department of Health, Education, and Welfare, 1976).

3. Serrano v. Priest, 5 Cal. 3d. 584, 96 Cal. Rptr. 601, 487 p. 2d, 1241 (1971).

4. The source for the disparity ratios within states is "Intrastate and Interstate Disparities in Current Operating Expenditures per Pupil 1971–1972," National Center for Educational Statistics, *Bulletin Number 18* (March 25, 1974), supplemented by data obtained directly from state statistical personnel in Montana and Wisconsin.

5. A valuable overview on traditional and contemporary approaches to school finance reform is presented in John Pincus, ed., *School Finance in Transition* (Cambridge, Mass.: Ballinger Publishing Company, 1974).

6. The difficulties of specifying national adjustments for special local circumstances is typified by the problems associated with adjusting for cost of education differences. A general index such as the Consumer Price Index (CPI) is not entirely satisfactory for this purpose as it may fail to reflect accurately factors that affect the education costs of an area. For instance, a district's teacher salary level, the largest component of school expenditures, is related to the general achievement level of its children, the presence of violence in the schools, unionism, and the potential supply of certified teachers in the population.

Rather than using a general index like the CPI, one could construct a cost of education index based on geographic differences in the prices of equivalent education inputs. The problem here is to separate cost from quality components of higher input prices. How accurately this separation can be achieved is a subject of considerable controversy. Two different views of the feasibility of separating quality (demand factors) from cost (supply factors) for teachers, are presented by Harvey Brazer, "Adjusting for Differences Among School Districts in the Costs of Educational Inputs: A Feasibility Report," in *Selected Papers in School Finance, 1974,* U.S. Office of Education; and by Norton Grub, "Identifying Teacher Supply Functions and Constructing Cost Indices: Methodological Explorations with California Unified School Districts," in draft for the Office of Education, Contract OEC-300-75-0320.

7. John J. Callahan et al., *Impact Aid and Basic State School Finance Programs: Can They Be Made More Compatible?* (Washington, D.C.: Legislators' Education Action Project, National Conference of State Legislatures, October 8, 1976).

8. ACIR state revenue capacity estimates used in this paper were updated to 1971–1973 by The Brookings Institution. See Richard P. Nathan et al., *Monitoring Revenue Sharing* (Washington, D.C.: The Brookings Institution, 1975).

Note that although the ACIR index is normally calculated on a per capita basis, we have converted it to a per pupil measure. Although per capita measures of capacity reflect more realistically a state's ability to finance total public service demands, converting to a per pupil base facilitates discussion of interstate equalization strategies for education. In addition, equalizing on a per capita capacity would mean that states of equal per capita capacity would raise at equal tax efforts different amounts of revenue per pupil depending on the fraction of their population in the public schools. For example, the District of Columbia (with a low proportion of its population in the public schools) appears relatively less well off on a per capita than on a per pupil revenue capacity measure (i.e., 119 percent of the national average, per capita, and 139 percent of the national average, per pupil).

9. Revenue capacity is defined as the total amount that would be obtained by applying within any particular state the national average rate of each of many kinds of state and local taxes and other revenue sources in use in the nation. The ACIR developed separate potential yield figures for fourteen kinds of state taxes, nine local taxes, and an even larger number of nontax revenue sources. See Advisory Commission on Intergovernmental Relations, *Measuring the Fiscal Capacity and Effort of State and Local Areas* (1971).

10. In the absence of a federal education block grant, the rate of revenue substitution is not directly measurable but may be approximated by observing substitution rates for similar types of programs. A comparatively sophisticated estimation model applied to the state of Massachusetts predicted a substitution rate of a state block grant for local revenue of from 45 to 55 percent. (David Stern, "Effects of Alternative State Aid Formulas on the Distribution of Public School Expenditures in Massachusetts," *The Review of Economics and Statistics,* [February 1973], pp. 91–97.) One recent study of the federal AFDC aid program found that the stimulative effect of the federal grant was attributable almost entirely to the price effect of the matching formula and that its income effect was not significantly different from zero. Larry Orr, "Income Transfers as a Public Good: An Application to AFDC *Technical Analysis Paper No. 4,* (Washington, D.C.: Office of Income Security Policy, Office of the Assistant Secretary for Planning and Evaluation, Department of Health, Education, and Welfare, May 1975).

11. For example, Maine's school finance reform was subsidized in large part by revenue-sharing movies. As Nathan and Adams report, the state decided at the beginning of the revenue-sharing program to use shared revenues as a means of meeting its goal of increasing the state's share of local school costs from one-third to one-half. See Richard P. Nathan and Charles F. Adams, Jr. et al., *Revenue Sharing: The Second Round* (Washington, D.C.: The Brookings Institution, 1977), p. 49.

12. For a detailed description of the federal revenue-sharing program and an excellent description of the events leading to its passage an implementation, see Richard P. Nathan et al., *Monitoring Revenue Sharing* (Washington, D.C.: The Brookings Institution, 1975).

13. Robert D. Reischauer, *General Revenue Sharing: Its Impact on and Relation to the Education Sector* (Washington, D.C.: U.S. Office of Education, June 1975).

14. Ibid., pp. 44–47.

15. "Bill Lets Locals Use Revenue Sharing for Education," *Education Daily,* 9 (April 21, 1976).

16. Ibid.

17. See Department of the Treasury, General Accounting Office, *Revenue Sharing Fund Impact on Midwestern Townships and New England Counties* (Washington, D.C.: Department of the Treasury, April 22, 1976), pp. i–iv.

18. These fears were expressed early during introduction of the first revenue-sharing bill. Wilbur Mills, then Chairman of the House Ways and Means Committee, detailed the provisions proposed and addressed the omission of education from the legislation by saying, "There is an additional reason (why school districts are omitted from the legislation). If they had been included in the bill, there would be considerable danger that (the annual grant) to local governments would be spread so thin that it would not be effective in accomplishing its purpose." 118 *Congressional Record H5879* (Daily Edition, June 21, 1972).

19. In 1974–1975 local revenues for public elementary and secondary education amounted to about $29.7 billion. This was about 30.4 percent of the approximately $97.8 billion of total local own-source revenues recorded for the same period. Source for total local education revenues: National Center for Educational Statistics, *Digest of Education Statistics 1975 Edition*, Table 63; Source for local own-source revenues: U.S. Bureau of the Census, *Governmental Finances in 1974–1975*, Series GF 75-5, Table 4.

20. Of course this division would vary by state with some states absorbing more and others less than 50 percent of all public service expenditures. See, Richard Nathan et al., op. cit., pp. 151–155.

DATA SOURCES USED FOR TABLE 5-2

Income/Enrollment—1974 aggregate personal income: Department of Health, Education, and Welfare, National Center for Educational Statistics, *Digest of Education Statistics, 1975*; 1975 fall enrollment for elementary and secondary public schools; Department of Health, Education, and Welfare, National Center for Educational Statistics, *Statistics of Public Elementary and Secondary Day School*, Fall 1975.

Nonfederal Revenue/Enrollment—Composite of state and local revenue receipts for 1975–1976 per total elementary and secondary fall 1975 enrollment. Department of Health, Education, and Welfare, National Center for Educational Statistics, *Statistics of Public Elementary and Secondary Day Schools*, Fall 1975, Tables 10, 4.

Federal Revenue/Enrollment—Federal revenue receipts for 1975–1976 per total elementary and secondary fall 1975–1976 enrollment. Department of Health, Education, and Welfare, National Center for Educational Statistics, *Statistics of Public Elementary and Secondary Day Schools*, Fall 1975, Tables 10, 4.

Total Revenue/Enrollment—Aggregate of federal, state, and local revenue receipts for 1975–1976 per total elementary and secondary fall 1975–1976 enrollment. Department of Health, Education, and Welfare, National Center for Educational Statistics, *Statistics of Public Elementary and Secondary Day Schools,* Fall 1975, Tables 10, 4.

Nonfederal Revenue/Personal Income—Composite of state and local revenue receipts divided by 1974 total aggregate personal income. Department of Health, Education, and Welfare, National Center for Educational Statistics, *Statistics of Public Elementary and Secondary Day Schools,* Fall 1975; Department of Health, Education, and Welfare, National Center for Educational Statistics, *Digest of Educational Statistics,* 1975.

DATA SOURCES USED FOR TABLE 5-6: SELECTED MEASURES OF STATE NEED AND CAPACITY

Income/Enrollment—1974 aggregate personal income: Department of Health, Education, and Welfare, National Center of Educational Statistics, *Digest of Education Statistics,* 1975; 1975 fall enrollment for elementary and secondary public schools: Department of Health, Education, and Welfare, National Center for Educational Statistics, *Statistics of Public Elementary and Secondary Day Schools,* Fall 1975.

Estimated General Revenue Capacity—Richard P. Nathan, Allen D. Manvel, and Susannah E. Calkins, *Monitoring Revenue Sharing,* (Washington, D.C.: Brookings Institution, 1975), Table B-4 restated as a per pupil measure using enrollment.

Average Teachers Salary—for classroom teachers. Department of Health, Education, and Welfare, National Center for Education Statistics, *Statistics of Public Elementary and Secondary Day Schools,* Fall 1975.

Enrollment/Teachers—1975 fall enrollment for elementary and secondary public schools; 1975 total professional educational staff: Department of Health, Education, and Welfare, National Center for Educational Statistics, *Statistics of Public Elementary and Secondary Day Schools,* Fall 1975.

Percent Disadvantaged—Composite based on percent Title I children and percent children with Limited English Speaking Ability (LESA) as a proportion of total elementary and secondary enrollment. Title I children, preliminary statistics from Department of Health, Education, and Welfare, Office of Education, P.L. 89–10 Title I, Part A, fiscal year 1976. LESA figures are restructured from the U.S. Bureau of the Census, Census of the Population: *1970 General Social and Economic Characteristics,* Final Report PC(1)–CI US Summary, Table 146, 147.

Title I Revenue per Pupil—Estimated total Title I funds under provision of P.L. 89–10, Title I, Part A, as amended, school year 1976–1977. (Fiscal Year 1977) per total elementary and secondary public school enrollment, school year 1975–1976. Department of Health, Education, and Welfare, National Center for Educational Statistics, *Statistics of Public Elementary and Secondary Day Schools,* Fall. 1975.

APPENDIX 5-A

Table 5A-1 in this appendix shows selected fiscal variables for each state, region, and for the entire nation. The district classifications are identical to those in Tables 5-1 and 5-4. The regional groupings are for each of the four principal U.S. Census geographic regions: Northeast, Middle West, South, and West. The entries for each region and the nation are computed by weighting the corresponding entries for each state by the respective number of pupils. By including variables showing personal income on a per pupil and per capita basis, the appendix table augments the text tables. These income measures should be of a general interest to many readers.

Table 5A–1. Selected Fiscal Characteristics for School Districts, by States, 1970

	EPV PER ADA (A)	EPV PER POP (B)	INC PER ADA (C)	INC PER POP (D)	DISAD (E)	AVG TEACH SAL (F)	LOC REV/ ADA (G)	ST REV/ ADA (H)	SAL REV/ ADA (I)	FED REV/ ADA (J)	TOTAL REV/ ADA (K)	LOC REV/ EPV (L)
ALABAMA												
EQUALIZED PROPERTY VALUE PER ADA												
LOW 25%	—	—	—	—	—	—	—	—	—	—	—	—
MIDDLE 50%	—	—	—	—	—	—	—	—	—	—	—	—
HIGH 25%	—	—	—	—	—	—	—	—	—	—	—	—
DEGREE OF URBANIZATION												
CENTRAL CITY	—	—	12355.	2658.	27.33	7513.0	126.4	274.5	400.9	69.4	470.3	—
LARGEST CI	—	—	11387.	2419.	29.21	7377.8	125.5	273.6	399.1	50.0	449.1	—
SURBURBAN*	—	—	10740.	2408.	24.49	7291.0	125.7	282.0	407.7	66.5	474.2	—
NON METRO**	—	—	9071.	2018.	33.70	6775.2	99.5	310.0	409.5	85.2	494.7	—
AVERAGE	—	—	10366.	2284.	29.93	7140.2	112.8	293.9	406.7	76.7	483.4	—
ALASKA												
EQUALIZED PROPERTY VALUE PER ADA												
LOW 25%	—	—	—	—	—	—	—	—	—	—	—	—
MIDDLE 50%	—	—	—	—	—	—	—	—	—	—	—	—
HIGH 25%	—	—	—	—	—	—	—	—	—	—	—	—
DEGREE OR URBANIZATION												
CENTRAL CITY	—	—	—	—	—	—	—	—	—	—	—	—
LARGEST CI	—	—	—	—	—	—	—	—	—	—	—	—
SURBURBAN*	—	—	—	—	—	—	—	—	—	—	—	—
NON METRO**	—	—	16244.	3755.	20.52	11099.2	308.2	703.5	1011.7	302.0	1313.7	—
AVERAGE	—	—	16244.	3755.	20.52	11099.2	308.2	703.5	1011.7	302.0	1313.7	—
ARIZONA												
EQUALIZED PROPERTY VALUE PER ADA												
LOW 25%	4059.	842.	12594.	2467.	29.38	8292.8	115.0	436.8	551.8	89.8	641.6	0.0290
MIDDLE 50%	8989.	1297.	22445.	3011.	24.45	9462.3	302.0	396.5	698.5	58.5	757.0	0.0350
HIGH 25%	23238.	2032.	43441.	3071.	21.83	10132.2	461.4	455.0	916.4	69.8	986.2	0.0220
DEGREE OF URBANIZATION												
CENTRAL CITY	13762.	1166.	34985.	2984.	26.40	10546.7	413.9	442.0	855.9	65.7	921.6	0.0340
LARGEST CI	7370.	989.	22199.	2979.	24.67	10267.9	304.9	398.3	703.2	50.4	759.6	0.0410
SUBURBANa	9051.	1247.	24264.	3146.	18.08	9113.8	261.1	420.3	681.4	33.4	714.8	0.0310
NON METROb	13696.	1779.	18674.	2300.	37.63	8284.6	259.3	404.8	664.1	143.4	807.5	0.0260
AVERAGE	11318.	1367.	25231.	2890.	25.03	9337.3	295.1	421.1	716.3	69.2	785.4	0.0300

aIncludes all noncenter-city metropolitan area.
bIncludes rural and all other nonmetropolitan area.

Table 5A–1. (continued)

	EPV PER ADA (A)	EPV PER POP (B)	INC PER ADA (C)	INC PER POP (D)	DISAD (E)	AVG TEACH SAL (F)	LOC REV/ ADA (G)	ST REV/ ADA (H)	SAL REV/ ADA (I)	FED REV/ ADA (J)	TOTAL REV/ ADA (K)	LOC REV/ EPV (L)
ARKANSAS												
EQUALIZED PROPERTY VALUE PER ADA												
LOW 25%	3277.	806.	7647.	1793.	38.53	6262.9	137.4	253.0	390.4	99.2	489.7	0.0420
MIDDLE 50%	4835.	1060.	9786.	2096.	30.95	6436.2	214.3	232.9	447.2	90.1	537.3	0.0440
HIGH 25%	7410.	1450.	13118.	2473.	28.64	6865.3	323.3	198.6	521.9	64.1	586.0	0.0440
DEGREE OF URBANIZATION												
CENTRAL CITY	7305.	1342.	15293.	2807.	23.51	6911.8	345.5	182.0	527.3	59.8	587.3	0.0480
LARGEST CI	8828.	1567.	17633.	3130.	23.17	7287.0	402.3	168.8	571.2	53.0	624.1	0.0460
SUBURBAN *	3721.	1004.	7953.	2071.	32.75	6336.5	177.0	227.1	404.1	68.2	492.3	0.0470
NON METRO **	4891.	1058.	9383.	1969.	34.13	6450.8	204.6	240.5	445.1	91.3	536.4	0.0420
AVERAGE	5089.	1094.	10084.	2115.	32.27	6500.1	222.3	229.4	451.7	85.9	537.6	0.0440
CALIFORNIA												
EQUALIZED PROPERTY VALUE PER ADA												
LOW 25%	6568.	1791.	11868.	3204.	17.18	11290.7	340.1	411.6	751.7	54.3	806.0	0.0520
MIDDLE 50%	12038.	2530.	17811.	3620.	21.73	11756.4	560.3	304.9	865.2	47.5	912.7	0.0460
HIGH 25%	23668.	3366.	30272.	3918.	19.51	12454.2	781.1	256.2	1037.3	42.9	1080.2	0.0360
DEGREE OF URBANIZATION												
CENTRAL CITY	13838.	2393.	20441.	3645.	24.00	12446.5	607.2	319.4	926.6	57.6	984.2	0.0460
LARGEST CI	14146.	2493.	21743.	3832.	27.24	11871.1	698.7	313.7	1012.4	53.8	1066.2	0.0490
SUBURBAN *	13165.	2553.	19336.	3634.	16.44	11625.5	521.3	325.3	846.6	40.0	886.6	0.0450
NON METRO **	16475.	3689.	13261.	2860.	21.12	10419.1	548.4	271.5	819.8	45.3	865.1	0.0360
AVERAGE	13577.	2554.	19440.	3591.	20.04	11814.2	560.5	319.4	879.8	48.0	927.9	0.0450
COLORADO												
EQUALIZED PROPERTY VALUE PER ADA												
LOW 25%	5445.	1545.	10672.	2843.	18.10	8060.8	346.2	278.7	624.9	79.4	704.3	0.0650
MIDDLE 50%	8582.	2031.	13347.	3123.	15.01	8404.4	525.2	236.6	761.8	52.8	814.7	0.0620
HIGH 25%	16366.	3161.	18995.	3524.	21.54	9744.1	771.3	165.2	936.6	62.2	998.7	0.0490
DEGREE OF URBANIZATION												
CENTRAL CITY	12435.	2239.	17999.	3261.	22.26	9718.0	657.1	191.5	848.6	84.1	932.7	0.0530
LARGEST CI	15105.	2534.	20968.	3545.	23.50	10358.1	798.0	156.0	954.1	78.4	1030.4	0.0530
SUBURBAN *	7169.	1917.	13102.	3390.	11.61	8414.7	495.7	246.0	741.7	52.7	794.4	0.0700
NON METRO **	11044.	2582.	11582.	2662.	21.64	7886.4	495.6	242.0	737.6	53.0	790.6	0.0490
AVERAGE	9744.	2192.	14090.	3153.	17.42	8653.4	542.0	229.3	771.3	61.8	833.1	0.0590

Table 5A-1. (continued)

	EPV PER ADA (A)	EPV PER POP (B)	INC PER ADA (C)	INC PER POP (D)	DISAD (E)	AVG TEACH SAL (F)	LOC REV/ ADA (G)	ST REV/ ADA (H)	SAL REV/ ADA (I)	FED REV/ ADA (J)	TOTAL REV/ ADA (K)	LOC REV/ EPV (L)
									CONNECTICUT			
EQUALIZED PROPERTY VALUE PER ADA												
LOW 25%	22130.	5360.	14796.	3514.	14.15	8936.0	515.3	260.7	775.9	22.6	798.6	0.0250
MIDDLE 50%	41270.	8562.	18770.	3889.	15.45	9619.6	694.1	211.1	905.3	23.4	928.7	0.0170
HIGH 25%	66246.	12287.	24525.	4584.	19.45	10698.5	790.4	214.5	1004.9	41.0	1046.0	0.0120
DEGREE OF URBANIZATION												
CENTRAL CITY	48732.	8364.	20095.	3502.	24.11	9942.9	686.5	208.8	895.3	59.8	955.1	0.0150
LARGEST CI	68192.	11761.	17901.	3087.	34.24	10865.7	704.5	294.8	1061.4	67.1	1129.5	0.0110
SUBURBAN*	41978.	9318.	19412.	4323.	12.29	9782.9	704.3	217.8	922.1	13.9	936.0	0.0190
NON METRO**	35474.	7669.	17400.	3817.	13.37	8931.0	578.6	264.0	842.7	12.3	855.0	0.0200
AVERAGE	42733.	8693.	19215.	3969.	16.13	9718.4	673.5	224.4	897.9	27.6	925.5	0.0180
									DELAWARE			
EQUALIZED PROPERTY VALUE PER ADA												
LOW 25%	15003.	3779.	10932.	2754.	14.12	8943.1	170.6	563.5	734.1	75.1	809.2	0.0110
MIDDLE 50%	21242.	4766.	14888.	3307.	11.15	9430.1	238.9	587.8	826.7	15.6	842.3	0.0110
HIGH 25%	31798.	6140.	19011.	3647.	23.33	10837.9	319.3	627.4	946.8	89.7	1036.6	0.0100
DEGREE OF URBANIZATION												
CENTRAL CITY	30800.	5178.	17632.	2964.	34.97	11979.5	323.3	669.7	993.0	164.0	1157.0	0.0100
LARGEST CI	30800.	5178.	17632.	2964.	34.97	11979.5	323.3	669.7	993.0	164.0	1157.0	0.0100
SUBURBAN*	21516.	4686.	17017.	3709.	8.88	9705.2	282.4	580.8	863.2	6.4	869.6	0.0100
NON METRO**	20806.	5048.	10601.	2604.	18.18	8810.8	148.5	583.1	731.6	60.5	812.1	0.0070
AVERAGE	22321.	4863.	14929.	3254.	14.94	9660.2	242.0	591.6	833.6	49.0	882.6	0.0110
									DISTRICT OF COLUMBIA			
EQUALIZED PROPERTY VALUE PER ADA												
LOW 25%												
MIDDLE 50%					"NOT APPLICABLE"							
HIGH 25%												
DEGREE OF URBANIZATION												
CENTRAL CITY												
LARGEST CITY												
SUBURBAN*												
NON METRO**												
AVERAGE												

Table 5A–1. (continued)

	EPV PER ADA (A)	EPV PER POP (B)	INC PER ADA (C)	INC PER POP (D)	DISAD (E)	AVG TEACH SAL (F)	LOC REV/ ADA (G)	ST REV/ ADA (H)	SAL REV/ ADA (I)	FED REV/ ADA (J)	TOTAL REV/ ADA (K)	LOC REV/ EPV (L)
FLORIDA												
EQUALIZED PROPERTY VALUE PER ADA												
LOW 25%	14996.	3513.	11548.	2684.	23.46	8273.6	103.6	486.5	670.1	82.9	753.0	0.0130
MIDDLE 50%	23958.	4555.	15934.	2959.	24.13	9855.2	290.7	482.1	772.8	71.8	844.6	0.0120
HIGH 25%	35630.	6336.	19934.	3480.	23.38	9576.7	429.1	453.2	882.3	58.0	940.3	0.0120
DEGREE OF URBANIZATION												
CENTRAL CITY	20317.	3899.	14595.	2801.	22.54	8227.0	263.5	486.8	750.3	65.7	816.0	0.0130
LARGEST CI	20091.	3862.	14422.	2786.	22.63	8227.0	254.7	482.5	737.2	70.6	807.8	0.0130
SUBURBAN*	25488.	4643.	18152.	3308.	22.97	10046.3	320.0	466.8	786.8	69.4	0.0130	0.0110
NON METRO**	24322.	5097.	12449.	2616.	25.35	8418.8	272.8	468.0	760.8	75.1	835.9	0.0110
AVERAGE	24635.	4739.	15838.	3020.	23.77	9395.2	298.5	476.0	774.5	71.1	843.6	0.0120
GEORGIA												
EQUALIZED PROPERTY VALUE PER ADA												
LOW 25%	16573.	3999.	9108.	2107.	29.69	6639.2	113.1	350.9	464.0	66.7	530.7	0.0070
MIDDLE 50%	23852.	5572.	10762.	2479.	24.99	7161.8	187.1	326.8	513.9	67.5	581.4	0.0080
HIGH 25%	37037.	7741.	16431.	3384.	18.48	8221.8	394.8	283.6	678.4	39.3	717.7	0.0110
DEGRESS OF URBANIZATION												
CENTRAL CITY	36192.	7791.	12546.	2909.	27.11	8216.1	345.2	289.6	634.8	65.5	700.3	0.0090
LARGEST CI	46079.	10006.	14871.	3229.	28.23	8957.9	488.2	255.7	744.0	52.9	796.9	0.0110
SUBURBAN*	26394.	5711.	15293.	3249.	14.09	7613.4	277.7	307.0	564.7	62.0	636.7	0.0100
NON METRO**	21349.	5066.	9489.	2185.	28.78	6730.4	153.0	339.7	492.7	62.5	555.3	0.0070
AVERAGE	25328.	5721.	11765.	2612.	24.54	7296.1	220.5	322.1	542.5	60.2	602.8	0.0080
HAWAII												
EQUALIZED PROPERTY VALUE PER ADA												
LOW 25%												
MIDDLE 50%												
HIGH 25%												
						"NOT APPLICABLE"						
DEGREE OF URBANIZATION												
CENTRAL CITY												
LARGEST CI												
SUBURBAN*												
NON METRO**												
AVERAGE												

Table 5A-1. (continued)

	EPV PER ADA (A)	EPV PER POP (B)	INC PER ADA (C)	INC PER POP (D)	DISAD (E)	AVG. TEACH SAL (F)	LOC REV/ ADA (G)	ST REV/ ADA (H)	SAL REV/ ADA (I)	FED REV/ ADA (J)	TOTAL REV/ ADA (K)	LOC REV/ EPV (L)
IDAHO												
EQUALIZED PROPERTY VALUE PER ADA												
LOW 25%	12674.	3192.	10599.	2636.	15.06	6995.4	164.5	316.9	491.4	76.4	567.8	0.0140
MIDDLE 50%	16922.	4136.	11291.	2671.	14.08	7051.7	240.3	301.3	541.6	42.2	583.8	0.0140
HIGH 25%	27358.	21244.	10178.	2465.	16.02	6760.1	313.9	254.1	568.0	72.4	640.3	0.0120
DEGREE OF URBANIZATION												
CENTRAL CITY	17130.	3700.	14825.	3202.	10.24	0.0	274.5	290.3	564.7	27.9	592.7	0.0160
LARGEST CI	17130.	3700.	14825.	3202.	10.24	0.0	274.5	290.3	564.7	27.9	592.7	0.0160
SUBURBAN*	15637.	4124.	10256.	2731.	12.47	5298.3	183.6	274.4	458.0	20.9	478.9	0.0120
NON METRO**	18735.	8928.	10274.	2522.	15.53	7007.4	239.0	294.4	533.4	63.6	597.0	0.0130
AVERAGE	18469.	8177.	10840.	2611.	14.81	6964.7	242.2	293.4	535.6	58.3	593.9	0.0130
ILLINOIS												
EQUALIZED PROPERTY VALUE PER ADA												
LOW 25%	39956.	28699.	19475.	3206.	12.44	8788.0	514.8	407.5	922.3	28.5	950.8	0.0150
MIDDLE 50%	61467.	11206.	21015.	3412.	18.55	9724.1	676.9	350.5	1027.4	54.7	1082.01	0.0110
HIGH 25%	153614.	15167.	45350.	3910.	11.76	9455.6	1182.8	179.2	1362.0	20.3	1382.3	0.0080
DEGREE OF ORGANIZATION												
CENTRAL CITY	59905.	8889.	22996.	3409.	26.25	10708.9	731.0	372.6	1103.6	82.9	1186.4	0.0120
LARGEST CI	61672.	8821.	23796.	3404.	29.50	10753.9	752.9	370.1	1123.0	94.2	1217.2	0.0120
SUBURBAN*	91624.	22286.	32843.	3833.	11.00	9081.4	843.5	296.8	1140.3	22.5	1162.9	0.0110
NON METRO**	72504.	12277.	16949.	2776.	12.72	8297.3	614.7	321.5	936.2	29.0	965.2	0.0090
AVERAGE	79123.	16569.	26712.	3485.	15.32	9422.9	762.8	322.0	1084.7	39.5	1124.3	0.0110
INDIANA												
EQUALIZED PROPERTY VALUE PER ADA												
LOW 25%	21632.	5008.	12978.	2985.	8.83	9474.8	296.0	301.6	597.6	23.0	620.5	0.0140
MIDDLE 50%	31179.	6791.	14352.	3085.	12.54	10406.9	402.9	264.9	667.8	27.5	695.3	0.0130
HIGH 25%	46852.	10195.	15156.	3239.	10.53	10210.9	516.2	211.7	723.0	12.5	740.5	0.0120
DEGREE OF URBANIZATION												
CENTRAL CITY	33388.	6906.	14972.	3082.	15.59	11264.1	410.1	254.8	664.9	37.6	702.5	0.0130
LARGEST CI	30020.	6454.	14148.	3042.	16.27	11311.4	437.6	260.7	698.3	36.2	734.5	0.0150
SUBURBAN**	32385.	7282.	14910.	3310.	8.19	9697.8	425.8	263.9	689.7	18.0	707.7	0.0130
NON METRO**	32448.	7353.	12992.	2928.	10.05	9583.7	381.5	263.0	644.4	14.6	659.1	1.0140
AVERAGE	32709.	7196.	14209.	3098.	11.11	10124.7	404.5	260.8	665.3	22.6	687.9	0.0130

Table 5A-1. (continued)

	EPV PER ADA (A)	EPV PER POP (B)	INC PER ADA (C)	INC PER POP (D)	DISAD (E)	AVG TEACH SAL (F)	LOC REV/ ADA (G)	ST REV/ ADA (H)	SAL REV/ ADA (I)	FED REV/ ADA (J)	TOTAL REV/ ADA (K)	LOC REV/ EPV (L)
IOWA												
EQUALIZED PROPERTY VALUE PER ADA												
LOW 25%	33372.	7279.	14381.	3131.	11.32	10070.5	660.5	258.8	919.2	30.5	949.7	0.0200
MIDDLE 50%	47885.	10988.	12636.	2787.	13.92	9020.6	653.0	248.0	901.0	28.4	929.4	0.0140
HIGH 25%	76971.	17514.	12236.	2718.	16.55	8176.9	771.2	239.4	1010.5	31.3	1041.9	0.0100
DEGREE OF URBANIZATION												
CENTRAL CITY	37788.	7595.	15854.	3186.	11.47	9959.0	683.9	274.8	958.7	31.9	990.5	0.0180
LARGEST CI	38432.	7687.	16927.	3386.	11.56	11026.6	624.6	301.7	926.3	42.4	968.7	0.0160
SUBURBAN *	48901.	10023.	13577.	2674.	13.56	8425.4	691.0	258.3	949.4	27.6	976.9	0.0170
NON METRO **	56791.	13492.	11854.	2740.	14.84	8941.5	682.8	237.2	920.0	29.5	949.5	0.0130
AVERAGE	51528.	11692.	12972.	2855.	13.93	9072.0	684.4	248.5	932.9	29.7	962.6	0.0150
KANSAS												
EQUALIZED PROPERTY VALUE PER ADA												
LOW 25%	7418.	1663.	14298.	3033.	13.62	8881.0	385.0	271.0	656.0	82.5	738.5	0.0540
MIDDLE 50%	11071.	2309.	15172.	3093.	12.36	8178.1	395.0	260.6	655.7	48.4	704.1	0.0370
HIGH 25%	27473.	6427.	10856.	2471.	18.56	7754.8	593.6	291.2	884.8	39.3	924.1	0.0240
DEGREE OF URBANIZATION												
CENTRAL CITY	8635.	1711.	15934.	3155.	15.50	9122.9	422.2	261.5	683.7	70.2	753.9	0.0490
LARGEST CI	8524.	1739.	16273.	3300.	14.01	9672.9	436.4	286.7	723.1	61.5	784.9	0.0510
SUBURBAN *	10921.	2614.	14932.	3560.	8.18	8433.4	442.0	248.1	690.0	55.0	745.0	0.0460
NON METRO **	17944.	4016.	12590.	2571.	16.09	7807.3	450.6	283.9	734.5	48.0	782.5	0.0300
AVERAGE	14258.	3177.	13875.	2922.	14.22	8248.0	442.2	270.9	713.0	54.7	767.7	0.0380
KENTUCKY												
EQUALIZED PROPERTY VALUE PER ADA												
LOW 25%	14568.	3175.	7825.	1629.	44.05	7076.1	81.1	411.9	493.0	131.8	624.9	0.0050
MIDDLE 50%	29522.	5860.	13081.	2524.	21.77	7300.6	219.1	371.9	590.9	80.8	671.7	0.0070
HIGH 25%	39072.	7358.	15093.	2810.	19.39	8219.8	347.5	329.7	677.2	51.0	728.2	0.0090
DEGREE OF URBANIZATION												
CENTRAL CITY	35305.	6379.	15228.	2751.	25.51	8992.2	347.1	324.4	671.5	63.7	735.2	0.0100
LARGEST CI	35251.	6394.	14967.	2715.	28.27	9258.9	363.7	318.8	682.4	63.4	745.9	0.0100
SUBURBAN *	34205.	6433.	16739.	3136.	11.07	7858.2	331.0	325.8	657.8	34.9	692.7	0.0100
NON METRO **	24492.	5066.	9905.	1987.	33.63	7075.8	147.7	397.6	545.3	111.4	655.7	0.0060
AVERAGE	28171.	5563.	12270.	2372.	26.74	7474.2	216.7	371.3	588.0	66.1	674.1	0.0070

Table 5A-1. (continued)

	EPV PER ADA (A)	EPV PER POP (B)	INC PER ADA (C)	INC PER POP (D)	DISAD (E)	AVG TEACH SAL (F)	LOC REV/ ADA (G)	ST REV/ ADA (H)	SAL REV/ ADA (I)	FED REV/ ADA (J)	TOTAL REV/ ADA (K)	LOC REV/ EPV (L)
LOUISIANA												
EQUALIZED PROPERTY VALUE PER ADA												
LOW 25%	—	—	—	—	—	—	—	—	—	—	—	—
MIDDLE 50%	—	—	—	—	—	—	—	—	—	—	—	—
HIGH 25%	—	—	—	—	—	—	—	—	—	—	—	—
DEGREE OF URBANIZATION												
CENTRAL CITY	—	—	13872.	2683.	33.50	8114.1	311.8	379.7	691.5	48.8	740.3	0.0190
LARGEST CI	—	—	16835.	2714.	39.66	8395.4	301.2	361.7	662.9	69.3	732.3	0.0180
SUBURBAN *	—	—	12905.	2664.	23.37	7190.6	259.2	401.9	661.2	92.6	713.8	0.0180
NON METRO **	—	—	7908.	1831.	47.10	7334.4	183.2	453.4	636.6	77.9	714.6	—
AVERAGE	—	—	10722.	2551.	38.40	7546.1	237.2	421.0	658.1	64.2	722.3	0.0180
MAINE												
EQUALIZED PROPERTY VALUE PER ADA												
LOW 25%	11764.	3347.	8077.	2249.	23.49	7264.4	228.9	457.6	686.5	53.3	739.8	0.0190
MIDDLE 50%	20981.	5058.	10920.	2605.	17.23	8017.9	383.5	287.8	671.3	36.5	707.8	0.0180
HIGH 25%	34297.	7513.	13298.	2795.	20.77	7913.3	624.9	156.2	781.1	37.1	818.2	0.0180
DEGREE OF URBANIZATION												
CENTRAL CITY	29326.	5604.	14259.	2736.	24.48	8039.4	504.8	148.9	653.7	41.4	695.2	0.0170
LARGEST CI	30325.	6077.	14008.	2802.	21.32	8584.6	590.6	155.4	746.0	50.9	796.9	0.0190
SUBURBAN *	24794.	6017.	12781.	3111.	9.58	8350.2	563.3	221.5	784.8	25.2	810.0	0.0230
NON METRO **	20210.	5057.	9851.	2446.	20.36	7665.7	362.1	336.8	698.9	43.2	742.1	0.0180
AVERAGE	22009.	5245.	10803.	2563.	19.68	7803.3	405.3	297.3	702.6	40.8	743.5	0.0180
MARYLAND												
EQUALIZED PROPERTY VALUE PER ADA												
LOW 25%	21392.	4114.	14884.	2834.	26.19	9772.1	497.3	431.2	928.5	79.4	1007.9	0.0230
MIDDLE 50%	28456.	6080.	15972.	3403.	10.79	9455.0	581.5	336.5	918.0	62.5	980.4	0.0200
HIGH 25%	41880.	9034.	21281.	4549.	10.04	11253.1	776.0	330.0	1106.0	62.6	1168.6	0.0190
DEGREE OF URBANIZATION												
CENTRAL CITY	21446.	3945.	15619.	2873.	27.55	10117.3	537.1	432.8	970.0	75.6	1045.6	0.0250
LARGEST CI	21446.	3945.	15619.	2873.	27.55	10117.3	537.1	432.8	970.0	75.6	1045.6	0.0250
SUBURBAN *	33665.	7212.	18720.	3996.	9.44	10221.7	675.1	318.8	993.9	58.2	1052.1	0.0200
NON METRO **	26897.	5906.	12297.	2668.	17.95	8913.8	445.9	418.3	864.2	88.1	952.4	0.0170
AVERAGE	30046.	6327.	17027.	3547.	14.55	9985.0	609.1	358.6	967.6	66.7	1034.4	0.0210

Table 5A-1. (continued)

	EPV PER ADA (A)	EPV PER POP (B)	INC PER ADA (C)	INC PER POP (D)	DISAD (E)	AVG TEACH SAL (F)	LOC REV/ ADA (G)	ST REV/ ADA (H)	SAL REV/ ADA (I)	FED REV/ ADA (J)	TOTAL REV/ ADA (K)	LOC REV/ EPV (L)
MASSACHUSETTS												
EQUALIZED PROPERTY VALUE PER ADA												
LOW 25%	20411.	4265.	15060.	3028.	17.15	9320.2	632.7	244.5	877.1	49.0	926.1	0.0310
MIDDLE 50%	27875.	5194.	19079.	3371.	16.36	9838.3	818.2	235.8	1053.9	35.2	1089.1	0.0300
HIGH 25%	49463.	8435.	25194.	3983.	14.15	9825.7	1020.1	155.3	1175.3	27.1	1202.4	0.0220
DEGREE OF URBANIZATION												
CENTRAL CITY	24408.	3651.	20715.	3037.	24.42	10001.5	706.9	264.4	971.3	67.5	1038.7	0.0290
LARGEST CI	25032.	3120.	24699.	3078.	27.49	10577.8	798.3	308.8	1107.1	73.0	1180.0	0.0320
SUBURBAN *	31718.	6295.	18905.	3685.	12.52	9746.8	882.6	209.6	1092.2	22.3	1114.5	0.0290
NON METRO **	40027.	6946.	20407.	3160.	16.06	9100.7	778.7	181.1	959.8	42.1	1001.9	0.0230
AVERAGE	31404.	5772.	19602.	3438.	16.00	9705.5	822.2	217.8	1040.0	36.6	1076.6	0.0280
MICHIGAN												
EQUALIZED PROPERTY VALUE PER ADA												
LOW 25%	11202.	2766.	12521.	3032.	11.23	10274.4	352.2	507.0	859.3	20.7	880.0	0.0320
MIDDLE 50%	17638.	3755.	15897.	3319.	15.16	11441.3	542.9	435.2	978.1	41.1	1019.3	0.0310
HIGH 25%	27916.	5701.	18856.	3744.	13.44	12437.0	837.3	397.0	1234.4	36.1	1270.5	0.0310
DEGREE OF URBANIZATION												
CENTRAL CITY	21021.	3720.	18506.	3246.	20.79	12977.5	624.4	433.3	1057.7	76.4	1134.2	0.3000
LARGEST CI	20203.	3433.	18895.	3210.	24.52	12997.7	488.7	429.4	918.1	93.9	1012.0	0.0240
SUBURBAN *	18505.	4232.	16149.	3660.	10.39	11361.4	606.3	446.3	1052.6	18.2	1070.8	0.0340
NON METRO **	16275.	3756.	12174.	2791.	13.80	9793.5	428.1	448.6	876.7	28.0	904.7	0.0270
AVERAGE	18598.	3994.	15792.	3354.	13.75	11398.2	568.8	443.6	1012.4	34.8	1047.2	0.0310
MINNESOTA												
EQUALIZED PROPERTY VALUE PER ADA												
LOW 25%	14054.	3828.	10571.	2830.	16.44	9513.4	398.8	500.0	898.8	45.3	944.2	0.0320
MIDDLE 50%	25979.	6233.	12819.	3076.	15.76	9900.4	491.1	462.3	953.4	33.4	986.7	0.0190
HIGH 25%	48770.	8983.	17738.	3012.	21.20	10239.8	587.8	340.2	928.0	64.5	992.5	0.0120
DEGREE OF URBANIZATION												
CENTRAL CITY	41215.	6418.	20959.	3363.	16.39	11187.6	608.5	303.7	912.1	74.6	986.7	0.0210
LARGEST CI	52689.	7702.	23883.	3478.	19.65	11656.2	717.6	247.7	965.3	78.9	1044.2	0.0140
SUBURBAN *	20640.	5335.	13764.	3579.	10.18	10230.6	505.3	477.6	982.9	16.9	999.8	0.0260
NON METRO **	30093.	7068.	10249.	2386.	23.35	9089.9	434.8	467.5	902.3	53.7	955.5	0.0160
AVERAGE	28694.	6319.	13487.	2998.	17.29	988.4	492.2	441.2	933.4	44.1	977.5	0.0210

Table 5A-1.   (continued)

	EPV PER ADA (A)	EPV PER POP (B)	INC PER ADA (C)	INC PER POP (D)	DISAD (E)	AVG TEACH SAL (F)	LOC REV/ ADA (G)	ST REV/ ADA (H)	SAL REV/ ADA (I)	FED REV/ ADA (J)	TOTAL REV/ ADA (K)	LOC REV/ EPV (L)
MISSISSIPPI												
EQUALIZED PROPERTY VALUE PER ADA												
LOW 25%	2903.	748.	7007.	1765.	42.95	6064.0	88.4	290.4	378.8	64.3	443.1	0.0320
MIDDLE 50%	4734.	1143.	7170.	1693.	47.30	6238.0	114.8	282.5	397.4	107.3	504.6	0.0250
HIGH 25%	10489.	2291.	11153.	2430.	32.36	7015.1	231.4	278.8	510.2	39.9	550.1	0.0220
DEGREE OF URBANIZATION												
CENTRAL CITY	11912.	2495.	13126.	2702.	27.28	7497.2	242.7	222.0	464.8	65.6	530.3	0.0190
LARGE CI	15053.	3201.	13420.	2853.	29.81	7921.3	320.5	263.9	584.4	29.7	614.1	0.0210
SUBURBAN *	4593.	1266.	7185.	1939.	34.06	6660.8	151.6	297.9	449.5	101.8	551.3	0.0340
NON METRO **	5020.	1188.	7568.	1788.	45.15	6203.0	122.6	290.2	412.8	79.6	492.4	0.0260
AVERAGE	5715.	1331.	8125.	1895.	42.48	6375.5	137.3	283.6	420.9	79.7	500.6	0.0260
MISSOURI												
EQUALIZED PROPERTY VALUE PER ADA												
LOW 25%	17552.	9848.	11614.	2816.	13.60	7392.9	259.2	321.7	580.9	55.1	636.0	0.0150
MIDDLE 50%	29897.	5963.	16135.	3169.	12.01	7984.9	450.3	264.9	715.1	37.0	752.1	0.0150
HIGH 25%	48523.	8431.	22270.	3759.	15.53	9127.3	675.3	228.8	904.1	36.6	940.7	0.0140
DEGREE OF URBANIZATION												
CENTRAL CITY	28133.	4953.	16197.	2849.	12.48	7912.4	391.7	277.0	668.7	29.4	698.1	0.0140
LARGEST CI	28111.	5107.	15644.	2842.	12.99	8558.0	411.6	282.2	693.8	31.0	724.8	0.0150
SUBURBAN *	33709.	6574.	18366.	3589.	10.20	8614.3	527.2	258.6	785.8	29.9	815.7	0.0160
NON METRO **	26591.	11011.	11781.	2392.	21.78	6819.0	298.6	298.2	596.8	76.1	673.0	0.0120
AVERAGE	31467.	7551.	16538.	3228.	13.29	8122.3	458.7	270.1	728.8	41.4	770.2	0.0150
MONTANA												
EQUALIZED PROPERTY VALUE PER ADA												
LOW 25%	4801.	850.	16596.	2881.	15.17	10771.0	247.5	252.6	500.2	172.6	672.8	0.0510
MIDDLE 50%	7475.	1197.	18147.	2700.	17.22	10155.1	285.9	221.3	507.3	43.1	550.3	0.0400
HIGH 25%	16004.	1144.	41696.	2803.	15.08	7493.8	400.3	256.2	656.5	56.3	712.8	0.0260
DEGREE OF URBANIZATION												
CENTRAL CITY	8936.	954.	25741.	2929.	14.91	10484.4	305.1	256.6	561.7	152.7	714.3	0.0420
LARGEST CI	5675.	929.	17794.	2921.	14.85	12330.0	270.9	256.8	527.7	193.3	721.0	0.0480
SURBURBAN *	11743.	1213.	24939.	2570.	18.88	7878.9	304.5	259.3	563.8	20.7	584.5	0.0270
NON METRO **	8921.	1145.	22772.	2727.	16.49	9431.7	304.9	229.5	534.4	54.2	588.6	0.0390
AVERAGE	8939.	1097.	23646.	2771.	16.18	9643.7	304.9	237.9	542.8	78.8	621.6	0.0390

Table 5A-1.   (continued)

	EPV PER ADA (A)	EPV PER POP (B)	INC PER ADA (C)	INC PER POP (D)	DISAD (E)	AVG TEACH SAL (F)	LOC REV/ ADA (G)	ST REV/ ADA (H)	SAL REV/ ADA (I)	FED REV/ ADA (J)	TOTAL REV/ ADA (K)	LOC REV/ EPV (L)
NEBRASKA												
EQUALIZED PROPERTY VALUE PER ADA												
LOW 25%	7316.	2003.	9773.	2870.	15.51	7627.6	378.3	146.5	524.7	65.6	590.4	0.0530
MIDDLE 50%	11693.	2342.	15998.	3054.	14.52	8141.6	493.3	145.5	658.8	36.8	675.7	0.0420
HIGH 25%	20749.	4709.	12071.	2691.	17.38	6954.1	623.9	131.3	755.1	27.1	782.3	0.0320
DEGREE OF URBANIZATION												
CENTRAL CITY	11681.	2055.	17784.	3133.	14.29	8390.0	497.7	150.2	647.9	35.7	683.5	0.0430
LARGEST CI	12270.	2130.	17914.	3110.	16.30	8332.9	482.9	148.4	631.3	16.3	647.6	0.0390
SUBURBAN*	10579.	2758.	12427.	3332.	9.46	7798.8	438.6	148.8	587.4	83.0	670.4	0.0460
NON METRO**	14201.	3354.	11125.	2580.	17.85	7202.3	512.8	135.6	648.4	33.9	682.3	0.0410
AVERAGE	12862.	2849.	13460.	2867.	15.48	7716.2	497.2	142.2	639.4	41.6	681.0	0.0420
NEVADA												
LOW 25%	2246.	500.	17870.	3805.	12.55	9313.6	532.7	297.7	830.3	42.8	873.1	0.3060
MIDDLE 50%	12918.	3087.	14727.	3515.	13.04	9866.5	452.4	341.5	793.9	94.1	888.0	0.0350
HIGH 25%	19668.	4671.	14125.	3361.	14.51	9424.1	576.5	330.9	907.4	86.2	993.6	0.0310
DEGREE OF URBANIZATION												
CENTRAL CITY	1683.	354.	18508.	3891.	12.33	9303.8	568.3	276.9	845.1	32.9	878.1	0.3380
LARGEST CI	1683.	354.	18508.	3891.	12.33	9303.8	568.3	276.9	845.1	32.9	878.1	0.3380
SUBURBAN*	13130.	3122.	14891.	3541.	13.17	10019.3	462.4	327.2	789.7	95.9	885.5	0.0350
NON METRO**	19928.	4779.	13206.	3194.	14.66	8817.3	547.9	386.3	934.2	83.9	1018.1	0.0290
AVERAGE	11937.	2836.	15362.	3549.	13.28	9617.7	503.5	327.9	831.4	79.3	910.7	0.1020
NEW HAMPSHIRE												
EQUALIZED PROPERTY VALUE PER ADA												
LOW 25%	16510.	4031.	11951.	2921.	13.39	7276.1	567.4	118.8	686.2	13.3	699.5	0.0350
MIDDLE 50%	25697.	5080.	15797.	3045.	14.36	7787.4	687.2	45.9	733.1	41.3	774.4	0.0270
HIGH 25%	43864.	7112.	20569.	3041.	16.50	7913.8	914.8	49.9	964.7	29.5	994.2	0.0210
DEGREE OF URBANIZATION												
CENTRAL CITY	31619.	4888.	19829.	3079.	20.91	7935.0	670.2	34.3	704.5	39.1	743.6	0.0210
LARGEST CI	34259.	5167.	19509.	2940.	22.58	8009.1	651.4	41.1	702.5	46.0	748.6	0.0190
SUBURBAN*	21342.	4518.	15111.	3228.	12.40	7528.6	711.8	65.0	776.8	14.2	791.0	0.0340
NON METRO**	27978.	5529.	13295.	2970.	13.55	7857.6	724.3	72.1	796.4	31.8	828.2	0.0280
AVERAGE	27942.	5326.	16028.	3013.	14.66	7691.2	714.1	65.1	779.3	31.3	810.6	0.0270

Table 5A-1. (continued)

	EPV PER ADA (A)	EPV PER POP (B)	INC PER ADA (C)	INC PER POP (D)	DISAD (E)	AVG TEACH SAL (F)	LOC REV/ ADA (G)	ST REV/ ADA (H)	SAL REV/ ADA (I)	FED REV/ ADA (J)	TOTAL REV/ ADA (K)	LOC REV/ EPV (L)
NEW JERSEY												
EQUALIZED PROPERTY VALUE PER ADA												
LOW 25%	19153.	3918.	17374.	3137.	15.71	8888.7	569.4	277.7	847.0	52.5	899.5	0.0300
MIDDLE 50%	30500.	5717.	21452.	3639.	17.00	9853.2	781.8	209.5	991.3	47.5	1038.9	0.0260
HIGH 25%	53754.	8500.	30006.	4618.	15.04	10672.8	961.0	161.3	1122.3	19.5	1141.9	0.0190
DEGREE OF URBANIZATION												
CENTRAL CITY	28646.	4315.	19064.	2861.	31.23	10257.7	615.8	293.6	909.4	129.1	1038.4	0.0230
LARGEST CI	25477.	4014.	15774.	2485.	38.31	10456.6	674.3	392.0	1066.3	181.4	1247.6	0.0260
SUBURBAN *	36255.	6283.	24337.	4016.	14.01	9850.6	805.8	204.4	1010.2	27.8	1038.0	0.0240
NON METRO **	29850.	6023.	20117.	3592.	13.88	9528.1	775.4	199.0	974.3	31.4	1005.8	0.0280
AVERAGE	33624.	5963.	22570.	3758.	16.19	9816.7	773.5	214.5	988.0	41.8	1029.7	0.0250
NEW MEXICO												
EQUALIZED PROPERTY VALUE PER ADA												
LOW 25%	4623.	1226.	8174.	2190.	48.20	7379.7	63.4	495.9	559.3	208.2	767.6	0.0140
MIDDLE 50%	7864.	1935.	10957.	2655.	36.35	7720.6	108.6	467.1	575.8	93.3	669.0	0.0140
HIGH 25%	18404.	5071.	8161.	2201.	41.61	7936.3	138.9	520.3	659.2	109.4	768.6	0.0080
DEGREE OF URBANIZATION												
CENTRAL CITY	7931.	1901.	11962.	2867.	31.88	7932.7	104.3	455.2	559.5	79.2	638.7	0.0130
LARGEST CI	7931.	1901.	11962.	2867.	31.88	7932.7	104.3	455.2	559.5	79.2	638.7	0.0130
SUBURBAN *	0.	0.	0.		0.0	0.0	0.0	0.0	0.0	0.0	0.0	0.0
NON METRO **	10444.	2817.	8532.	2236.	44.39	7584.4	105.2	501.6	606.7	146.2	752.9	0.012
AVERAGE	9689.	2542.	9562.	2425.	40.63	7689.0	104.9	487.6	592.5	126.0	718.6	0.0120
NEW YORK												
EQUALIZED PROPERTY VALUE PER ADA												
LOW 25%	15447.	5563.	12309.	3009.	12.65	10561.1	406.3	866.9	1273.2	21.4	1294.0	0.0260
MIDDLE 50%	33083.	6970.	21074.	3697.	18.14	11399.6	697.7	629.4	1327.2	50.7	1377.9	0.0220
HIGH 25%	53135.	7270.	31247.	4030.	30.66	11750.9	977.0	573.2	1550.3	102.7	1652.9	0.0180
DEGREE OF URBANIZATION												
CENTRAL CITY	46004.	5563.	30442.	3611.	33.20	11333.6	799.5	616.8	1416.4	118.4	1534.7	0.0170
LARGEST CI	49517.	5728.	32169.	3721.	35.48	11301.0	569.7	621.1	1490.0	119.7	1610.6	0.0180
SUBURBAN *	27894.	7112.	17829.	3844.	12.14	11571.9	691.9	673.8	1365.7	21.4	1387.1	0.0260
NON METRO **	22221.	5129.	12423.	2818.	14.76	10191.0	460.2	812.5	1272.7	28.7	1301.4	0.0210
AVERAGE	33687.	6273.	21426.	3608.	19.90	11277.7	694.7	674.7	1369.4	56.4	1425.8	0.0220

Table 5A–1.   (continued)

	EPV PER ADA (A)	EPV PER POP (B)	INC PER ADA (C)	INC PER POP (D)	DISAD (E)	AVG TEACH SAL (F)	LOC REV/ ADA (G)	ST REV/ ADA (H)	SAL REV/ ADA (I)	FED REV/ ADA (J)	TOTAL REV/ ADA (K)	LOC REV/ EPV (L)
NORTH CAROLINA												
EQUALIZED PROPERTY VALUE PER ADA												
LOW 25%	20200.	4737.	9164.	2064.	32.85	7616.2	119.5	423.8	543.3	88.5	631.8	0.0060
MIDDLE 50%	32442.	7210.	11922.	2589.	22.80	7645.1	183.4	410.5	593.9	62.0	655.9	0.0060
HIGH 25%	59625.	12807.	12678.	2599.	18.15	9478.6	206.7	410.0	617.5	49.3	666.8	0.0040
DEGREE OF URBANIZATION												
CENTRAL CITY	36386.	7769.	14827.	3166.	18.00	7968.2	248.8	398.4	647.1	44.1	691.2	0.0070
LARGEST CI	34980.	7614.	15219.	3313.	16.06	7581.3	321.1	397.0	718.1	32.7	750.8	0.0090
SUBURBAN *	56278.	11841.	12679.	2547.	19.63	7260.4	194.4	397.1	591.5	63.2	654.7	0.0040
NON METRO **	32287.	7332.	10064.	2213.	27.03	7612.3	144.5	422.1	566.6	72.9	639.5	0.0050
AVERAGE	36176.	7991.	11421.	2460.	24.15	7596.2	173.3	413.9	587.1	65.5	652.6	0.0050
NORTH DAKOTA												
EQUALIZED PROPERTY VALUE PER ADA												
LOW 25%	23585.	6722.	9412.	2672.	17.20	8018.0	283.1	207.2	490.3	159.3	649.7	0.0120
MIDDLE 50%	34870.	8126.	11371.	2554.	22.57	7668.9	387.6	204.7	592.2	36.9	629.1	0.0110
HIGH 25%	56225.	13891.	10154.	2437.	31.14	7008.5	412.0	200.3	612.3	52.4	664.4	0.0080
DEGREE OF URBANIZATION												
CENTRAL CITY	37996.	7152.	16338.	3075.	12.66	9179.8	605.0	160.6	765.5	31.5	797.0	0.0160
LARGEST CI	37996.	7152.	16338.	3075.	12.66	9179.9	605.0	160.6	765.5	31.5	797.0	0.0160
SUBURBAN *	40714.	11216.	9277.	2560.	18.91	7303.0	381.8	168.0	549.8	23.4	573.3	0.0100
NON METRO **	37205.	9362.	10018.	2499.	24.65	7433.4	342.1	210.1	552.2	77.2	629.4	0.0100
AVERAGE	37386.	9216.	10577.	2554.	23.37	7591.0	367.5	204.2	571.7	71.4	643.1	0.0100
OHIO												
EQUALIZED PROPERTY VALUE PER ADA												
LOW 25%	23801.	6185.	10839.	2783.	9.84	7147.2	400.7	297.2	697.9	28.4	726.3	0.0170
MIDDLE 50%	39643.	8590.	14546.	3117.	12.54	8236.4	591.4	220.2	611.6	37.4	849.0	0.0150
HIGH 25%	57612.	11644.	18534.	3524.	17.58	9862.3	828.5	180.9	1009.4	52.9	1062.3	0.0150
DEGREE OF URBANIZATION												
CENTRAL CITY	47579.	8665.	16959.	3076.	20.29	9899.5	733.6	199.9	933.9	69.2	1002.7	0.0160
LARGEST CI	52739.	9395.	15965.	2844.	28.70	10932.4	892.7	207.0	1099.7	92.9	1102.6	0.0170
SUBURBAN *	40793.	9358.	15582.	3450.	9.93	8194.0	641.1	231.1	872.2	28.3	900.5	0.0160
NON METRO **	32519.	7344.	11064.	2682.	11.28	7302.2	428.0	254.6	682.6	27.3	709.9	0.0140
AVERAGE	40174.	8752.	14616.	3135.	13.13	8370.5	603.0	229.7	832.6	39.0	871.6	0.0150

Table 5A-1. (continued)

	EPV PER ADA (A)	EPV PER POP (B)	INC PER ADA (C)	INC PER POP (D)	DISAD (E)	AVG TEACH SAL (F)	LOC REV/ ADA (G)	ST REV/ ADA (H)	SAL REV/ ADA (I)	FED REV/ ADA (J)	TOTAL REV/ ADA (K)	LOC REV/ EPV (L)
OKLAHOMA												
EQUALIZED PROPERTY VALUE PER ADA												
LOW 25%	3012.	822.	9878.	2414.	22.05	6975.5	141.6	274.6	416.1	82.4	498.5	0.0470
MIDDLE 50%	5697.	1220.	13318.	2788.	1924.	7403.6	171.8	222.9	394.7	36.5	431.3	0.0330
HIGH 25%	9398.	2124.	14445.	3161.	16.29	6996.2	446.8	186.6	633.4	26.6	659.9	0.0480
DEGREE OF URBANIZATION												
CENTRAL CITY	7316.	1520.	15867.	3273.	18.03	7632.4	251.6	186.1	437.7	36.0	473.7	0.0330
LARGEST CI	8842.	1891.	16208.	3466.	15.55	7632.4	499.1	161.5	660.6	17.9	676.5	0.0560
SUBURBAN *	4889.	1282.	11919.	2911.	13.03	6883.4	210.7	230.0	440.7	49.2	489.9	0.0440
NON METRO **	5700.	1273.	11192.	2396.	23.70	7193.3	234.3	251.3	485.6	49.4	533.0	0.0420
AVERAGE	5951.	1347.	12740.	2787.	19.21	7194.7	233.0	226.7	459.7	45.5	505.2	0.0400
OREGON												
EQUALIZED PROPERTY VALUE PER ADA												
LOW 25%	22221.	4507.	15909.	2933.	13.96	9125.1	441.9	273.9	715.9	32.6	748.5	0.0220
MIDDLE 50%	33603.	6084.	16465.	3116.	12.29	9845.2	613.0	203.7	816.7	32.5	849.1	0.0180
HIGH 25%	51272.	10167.	19074.	3305.	16.32	9911.33	528.7	160.2	686.9	65.9	754.8	0.0110
DEGREE OF URBANIZATION												
CENTRAL CITY	42534.	7258.	20133.	3445.	14.37	10465.3	552.2	155.9	708.0	65.0	773.0	0.0140
LARGEST CI	48271.	7756.	22450.	3607.	16.63	10329.9	470.6	139.2	609.8	77.9	687.7	0.0100
SUBURBAN *	28262.	5701.	17847.	3246.	11.95	9198.6	602.8	241.8	844.6	26.6	871.2	0.0230
NON METRO **	36347.	8124.	14298.	2809.	14.77	9441.2	502.8	218.1	720.8	37.7	758.5	0.0150
AVERAGE	35174.	7111.	16978.	3118.	13.71	9686.6	549.2	210.4	759.5	40.9	800.4	0.0170
PENNSYLVANIA												
EQUALIZED PROPERTY VALUE PER ADA												
LOW 25%	10875.	2431.	11665.	2579.	13.02	8862.7	305.4	499.4	804.8	20.5	825.3	0.0320
MIDDLE 50%	18082.	3631.	15901.	3152.	13.21	8859.8	509.4	405.0	914.5	20.1	934.6	0.0280
HIGH 25%	28414.	4155.	23799.	3438.	19.92	11154.7	669.6	389.1	1058.7	85.3	1144.0	0.0240
DEGREE OF URBANIZATION												
CENTRAL CITY	25090.	3378.	22273.	3000.	23.62	11620.0	558.0	484.7	1042.6	111.5	1154.1	0.0220
LARGEST CI	15918.	3251.	24077.	3029.	25.97	13011.5	556.1	569.3	1125.3	149.1	1274.4	0.0210
SUBURBAN *	19320.	3821.	16950.	3344.	12.25	8901.8	546.2	385.1	931.3	17.0	948.3	0.0280
NON METRO **	13009.	2755.	12263.	2575.	13.16	8873.7	349.0	463.0	812.0	19.9	831.9	0.0310
AVERAGE	18863.	3462.	16816.	3030.	14.74	9434.1	498.4	424.6	923.1	36.5	959.6	0.0280

Table 5A–1. (continued)

	EPV PER ADA (A)	EPV PER POP (B)	INC PER ADA (C)	INC PER POP (D)	DISAD (E)	AVG TEACH SAL (F)	LOC REV/ ADA (G)	ST REV/ ADA (H)	SAL REV/ ADA (I)	FED REV/ ADA (J)	TOTAL REV/ ADA (K)	LOC REV/ EPV (L)
RHODE ISLAND												
EQUALIZED PROPERTY VALUE PER ADA												
LOW 25%	28429.	5549.	16543.	3144.	20.80	8443.5	417.0	313.7	730.7	46.4	777.1	0.0150
MIDDLE 50%	35279.	6868.	16961.	3269.	17.74	8867.3	534.3	246.9	781.2	40.5	821.8	0.0150
HIGH 25%	51886.	6915.	23174.	3041.	25.61	9463.5	688.1	282.1	970.2	64.1	1034.3	0.0130
DEGREE OF URBANIZATION												
CENTRAL CITY	44739.	6719.	21116.	3174.	23.03	9802.5	653.7	180.4	934.1	53.8	987.9	0.0150
LARGEST CI	54643.	6593.	25760.	3108.	31.57	10144.1	783.1	316.4	1099.5	93.6	1193.0	0.0140
SUBURBAN*	33755.	6445.	17120.	3250.	19.57	8412.8	492.3	248.9	741.1	38.7	779.8	0.0150
NON METRO**	36956.	6560.	17353.	2972.	16.48	8792.7	496.2	311.9	828.1	66.1	694.1	0.0140
AVERAGE	37720.	6550.	18410.	3181.	20.47	8910.4	543.5	272.4	815.8	47.9	863.7	0.0150
SOUTH CAROLINA												
EQUALIZED PROPERTY VALUE PER ADA												
LOW 25%	1313.	335.	7424.	1884.	40.39	6795.6	104.3	309.6	414.0	105.2	519.2	0.0790
MIDDLE 50%	2141.	494.	10265.	2322.	28.16	7165.3	161.1	318.6	479.6	88.3	567.9	0.0750
HIGH 25%	2922.	620.	12499.	2643.	20.72	7309.7	242.9	388.8	631.7	49.1	680.8	0.0850
DEGREE OF URBANIZATION												
CENTRAL CITY	2460.	515.	13000.	2721.	17.16	7567.4	248.3	340.4	588.6	33.9	622.5	0.1010
LARGEST CI	2460.	515.	13000.	2721.	17.16	7567.4	248.3	340.4	588.6	33.9	622.5	0.1010
SUBURBAN*	2214.	478.	11662.	2523.	26.33	7189.5	181.9	364.4	546.3	84.0	630.3	0.0840
NON METRO**	2045.	485.	9006.	2128.	32.42	7004.3	149.5	319.0	468.5	88.9	557.4	0.0730
AVERAGE	2129.	486.	10113.	2293.	29.36	7108.9	167.3	333.9	501.2	82.7	584.0	0.0780
SOUTH DAKOTA												
EQUALIZED PROPERTY VALUE PER ADA												
LOW 25%	19830.	4979.	10085.	2537.	20.58	8015.4	417.8	104.9	522.7	131.8	654.5	0.0200
MIDDLE 50%	33241.	7818.	10892.	2432.	21.23	7572.8	532.0	91.3	623.2	53.5	767.7	0.0160
HIGH 25%	53988.	12960.	9104.	2151.	34.03	5826.6	547.4	93.1	640.5	55.9	695.4	0.0110
DEGREE OF URBANIZATION												
CENTRAL CITY	28269.	6442.	12624.	2877.	12.31	8868.2	557.4	92.2	649.6	36.6	656.2	0.0200
LARGEST CI	28269.	6442.	12624.	2877.	12.31	8868.2	557.4	92.2	649.6	36.6	656.2	0.0200
SUBURBAN*	46514.	12414.	8614.	2316.	18.75	6895.6	643.1	80.6	723.7	19.4	743.1	0.0140
NON METRO**	35702.	8557.	9972.	2327.	25.93	7024.0	497.8	99.8	593.6	79.7	673.3	0.0160
AVERAGE	35075.	8393.	10243.	2388.	24.27	7246.9	507.3	95.1	602.4	73.7	676.1	0.0160

Table 5A-1. (continued)

	EPV PER ADA (A)	EPV PER POP (B)	INC PER ADA (C)	INC PER POP (D)	DISAD (E)	AVG TEACH SAL (F)	LOC REV/ADA (G)	ST REV/ADA (H)	SAL REV/ADA (I)	FED REV/ADA (J)	TOTAL REV/ADA (K)	LOC REV/EPV (L)
									TENNESSEE			
EQUALIZED PROPERTY VALUE PER ADA												
LOW 25%	13718.	3305.	8212.	1939.	32.80	6931.3	134.8	230.3	367.2	86.0	453.1	0.0190
MIDDLE 50%	24277.	4822.	12801.	2534.	24.58	7935.2	239.2	191.0	430.2	66.7	496.9	0.0100
HIGH 25%	54768.	13588.	12350.	2597.	19.83	7717.7	220.2	248.9	469.1	44.1	513.2	0.0050
DEGREE OF URBANIZATION												
CENTRAL CITY	23955.	4775.	13763.	2738.	27.01	8573.1	320.9	87.4	408.3	68.8	477.1	0.0130
LARGEST CI	22649.	4523.	14070.	2785.	27.37	8701.4	319.7	0.0	319.7	56.3	376.0	0.0140
SUBURBAN*	45848.	11568.	13851.	2887.	17.07	8250.9	290.7	220.7	511.4	44.7	556.1	0.0080
NON METRO **	23833.	5120.	9734.	2067.	28.58	6937.6	133.0	258.4	391.4	74.1	465.5	0.0110
AVERAGE	29260.	6634.	11541.	2401.	25.45	7624.3	208.9	215.3	424.2	65.8	490.0	0.0110
									TEXAS			
EQUALIZED PROPERTY VALUE PER ADA												
LOW 25%	20209.	4778.	9676.	2253.	43.84	6813.5	175.4	300.8	476.2	81.0	557.2	0.0090
MIDDLE 50%	38295.	8145.	14104.	2930.	20.50	7819.6	283.9	292.1	576.0	38.4	614.4	0.0080
HIGH 25%	95150.	21885.	14157.	2925.	27.81	8093.0	464.0	249.0	713.0	43.5	756.4	0.0060
DEGREE OF URBANIZATION												
CENTRAL CITY	37483.	7635.	14561.	1972.	29.39	7855.4	303.6	268.8	572.4	51.2	423.7	0.0080
LARGEST CI	55094.	10577.	17477.	3355.	24.59	7998.1	368.3	242.8	611.1	23.6	634.7	0.0070
SUNBEAM*	43039.	10162.	12595.	2868.	24.13	6462.1	298.1	287.2	585.4	52.7	638.1	0.0080
NON METRO **	67347.	15757.	11058.	2361.	29.56	7631.7	301.9	302.3	604.1	47.1	651.3	0.0060
AVERAGE	47985.	10738.	13010.	2759.	28.16	7636.4	301.8	283.5	585.3	50.3	635.6	0.0070
									UTAH			
EQUALITIES PROPERTY VALUE PER ADA												
LOW 25%	16854.	5236.	8706.	2718.	9.01	8321.5	169.3	442.3	611.6	65.4	677.0	0.0100
MIDDLE 50%	25149.	7035.	9452.	2597.	12.15	8459.7	272.2	410.9	683.1	32.8	715.8	0.0110
HIGH 25%	44101.	10949.	12117.	2770.	16.06	8893.0	447.3	305.4	752.6	43.8	796.4	0.0100
DEGREE OF URBANIZATION												
CENTRAL CITY	39835.	7682.	15392.	3007.	17.36	9430.4	400.2	527.1	727.3	51.7	779.1	0.0100
LARGEST CI	50336.	9269.	17654.	3251.	19.29	9788.1	491.5	278.2	769.7	49.7	819.1	0.0100
SUBURBAN*	22720.	7053.	8757.	2693.	9.37	8246.9	247.9	402.7	650.6	35.6	686.2	0.0110
NON METRO **	30121.	8705.	8216.	2333.	13.90	8478.8	300.8	422.0	722.8	56.5	779.3	0.0100
AVERAGE	27813.	7564.	9932.	2670.	12.34	8533.5	290.2	392.4	682.6	43.7	726.3	0.0110

Table 5A–1.   (continued)

	EPV PER ADA (A)	EPV PER POP (B)	INC PER ADA (C)	INC PER POP (D)	DISAD (E)	AVG TEACH SAL (F)	LOC REV/ ADA (G)	ST REV/ ADA (H)	SAL REV/ ADA (I)	FED REV/ ADA (J)	TOTAL REV/ ADA (K)	LOC REV/ EPV (L)
VERMONT												
EQUALIZED PROPERTY VALUE PER ADA												
LOW 25%	19173.	4463.	14173.	2860.	13.85	7603.5	500.9	395.3	896.2	23.8	920.0	0.0270
MIDDLE 50%	30281.	5200.	17184.	2893.	15.46	7887.9	704.3	386.1	1090.3	35.1	1125.4	0.0230
HIGH 25%	56054.	7026.	23757.	2863.	14.33	10149.2	1119.8	430.9	1550.7	41.2	1591.9	0.0210
DEGREE OF URBANIZATION												
CENTRAL CITY	—	—	—	—	—	—	—	—	—	—	—	—
LARGEST CI	—	—	—	—	—	—	—	—	—	—	—	—
SUBURBAN *	—	—	—	—	—	—	—	—	—	—	—	—
NON METRO **	33944.	5472.	18074.	2877.	14.77	8382.0	757.2	399.6	1156.8	33.8	1190.6	0.0240
AVERAGE	33944.	5472.	18074.	2877.	14.77	8382.0	757.2	399.6	1156.8	33.8	1190.6	0.0240
VIRGINIA												
EQUALIZED PROPERTY VALUE PER ADA												
LOW 25%	18988.	4269.	9761.	2185.	27.61	7456.3	295.9	310.5	606.4	86.4	692.8	0.0160
MIDDLE 50%	25990.	5881.	12360.	2712.	19.55	8167.1	365.3	256.6	621.8	67.1	688.9	0.0140
HIGH 25%	41715.	8295.	19477.	3843.	15.63	9488.9	620.3	219.6	839.9	109.8	949.7	0.0160
DEGREE OF URBANIZATION												
CENTRAL CITY	25088.	5001.	15010.	2969.	20.64	8575.6	482.5	244.4	727.0	87.4	814.3	0.0190
LARGEST CI	25689.	4303.	16659.	2790.	28.81	9616.5	403.8	237.0	640.8	153.2	794.0	0.0160
SUBURBAN *	32905.	6874.	16185.	3277.	12.69	8683.9	439.7	246.5	666.2	67.9	754.1	0.0140
NON METRO **	27231.	6167.	11550.	2620.	24.33	8036.1	367.8	274.7	642.5	87.6	730.1	0.0140
AVERAGE	28170.	6082.	13489.	2863.	20.59	8319.7	411.6	260.8	672.5	82.6	755.1	0.0150
WASHINGTON												
EQUALIZED PROPERTY VALUE PER ADA												
LOW 25%	26122.	6875.	12206.	3159.	10.94	9630.2	304.0	340.0	846.0	64.3	910.3	0.0120
MIDDLE 50%	42560.	10332.	14208.	3343.	14.03	10551.1	360.4	531.0	891.4	64.1	955.5	0.0090
HIGH 25%	94745.	18674.	19223.	3548.	14.47	11252.4	547.5	432.5	979.9	50.7	1030.7	0.0060
DEGREE OF URBANIZATION												
CENTRAL CITY	70509.	11723.	21492.	3630.	15.35	12146.4	516.5	460.2	976.4	53.6	1030.0	0.0080
LARGEST CI	97877.	14843.	26784.	4062.	15.66	12398.9	647.2	390.6	1037.8	51.1	1068.9	0.0070
SUBURBAN *	40114.	10121.	14131.	3556.	10.17	10357.6	399.1	553.4	952.5	31.1	983.6	0.0110
NON METRO **	54441.	13325.	11932.	2897.	16.32	9637.1	308.9	480.4	789.4	104.3	893.6	0.0070
AVERAGE	51496.	11553.	14961.	3348.	13.37	10496.1	393.6	508.6	902.2	60.8	963.0	0.0090

Table 5A-1. (continued)

	EPV PER ADA (A)	EPV PER POP (B)	INC PER ADA (C)	INC PER POP (D)	DISAD (E)	AVG TEACH SAL (F)	LOC REV/ ADA (G)	ST REV/ ADA (H)	SAL REV/ ADA (I)	FED REV/ ADA (J)	TOTAL REV/ ADA (K)	LOC REV/ EPV (L)
WEST VIRGINIA												
EQUALIZED PROPERTY VALUE PER ADA												
LOW 25%	18672.	4772.	7335.	1864.	36.43	8054.2	193.4	405.8	599.2	99.3	698.5	0.0110
MIDDLE 50%	29719.	6190.	11118.	2303.	23.69	7785.4	231.6	366.7	598.3	79.1	677.5	0.0080
HIGH 25%	44840.	8676.	14325.	2758.	18.33	9132.1	361.4	348.1	709.7	49.8	759.5	0.0080
DEGREE OF URBANIZATION												
CENTRAL CITY	48938.	8726.	16377.	2800.	16.68	8854.0	351.0	353.0	703.9	37.5	741.4	0.0070
LARGEST CI	45190.	8214.	15202.	2763.	18.00	8316.5	308.7	362.9	671.6	47.3	718.9	0.0070
SUBURBAN *	38429.	8159.	12751.	2710.	19.73	9214.4	350.3	346.3	696.8	58.4	755.2	0.0090
NON METRO **	26041.	5668.	9718.	2115.	20.38	7614.2	214.6	381.5	596.1	87.5	683.6	0.0090
AVERAGE	30737.	6457.	10974.	2307.	25.53	8189.3	254.6	371.8	626.4	76.9	703.2	0.0090
WISCONSIN												
EQUALIZED PROPERTY VALUE PER ADA												
LOW 25%	22224.	5216.	11431.	2655.	17.48	8722.0	479.0	434.6	913.7	27.6	941.2	0.0220
MIDDLE 50%	34084.	6752.	15821.	3088.	15.14	9700.0	693.8	240.1	933.9	27.3	961.2	0.0200
HIGH 25%	55487.	8049.	24876.	3600.	15.73	10492.3	891.7	176.6	1068.3	28.0	1096.3	0.0170
DEGREE OF URBANIZATION												
CENTRAL CITY	37787.	6503.	18637.	3203.	17.51	10611.9	738.3	235.3	973.7	41.2	1014.8	0.0200
LARGEST CI	39239.	6253.	20047.	3194.	22.46	11478.9	803.6	277.4	1081.0	54.5	1135.5	0.0200
SUBURBAN *	41355.	7420.	20059.	3552.	12.05	9682.6	765.3	268.1	1033.4	13.7	1047.1	0.0200
NON METRO **	31443.	6235.	13205.	2670.	17.80	8897.7	590.3	305.1	895.4	28.7	924.1	0.0200
AVERAGE	36470.	6692.	16987.	3108.	15.88	9653.5	689.6	272.8	962.4	27.6	990.0	0.0200
WYOMING												
EQUALIZED PROPERTY VALUE PER ADA												
LOW 25%	6070.	1561.	11402.	2900.	17.22	9115.4	138.7	390.3	529.1	73.6	602.7	0.0230
MIDDLE 50%	11192.	2773.	12397.	2958.	13.41	8659.1	221.2	326.3	547.5	28.3	575.7	0.0200
HIGH 25%	31761.	6786.	14399.	2894.	13.49	8384.1	469.0	213.0	682.0	32.6	714.6	0.0160
DEGREE OF URBANIZATION												
CENTRAL CITY	—	—	—	—	—		—	—	—	—	—	—
LARGEST CI	—	—	—	—	—		—	—	—	—	—	—
SUBURBAN *	—	—	—	—	—	—	—	—	—	—	—	—
NON METRO **	14651.	3394.	12606.	2928.	14.41	8815.0	257.6	316.4	574.0	40.9	614.8	0.0200
AVERAGE	14651.	3394.	12606.	2928.	14.41	8815.0	257.6	316.4	574.0	40.9	614.8	0.0200

Table 5A-1.   (continued)

	EPV PER ADA (A)	EPV PER POP (B)	INC PER ADA (C)	INC PER POP (D)	DISAD (E)	AVG TEACH SAL (F)	LOC REV/ ADA (G)	ST REV/ ADA (H)	SAL REV/ ADA (I)	FED REV/ ADA (J)	TOTAL REV/ ADA (K)	LOC REV/ EPV (L)
NORTHEAST												
EQUALIZED PROPERTY VALUE PER ADA												
LOW 25%	16057.	3684.	13393.	2940.	14.21	9463.2	438.2	538.0	976.2	30.1	1006.3	0.0290
MIDDLE 50%	28508.	5746.	19034.	3479.	16.21	10039.6	666.3	410.5	1076.8	38.0	1114.8	0.0250
HIGH 35%	46821.	7127.	27278.	3935.	22.16	10975.5	875.4	368.8	1244.2	69.3	1313.5	0.0200
DEGREE OF URBANIZATION												
CENTRAL CITY	38354.	5066.	25488.	3333.	28.94	10948.0	709.1	474.1	1183.1	104.3	1287.4	0.0200
LARGEST CI	42948.	5192.	28893.	3467.	33.10	11442.4	792.9	562.4	1355.3	122.1	1477.4	0.0190
SUBURBAN*	28537.	6090.	18943.	3734.	12.68	10128.0	694.2	412.0	1106.2	21.3	1127.5	0.0260
NON METRO**	23919.	4955.	14907.	2939.	14.53	9182.1	532.8	430.9	963.7	28.5	992.2	0.0250
AVERAGE	29972.	5576.	19684.	3458.	17.20	10129.3	661.4	431.9	1093.5	43.8	1137.3	0.0240
MIDWEST												
EQUALIZED PROPERTY VALUE PER ADA												
LOW 25%	23100.	9745.	13408.	2946.	12.31	8783.2	416.4	369.0	785.4	35.1	820.5	0.0230
MIDDLE 50%	36277.	7440.	15961.	3167.	14.89	9504.1	565.4	305.8	871.3	39.6	910.8	0.0190
HIGH 25%	68726.	10629.	23198.	3451.	15.40	9960.3	823.7	237.3	1061.0	35.5	1096.5	0.0160
DEGREE OF URBANIZATION												
CENTRAL CITY	39429.	6788.	18493.	3206.	19.59	10761.4	640.6	294.0	934.6	63.4	998.0	0.0200
LARGEST CI	42074.	6690.	19951.	3235.	24.05	11125.5	657.9	322.0	979.9	77.2	1057.0	0.0190
SUBURBAN*	45899.	10638.	20266.	3597.	10.37	9452.5	652.1	313.7	965.7	23.6	989.3	0.0200
NON METRO**	36539.	8076.	12419.	2671.	15.44	8455.3	487.8	301.0	788.8	35.5	824.3	0.0170
AVERAGE	41094.	8814.	17131.	3183.	14.37	9437.8	592.7	304.5	897.2	37.4	934.6	0.0190
SOUTH												
EQUALIZED PROPERTY VALUE PER ADA												
LOW 25%	15443.	3581.	9595.	2193.	34.02	7433.2	180.9	350.0	530.9	25.7	616.6	0.0180
MIDDLE 50%	25495.	5429.	12892.	2693.	22.93	7958.0	265.1	324.2	589.4	63.3	652.7	0.0160
HIGH 25%	49009.	10671.	15555.	3121.	21.30	8551.6	410.6	306.7	717.4	53.6	771.0	0.0160
DEGREE OF URBANIZATION												
CENTRAL CITY	30203.	6119.	14442.	2912.	26.37	8274.4	313.6	291.0	604.6	58.1	662.6	0.0150
LARGEST CI	30340.	5942.	15398.	2978.	25.91	8603.3	367.2	291.8	659.0	54.8	713.8	0.0210
SUBURBAN*	31046.	6715.	15023.	3114.	18.80	8662.3	338.3	337.5	675.8	59.0	734.5	0.0180
NON METRO**	26891.	6085.	10039.	2206.	30.70	7304.2	205.5	344.6	550.1	75.9	626.1	0.0170
AVERAGE	28860.	6277.	12482.	2628.	26.32	7887.8	268.4	330.0	598.4	66.9	665.3	0.0170

Table 5A-1. (continued)

	EPV PER ADA (A)	EPV PER POP (B)	INC PER ADA (C)	INC PER POP (D)	DISAD (E)	AVG TEACH SAL (F)	LOC REV/ ADA (G)	ST REV/ ADA (H)	SAL REV/ ADA (I)	FED REV/ ADA (J)	TOTAL REV/ ADA (K)	LOC REV/ EPV (L)
WEST												
EQUALIZED PROPERTY VALUE PER ADA												
LOW 25%	10086.	2615.	12003.	3034.	17.71	9880.6	306.4	405.6	712.1	67.5	779.6	0.0450
MIDDLE 50%	17061.	3827.	16313.	3344.	19.46	10391.2	472.3	335.1	807.4	51.0	858.3	0.0360
HIGH 25%	33908.	6403.	25715.	3554.	19.38	10912.3	650.3	288.6	938.9	52.7	991.6	0.0270
DEGREE OF URBANIZATION												
CENTRAL CITY	19512.	3354.	20499.	3527.	22.56	11440.7	562.1	321.5	883.6	61.2	944.8	0.0430
LARGEST CI	23057.	3871.	21020.	3670.	24.48	10639.7	607.3	305.3	912.5	59.6	972.1	0.0460
SUBURBAN*	16969.	3757.	17788.	3492.	14.76	10646.0	472.7	353.2	825.8	39.7	865.6	0.0390
NON METRO**	24510.	6186.	12959.	2719.	21.85	8901.8	347.8	363.7	711.5	88.1	799.6	0.0220
AVERAGE	19524.	4167.	17571.	3324.	19.02	10403.0	473.5	345.0	818.5	58.2	876.7	0.0360
NATIONAL												
EQUALIZED PROPERTY VALUE PER ADA												
LOW 25%	16955.	5259.	11993.	2726.	20.36	8782.2	330.4	408.3	738.7	54.9	793.7	0.0260
MIDDLE 50%	27975.	5830.	15780.	3122.	18.44	9381.6	480.5	340.6	821.1	48.4	869.5	0.0220
HIGH 35%	51815.	9135.	22191.	3478.	19.45	10007.3	679.2	297.7	976.9	51.8	1028.7	0.0190
DEGREE OF URBANIZATION												
CENTRAL CITY	32329.	5467.	19188.	3210.	24.32	10352.1	538.9	337.9	876.8	70.2	947.0	0.0230
LARGEST CI	35637.	5496.	21489.	3325.	27.08	10528.9	612.2	376.8	989.0	80.3	1069.3	0.0250
SUBURBAN*	32230.	7174.	18191.	3503.	13.83	9709.1	558.1	355.1	913.2	34.2	947.4	0.0250
NON METRO**	29053.	6516.	11724.	2500.	23.13	8137.8	347.3	346.9	694.2	59.0	753.2	0.0190
AVERAGE	31179.	6513.	16208.	3080.	19.75	9308.4	480.1	347.8	827.9	52.1	880.0	0.0220

Source: U.S. Census and Eluegia 1970 data base supplemented with a special survey to collect data on equalized property values.

Definitions:
A. Equalized property value per pupil (ADA).
B. Equilized property value per pupil (ADA).
C. Personal income per pupil (ADA).
D. Personal income per resident.
E. Orshansky Poverty Population of school-age (5-17) children plus 35% of the estimated number of school-age children from families with non-English language mother tongue.
F. Average salary of instructional staff.
G. Local revenue per pupil (ADA).
H. State revenue per pupil (ADA).
I. Combined state and local revenues per pupil (ADA).
J. Federal revenue per pupil (ADA).
K. Total revenue per pupil (ADA).
L. Local revenue per equalized property value.

Table 5A-2. Trends in Educational Expenditures and Services

Year	Total Expenditures per Pupil Unadjusted Dollars (1)	Constant (1972-73 Dollars) (2)	Pupils per Classroom Teacher (3)	Average Instructional Staff Salary Unadjusted Dollars (4)
1951–1952	313	510	24.2[b]	3,450
1953–1954	351	559	24.8	3,925
1955–1956	388	618	24.5	4,156
1956–1958	449	672	24.0	4,702
1959–1960	472	688	24.0	5,174
1961–1962	530	755	23.8	5,700
1963–1964	559	776	23.9	6,240
1965–1966	654	877	22.9	6,935
1967–1968	786	989	21.9	7,885
1969–1970	970	1,099	20.8	8,840
1970–1971	1,008[a]	1,087[a]	20.7	9,570
1971–1972	1,100[a]	1,144[a]	20.6	10,100[a]
1972–1973	1,182[a]	1,182[a]	20.2	10,608[a]

Source: Expenditures and Average Instructional Staff Salary: Department of Health, Education and Welfare, Office of Education, "Digest of Education Statistics," 1973. (1), (2), and (4). Pupils (in Average Daily Attendance) 1951-52, 1969-70: Department of Health, Education, and Welfare, Office of Education, "Statistics on State Public School Systems," 1969-70 ed., 1970-71, 1973-74: USOE: Statistics of Public Elementary and Secondary Day Schools, Annual (3).

[a]Estimated by USOE.

[b]Includes guidance personnel, librarians, and psychologists, and so on.

Chapter Six

Federal Assistance to National Target Groups: The ESEA Tital I Experience

Robert J. Goettel*

The purpose of this chapter is to examine the national interest in federal aid programs designed to serve target groups of students. Such groups include the economically and educationally disadvantaged, the handicapped, and those who can benefit from occupational education programs. While the federal government's interest and involvement in improving instructional opportunities in these areas dates back sixty years to the Smith-Hughes Act of 1917, the purposes to be served and the strategies employed to achieve those purposes have changed substantially, most notably since passage of the Elementary and Secondary Education Act of 1965 (ESEA). These changes have dramatically affected intergovernmental relationships in education, the expectations placed upon educational institutions, and our general understanding of the possibilities open to the federal government for affecting educational programs and improving the learning outcomes of target children, and the limits on its ability to bring about change.

The federal government's basic purposes for each of the target groups have been to ensure the provision of services where they were not being provided and to improve the instructional characteristics of those services. In the past, approaches toward achieving these purposes emphasized federal aid as an incentive to states and local school districts to respond to national goals. Indeed, until the mid-1960s the federal strategy was predicated on a belief in the "inherent right of local school districts to determine the nature and scope of the educational enterprise."[1] Accordingly, the U.S. Office of Education (USOE)

---

*Dr. Goettel wishes to emphasize that his views are based in important part upon recent experience as a participant in a study of the administration at the state and local levels of Title I ESEA conducted by the Syracuse Research Corporation and Booz-Allen and Hamilton, Inc., but not upon analysis of the data that the study collected.

relied upon routine grant management and technical assistance procedures that reflected a preoccupation with fiscal accountability for federal funds and permitted considerable state and local discretion in program design.

In the last half-dozen years, however, the federal posture has shifted, particularly with respect to the administration of the annual $2 billion Title I program. Faith in the capacity of local education agencies (LEAs) to embrace national purposes has been largely abandoned, and the federal government has begun to exert authority and leadership out of proportion to its contribution of only 7 percent to educational revenues for elementary and secondary schools. Greater specificity in legislation, detailed federal regulations and guidelines, and, at least in comparative terms, more aggressive program-monitoring procedures have produced a new climate that has prompted fears by some state officials that the "junior partner"—the federal government—is now running the firm. Indeed, Joseph Cronin, Superintendent of Public Instruction in Illinois, contends that "slowly, inexorably, and incrementally, the federal government is taking over education. Especially since 1965, the country has moved—almost every year—toward a national system of education."[2]

Whether education is on the road toward a federal takeover or whether the more prescriptive and assertive federal role is, as some reformers argue, only a reflection of congressional impatience with states and local districts for their inability or unwillingness to respond on their own,[3] local districts that are ultimately responsible for providing educational services find much to criticize at both the federal and state levels. For example, the Finance/Funding Committee of the National Federation of Urban-Suburban School Districts summarized the major complaints from the local level as follows:[4]

- Conflict between Congress and the president regarding the role of the federal government has prevented the orderly delivery of services, disrupted basic planning, created serious staffing problems, and precluded efficient program implementation.
- Lack of coordination between the various federal, state, and local agencies restricts, and in some cases prohibits, participation by intended recipients of federal support programs.
- Inconsistencies in the interpretation of federal programs, legislation, and the resultant regulations developed by HEW hamper the administration of many programs and sometimes result in the denial of services to intended beneficiaries.
- Many federal grants are highly categorical in nature, which limits the ability of local school districts to provide services to many needy children.
- SEAs receive funds for federal program administration that they are often not equipped to provide.
- In some federal programs certain states are channeling or draining off unusually large amounts of federal funds for state administrative activities before funds reach the target or main objective of the program.

Despite such concerns at the state and local levels, the thrust toward greater federal direction and assertiveness regarding the ways federally funded programs are administered by states and local districts has many supporters at the national level, and not only in the area of compensatory education programs. The new All Handicapped Children Act of 1975 (PL 94-142), which some analysts estimate will cost Washington over $3 billion annually by 1982,[5] will be accompanied by detailed regulations and guidelines and a need for comprehensive leadership and monitoring of compliance at least as great as that currently required for Title I. Equally important, PL 94-142 seems to refine and expand three implied principles regarding the state and federal partnership to provide educational services to target groups of pupils. First, the federal government has the obligation to assure that *appropriate* educational services are provided for all target pupils irrespective of the state or district in which they live. Second, the federal government also has the responsibility to fund all or a substantial proportion of the *extra costs* of educational services to target pupils. Third, the federal government can and should prescribe *specific instructional strategies* to be used with target pupils, in the case of this act, the mainstreaming of mildly handicapped pupils. The principles as embodied in PL 94-142 seem a reasonably accurate reflection of the current congressional conception of the appropriate federal role in education at least insofar as that role has an impact upon pupils with special educational needs.

Even vocational education aid programs, the oldest programs and also most heavily influenced by state and local political cultures and historical practices, have not escaped the thrust toward greater federal control. Both a recent Government Accounting Office (GAO) report to Congress and a report prepared for the USOE by Project Baseline of Northern Arizona University[6] urge stronger federal control over how states use Vocational Education Act funds, particularly how they use them in comprehensive planning and evaluation, how state education agencies (SEAs) use administrative funds, and how funds and programs for the disadvantaged and for central-city school districts are set up, thus assuring that these funds and programs are available.

There is general agreement, therefore, that a new federal posture is emerging both in legislation and in the management of the major groups of federal aid programs designed to serve the special educational needs of target pupils. Evidence of increased federal control over state and local decisionmaking and management practices has been relatively recent—in legislation, since the passage of ESEA in 1965 and, in fact, predominately in the administration of Title I of that act over the past five or six years. Title I's first decade can be instructive, particularly to answer two fundamental questions that must continually be asked about the federal-state-local partnership for meeting the needs of target groups of pupils.

The first question is whether or not the system of controls works. Specifically does firm direction, coupled with assertiveness by the federal government and, in turn, by the states, get the funds where they are intended to go and hold the promise of improved instructional programs and pupil achievement? The conventional view is that the system does not work very well, that states and local school districts find ways to make federal funds work for their own purposes, purposes that are often at variance with national goals. This occurs, it is asserted, in part because state and local education agencies are dominated by their past histories and political cultures. The federal government is seen as unable to overcome the dominance of localism because (1) federal program goals have not been accepted by all of the partners, (2) administrators do not know how to comply with federal requirements and how to improve instructional programs, (3) the USOE, the SEAs, and the LEAs lack management capability, and (4) the USOE lacks both a will and a way to exert the authority required to assure compliance with federal expectations.

The second fundamental question is both more complex and more critical to the success of the federal-state-local partnership. Even if the controls work, are they necessary? Does the national interest in reforming the flow of funds to target groups of pupils, such as the educationally disadvantaged, require the types of federal-state-local administrative controls that currently characterize Title I and will most certainly also characterize the administration of PL 94-142? Does the nature of the educational programs supported by those funds require controls? The common state and local argument is that such controls are not only not necessary, but that they also get in the way of effective implementation of effective programs. The claim is that the educational purposes of the federal government's relatively minor fiscal contribution would be better served by devoting the energies of state and local officials to program improvement rather than to trying to comply with overly specific regulations.

Answers to these two questions will never be clear-cut. One's view of the operation of the federal programs is very much controlled by what a person believes the federal government's role should be in relation to states and local districts. In addition, the two questions are not quite so separable as they might appear to be at first glance. For example, one way to view the differences between the states, their local school districts, and the federal government is within the context of the perennial question about whether federal aid should be categorical or general purpose in character.

Some observers hold that state and local officials will not be satisfied until they are able to tap into the federal revenue system through federal aid grants that are not fettered by any form of control, so that there will be no federal requirements to conflict with local values. While state and local officials rationalize the appropriateness of a "no strings attached" approach by citing the infinite variability of local conditions and their own unique ability to design programs to meet children's needs that are associated with those conditions, reformers see state and local officials as really wanting no more than to "take the money and run." In the eyes of reformers at the federal level, state and local resistance to federal aid programs and to the controls that accompany federal dollars seems based on the assumption that the goals and procedures of the major aid programs for target groups are "Washington" goals that will not be willingly embraced by state and local officials. The folks "out there" are too often seen as the bad guys.

While preferences for general aid, instinctive resistance to anything that Washington identifies as important, and, above all, abhorence of regulations and guidelines for spending federal aid probably represented the attitude of most state and local officials in the mid-1960s, such hard-core resistance may not be the rule as we start the second decade of ESEA. Moreover, evidence is emerging to indicate that the federal government does influence state and local program management positively and to justify the basic assumptions under which ESEA was originally formulated. Wise decisions about how to improve ESEA, administer PL 94-142, and modify vocational education aid programs within the framework of an enduring federal, state, and local partnership must be based upon a realistic understanding of what has already been accomplished, what the limits to federal influence are, and how the real problems of state and local officials can be addressed by the federal government to better meet the needs of children.

This chapter is organized in six sections. In the second section, which follows, the principal studies of the administrative implementation of ESEA are reviewed and the common perception of the effectiveness of the federal role is presented. A somewhat more optimistic view is presented, and the reasons for that optimism, based upon current observations of federal and state oversite of the aid program, are discussed. The third, fourth, and fifth sections concern specific issues relating to Title I in particular and education grant programs in general. The process by which allocative goals are achieved is the subject of the third section; the fourth section addresses the difficult issues of needs assessment and program evaluation; the fifth section discusses parent involvement and the coordination of Title I with other federal and state programs serving essentially the same target group. Finally, in the sixth section the key implications of this review of the Title I experience are summarized.

THE INTERGOVERNMENTAL PARTNERSHIP IN ADMINISTERING TITLE I PROGRAMS

Previous Studies of the Administrative Process
The status of the federal-state-local partnership in administering ESEA Title I over the past decade is the most instructive illustration of both the problems and possibilities that confront educational reformers in their attempts to improve learning in target groups. The major studies that have examined administration of the program up through 1974 are the following:

- *Federal Aid to Education: Who Benefits? Who Governs?*, in which a study team, under the auspices of the Syracuse University Research Corporation and directed by Joel S. Berke and Michael W. Kirst, examined intrastate distribution patterns and state education agency administrative procedures for eight major federal aid programs.[7]

- *Evaluation and Reform: The Elementary and Secondary Education Act of 1965, Title I,* by Milbrey W. McLaughlin of the Rand Corporation, in which McLaughlin considers efforts to assess the effects of Title I and turn the result into more effective administrative practices.[8]
- *The Silken Purse,* the final report by the Planar Corporation of a study of administrative practices of the USOE and of selected state education agencies and local districts.[9]

Who Benefits? Who Governs?

The Berke and Kirst comparative case studies of federal aid adminis-tration in New York, Michigan, California, Massachusetts, Texas, and Virginia were conducted in 1969 and 1970. Well grounded in early studies of the politics of education at the state level, Berke and Kirst emphasized the great importance of differences in state political cultures in determining the outcomes of federal policy, even in states that are as metropolitan as the ones examined in the study.

> The variety of ways by which federal aid is administered stems primarily from differences in state political cultures. Federal aid is channeled into an existing state political system and emerges as a mixture of federal priorities and frequently quite different, if not conflicting, state priorities. This combined delivery mechanism en-sures that the implementation policies will not be uniform among the states, especially since the sanctions and incentives available to the federal government are insufficient to alter significantly the tra-ditional patterns of state educational policy. Yet, over a long period of time, federal administrators and guidelines do exert a perceptible impact on state policies, so long as federal objectives are not changed.[10]

Though state education bureaucracies usually predominate over governors, legislatures, and pressure groups, Berke and Kirst found that SEA ad-ministrative procedures are affected by federal regulations that signal a manda-tory change. In addition, while SEA relationships with local districts proceed according to historical patterns of behavior, those relationships and the on-going routines and procedures of the SEA vary widely among states. Of particu-lar importance to the administration of federal programs are differences among SEAs in the extent to which they exhibit assertive versus passive behavior toward local districts, in the nature of state leadership shown, particularly by the chief state school officer, and in the extent to which the SEAs exhibit an "audit mentality" versus a leadership one.

Berke and Kirst recommended that USOE oversight of SEAs be characterized by a *differential administration* that would permit the more assertive and leadership-oriented states greater flexibility in their administration of federal programs. They urged wider participation by legislators, teachers, students, and community agencies and also by parents to reverse the "top-down" compliance strategy. Berke and Kirst also recommended that the federal government encourage state-level comprehensive planning toward meeting educational needs and systematic state assessment of program effectiveness.

Evaluation and Reform

Milbrey McLaughlin sets forth what in the early 1970s was the common assessment of the administrative effectiveness of ESEA, an assessment that by and large presents a negative view. She concluded that in the late 1960s and early 1970s the trend to tighten up the legislation, rules, and guidelines had been based on an unrealistic view of administrative behavior. Successful implementaton of Title I programs, she contends, is determined by the interdependent relationship among four factors. The first is *common goals*: officials at the state and local levels must understand and share the objectives of the program that they are expected to implement. The second factor is *knowledge*: officials at each level of the enterprise must know how to achieve an objective effectively and have the information they need for determining how successfully subordinate agencies and institutions are carrying out mutually agreed upon plans. Third, there must be *incentives* for compliance or effective performance, that is, a workable system of rewards. Finally, the federal government and, in turn, the states must possess *effective authority* to ensure compliance, that is, have an ultimate ability to punish as well as reward. This authority, however, should be one in which the "rewards and sanctions are removed to the background."[11]

In her study McLaughlin found little common agreement about the specific goals of Title I. This condition is usually attributed to the conflicting expectations of supporters of the legislation in 1965 and is usually thought of as indicative of the contextual differences among states and districts. But compounding the differences among federal, state, and local officials over the broad purposes to be served by Title I are the often conflicting interpretations of the rules and regulations that emanated from USOE in the early years and made it even more difficult for state and local officials with the best of intentions to identify the specific objectives that they were expected to share with their federal counterparts. Lack of understanding of objectives made it difficult for such officials to design compliant programs and particularly easy for officials who did not share the broad goals of Title I to hide behind the ambiguities.

More important, educators were seen by McLaughlin as not really knowing how to design and implement programs that would improve learning for the educationally disadvantaged. Nor, she felt, did state and local officials know how to evaluate programs to determine the relative effectiveness of alternative learning strategies.

McLaughlin also found that the incentives and authority available to federal and state officials were generally inadequate. They did not adequately use the critical tools of program approval and the monitoring of project implementation. State officials either had too few sanctions and controls, applied them too late, or were unwilling to use those powers that they did have. According to McLaughlin, neither the USOE nor the SEAs "have enforced program regulations with much rigor, enthusiasm or success."[12] A major focus of criticism was the federal government's audit procedures and its reluctance to enforce audit exceptions and recover the full amount of funds that had been expended in violation of legal requirements.

Given these shortcomings in the intergovernmental administration of Title I, McLaughlin suggested that, perhaps, "Title I programs, as they have been evaluated, have never existed—that Title I has not yet been implemented as intended by reformers."[13] The failure of Title I may, therefore, be a failure of federal policy to bring about these programs on the local level. To fulfill the intentions of the legislation, McLaughlin concludes that federal policymakers must formulate realistic incentives that would encourage local districts to establish programs for the educationally disadvantaged.

The Silken Purse

The study by the Planar Corporation comes to similar conclusions about the effectiveness of administrative practices in implementing the intentions of the federal government at the state and local levels. Planar staff conducted extensive interviews with USOE Area Desk personnel responsible for monitoring the practices of SEAs, made site visits to five states, and administered a survey to ten additional states and thirty-six local districts. Like Berke and Kirst, the Planar staff assumed that the political climate of the states was a major determinant of administrative practices, and they found those practices to vary considerably from state to state. Recognizing that change was occurring in the administration of the program, they note that "the quality and pace of the changes have varied from state-to-state to the point where today it is almost a contradiction in terms to refer to a national Title I program."[14] In practice, the Planar staff found Title I to be conceptually related to revenue sharing; that is, many districts seemed to be using the funds as general purpose aid.

The policy recommendations drawn by the Planar staff from their study emphasized five themes:

1. Title I should have a relatively small set of streamlined regulations.
2. Specific standards for program operation should be established in the regulations.
3. The legislation and regulations should provide for considerable flexibility in SEA management of Title I.
4. Strong incentives should be provided for SEAs and LEAs to comply with the standards in order to minimize resort to the sanction of demanding repayment of amounts misspent.

5. The legislation should promote administrative accountability at all levels of operation.

In general, the specifics of the Planar recommendations primarily involve the development of incentives to enhance the capacity of state education agencies and local districts to operate more effective Title I programs. Considerable attention is given in the report to developing new ways to calculate the state administrative set-aside, so as to better meet the needs of small states with large numbers of programs to monitor and encourage states to provide more services to local districts.

Factors That Affect the Attainment of National Goals in Federal Categorical Aid Programs

Table 6-1 summarizes the responsibilities or functions performed by HEW and USOE, the SEAs, LEAs, and individual schools in operating Title I programs. Also included in Table 6-1 are those factors that influence the way the federal program is operated at each level. The influencing factors are drawn from the Berke and Kirst, McLaughlin, and Planar reports as well as from observations made from the current National Institute of Education (NIE) studies of the administration of Title I.

One of the striking aspects of the list of influencing factors is the number of factors over which a superordinate level of government has only marginal ability to either control or affect program implementation. For example, the personal and leadership capabilities of district and school staff; the basic fiscal condition of each district; and the nature, quality, and history of relations between LEA and SEA staff are but a few of the many local contextual factors that will in the short term dominate the character of a program. Indeed, when a federal policy such as the Title I requirements is traced down from the USOE to the individual school, one should probably be surprised to find any characteristic of a program that is directly attributable to the federal role.

In the long term, however, the state and local context in which federal program administration occurs can incrementally compensate for and adapt to factors that in the short run appear to be uncontrollable and unchangeable. Within the framework of the rules and regulations that represent minimum standards, mutual adaptation should be expected over time between the USOE and SEAs, LEAs, and, in many cases, LEAs and the individual schools.

The predominant view of Title I is that, to the extent that mutual adaptation occurred, it has resulted in a subversion of the purposes and principles of the federal program and only a relatively low level of conformance with legislative expectations has been achieved. The usual assertion is that Title I is not a national program for the educationally disadvantaged, but rather a somewhat restricted general purpose aid used by state and local education agencies to meet their own sets of needs—some educational, some fiscal, and some political. In fact, compliance strategies based primarily upon "top-down"

Table 6-1.   The Context of Intergovernmental Relations in the Administration of ESEA Title I

Responsibilities	Factors That Influence Program Operation
HEW and USOE	
• Determine county (and therefore state) allocations	• Congressional expectations
• Determine program regulations	• Reactions from state and local agencies
• Approve state plans	• Reactions from interest groups
• Monitor SEA and LEA performance	• Capacity
• Access program effectiveness	Resources: availability of staff and support funds
• Provide technical assistance to states	Skills and experience of staff
• Interpret rules and regulations	• Intraagency coordination and competition
	• Posture toward SEAs and LEAs (assertive v. passive)
	• Resolution of conflicts with particular states
States	
• Develop and submit state plan	• Political and social context in which educational decisions are made and implemented
• Provide assurance to federal government of intent to operate program in compliance with regulations	• Historical relationship between SEA and LEAs
• Approve project applications from LEAs	• Political influence of particular LEAs
• Monitor local projects to assure operation of program in accordance with application "contract"	• Adminstrative style
• Establish complaint procedure	Compliance v. program improvement
• Submit annual evaluation report to federal government	Assertive v. passive
• Submit annual fiscal report to federal government	• Capacity
• Submit funds distribution and use report to federal government	Resources: availability of staff and support funds
• Determine subcounty allocations	Skills and experience of staff
• Provide technical assistance to LEAs	• Prior experience with federal agencies
To assure compliance	Audits
To improve program operations	Management team reviews
	Idiosyncratic interpretations of requirements
	• Values of key actors
	Chief state school officer
	Federal programs or Title I director
	• Nature and relationship of state compensatory education program
	Interest and involvement of governor and legislature
	Fiscal and programmatic relationship
	• Changing fiscal context
	• Number of LEAs and projects to be monitored

Responsibilities	*School Districts*	*Factors That Influence Program Operation*

School Districts

Responsibilities

- Conduct needs analysis and design projects to meet needs
- Determine allocation of funds to schools and pupils in compliance with federal regulations
- Involve parents in decisionmaking process
- Evaluate project effectiveness
- Maintain appropriate fiscal records
- Submit fiscal and programmatic reports to SEA
- Monitor project implementation in decentralized districts and schools

Factors That Influence Program Operation

- Size of district
- Size and importance of federal program
- Type of district
  - Urban
  - Suburban
  - Rural
- Changing fiscal context
- Management and programmatic capacity
- Leadership of superintendent
- Role and influence of Parent Advisory Council (PAC)
- Idiosyncratic characteristics and problems, e.g., desegregation
- Relationships between SEA and LEA program staff
- Prior experience with compliance issues
  - Audits
  - Monitoring reviews
- Basic educational style
- Presence, nature, and size of other categorical programs
- Collective bargaining contract

Schools

Responsibilities

- Identify participating pupils
- Design instructional activities for pupils (this will be a district function in many places)
- Implement project activities
- Coordinate project activities with regular and special programs
- Improve learning
- Involve parents in decision process

Factors That Influence Program Operation

- District policies and priorities
- Leadership of district staff
- Competence of district staff
- District program designs
- District oversight
- Leadership of principal
- Presence of other categorical programs (state and federal)
- Role and influence of parents
- Concentration of high-need pupils
- Turnover of staff
- Concentration of funds

administration of federal mandates that were constantly tightened—and, many would add, lengthened—was based upon an unrealistic view of administrative behavior in an intergovernmental setting. In many ways this view was capsulized by William Wayson when he observed that "The failure of ESEA was (and is) a local and state victory over federal attempts to use education to improve the status of the poor. From the earliest days, the funds were used differently from what Congress had intended."[15]

Most of the negative attitudes currently held by federal officials, policy analysts, and reformers about the extent to which the federal controls have been effective in implementing Title I programs evolved from experiences during the very early years of implementation when abuses at state and local levels abounded and there was widely recognized maladministration at the federal level. Those major abuses are well documented and do not need to be repeated here.[16] In addition, the assumptions of failure were also formed by the general lack of evidence of improved learning by Title I pupils, attributable at least in part to the inadequacy of Title I evaluations. In addition, the knowledge that only a very small percentage of the funds identified in federal audits as misused by states and local districts has actually been returned contributes to the belief that the controls are not working, as does the apparently successful resistance to federal controls by the state education department in California.

A More Current View

The common view of Title I administration may be overly pessimistic and unjustified. A more current "end of the first decade" view of the federal-state-local partnership could provide a good deal more confidence in the ability of the federal government to influence the operation of categorical programs in local school districts. Though the jury is certainly still out, initial observations support the belief that the fundamental principles and purposes of a federal aid program directed to disadvantaged pupils are currently widely if not universally accepted.[17] For example, compliance with the major funds allocation regulations is probably no longer a major issue, though it will continue to be a concern that deserves routine and, in some cases, vigorous attention. While much variation in administrative practices and effectiveness continues to exist at both state and local levels, instances of outright malfeasance and noncompliance are probably quite rare. Equally important, there has been a general upgrading of the norms of administrative practice at each level of the partnership. This is not to say that successful implementation of Title I as intended by the federal government is universal and that there are no problems. Rather, it is to say that the first decade of Title I has produced a working and viable accountability system that is largely responsible for reducing the incidence of major infractions or problems to a manageable minimum, and the system provides a vehicle through which ongoing and persistent problems can be identified and addressed. There may also be reason to believe that the institutional and personal capabilities of professional staff dealing with compensatory education, both in grant management and program improvement skills, have been significantly upgraded. On balance, there is evidence to indicate that USOE administrative practices have contributed to this improved environment at the state level and that, in turn, state administrative practices have had a positive influence on local districts. In the research presently being undertaken[18] to confirm these preliminary impressions, the implications for the long-term nature of the federal-state-local partnership in programs serving target groups will be extremely important.

Changes in Federal Oversight and SEA
Management of Title I

Effective programs begin with sound management, and progress has been substantial at both the federal and state levels over the past five years. For example, many SEA personnel are seriously concerned with implementing and enforcing the regulations. They accept the regulations as objectives and are really trying. In many states if the Title I directors are not actually receiving substantial support from the chief state school officer, they are at least enjoying greater latitude in dealing with local districts than was the case in the late 1960s.

The apparent willingness of state officials to adopt federal objectives stems from a number of factors. One of the more important is that many state officials have had much experience in dealing with Title I. Though our information is as yet incomplete, we have been struck by the number of Title I directors, field consultants, and fiscal personnel who have been with the program since its inception in 1965. They have worked out the basic procedures and understandings between federal and local officials about the program's requirements. While the conventional wisdom holds that familiarity creates deference to state and local priorities and an overriding of the federal interest, at least in those regulatory areas where the requirements are unambiguous, long-term relationships seem to have promoted compliance.

Federal actions also may have an important role to play in improving state management practices. Despite the bad reputation association with the federal government's audit procedures—only $750,000 of an estimated $266 million of potential violations has been returned to the federal government—many state officials apparently find it easier to enforce the regulations than to become involved in an audit exception. The post-Watergate concern with trust in government apparently has also "encouraged" state officials to enforce the regulations. Disagreement with a federal requirement may no longer be seen as sufficient reason for not complying with legal responsibilities and for running the risk of an audit exception.

In addition, the USOE Area Desk staff in the Office of Compensatory Education has played an important role in improving state management procedures. Each area desk has four professional staff members who perform annual management team reviews of the Title I operation in each state. Such reviews usually take about one week per state and involve site visits to several LEAs as well as interviews and examinations of records and documents at the SEA. We have examined the composite results of these reviews for all fifty states and the separate review reports and state responses for more than a dozen. At the very least, the management team review process has produced incremental progress in state management procedures, even in those states considered to have outstanding programs. But more important, the reviews and year-round relationship between the staff of the area desk, as well as others in the office, and SEA officials have contributed to substantial changes in many states. The overall upgrading of SEA Title I administration in many of the southeastern states that, up to 1970, had a good deal less than exemplary reputations for their acceptance of federal purposes and procedures seems both real and impressive.

The management team reviews by USOE not only address compliance issues, but also concern themselves with the management capacity of the SEA to attain compliance and to promote more effective programs. Each review report "suggests" ways for the SEA to improve its operating procedures. The important point here is that the USOE has addressed the *process* of state administration, and many SEAs seem to have responded by changing their management procedures. Although some might describe the SEA-USOE relationship as too cozy to foster the real improvement that some reformers desire, it has seemed a realistic approach to moving each state from where it currently is to a more effective level of management practice.

The USOE Area Desk teams have encouraged SEAs to monitor LEAs in virtually the same way as the SEAs are themselves monitored by the USOE. Effective enforcement of regulations and, indeed, effective encouragement of specific programmatic goals and evaluation procedures begin with a comprehensive and detailed evaluation of the annual program application of each LEA. Not only should information from prior evaluations of the district's program be used at the time of the application review, but the district's own evaluation procedure design should also be examined. Once approved, the application and project budget become a "contract" between the LEA and the SEA. The SEA must then monitor each LEA's performance in implementing the "contract." Monitoring occurs through written reports submitted to the SEA, informal contact between local and state personnel, formal on-site monitoring visits conducted by field consultants, and on-site audits by state fiscal auditors, who typically operate independently of the federal program staff. The USOE–Management Review teams have emphasized the importance of frequent on-site reviews for each participating district; the informal standard seems to be to visit each district at least once every two years with annual visits to the large districts in each state. Particular stress is placed on instruments or checklists to be used by the SEA review team (just as the USOE teams employ checklists and set procedures for examining SEA records). At the same time the USOE encourages SEAs to commit resources from state administrative set-aside funds for technical assistance to LEAs, for dissemination activities, and for evaluating local programs. To date, however, technical assistance seems to be addressed primarily to showing LEA officials how to run compliant programs. There is little evidence that much attention is devoted to helping LEAs design and evaluate activities in order to provide more effective programs.

One of the reasons for the progress made over the past few years in state administration of Title I is the widespread acceptance of the management model reflected in the USOE team reviews. Where, in USOE's view, SEAs have not been adequately ensuring the implementation of authentic Title I programs, USOE has pushed SEAs to make the changes necessary for bringing programs into compliance. One of the more common thrusts has been to centralize control over Title I operations under the state director in those states where various functions and, therefore, controls had been widely dispersed throughout a state agency.

The point here is that USOE monitoring of SEA administrative practices has covered not ony *what* states must do to bring programs into compliance, but also *how* to achieve that end. Perhaps more significant for the future both of Title I and of such legislation as PL 94–142 is the fact that the states seem to have responded to the USOE by making the adjustments required. This is in large measure a function of the control that the USOE can exert over the use of state administrative set-aside funds. The USOE-SEA relationship suggests that the federal government may be beginning to establish a type of authority where rewards and sanctions are moved to the background. For those few states where a serious gap remains between federal expectations and state implementation, however, assertive exercise of federal authority will continue to be necessary.

From the states' perspectives, a number of problems still remain, and while most are potentially solvable, they are currently proving particularly troublesome. The most notable may be the different interpretations of the requirements, interpretations that depend on who in HEW made them. Critics have long charged that ambiguities in the rules, guidelines, and other published materials make compliance difficult. The Lawyers Committee for Civil Rights Under Law has prepared for the NIE an analysis of conflicts in interpretations that should serve as an important first step in clearing up many of the differences. Our contacts with SEA personnel lead us to conclude that the reality of current ambiguities and their real impact on state and local operations are probably far less than is generally believed. Those that exist could be largely resolved if the USOE would develop usable examples or models as illustrations of acceptable approaches to program implementation.

States seem particularly concerned about differences in the interpretations of rules and regulations made by USOE administrative personnel and those by HEW auditors. The auditors work out of the ten HEW regional offices, and their responsibilities cover many federal programs in addition to those administered by the education division. Accordingly, the potential for misinterpretation is higher than it would be if only ESEA, or even only education programs, were being audited. Though procedures for resolving differences before final resolution of audit exceptions exist, generally poor communications between USOE staff and HEW audit personnel represents one of the more troublesome points in the federal government's process of auditing categorical grant programs.

Summary

The first ten years of ESEA Title I have produced a set of administrative procedures and relationships through which state and local officials can be held accountable for implementation of the program in accordance with national goals and expectations. The experiences in Title I have several implications for federal programs serving other target groups of pupils, such as the new All Handicapped Children Act, as well as for the possibility of greater federal control over vocational education aid. First, ESEA required a major restructuring of federal-state-local relationships that was probably more extensive and more complex than was recognized or understood in 1965. Though the quality of intergovernmental relationships established between compensatory education officials at each level may be partially transferable within each state to areas of special and vocational education, relationships between government officials tend to be subject specific. This suggests that several years experience with PL 94-142 may be required before the partnership in special education is also institutionalized and that at the outset progress may be very uneven. Second, given the kinds of new relationships that were required, long-term estimates of the viability of the federal-state-local partnership based on the frequent difficulties of the early years were probably overly pessimistic. Only within the past two or three years have the normative patterns of SEA and LEA administrative behavior begun to indicate that a workable system might be in place. Third, although in the short run the federal government lacks authority or control over the political and cultural context within which states and local school districts administer Title I, in the long term the federal role appears to be a significant factor in changing state and local practices. In other words, the lever of federal aid seems to be working.

Finally, the first decade of the ESEA has not only produced a workable accountability system, but it has also provided a major experience in capacity building at the state level that goes far beyond the general conception of Title V, which was designed expressly for that purpose. Indeed, ESEA has emphasized the key role of the state in implementing and improving programs for target groups of pupils. In many states there is increasing pressure from local districts to reduce state as well as federal control over local decisionmaking.

The future success of federal programs designed to meet national priorities may depend on the federal government's capacity to assist states and provide incentives for them to move from a simplistic, compliance-oriented administrative style to a leadership posture in their own relations with local districts.

If this picture of Title I is relatively accurate, assuring maintenance and continued improvement in compliance areas by states and local districts will become a routine administrative activity. The major task will then be to focus administrative energy predominately on issues of program effectiveness to assure that the educational goals of Title I are achieved. Issues of program design, evaluation, and improvement are far more difficult to resolve than the primarily regulatory concerns that represent the major accomplishment of the first decade.

The remainder of this chapter focuses on specific components of Title I that have implications for the effectiveness of compensatory education and for other federal categorical programs. The discussion will consider the effects of federal requirements on local districts, with particular attention given to implications for program consolidations and to a strategy for providing states with greater flexibility in adapting the federal program to their own conditions and procedures.

ALLOCATING FUNDS TO TARGET PUPILS

The most critical step in improving the educational opportunities of a target group of pupils is to get the funds from Washington to the appropriate individual school and classroom sites so that they can be converted into resources for instructional programs. The two basic policy questions are: first, how are the target pupils to be defined and identified, and second, among the target-group pupils which ones are actually to receive services?

Under Title I the process works as follows:

- The federal government makes the county and therefore the aggregate state allocation on the basis of a poverty criterion.
- The SEAs make subcounty allocations, also using a poverty criterion.
- LEAs select eligible schools on the basis of a poverty criterion.
- LEAs make the allocations to schools, usually on the basis of educational needs, but sometimes on the basis of poverty criteria.
- Schools identify pupils to be served on the criterion of educational needs (achievement).

The operating principles behind this process are that (1) all states and all counties receive Title I funds; (2) all LEAs are eligible for funds; (3) only those pupils in school target areas in which the concentration of poverty pupils as defined by the poverty criteria used for subdistrict allocations exceeds the district average are *eligible* to receive funds; (4) only those pupils whose educational need is greater than a district criterion and who are also in eligible schools are *eligible* to receive services; and (5) only those eligible pupils in schools with the highest concentrations of economic need pupils *actually receive* services. These procedures in Title I are designed to assure that those districts with the greatest need receive the most funds; that, within each district, those pupils with the greatest need compared to others within the district receive the services; and that a critical mass of funds is available to those who actually participate in the Title I program.

This process of administering procedures for funds allocation under Title I is generally under control, with far fewer examples of efforts to subvert the rules and regulations than was the case four or five years ago. For example, clarification of the comparability procedures for the 1974–75 school year has gone a long way toward achieving actual attainment of the congressional purpose. While some technical problems remain and SEAs handle numerous queries from LEAs about specific concerns idiosyncratic to each district, a very high order of compliance should be the norm in the immediate future. It is particularly worth noting that the comparability requirement has a specific, immediate, and reasonable penalty that must be applied to LEAs found to be out of compliance. SEAs are required to not pay LEAs for costs of Title I programs incurred during each day that the district is noncomparable. This penalty has been invoked by some states.

However, a number of policy issues about procedures for funds allocation continue to require attention. They include the following:

- Should allocations more effectively reflect the high expenditure levels of those major metropolitan states who "lost" funds under the 1974 amendments?
- Should there be adjustments in county and subcounty allocation formulas to recognize the effects of higher concentrations of disadvantaged pupils in some districts? Should all LEAs be eligible for Title I funds?
- At what levels and in what ways should an education needs criterion be used in place of a poverty criterion?
- Should schools with very high concentrations of Title I pupils be exempted from the requirement to serve only target pupils?

Fiscal Needs of High Expenditure States

The Education Amendments of 1974 included a new formula for allocating Title I funds to the states; they effectively redistributed federal aid from metropolitan states with high expenditures to states that were more rural and had lower expenditures, as well as from urban to rural areas within states. Title I is an extremely important revenue source for many city school districts caught in the fiscal bind of declining growth or, at best, growth in the tax base that is much slower than average, expanding demands on municipal budgets, and declining as well as changing enrollment patterns. Indeed, the new allocation policy essentially shifted federal funds from states and cities that *look* relatively wealthy as a result of their average income and per pupil expenditure characteristics, but who are experiencing very slow economic growth, to a number of states enjoying substantial economic growth. Between 1974 and 1976 the three largest cities in New York had their Title I allotments reduced between 27 and 31 percent; Cleveland, Ohio, and Camden, New Jersey, each lost 31 percent, Minneapolis and St. Paul, 23 and 14 percent, respectively, and Los Angeles, 13 percent. Even in the Southeast where economic growth was impressive, Atlanta lost 10 percent of its Title I aid, Charlotte was reduced 9 percent and Winston-Salem 23 percent. The numbers of pupils requiring compensatory education services in these cities had not declined at rates at all close to the reductions in aid.

Two provisions in the new formula contributed to the shift of Title I aid away from urban areas. First, while the new poverty measure from the census of 1970 increased the incidence of poverty in rural areas, it did not consider important urban-rural cost differences other than food that contribute to the effects of low income. Second, the count of pupils in families above the poverty level receiving Aid to Dependent Children (ADC) payments, which is used in addition to the census data, was reduced to two-thirds of each actual pupil. Cities have far higher proportions of ADC pupils than rural areas. In addition, given greater reliance on census data, urban areas may have been more affected by an estimated undercounting in the census of 1970 of 5.3 million persons, most of whom are believed to be low-income city residents.

State Title I allocations are also based on each state's average per pupil expenditure. The calculation of that average, however, includes an implicit interstate equalization provision since the figure cannot be less than 80 percent nor more than 120 percent of the national average. Connecticut, Illinois, Maryland, New York, New Jersey, and Alaska spend more than the 120 percent of the cutoff. Since some of these states have been among the pacesetters in developing state-level compensatory education and special education programs, the lack of consideration of their higher per pupil expenditures in the aid formulas would seem to be inconsistent with current national goals.

It is probably not possible to find one poverty measure or one formula that would meet all the criteria that might reasonably be used to judge a distribution plan. The selection of a formula, therefore, will always be based in large measure on personal values and the political process. Staff at both HEW and the NIE are analyzing alternative formulas for consideration during the congressional debate over renewal of ESEA in 1978, and some of those alternatives can be expected to be responsive to the fiscal problems of urban states. It is quite possible, of course, that using only current data will show that the patterns of poverty are shifting away from rural areas to those states traditionally seen as having greater capacity to support governmental services. If that is the case, the existing formula and the redistributions that would result from the use of new data for "old" formula measures may direct a greater share of Title I funds to urban states. Whatever the case, the fiscal and educational needs of the high-expenditure metropolitan states and their major cities deserve greater consideration than they received from Congress in 1974.

Recognition in the Formulas of Higher
Concentrations of Eligible Pupils

As noted earlier, the funding formulas and regulations for selecting target areas and pupils are designed to make all LEAs eligible to receive funds, but they are not necessarily designed to ensure that all pupils in a state who are similarly situated, either as to poverty status or as to educational need, will receive services. Given two schools with, say, 12 percent of their enrollment from low-income families, but with districtwide averages of 10 and 15 percent, pupils in the school located in the district with 15 percent *will not* be eligible for services. A recent study prepared for the USOE by the Educational Testing Service found that "25 percent more of the students in high poverty schools would have qualified for compensatory services had they attended low poverty schools."[19] In short, the principle of providing services to a special target group when the standard for funds allocation is the concentration of pupils from that target group in a particular area or school apparently works more effectively in addressing variations school by school within districts than variations among districts.

Similarly, if the school with a 12 percent concentration of eligible pupils is located in a district with, say, an average of 10 or 11 percent concentration, pupils in that school still may not actually receive services because of the requirement to concentrate funds and services in those schools with the greatest needs—and there may not be sufficient funds to go around to all eligible schools. The net effect of the current formulas, particularly when combined with the regulations for concentrating funds in high-need schools and concentrating services on high-need pupils, is to leave many high-need pupils without Title I services, simply because they attend schools whose percentage of low-income pupils is lower than their district's average. In many cities those pupils are experiencing absolute reductions in instruction and support services as a result of severe fiscal pressures at both the municipal and state levels. Although many such city districts continue to appear property wealthy, they are unable to use that tax base for school purposes.

In order to target additional funds to such districts, consideration should be given to a funding formula that recognizes the effects of unusually high concentrations of educationally deprived pupils. But such a "high-concentration" formula should also be combined with a provision that would permit LEAs to distribute funds to more schools and pupils. Whatever standard is used to permit wider distribution of Title I services within high-concentration districts, increased funding would probably also be necessary, and thus services going to schools and pupils already participating in the program would not be reduced.

On the other hand, perhaps now is the time seriously to consider whether all school districts should continue to be eligible to receive Title I funds. In order to obtain passage of ESEA in 1965, a formula based on eligibility for every district in the United States was a political necessity. Since then it has been assumed that the large constituency of Title I districts continued to be politically necessary for maintaining and increasing the size of the annual appropriation, though appropriation increases have fallen short of the rise in costs due to inflation. The principle of serving those schools with the highest concentration of high-need pupils *within* individual school districts is clearly in conflict with the principle of providing funds for *all* districts in each state no matter what their relative need. Perhaps only those LEAs whose concentration of Title I pupils is greater than the state average should be eligible to receive funds. In Michigan, for example, state compensatory education program funds are allocated to all eligible pupils in only those districts with the largest numbers and concentrations of such pupils, 85 out of 570 districts, whereas Title I provides services for *some* pupils in *all* districts in Michigan. Unfortunately, in most states, data are not available that would show the effects of redistributing funds from low-concentration districts to high-concentration districts. Given the relatively small proportion of funds currently going to low-concentration districts, the political costs incurred in trying to make such a formula change may not be worth the redistributional benefits that would occur. Such a change should, nevertheless, be explored.

Education Needs Versus Poverty as an Allocation Criterion

Interest can be expected to continue in using a criterion of educational needs based on achievement test data rather than a poverty indicator for determining the allocation of Title I funds within LEAs. Currently educational need is used to identify pupils who will receive Title I services once the participating school has been selected using a poverty indicator. In many districts the number of low-achieving pupils in each eligible school is also used to determine the school allocations. Two states, Michigan and New York, allocate state compensatory education funds to LEAs using test score results as the measure of need.

The NIE is currently monitoring demonstration projects in thirteen LEAs to determine whether alternative ways of allocating funds to schools within each district would result in more effective programs. All of the thirteen districts, when granted permission to change the criteria used for determining Title I eligible schools, elected to use an achievement criterion. Many local officials prefer an achievement measure because it has the attractive feature of being directly related to what many believe to be the fundamental purpose of the act and it may be easier to administer in urban districts undergoing desegregation.

The issue of employing a criterion of educational needs for sub-county allocations to school districts is also likely to persist. Congressman Quie has proposed that states be permitted to make distributions to districts based on test scores rather than on poverty data. While Guthrie and Frentz found that large urban school districts tend to lose funds when achievement tests are used in place of poverty measures, alternatives other than the ones that they simulated might produce different distributional results.[20] More evidence is clearly required before states should be permitted to make the change.

Serving All Pupils in High-Concentration
Title I Schools

The most fundamental principle guiding the administration of Title I programs is that such programs meet the special educational needs of educationally deprived children rather than assist a school district in carrying out its regular program of instruction. Only children eligible for Title I should receive the benefits of services funded by Title I. During the early years of ESEA the requirement that Title I funds not be used for general aid purposes was probably the most flagrantly abused provision of the legislation. It will continue to be an area of compliance that must be closely and continually watched. The fiscal pressures facing many school districts provide considerable motivation to use federal funds to maintain for all pupils services that are scheduled to be reduced or eliminated. The problem of program cutbacks is especially troublesome to teachers and parents when the pupils so affected have achievement levels below the average but whose need for extra services is not as great as those who qualify for Title I services. An exaggerated form of the problem occurs in those schools where the concentration of Title I eligible pupils is extremely high and the vast majority of all pupils in the school achieves below national norms. In such schools teachers, aides, and parents often view the school itself as "disadvantaged," and their desire to serve more pupils or structure their Title I programs within the basic instructional program is not motivated by a wish to serve high-achieving or high socioeconomic status (SES) pupils. Rather, they are making a legitimate attempt to provide a more effective basic instructional program, one already designed around the special needs pupils.

Perhaps the rules and regulations of Title I should be modified to permit such schools to use Title I funds for all pupils in the school through the regular instructional program. If, say, as many as 50 percent of a school's pupils were eligible for Title I or if at least 75 percent were below national reading norms, the usual rules for servicing only Title I pupils could be waived.

DESIGNING, EVALUATING, AND IMPROVING
INSTRUCTIONAL PROGRAMS

As has been noted, there seems to be increasing though not universal compliance with funds allocation regulations that reflects an operational acceptance of the allocative goals of Title I as those goals are currently conceptualized. Much of the administrative energy of the first decade has sought to assure the attainment of those goals. Additional concern throughout the first decade has focused on the extent to which compensatory education funds and services have, in fact, raised pupil achievement. Not surprisingly, the major studies of the program have sought to answer that question,[21] and Congress, in Section 151 of the Education Amendments of 1974, required the USOE to provide greater direction to states and local districts in the content of program evaluations.

Just as there is substantial compliance with the funds allocation requirements of Title I, there is also general compliance with the nominal requirements of needs assessment and evaluation, though the capacity of agency personnel and the quality of practices vary widely among SEAs and LEAs. Several state officials with whom we talked over the last few months have indicated that, now that their administrative procedures for assuring compliance with the funds allocation requirements are in place, they are in a position to give greater attention to improving needs assessments, program designs, and evaluations. The basic question is how can the USOE most effectively enhance the capacity of SEAs to assist districts to identify pupils most in need of services and improve programs so that they more effectively meet the needs of those pupils?

The task of helping states to become effective agents of change will be far more difficult to achieve than the overall upgrading of SEA performance in the management of federal grants, the major accomplishment of the first decade of ESEA. Three obstacles are significant. First, after a decade of Title I, the specific compensatory education programs provided by school districts have been largely institutionalized by local officials into the continuing instructional program. Change, even incremental improvement, is far more difficult to promote when instructional approaches are well entrenched, particularly when there may be a lack of receptiveness to change. Second, though the technology of evaluating instructional programs may be in its embryonic stages, it is probably still far ahead of the capacity of principals and teachers to use the results of evaluations to improve instruction. This leads to the third obstacle. Even when evaluation results are clear and accepted by principals and teachers, the lack of knowledge about how to change instructional strategies, as Milbrey McLaughlin has noted, continues to inhibit change.[22]

Taken together these obstacles should not be cause for overreaction; the baby of compensatory education should not be thrown out with the bathwater of fiscal prudence. Indeed, these problems are characteristic of all instructional areas, not just of compensatory education programs. In terms of federal programs for target groups of pupils, concern with improving instruction and demonstrating measurable gains in achievement is probably more visible in compensatory education, bilingual education, and the special education areas of learning disabilities and the mildly handicapped than in programs for the severely handicapped or in vocational education. The implication is that during the second decade of massive federal involvement in local instructional programs the energies of the federal government should be directed toward improving the capacity of SEAs and LEAs to conduct needs assessments, evaluate programs, and implement new instructional strategies.

Needs Assessment and Program Design

Title I requires that local school districts conduct annual needs assessments to determine which instructional and support services are most needed, which grade levels should receive priority services, and which individual pupils at the selected grade levels should be eligible for participation in Title I programs. The intent is to have each local school district focus its Title I funds where the need for those funds is greatest, with those needs identified and given priority through a systematic process that includes parent involvement. Over the past several years the federal government has made its expectations about this process more explicit, most recently in the regulations that will govern the implementation of the 1974 Amendments to ESEA published in September 1976. Among a number of changes, the regulations require the use of procedures and instruments sufficient to determine the instructional and noninstructional needs of children who will participate in Title I projects and the establishment of specific criteria for identifying children with the greatest need and those who no longer require Title I services.[23]

The federal government has also strengthened its urging that the majority of Title I funds be used to improve basic skills, and some states have responded to that expectation by greatly reducing the discretion of LEAs in deciding which services will be provided and which grade levels will be served. States have either prescribed the purposes for which funds should be used or have left such decisions to the district if a district can demonstrate having conducted the required needs assessment. It seems axiomatic that the SEAs will play the key role in improving the designs of instructional programs and that successful implementation will just as clearly be determined by the extent to which LEAs can adapt general approaches to their specific needs and conditions. The ability of SEAs to help LEAs will be determined by the quality of the help that can be provided and the availability of assistance.

Program Evaluation

That the decade has been ten years of frustration with respect to evaluations of the effectiveness of Title I is exceedingly well documented. The basic tension over the past decade has been between the need for evaluation as a tool for improving the design and implementation of programs at the local level and the federal government's need for data about the overall effectiveness of Title I as a national program. Both goals have their advocates, and USOE efforts have often reflected unworkable compromises between the two. What would seem to be critical at this juncture is for the federal government—the Congress and the USOE—to have a realistic understanding about the extent to which these goals can be attained in the near future, either singly or in conjunction with each other, and about how requirements under Title I as well as under other federal programs serving target groups of pupils can contribute to their attainment.

Can an evaluation reporting system be designed that is capable of providing federal-level policymakers with the type of information they want about the educational effectiveness of Title I? That goals seems unattainable, at least in the short term, even if the reporting system is designed *exclusively* to meet national information needs. More important, however, the increasing realization of the importance of the states in the intergovernmental partnership suggests that emphasis should be placed instead on building the capacity of SEAs and LEAs to evaluate their own programs. Indeed, the most pressing need is to develop a reasonable level of technological competence in the area of evaluation in each SEA and LEA. Some SEAs do not have the services of a staff member specifically trained in educational evaluation to help with the Title I program.

Close behind the need for technological skills is the need for local- and state-level evaluation studies for guiding policy decisions. The recent Education Turnkey Study to evaluate compensatory education programs in Michigan is one example of such studies. Based on the results of the Education Turnkey Study,[24] SEA staff members in Michigan have already begun to require modification of LEA project designs—most notably by reducing heavy use of teacher aides—before approving applications.

OTHER MANAGEMENT AND PROGRAMMATIC ISSUES

This section addresses three issues: parent involvement, coordination with state compensatory education programs, and coordination with other federal programs.

Parent Involvement

The effort to achieve parent involvement in Title I programs has been viewed as one of the major reforms in the act, but implementation of parent advisory councils (PACs), which play a continuing and important role in program decisionmaking, may exhibit as much variation as any regulatory or programmatic issue. This is particularly true at the school-building level in districts where PACs have been required only since the Education Amendments of 1974. It had been hoped and expected that strong and active PACs would complement the basically top-down administrative orientation of the usual enforcement procedures.

Participation of parents in local program decisions seems to follow three general patterns. In some LEAs there is a strong commitment to parent participation, often predating the Title I requirements, and parent councils at both the district and school levels have considerable influence. As a result of parent-training workshops and frequent meetings, the level of knowledge and understanding is exceptional. In other districts, administrators seem to support parent involvement and the districtwide PAC functions regularly, but building-level commitment and participation vary markedly. In still other districts, real parent involvement is minimal or nonexistent, either because parents are unconcerned or because school administrators block attempts at change and frustrate the community, largely to protect their own interests.[25]

By and large very little is known about the level, quality, or effectiveness of parent participation in Title I decisionmaking. Where parents are seriously involved, school officials probably comply fully with the letter as well as with the spirit of the rules and regulations. Beyond such minimum standards, the line between coaptation of parents by school officials and legitimate respect for and deference to school officials by parents may be very thin indeed. At the school-building level, aside from the level of commitment to parent participation exhibited by the professional staff, the most important factor may be the extent to which important programmatic decisions about Title I have been delegated to building personnel. If all or most key decisions about the program offered in each school are made at the district level so that the only major remaining concern is with the selection of participating pupils, there is little incentive for parent participation.

Three issues concerning parent involvement in Title I have important implications for decisionmaking in the program as well as in other categorical federal programs. First, should Title I parents who are employees of the school district be allowed to participate in PACs, and if so, should they be permitted to vote? Though not a concern in the vast majority of LEAs, occasionally the considerable influence of parent-employees has made it virtually impossible for school officials to alter programs by reducing aide positions, even when Title I funds are reduced. One district studied withdrew the authority of individual schools to make many programmatic decisions, a move that in large measure was designed to eliminate the ability of the school PAC, though not the district PAC, to retain aide positions for members of the community.

Second, should a criterion for requiring building-level PACs be established so that schools with very few Title I services would be exempted from the requirement? At present small school districts are exempted.

Third, should LEAs and schools with several parent councils, each required by a different categorical program, be permitted to organize in a manner different from the Title I rules and regulations? Some schools within districts have as many as four or five parent committees, frequently with overlapping membership and interests. More efficient uses of both parent and staff time would seem to warrant a more flexible approach to the organization of parent councils. At the very least, grant consolidation proposals should directly address this issue.

Coordination with State Compensatory Education Programs

More than a dozen states have their own state-level compensatory education programs. Five of these states plus another eight also have state-level bilingual programs.[26] The relationships between the federal and state programs can tell much about the extent and nature of a state's commitment to compensatory education as well as provide clues about how the federal program would be administered were states given greater discretion over the program's operation.

The compensatory education programs in the large industrial states of California, New York, Michigan, and Ohio account for approximately 90 percent of state-level compensatory education funds and offer considerable contrast in their relationships to Title I. In general, even when the state programs utilize the grant application and state approval process, local districts are given considerably more discretion over use of funds than they currently have under Title I. While some of that discretion occurs by intent, much occurs by default because legislatures have not provided funds for SEAs to monitor local programs.

In New York's Chapter 241 program for Pupils with Special Educational Needs (PSEN), for example, pupils scoring below the twenty-fourth percentile in the distribution of the statewide achievement test scores are weighted 25 percent more than other pupils for aid distributed through the state's foundation formula. LEAs are required to demonstrate that the funds have been used for target pupils in three priority areas: reading, math, and bilingual education. They do not have to submit applications for approval, but annual evaluations are required. The SEA is attempting to exert greater control over the conduct of local projects, but since the legislation did not provide "new" money for "new" programs in most districts, LEAs often view such actions as an attempt by the state to get more control without more money.

Ohio's Disadvantaged Youth Program (DYP) utilizes the grant application process and is conceptually related to Title I. The SEA staff responsible for the program is very small, and thus program monitoring and evaluation are more limited than in Title I. In addition, the staff is both physically and organizationally separate from federal program officials.

The Michigan Chapter 3 program provides funds to approximately eighty-five LEAs, and allocations are based on the number of pupils in grades K–6 scoring in the lowest 15 percent on the Michigan tests for needs assessment.

Funds are expected to follow pupils, and each district must design an individual program for *each* participating pupil. In addition, LEAs must submit evaluation results to the SEA for each school building conducting a Chapter 3 program. Considerable conflict has centered around a provision to penalize LEAs in which less than 75 percent of the pupils achieve gains in grade equivalency scores of less than 75 percent for one year, although that penalty has never been actually invoked. However, the SEA is expected to recommend to the legislature that districts with participating school buildings not meeting the standard of 75 percent be required to submit a revised compensatory education program plan to be approved by the SEA in order to receive continued authorization for funding. In short, the new penalty would require that LEAs with unsuccessful programs have their state Chapter 3 programs subjected to the same supervision of their program design and evaluation procedures that is currently applied to all Title I projects. Currently, only one SEA staff consultant and two technicians are assigned to Chapter 3 supervision compared to ten field consultants for Title I, though those consultants do give some attention to Chapter 3 programs when they visit schools that have both.

The California situation is by far the most complex and at the same time perhaps the most illustrative of what can occur in state-level program implementation when the basic goals of compensatory education are embraced by a state but a number of the key operating principles are rejected. The California Legislature has appropriated funds for a major early childhood education (ECE) program as well as for programs for disadvantaged youth and compensatory reading. The funding from state sources almost matches the $155 million the state receives under Title I. In the first phase of what the SEA hopes will eventually become a program in all schools, ECE is currently focused on those districts and schools serving disadvantaged pupils. The fundamental purpose of ECE is to improve programs at the school-building level. To this end the SEA utilizes a consolidated application form for projects funded under all categorical funding sources available to a school.

The USOE Management Review Teams have been highly critical of the California approach because Title I funds are commingled with funds from other sources for which requirements and criteria differ from Title I; thus there is no audit trail for the federal program. Consolidated programs benefit an entire school population, which includes both educationally deprived pupils and those who are not educationally deprived. USOE contends that applications from LEAs are approved by the SEA even though such applications do not describe a discrete project designed to meet the special needs of educationally deprived children. Since discrete projects are not conducted by California schools, many other provisions of Title I cannot be assessed by either the SEA or the federal government.

Several audit exceptions are currently pending in California, including one directed at the support of SEA staff from the Title I state administrative set-aside. While the SEA has instituted record-keeping procedures designed to correct the deficiencies cited in that audit exception, SEA staff working on compensatory education are, nevertheless, widely dispersed throughout many divisions of the agency. This organizational arrangement precluded the creation within the SEA of a Title I unit that would effectively serve as an advocate for the special interest of educationally deprived children and compensatory education programs. The commingling of federal and state funds might be less of an issue if that were the case and it were clear that extra resources were devoted to high-need pupils regardless of the source of funding.

Though most SEA officials express the preference for much greater coordination between Title I and their state program, only California has produced an important conflict with federal officials.[a] This presents the federal government with a major dilemma. How can the integrity of the funds allocation regulations, which are designed to guarantee that federal funds actually reach the target group of pupils, be maintained while at the same time encouraging the initiative and creativity of SEA leadership? As long as both objectives remain in competition the only assured outcome will be a continuation of tension between state and federal officials.

Accountability for use of funds and for program effectiveness need not be in competition with creative program leadership. Often the claim that "creativity is inhibited by federal requirements" has been convenient rhetoric for doing business as usual instead of focusing categorical funds on those pupils most in need of special services. Where this has been the case, the concerns of federal officials, congressional advocates of compensatory education, and reformers have certainly been justified. Examples of such rhetorical resistance to the federal role have been numerous, particularly in the early years of ESEA. But in the past three to five years the specificity of federal requirements, particularly those that assure the fulfillment of allocative goals, has made it possible for many state and local officials to make allocative and programmatic decisions that would have been impossible if those decisions had occurred solely within the context of state and local political cultures and administrative relationships. In those states and local districts where the current operation of compensatory education programs reflects an institutionalization of national priorities, the federal government should consider permitting alternative paths that would allow federal programs to be adapted to the particular needs, conditions, and initiatives of each state.

In practice, some degree of differential administration of SEA management practices by USOE already occurs, even within a single area desk. A formal procedure for responding to the greater initiative demonstrated by those states that have their own compensatory education programs could serve as an incentive to others. Moreover, since the overall level of compliance with Title I regulations generally meets acceptable minimum standards, the climate

---

[a]In all states with compensatory education programs, however, evaluation results are confounded because it is impossible to separate the unique contribution of the state program from that of the Title I.

is probably right to begin to treat states differently according to the quality and creativity of their planning and their implementation of compensatory education programs.

The largely effective regulatory accountability that currently characterizes Title I could evolve into an accountability system based on comprehensive state plans that represent a contractual arrangement between the state and the federal government. The current application approval–program monitoring–evaluation procedure that exists between SEAs and LEAs and the similar arrangements between many large school districts and individual schools could serve as models for the federal-state contract. For such a procedure to work effectively and maintain ultimate authority at the federal level, the federal-state contract would have to include the following:

- Evidence would be needed in the plan-contract that allocation and pupil participation procedures *will* conform to the key principle of serving those pupils most in need of compensatory education services in those schools with the highest concentrations of such pupils.
- The plan-contract would be restricted to a limited period of time, say, three to five years and would not be automatically renewable.
- SEA management procedures to be used in administering the federal or federal-state combined program would be specified.
- Procedures for evaluating SEA implementation of the plan-contract would be specified and the results of the evaluation used to judge the viability of the federal government's entering into subsequent plan-contracts with the state.
- USOE approval of the plan would be required. In the absence of an approved plan-contract, all regular rules and regulations would govern administration of the federal program.

The idea of differential administration has not been particularly popular at the federal level. Top USOE officials seem less than enthusiastic about having to make public their qualitative judgments about differences in the performance of states. In addition, in Congress equitable or consistent treatment of states is probably a more dominant value than differential treatment.[27] Some concerns are also based on doubts about the ability of the federal bureaucracy to administer "state-federal contracts," in which some states are permitted greater latitude than others, as well as doubts about USOE's effective authority to withdraw that latitude for lack of performance by a state. Nevertheless, qualitative, and in some cases quantitative, criteria are available for assessing the performance of SEAs in the relatively narrow area of the administration of compensatory education. Federal encouragement of imaginative and creative SEA level leadership in states already exhibiting sound program administration may well be dependent upon a formal process of differential treatment that recognizes the need for both SEAs and LEAs to obtain prior approval for their more innovative ideas and encouragement and support for implementation of those ideas.

Coordination with Other Federal Programs

Individual pupils and the schools that they attend can be the recipients of federal funds from several different sources. For example, compensatory education programs can be funded not only by Title I, but also by the federal bilingual program, the Indian Education Act, the Emergency School Assistance Act, the low-income housing provision of PL 874, and the Right to Read Act in addition to state-level compensatory education and bilingual programs. One local official has noted, "If each program focuses on the *same students* (most in need), those students will be overwhelmed with services, while other (less needy but still low achieving) students will not be served."[28] The contention that the separate and sometimes conflicting requirements of each program contribute to ineffective local planning is one rationale behind proposals to consolidate federal programs that are intended to serve the same types of pupils.

To what extent do the several programs serving target groups of pupils actually impede planning and coordination of instructional programs? It is too early in our study of Title I to have a definite answer to the question, but the situation may not be as bad as some local officials would have us believe. Where different services are supported by separate funding sources and the same SEA officials are responsible for administration of each program, accommodations can usually be worked out and individual pupils will not be overloaded with special services.

Problems arise when LEA officials must deal with different officials and administrative groups for each program at the state and federal levels. Bilingual, ESEA Title VII, Right to Read, and often Indian Education Act SEA officials frequently report to different deputies of the chief state school officer and, perhaps more important, may be in competition with each other. The Emergency School Assistance Act, which may contribute as much as any federal program to difficulties in planning and implementing local compensatory education programs in a coordinated fashion, is administered by the regional offices of HEW, and SEA officials are not directly involved. Given the requirements of the Education for All Handicapped Pupils Act (PL 94-142) for mainstreaming mildly handicapped and learning disabled pupils into regular classrooms, the potential for conflict with SEA special education staff also exists. In many cases the special services provided for mainstreamed pupils designated as handicapped will be exactly the same as those services provided under the label of compensatory education, especially if such pupils are economically as well as educationally disadvantaged.

The multiplicity of special categorical programs for different but often overlapping groups of pupils, and their often unique location within federal and state bureaucratic hierarchies, has its basis in the different political constituencies responsible for creating each program in the first place. These groups see program consolidation as reducing their special visibility and power. Concerns with visibility and power and competition for the right to control special programs that affect pupils in each constituent group—and perhaps a striving to expand the constituent group—exist at the state as well as the federal level. From the local perspective, at least some of this competition can be an impediment to effective program administration.

Program grant consolidation should be something more than either a disguised vehicle for letting states and local districts do whatever they wish with federal funds or only a cosmetic regrouping of grant programs still intended to maintain the integrity of federal support for the special needs of target pupils. If the purpose is to enhance the capability of LEAs to coordinate planning and implement programs for special needs pupils, administrative consolidation must begin at the federal level and should include attention to the relationship between day-to-day management activities and decisions and HEW audit function. Similar reorganization should be required at the SEA level, and evidence of an organizational structure that matches the categorical programs to be consolidated should be a prerequisite for approval of a consolidated state plan-contract. Finally, the process of management reviews of SEA administrative operations currently used only in Title I parts A and B and the migrant and neglected and bilingual programs should be expanded to cover at the least all such programs dealing with compensatory education. Such changes should help remove the real obstacles that sometimes get in the way of the efficient and effective management of federal grant programs at the local level and at the same time provide clarity about what is emerging as a very workable federal-state-local accountability system.

As an alternative to formal grant consolidation, USOE and the SEAs could be encouraged to reorganize on their own to facilitate ongoing coordination between all programs serving a particular target group of pupils. USOE could also take the leadership in developing prototype models of ways in which the several federal sources of funds could be provided at a given school and still comply with the separate requirements of each program. Either approach—formal consolidation or administrative reorganization—would retain the basic principles embodied in federal oversight of SEA administrative practices.

IMPLICATIONS OF THE EXPERIENCE OF THE
FIRST DECADE OF FEDERAL AID PROGRAMS
FOR TARGET GROUPS OF STUDENTS

The first decade of ESEA has been completed, and much has been accomplished. Evidence is beginning to emerge that demonstrates that a federal-state-local partnership for achieving a nationally determined educational goal can be made to work. Clarifications in the legislation and in the operating rules and guidelines have produced a large measure of understanding and acceptance of the basic purposes of compensatory education. Given time and a spirit of mutual adaptation by federal and state officials, no less should be expected of the new Education for All Handicapped Children Act.

Moreover, though it has taken almost the entire decade to achieve, a workable accountability system has been developed through which substantial compliance with funds allocation and programmatic requirements can be ensured. Though universal perfection has not been attained and some states and districts continue to fall short of acceptable performance standards, compliance no longer deserves to be a major reform issue; ongoing diligence and fine-tuning will be in order. The key role in this has been played by USOE. Although there were struggles in the early years, recently an effective working partnership has developed in most states, and USOE has been primarily responsible for this.

In addition, ESEA opened up new job opportunities at SEA and LEA levels, and a number of highly competent, creative, and experienced people are in place as program directors, field consultants, grant managers, and evaluation specialists. Many of these people are ready to shift their energies away from program compliance to issues of program improvement.

Although the federal government has played the determining role in the first decade, the key role for the future rests with the SEAs. This means that within the accountability framework already established, federal policy should be directed toward improving the capacity of SEAs to provide leadership and dirction to local districts. The challenges of planning, coordinating, implementing, and evaluating effective instructional programs for educationally deprived pupils—or for any target group of pupils—are considerably more difficult than the relatively simple task of attaining compliance with a set of grant management requirements.

The following strategies for building the capacity of SEAs to administer compensatory education programs deserve consideration at the federal level:

- The basic conception of compliance accountability embodied in Title I should be maintained.
- Coordination of *all* federal programs serving the educationally deprived should begin with administrative reorganization at USOE and the SEAs. Although legislative consolidation of grant programs may *not* be necessary to achieve administrative coordination, any plan helpful to local districts will require considerably more coordination among compensatory programs than is currently the case.
- Differences should be permitted among SEAs in management strategies, program evaluation procedures, and instructional priorities and strategies. SEA accountability should be maintained through a USOE-approved state

plan-contract and through consistent USOE technical assistance, monitoring, and enforcement procedures.

• Resources should be focused on improving the capacity of LEAs and SEAs to improve both the technology of their evaluation procedures and the use made of their evaluations. Fiscal incentives related to the state administrative set-aside should be provided to promote SEA leadership in this area.

In addition to issues of capacity building focused on SEA administration of compensatory education programs, the allocation formulas for both Title I and PL 94-142 should be reviewed. The current formula for determining Title I county allocations and the formulas used by states for subcounty allocations fail to take into consideration the fiscal effect of high concentrations of educationally deprived pupils in school districts, and both the Title I and PL 94-142 formulas ignore the very high costs of educational services in many industrialized states and metropolitan areas.

To summarize, this chapter has focused largely on federal policy about the educationally deprived target group of pupils. The new Education for All Handicapped Children Act is likely to face problems similar to those experienced in the first decade of Title I, and the lessons from the Title I experience should be instructive to the administrators of that act. Similarly in vocational education, the federal government's role may soon become more assertive, in response to criticism like that voiced in a recent report to USOE:

> The current [Vocational Education] legislation serves as a conscience, not as a blueprint. Attention to fine detail—the operational and administrative structures, the delivery system and fiscal responsibility necessary to accomplish the goals set forth—is missing.[29]

As was noted at the beginning of this chapter, state and local agencies can be expected to continue to resist an expanded federal role. If all fifty states could be counted upon to exert initiative in serving all of their target pupils, expansion would not be necessary. Until such time, however, the national priorities will probably require the continued development of a workable federal-state-local partnership similar to the one evolving in the administration of programs for the educationally deprived.

NOTES

1. *Federal Funding: Restructuring the Delivery of Assistance to Local School Districts* (Chicago: The National Federation of Urban-Suburban School Districts, October 1975).

2. Joseph M. Cronin, "The Federal Takeover: Should the Junior Partner Run the Firm?" *Phi Delta Kappan* (April 1976).

3. See, for example, Samuel Halperin, "Federal Takeover, State

Default or a Family Problem?" *Phi Delta Kappan* (June 1976) or the same article in *Compact.*

4. National Federation, *Federal Funding,* pp. 6, 10, 11.

5. "Federal and State Mandates Mean Still Higher Special Education Costs," *Dateline Washington,* (Washington, D.C.: National Legislative Conference, August 1976). For an analysis of the implications of the act see *Change in Education: Three Policy Papers on the Implementation of the "Education for All Handicapped Children Act"* (Washington, D.C.: Education Policy Research Institute of the Educational Testing Service, March 1976).

6. "What Is the Role of Federal Assistance for Vocational Education?" Report to the Congress by the Comptroller General of the United States, Washington, D.C., December 1974; and Mary L. Ellis, *A Report to the Nation on Vocational Education* (Flagstaff, Ariz.: Project Baseline, Northern Arizona University, November 1975).

7. Joel S. Berke and Michael W. Kirst, *Federal Aid to Education: Who Benefits? Who Governs?* (Lexington, Mass.: Lexington Books, D.C. Heath and Company, 1972).

8. Milbrey W. McLaughlin, *Evaluation and Reform: The Elementary and Secondary Education Act of 1965, Title I* (Santa Monica, Calif.: The Rand Corporation, R-1292-RC, January 1974); id. "Implementation of ESEA Title I: A Problem of Compliance," *Teachers College Record,* 77 Teachers College, Columbia University (February 1976); id. "Evaluation and Reform: The Case of ESEA Title I" (Santa Monica, Calif.: The Rand Corporation, 1974).

9. *The Silken Purse: Legislative Recommendations for Title I of the Elementary and Secondary Education Act* (The Planar Corporation, submitted to the Department of Health, Education, and Welfare, Contract HEW-05-72-224, Washington, D.C., October 1973). See also Peter G. Briggs, *A Perspective on Change: The Administration of Title I of the Elementary and Secondary Education Act* (Washington, D.C.: Department of Health, Education, and Welfare, Contract HEW-05-72-224, October 1973).

10. Berke and Kirst, op. cit.

11. McLaughlin, "Implementation of ESEA Title I."

12. Ibid.

13. Ibid.

14. *The Silken Purse,* op. cit.

15. William Wayson, "Decennial Views of the Revolution: The Negative Side," *Phi Delta Kappan* (November 1975).

16. See, for example, *Title I of ESEA: Is It Helping Poor Children?* (Washington, D.C.: Washington Research Report of the Southern Center for Studies in Public Policy and the NAACP Legal Defense and Educational Fund, 1969).

17. The National Institute of Education (NIE) was charged by Congress in the Education Amendments of 1974 (PL 93-380) to conduct a comprehensive study of compensatory education and report to Congress in late 1977, in time for the 1978 debate over renewal of ESEA. The NIE studies consider issues of funds, allocation, educational services, educational effectiveness, and the administration of compensatory education programs. NIE's interim

report is *Evaluating Compensatory Education* (Washington, D.C.: National Institute of Education, 1976).

18. The study of administrative practices of SEAs throughout the country and a comparative case analysis of the effect of those practices on the operation of LEA compensatory education programs was conducted for NIE by Booz-Allen and Hamilton, Inc., and the Syracuse Research Corporation. The results of that study are incorporated in NIE, *Administration of Compensatory Education* (Washington, D.C.: National Institute of Education, 1977).

19. Educational Testing Service, "A Study of Compensatory Reading Programs" (Washington, D.C.: U.S. Office of Education, 1976).

20. John A. Emrick, James W. Guthrie, Ann S. Frentz, and Rita M. Mize, "The Use of Performance Criteria to Allocate Compensatory Education Funds" (Menlo Park, Calif.: Stanford Research Institute, July 1974).

21. The major evaluations of Title I have been E.J. Mosback et al., *Analyses of Compensatory Education in Five School Districts: Summary* (Santa Barbara, Calif.: General Electric Co., TEMPO Division, 1968, processed); *Education of the Disadvantaged: An Evaluative Report on Title I of the Elementary and Secondary Education Act of 1965, Fiscal Year 1968* (Washington, D.C.: U.S. Office of Education, Government Printing Office, 1970); and Gene V. Glass et al., *Data Analysis of the 1968–1969 Survey of Compensatory Education (Title I)* (Washington, D.C.: U.S. Office of Education, Bureau of Elementary and Secondary Education (BESE), 1970).

22. McLaughlin, "Implementation of ESEA Title I."

23. See the *Federal Register* of September 28, 1976, for the new regulations governing the operation of Title I programs. The new regulations, which went into effect on October 28, 1976, reflect changes in the law made by Congress in PL 93–380.

24. *Study of the Cost-Effectiveness of Michigan Education Programs* (Washington, D.C.: Education Turnkey System, Inc., 1974).

25. Martin Chong, "The Role of Parents as Decision-Makers in Compensatory Education: A Review of the Literature" (Washington, D.C.: National Institute of Education, June 1976). (Xerox.)

26. Robert Bothwell, Richard Johnson, and Alan Hickrod, "Geographic Adjustments to School Aid Formulae," *School Finance Reform: A Legislator's Handbook* (Washington, D.C.: The Legislators' Education Action Project, National Conference of State Legislatures, February 1976) and also *State Compensatory Education Programs,* Department of Health, Education and Welfare Publication (OE) 75-07107, 1975.

27. For an excellent discussion of the problems and possible strategies for administering federal-state relationships based on differential treatment, see Jerome T. Murphy, *Grease the Squeaky Wheel: A Report of Title V of the Elementary and Secondary Education Act of 1965, Grants to Strengthen State Departments of Education* (Cambridge, Mass.: Center for Educational Policy Research, Harvard Graduate School of Education, February 1973).

28. Richard C. Benjamin, "Compensatory Education: A Perspective on Decision-Making at the Local District Level," prepared for the Educational Council of Michigan and the Michigan Educational Seminar, March 1976). (Xerox.)

29. Ellis, op. cit.

Chapter Seven

Federal Support for Improved Educational Practice

Paul Berman
Milbrey Wallin McLaughlin

If one word can describe the experience of social reformers during the past decade, it is frustration. The high aims of federal assistance and intervention efforts in urban development and renewal, health care and delivery, and criminal justice appear to have fallen far short of their expectations. New policies and practices in education have also followed the path of many other social reform efforts—from optimism and expansion to evaluation and finally to caution and retrenchment. Reform initiatives of the sixties were premised on the expectation that new technologies, more money, and more information could revitalize and redirect local educational practices. The result of these reforms, it was hoped, would be better educated students and greater "equality of educational opportunity."

Evaluations of federal efforts to reform American education showed the results to be generally disappointing. But it would be a mistake to write off the experience of the "decade of reform" as a failure. For there have been successes—albeit more modest than planners hoped. Federal enunciation of categorical priorities, for example, has led to increased awareness of the problems of special interest groups such as the disadvantaged or the handicapped and in some cases to effective state or local efforts to address these special needs. Or, at a more general level, the emerging role of the federal government as an external force for reform has promoted some of the most significant changes that large city school districts have experienced in the last half century. It is not that the federal efforts to promote reform in local educational practices have had "no effect," then; rather, the reform initiatives of the past decade have been less effective than planners had hoped. Second, the experiences of the past decade offer important lessons that can inform the next step in educational policy-making and contribute to the ongoing effort to define the federal role in education.

Two major empirical lessons seem almost self-evident in retrospect at least. First, federal policy, particularly the "Great Society" initiatives, was implicitly based on unrealistic expectations about the extent to which education could serve as an effective agent for social reform. We have learned that there are limits to what public schooling can accomplish in absolute terms as well as in terms relative to other social agencies (e.g., the family, peer groups, or the U.S. economic system). The need "to scale expectations downward" emerges clearly from the era of social reform; its current popularity as a political slogan should come as no surprise. The challenge for policymaking is to devise ways of adapting federal objectives—and expectations—to what schooling can and cannot do.

But to diagnose the presumed failure of social reform as being only or even primarily one of unrealistic expectations is to overlook or seriously misconstrue the second main lesson of the era: federal policymakers both underestimated and misconceived the problem of implementing planned change—that is, the problems associated with translating project proposals and federal guidelines into practice.

In the sixties and early seventies, reformers and social engineers sought to change what they perceived as an unresponsive educational system by stimulating and sponsoring innovations. The early federal approach can be characterized, albeit somewhat too simply, as technocratic. It focused on promoting the adoption of new and presumably better technologies or educational treatments. Its main policy instruments were the dissemination of information, the support of research and development, and the offer of federal money. For some programs, the acceptance of federal money had virtually no strings attached (e.g., ESEA Title III), whereas others had guidelines and evaluation-accountability requirements coupled with the threat of withdrawal of funds (e.g., ESEA Title I). Other federal programs (e.g., Right to Read, Career Education) employed guidelines less as a device to foster compliance than as a way to promote effective local planning. However, federal policies seldom addressed issues relating to the local process of implementation. Recent research findings suggest that a major reason why federal education policies have not produced the results intended is because of problems between federal inputs and local outputs—that is, implementation.[1]

One implementation problem could be called *slippage*—a lack of fit between federal policy goals and guidelines and the local response to these policy initiatives. Implementation slippage is apparent, for example, in ESEA Title I. This reform initiative, which allocated over $1 billion annually for the local establishment of "special educational programs for the disadvantaged," has yet to be implemented across the country as intended by Congress.[a]

---

[a]Great Society legislation inevitably had multiple, often inconsistent goals. One could cite conflicting objectives not only for the whole of the historic ESEA but also for each of its component titles. Many observers point to Title I as a classic case of multiple

Because the federal authority upon which local compliance depends does not extend to the direct control of local educational practices, the local projects funded by Title I have reflected dominantly *local* instead of *national* interest, goals, and priorities. Consequently, until recently many districts ignored program targeting guidelines and used Title I funds as general aid instead of using them to support programs for the disadvantaged. However, even though compliance, per se, is no longer a serious problem, the ancillary compensatory programs established by many districts are still at significant odds with the local commitment federal reformers had hoped to stimulate. Likewise, ESEA Title III—designed to support local initiated innovative practices—has sometimes been viewed by school officials primarily as a source of temporary soft money rather than as an opportunity to try out a new educational practice. In light of this country's strong tradition of federalism, slippage between federal intent and local implementation can be expected to continue to frustrate federal reform efforts when federal goals and guidelines are not *consonant* with local interests.

Whether or not consonance exists, a second flaw in a technocratic approach is the implicit tendency to equate adoption of a project (or goal or technology) with its implementation, or the promise of an educational method as demonstrated in one site with the outcome of the method in another school setting. In fact, federal incentives have been highly successful in stimulating local adoption of the latest innovations. But adoption has not provided a reliable forecast of the reality of project practice or the outcomes to be expected.

For example, as part of the federally sponsored Planned Variation Study, a particular Follow Through model (e.g., Bank Street) was adopted by a variety of different school districts. When federal program administrators asked what the consequences of the special Follow Through models were, they

---

goals (e.g., the desire to legitimate federal aid to public schools, on the one hand, and, on the other hand, the aim of helping minority children). But even the less popularly known Title III was thought of by some as "stimulating change in local schools" and by others as a funding device to provide federal funds for middle-class purposes to balance the "minority money" of Title I. Lest we ignore the obvious, several simple observations about assessing complex federal policies having multiple goals might be remembered.

It is a rare federal program that does not have political objectives distinguishable from delivery objectives and the realization of the one class of goals may have little to do with the realization of the other—or it may have everything to do with it. For example, Title IV of the Civil Rights Act has the delivery aim of providing technical assistance to school districts undergoing desegregation. Yet most knowledgeable commentators regard this delivery goal as decidedly secondary to the objective of establishing the federal government's commitment to desegregation, at least in a symbolic way. It seems pointless under these circumstances to judge Title IV as a failure if technical assistance has in fact accomplished little.

ESEA Title I illustrates a contrasting case. Title I enabled a redistribution of income to local school districts and must be judged an unqualified success relative to this goal. For this goal, implementation is a moot question. But the effects of this redistribution also can and should be judged. Have Title I programs achieved, for example, better education for low-income children? Implementation issues cannot be dismissed for this delivery goal.

implicitly assumed that when different school districts adopted the same educational model (technology) they in fact used the same model. Research showed this assumption to be erroneous.[2] The implemented educational practice differed from the adopted sponsor's design for any particular site; moreover, the same model resulted in distinctive practices across different sites. This phenomenon—the adaptation of a project to its institutional setting as it undergoes implementation—was so prevalent in our study of 300 innovations sponsored by four federal change agent programs that we labeled in *mutation*.[3] This study found that the mere adoption of a presumed better practice does not automatically or invariably fulfill its promose of supposedly better student outcomes; that projects generally mutate; and that implementation—rather than the adoption of a technology, the availability of information about it, or the level of funds committed to it—dominates the local innovative process and its outcomes.

To call attention to the critical significance of local implementation would have little policy relevance if the relationship between inputs and student outcomes were consistent regardless of what the mundane process of implementation happend to be. On the contrary, we found that local school systems vary in their capacity to deal with implementation of special projects. In particular, implementation is best understood as being embedded in the day-to-day operations of the school district. It is the product of the interplay between the local institutional setting with its heterogeneous and often conflicting environmental, cultural, and organizational factors and the features or requirements of project goals and means. Thus, effective implementation depends on how receptive local institutions are to planned change and the capacity of local personnel to manage change. School districts use federal resources (money, technology, and information) but are not usually influenced by them to change their commitments, motivations, or concern with innovation. The success of the project depends not only on institutional receptivity, but also on the implementation strategies that the district chooses—that is, training, planning format, type of user involvement, and so on. These specific local choices for the implementation of a special project tend to reflect the capacity of the district to manage change generally.

The interdependence of special project outcomes and local management capacity is particularly apparent as local districts face the issue of sustaining federally supported innovations at the end of federal seed money funding. The long-term effects of federal policies aimed at promoting innovation depend on the ability of local districts to incorporate so-called successful innovative practices into their district routine—an implementation problem of a different kind. Few districts, our research suggests, have the management skills to sustain even effective planned change efforts.[4] Federal efforts to reform educational practice have resulted in disappointingly few successful projects, primarily because of local implementation problems. But what is perhaps even more disturbing from the federal perspective is that, even where local efforts were successful, school managers were often unable to prevent the dissipation or disappearance of projects once federal funding stopped.

Two points summarize the implementation lessons of the past decade. First, the implementation of planned change in education is essentially a local process that is neither automatic nor assured. Short of a radical change in governance, it is not susceptible to direct control by federal efforts. Second, school districts need help and guidance. Generally speaking, they have not developed the management skills, motivations, or institutional capacity to implement or sustain planned change. The past decade demonstrates that federal policies can be successful in stimulating the adoption of categorical projects and in some cases in supporting effective local innovations. But these so-called successes will count for little unless the short- and long-term problems of implementing federal policies can be dealt with more effectively.

THE LOCAL PROCESS OF CHANGE

We believe the implementation of federal purposes has not been based on realistic assumptions about the local process of change—how it works and the local capacity to manage it. Federal concern with categorical programs, technical assistance, innovations, and dissemination seems appropriate and well intended. Yet the promise of these policies remains generally unrealized because they misperceive the ways in which local school districts use outside inputs. Because a major flaw of federal policy is that of perception rather than of intent or objectives, a more effective federal role in education requires a new and more realistic point of view about the relationship of central government to local school districts. As a starting point in understanding the limits and opportunities of federal policy, this section draws on our research to describe the nature of the local change process and suggests the factors that critically influence local planned change efforts.

The local process of change that characterizes a federally supported project is the result of the interplay between the federal input—in particular, special funds—and local choices, priorities, and institutional characteristics. This local process can be seen as comprising three phases: mobilization, implementation, and institutionalization. The phases of the local change process are not discrete; they are significantly interrelated as the choices and events in one phase profoundly influence events and outcomes in other phases.

Mobilization

The process of change begins with the decision to adopt a change agent project. This decision is made in a dynamic institutional reality in which events, demands, and priorities as well as behavior are constantly changing. In this local context, a federal change agent program is only a proximate cause of local change activities and decisions.

The initial motivation leading to local adoption of a federal project is a critical factor. Local school districts elect to initiate federally supported change agent projects for many different reasons. Many change agent projects are undertaken for essentially *opportunistic* reasons—that is, for reasons fundamentally unrelated to the educational delivery needs of the districts.[5] For example, local school officials may view the adoption of a change agent project primarily as an opportunity to garner extra short-term resources. In this instance, simply the availability of federal funds rather than the possibility of change in educational practice motivates project adoption. Or school managers may see change agent projects as an inexpensive way to cope with bureaucratic or political pressures on the system. For instance, innovation qua innovation often serves the purely bureaucratic objective of making the district appear up-to-date and progressive in the eyes of the community. Or a change agent project may function to mollify political pressures from groups in the community to "do something" about their special interests or needs. Whatever the particular motivation underlying opportunistic adoption of a change agent project, the effective absence of serious delivery or educational concerns means that the institutional interest and commitment necessary to effective implementation are also missing.

Conversely, a number of districts initiate change agent projects in what could be called a *problem-solving* mode. In this instance, federally supported change agent projects are initiated with the expectation that the project will address central educational needs of the district. Indeed, many change agent projects initiated in this manner represent expansion or refinement of educational strategies the district has already identified on a pilot or limited basis. A major finding of our research is that only when projects were initiated primarily out of delivery concerns did the adoption of a change agent project evidence the district commitment, concern, and energy necessary to the effective implementation and eventual institutionalization of the special project.[6]

However, there is another important aspect of the institutional commitment that characterizes the first phase of the change process. The decision to adopt a project is simply that—a decision. Plans must be made for project implementation—for example, selecting of sites and participants and decisions about resource allocation and evaluation. The *way* planning activities are conducted determines whether or not they serve another critical function in the change process—that is, generating of broad-based support within the system for the change agent project. An important lesson of our research is that the particular source of the idea for a change agent project—the central office or the "grass roots" staff—matters less to project outcomes than does the ultimate level of support built for the project within the system as a whole.

While essentially opportunistic projects rarely mobilize broad-based institutional support, problem-solving projects also often neglect the issue of mobilization. In particular, even where central office commitment and support for a project is high, steps must be taken during the planning process to generate similar enthusiasm and commitment from teachers and other staff who will ultimately be responsible for implementing the special project. Top-down directives, even when issued with the best of intentions, typically meet with indifference if not resistance at the school-building level. Similarly, grass roots projects are likely to founder in the long run if user-initiators do not enlist support and commitment from central office staff at the outset. Because the various organizational units in a local school system are only loosely related to one another, the commitment of staff at one level cannot be taken as proxy for the support of another. Full mobilization of the broad-based institutional support necessary to effective implementation and eventual institutionalization requires that planning activities include strategies to enlist the participation, input, and involvement of all principal actors in the local process of change—central office administrators, school staff, and, in many cases, community.

In summary, the beginning of a change agent project makes an important and pervasive difference to the activities and outcomes of other phases of the local change process. When the adopted project addressed a central educational need of the district and when active steps were taken to generate broad-based commitment and support, change agent projects were seen by staff as a widely supported district initiative, not simply "something the teachers wanted to do" or a "pet project of the superintendent." Consequently, staff was willing to work hard to implement the project, and its efforts were bolstered by the steady and explicit support of central office staff. An important observation from our research is that this level of institutional commitment—which is vital to effective implementation—typically cannot be generated once project operations begin.[7]

Implementation

The second phase of the local process of change—implementation—involves the translation of project plans and proposals into practice. In the cases we have examined, successful implementation and the promise of long-term institutional impact was characterized by a particular pattern of implementation: *mutual adaptation*.[8] Mutual adaptation describes a process in which the innovation was modified and the formal and informal organizational relationships among staff and among teachers and students were altered during the course of implementation. This process could involve a variety of adjustments in the project itself—for example, reduction or modification of idealistic project goals, amendment or simplification of project treatment, downward revision of ambitious expectations for behavioral change in the staff or of overly optimistic effects of the project on students, and unanticipated changes in standard practices by or relationships between staff and administrators. Mutual adaptation also signified genuine learning and change by the project staff—the acquisition of the skills and attitudes necessary to integration of project strategies into classroom practices.

The process of mutual adaptation does not represent a smooth or trouble-free course of project implementation. Indeed, from the perspective of an outside observer, the first year or so of project operations that follow this pattern are often seen as chaotic as staff tries hard to make the project work for them and to learn new skills and practices. In all the cases we observed, mutual adaptation occurred only if the project was preceded by the institutional attitudes and commitments associated with a problem-solving approach to project adoption and full mobilization of broad-based institutional support.

However, the receptiveness of the institutional setting to the change agent project is a necessary but not a sufficient condition for mutual adaptation or effective implementation. Mutual adaptation also requires the selection of a local implementation strategy that enables the support and commitment of administrators and staff to be fully engaged and adaptation to take place. These local management choices are distinct from a project technology; they relate to implementation choices about issues such as the mode and extent of staff participation in project decisionmaking, the type and sequencing of staff training, and the availability of resource assistance, staff meetings, and so on. These implementation strategies are important in providing feedback that can be used to modify project operations in promoting a sense of ownership among project staff and in furnishing the forum in which adaptation can occur.

In sum, mutual adaptation—which we believe is the key to serious change—requires both institutional support and the selection of implementation strategies that allow adaptation and learning to take place. Both requisites to effective implementation, in short, are *local* factors—factors typically not addressed by federal policies. The extent to which mutual adaptation has occurred during the implementation phase significantly determines the fate of a specially funded project during the third phase of the local change process, institutionalization.

Institutionalization

The third and last phase of the local change process that began with the adoption of a federally funded change agent project is institutionalization. During this phase federal funds are withdrawn, and the longer term effect of special funding on local practice becomes apparent. Institutionalization may mean many things—that is, the project design may be continued in part or whole or methods may be continued but materials dropped. Or the project may be continued at a reduced level of activity, it may be expanded, or it may continue to operate just as it did during the period of federal funding. Or it may go away altogether—methods, materials, concepts, and all.

At the most general level, the institutionalization of a change agent project involves incorporating project strategies in some form into standard district practice. However, the extent to which a special project is institutionalized after the end of federal funding depends both on district level decisions about whether or not and in what form the project should be continued as well as on the extent to which teachers and principals actually continue to use project methods and materials. It involves both the assimilation and acceptance of project concepts and methods by school staff as well as the incorporation of project procedures and supports into standard district level procedures. Thus, the extent to which a change agent project is institutionalized after the end of federal funding is determined by the *interplay* between decisions and choices at the district level and actual activities at the classroom level. Furthermore, as was the case in the original decision to adopt the change agent project, the main factors influencing this decision are likely to be a mix of organizational and political concerns weighed against the educational merits of the district.

Like the phases of the change process that precede this final phase, the process of institutionalization is an uncertain and often difficult process. That is, just as a decision to adopt a project is not an accurate forecast of implemented practice, neither is a tally of district continuation decisions an accurate indication of the return on the federal investment or the actual impact of the project on local educational practices. In particular, just as the commitment of district level staff could not be taken as proxy for commitment of staff at the school site during the first phase of the change process—the loosely coupled nature of the school system also means that continuation decisions made at one level of the system may or may not influence behavior at another level. A decision by central office adminstrators to continue a change agent project in some form may be operationally meaningless if the staff responsible for continuing the use of project strategies elect not to do so or are unable to do so because of inadequate training or institutional support. Similarly, individual teachers could choose to continue project strategies they had learned to use during the period of special project implementation with or without formal district sanction.

What factors affect the extent to which a project is continued at the district and classroom levels? For the projects we examined, the level of federal funding did *not* significantly influence the continuation status of a special project. Contrary to the fears of many grantmakers, expensive projects were no more or less likely to be continued than were less costly change agent projects.[9] Neither was continuation related to the educational methods employed by the projects. Instead, the extent to which a federally supported change agent project was institutionalized primarily depended on local choices and local institutional characteristics.

For the institutional motivations that were critical to the mobilization and operationalization continue to be vitally important as a change agent project ends. For example, projects that were initiated for opportunistic reasons are almost always dropped by the district after federal funding stops—that is, after they have fulfilled their primary purpose of bringing extra (if temporary) funds into the district.[10] It is important to note that this pattern of discontinuation occurs even where change agent projects are reportedly successful in meeting their objectives. Our research suggests that unless district level staff were committed to the project from the outset, it is usually not possible to mobilize support for the project once it is underway or at the time that decisions concerning institutional incorporation must be made.

But the decision to continue, like the decision to adopt, is simply that—a decision. If institutionalization of a change agent project is to result from a decision to continue, district officials must devise strategies to effectively implement that decision, and staff must have both the inclination and ability to continue project strategies.

In particular, because school districts are not generally well-integrated organizations, for the continued project to be institutionalized, the special status of the change agent project must be removed, and project support requirements must be accommodated in most if not all of five areas of district operations—budget, personnel, curriculum support activities, the instructional program, and facilities maintenance. Such accommodation of project support requirements (e.g., the ongoing training necessary to project operations, the technological maintenance costs, and centralized coordination) does not simply happen as a result of a decision to continue. Rather, incorporation of the project into district procedures requires the early and active attention of district managers to all relevant areas of system operations and the identification of effective institutionalization strategies to secure a place for the project in the operating budget and the support of community, school board members, and district staff.

Furthermore, because institutionalization typically involves a somewhat different set of actors than did the initiation and implementation of the special project, district managers must devise strategies to secure their support and commitment. For example, the authority to make district decisions to continue and support a project often does not rest with the same personnel or administrative unit that sanctioned project initiation. Likewise, if the district decides to expand project operations, the mobilization of support from teachers and principals is again a critical issue, and one that is often ignored. The outcome of a continuation decision often depends on the extent to which the commitment of these actors has been engaged.

Whether or not the efforts of school district administrators to continue the project in some form actually result in continuation also depends on whether or not the original project staff is able to carry on project activities. Unless implementation strategies were employed that allowed users to learn project strategies and integrate these new practices into their classroom operation, it is unlikely that the assimilation necessary to continuation will occur once the aegis of special project status is removed.

The key to institutionalization at the classroom level, then, is whether or not project teachers have assimilated project methods and materials into their classroom and whether or not the enthusiasm and commitment of new recruits are generated. The extent to which related changes are continued at the classroom level also depends on principal leadership and commitment. Unless a principal is committed to project conepts, project-related changes are unlikely to survive staff turnover or to be perceived in the professional self-interest of teachers.

But if teachers and principals are to receive the support they need to sustain project-related changes in the long run, the district managers must incorporate the necessary support arrangements—funding, training, technical assistance, and so on. These district level activities essentially comprise a process of remobilization and reimplementation and require the early, active attention of school managers.

In short, the process of institutionalization is no more certain or straightforward than the adoption or implementation of an innovation. Local management choices (i.e., implementation strategies and institutionalization activities) and institutional motivations continue to dominate this phase as they have throughout the local process of change. Unfortunately, our research suggests that very few school districts have the management capacity to develop and implement strategies that effectively institutionalize the changes resulting from successful innovation.[11]

In summary, the local process of change is a complex organizational process in which federal inputs—money, technology, or information—have only indirect or second-order effects. Any given federal policy input has an effect only in interaction with local institutional factors—specifically, local motivation and commitment and local management choices. Elements in the school setting such as perceived importance of the change agent project, implementation strategies that permit ownership to be generated and promote adaptation of the project to the needs and priorities of particular schools and classrooms, and continuation strategies that support the institutionalization of successful change agent projects directly determine both the short-term and the long-run effects of special federal funding. Furthermore, the ability of local personnel to effectively implement and sustain innovative projects reflects the management capacity of the district generally. Even the skills of an effective project leader will have only ephemeral or isolated impact on district practice if school managers are unable to plan for and carry out the institutionalization of successful change efforts. Managing the process of educational change requires highly developed leadership and administrative skills, staff commitment, and the institutional resources and capacity to change. Yet few districts possess these organizational requisites. It is precisely this complex local reality that defines the limits and opportunities for federal education policies.

RETHINKING THE FEDERAL ROLE IN EDUCATION

We have argued that the outcomes of change efforts depend primarily on local factors that federal policies typically have neither influenced nor addressed.

One inference from our analysis is that federal policies, *as presently conceived,* cannot be much more effective in the future than they have been in the past. Refining or tightening up existing federal policy instruments can only be expected to lead to change at the margins of educational practice in most school districts.

If present policies are unlikely to achieve federal objectives in education, what alternatives are available to federal policymakers? The preceding description of the local change process suggests two broad policy alternatives. One interpretation is that the federal government *cannot* influence local practices through its policies and so should greatly reduce its substantive (if not its financial) role in local school affairs. A second interpretation is that school systems do need and can use outside help in institutional development. This perspective argues for a significantly revised and substantively expanded federal role. The remainder of this discussion examines the assumptions and policy implementations of each position.

A Reduced Federal Role

A greatly reduced federal role could take either or both of two forms: one, effective substantive withdrawal from local affairs by switching to untied block grants to state and local agencies (this position has been characterized as "leave the money on the stump") or, two, cut back federal support for public education or hold it at its present level. This stance conveys skepticism about the possibilities of local change and the ability of the federal government to influence it. This position assumes that one or a combination of the following attributes characterizes school district motivation and capacity:

- Local school personnel do not want outside assistance and guidance and will resist it to the point of intransigence.
- School districts will use federal money to their own ends in disregard of federal guidelines and sanctions.
- The problem of local change is intractable with or without outside assistance.

Each of these assumptions contains partial truths; yet either individually or taken together they misrepresent the local reality. Let us consider the validity of each assumption in turn.

First, school districts generally do want outside help but do not want this assistance to be highly prescriptive or inflexible. For example, in addition to the extra resources provided by special federal programs, the categorical nature of federal funds is often valued by local officials because it provides a legitimacy for their efforts to mobilize support for special needs within the system. Many district officials have told us that if Title I funds were not earmarked for compensatory purposes, it would be difficult to sustain compensatory programs in the face of more powerful pressures within the district.

In short, the national priorities set by categorical programs can serve to catalyze local (and state) commitment when the local time is ripe.

Similarly, some forms of federal technical assistance and dissemination are often felt to be valuable. For example, the diffusion network begun under Section 306 of Title III is seen by many local school personnel as a source of good ideas and encouragement for their own efforts. The main limits on the willingness of local school systems to accept federal leadership and assistance is a requirement that federal policy not be dissonant with local interests and priorities and that means for achieving goals not be rigidly prescribed.

Second, it is true that school districts have used federal money for purposes other than those intended by federal policymakers and sometimes in disregard of federal guidelines and sanctions. However, this slippage occurs for a variety of reasons. There is malfeasance, of course, but we believe this is infrequent. A more important reason is opportunism—an attitude of "getting federal dollars just because they are out there" without any specific local plans to meet a central delivery need. We found that opportunistically conceived projects were likely to be implemented in a pro forma fashion and, in any event, were unlikely to be continued after federal funds were terminated. One federal response to opportunistic use of funds provided through categorical or entitlement programs, for example, might be to focus on compliance and enforcing accountability. However understandable such a response would be, it treats the symptom rather than the cause. Opportunism often reflects a shortsightedness by district officials in that free dollars sought for temporary bureaucratic or political advantage result in the hidden costs of dissipated staff energies and enthusiasm. The real payoff for federal policy would be in changing the attitudes and management perspectives that generate opportunism, not especially in eliminating the practice.[b]

A final reason why local behavior often departs from federal expectations stems from adaptation. Our research indicates that effective educational change requires adaptation of guidelines, programs, and technologies to local conditions. Oddly enough, such adaptations are sometimes thought of as deviations. We would hope that federal policy would encourage these largely healthy deviations.

Third, the intractability argument—that schooling cannot be changed in ways that significantly affect delivery—rests on several premises. Some critics contend that schooling cannot affect children more than it has because the main influences on learning come from nonschool factors; thus, change attempts short of radical transformation can have marginal results of best. Other critics,

---

[b]We suspect the costs of severely reducing opportunism would be substantial; they involve not only expensive monitoring, evaluation, and proposal selection mechanisms but also create an image of a federal enforcer that could damage program effectiveness. Thus, even if one defined the problem as compliance rather than one of helping school districts improve educational delivery, we doubt that the relatively small benefits of deterring opportunists would outweigh the costs of doing so.

ourselves included, believe that the key organizational dynamic of school districts comprises efforts to maintain the status quo; local school districts often use innovation to support these efforts rather than as an opportunity to seriously revise and redirect ongoing practices. For example, innovation qua innovation can serve to placate community or school board interests in being "up-to-date." Innovations also frequently are employed as a temporizing device—"We're trying something new to improve reading next year." The result of such maintenance activities is that little or no significant change is made in those delivery factors that might differentially affect student outcomes.

We share the frustration of social reformers and federal administrators with the extraordinary difficulty of changing local school district practice as well as with the cumulative evidence of "no significant difference." Yet while the aggregate evidence is discouraging, empirical research also gives some cause to be optimistic. Specifically, we have seen unusually effective practices; moreover, we and others have analyzed the process leading to such improved practices and found, as the preceding section of this chapter outlined, leverage points on this process. For example, management strategies can be devised that promote effective implementation. But as the preceding section also indicated, institutional receptivity is a necessary condition for implementation strategies to fulfill their promise. Our research suggests that such receptivity depends in large measure on basic district structural characteristics (e.g., the support given to schools and to efforts to change the incentive structure for school staff, authority relations, and information systems).

The critical question is if the fundamental organizational features of school districts are amenable to federal policy intervention. We think they can be. We have observed unusually effective districts that have learned how to manage change in ways that enhance delivery purposes. We have compared these unusual districts to several typical maintenance districts and attempted to define key differences between them in their management of change.[12] These differences we found have less to do with serendipity, "great men," exceptional staff, or even with exceptional resources than with the point of view in the district about the management of change and the role of professionals. Furthermore, this perspective generates organizational structures and arrangements that can be adapted by other districts. Our research suggests that federal policy may have an important role to play in promoting both the point of view and the structural requisites to effective institutional development.

In summary, changing schools in ways that matter is correctly seen as difficult; however, it is not intractable. This assumption about local motivations and capacity, like the other two assumptions that underlie the skeptical position, represents a misreading of reality. The policy inference drawn from these assumptions when taken together—that is, the federal government should severely reduce its substantive role—is unwarranted. A "no strings" block grant would be likely to facilitate healthy change in districts already possessing relatively developed institutional capacity. But the experience of the past decade indicates that these districts are disturbingly few and that federal money provided without other supports such as leadership and technical assistance could be expected to lead to little significant or enduring improvement in local educational practices.

A Revised Federal Role

A point of view consistent with the local process of change as we see it is one that might be called *localism.*[c] This perspective accepts the principle that change is essentially a local process and that school districts must ultimately take responsibility—in the fullest sense of the word—for delivering high-quality education. It sees a major federal role to be that of setting standards, defining national objectives, and providing technical assistance; it conceives of accountability as most effectively dealt with at the local level as part of the local political process. The effectiveness of localism as policy depends on the extent to which operational *interdependence* is achieved between local, state, and federal governments.

Localism and interdependence, like any broad concepts, should be seen only as ideals. However, our research suggests that these notions are an appropriate and useful conceptual starting point in rethinking the federal role in education. Specifically, the ideals of localism and interdependence suggest significant revisions in the way federal priorities are articulated and carried out.

Localism and interdependence imply that a new point of view about the relationship of the federal government to state and local governments should be adopted, a point of view that focuses federal policies on issues of institutional development. It suggests restructuring intergovernmental relations in education—a recurrent topic in Washington in the past few years. *How* this can be done clearly involves questions of politics as much as questions of substance and thus is beyond the scope of this chapter. However, our perspective argues that such a restructuring should involve issues like an expanded and routine participation of state and local administrators in the policymaking process and increased devolution of authority to state and local governments — a decentralization of effective power based on consensus about shared roles and separate responsibilities. The lack of trust expressed by participants at all levels of the system, for example, reflects a lack of information and an absence of agreement on function more than anything else.

Requisite to a renegotiation of the relationships between federal, state, and local education agencies is an effort to reach some agreement on the

---

[c]The comments of William B. Cannon, of the University of Chicago, at an April 21, 1976, American Educational Research Association Panel of the Implementation of Educational Policy, have been extremely helpful to us in thinking about "localism" and what a new "centralism" might entail.

broad goals of U.S. public education—a *national* education policy. The federal presence in state or local educational affairs is no longer at question; indeed, it appears to have become institutionalized. Thus, the disjointed and incremental (and somewhat apologetic) initiatives that have characterized federal education policymaking in the past no longer seem warranted. A clear and coherent national education policy would provide more consistent guidance to state and local officials, as well as provide new leadership opportunities for the U.S. Office of Education.

At least three lessons about school district behavior and the process of planned change are important to consider in renegotiating the federal (and so the state and local) role:

1. School district behavior is *inherently* variable. Local school districts differ in the problems they have; in their capacity to deal with their problems; and in their culture, structure, and setting. Given this variability, the desire to obtain programmatic *uniformity* is misguided and often counterproductive. Such efforts are likely to confirm the local suspicion that federal officials are not in touch with school district reality and also to preclude more effective local response to their particular situation.

2. Phases of the local change process require different types of technical assistance. Phases of the local change process are closely interrelated in practice; technical assistance that aims to promote change in local practices should reflect awareness of the various requirements of the entire process as it unfolds. Change agent policies should acknowledge the different and necessary function of each stage and differentiate technical assistance and planning requirements accordingly.

The policy aim for mobilization, for example, is to promote a problem-solving approach to choosing and initiating projects. The two components of mobilization—planning and support generation—may require different types of assistance. Districts should be discouraged from moving into implementation until broad-based support can be generated. Promotion of mutual adaptation should be the key objective of assistance for the operationalization phase. Institutionalization involves broader institutional issues of sustaining change that has in fact occurred.

3. Responsibility for implementation should be left to local personnel. Well-intentioned planners hope to solve the problem of implementation by giving assistance or designing means that would enable local staff to avoid (or minimize) the uncertainties attending the process of change. A packaged approach to change characterizes this point of view. Even were such supposedly implementation-proof assistance to prove effective for specific purposes of a project, this approach can create a dependency that causes more harm than good in the long run. For example, we observed situations in which local staff relied so heavily on technical assistance that they were unable to adapt project

materials and methods to their own needs and thus were unable to learn by doing. Similarly, the packaged management approaches we observed tended either to be dismissed as unworkable or to be viewed as a complete road map to innovation, in which case project participants failed to develop the flexibility to cope with unanticipated problems. Such efforts to help districts innovate seem to be motivated partially by interest in fiscal efficiency and in accelerating the innovative process. Outside assistance may produce savings under certain conditions, but our research suggests that innovation is by its nature a costly and time-consuming process. Attempts to speed up the process or to reduce its costs may achieve short-term efficiency at the expense of long-term benefits. In short, the responsibility for implementation should be left with the local staff, and assistance should focus on providing problem-solving skills, not solving problems.

What directions might federal policies take that would be consonant with these conditions and serve to facilitate local institutional development? An important and promising area of federal involvement suggested by our research is in local *staff development*. By staff development, we mean something much broader than the in-service education activities or training presently conducted by local districts and federal programs. Staff development in our view denotes a wide range of policies that share an objective of promoting the professionalism and initiative of teachers and administrators. Skill training in curricular areas is only one, and perhaps not the most important, development need of school personnnel. An effective approach in staff development would focus on providing opportunities for personnel to increase their planning or management skills and renew the commitment and interest they bring to their job. Examples of such strategies would be the provision of small amounts of discretionary funds to support development of the school site, sabbatical and travel funds for teachers, and small regional conferences for educators in support of the natural regional networks that exist between educators. Initiatives such as the present teachers' centers correctly point to the importance of user-initiated and designed development activities. However, efforts that focus primarily on teachers are likely to be disappointing unless attention also is given to the professional development needs of administrators. Frequently, teachers emerge from staff development activities only to find that the climate or practices of their school are incompatible with their new behavior and practice, or that the district is unable to provide the supports necessary to sustain it. The National Institute of Education, the regional labs, or even the professonal associations are examples of existing institutions that could facilitate and coordinate professional development activities for school district management personnel.

Federal attention to issues of local staff development appears particularly appropriate because in addition to the critical relationship of staff development to local institutional health, it also seems to be a concern that is consistently ignored or swept aside by local school districts. Most school districts operate in-service education programs that are widely seen as dull, irrelevant, and a waste of time. However, the issue of staff development is typically eclipsed at the local level by more apparently immediate or important concerns. In sum, the longer term issue of staff development in both essential to local institutional development and unlikely to receive attention from local personnel, especially as declining enrollments lead to tighter operating budgets.

Second, the federal government could help in making more effective technical assistance available to school districts by restructuring the present regional educational laboratories and centers to de-emphasize educational research and development and move toward a practitioner-based model of technical assistance. (Such a model operated successfully at the Northwest Regional Lab.) Technical assistance like this would be responsive to the needs and requests of practitioners and would focus on the process of local development— how to plan, how to encourage broad participation, how to motivate staff, and so on. Locating practitioner-based technical assistance in the regional labs and centers not only permits a timely and informed response, but also removes the assistance function from state or federal agencies where assistance is often seen by local personnel as entangled with regulation.

Third, federal categorical programs as well as federal programs supporting innovations (e.g., Title IV-C) could emphasize issues of local institutional development. Or the federal government could initiate a new program that explicitly addresses capacity building at the local level. An important lesson from our research is that the critical unit of intervention is not a particular curricular area or even a special target group, but rather the entire school system. Federal projects that attempt to fix one aspect of system operations are bound to represent unstable and short-lived remedies when they are dissonant with or not supported by broader institutional processes and routines. In other words, the problems addressed by special projects are rarely the root problem. Rather they are symptoms of more profound institutional deficiencies.

Through their application requirements, federal programs could encourage long-range planning at the district and school-site level and the integration of various federally funded efforts into the ongoing school program. Funds could be provided for technical assistance in accomplishing these institutional planning activities and strengthening the management capacity of school administrators. However, it is important to note that we do not envision a form of comprehensive planning as it is presently structured. Present planning requirements—because they focus on objectives, rather than on the planning process—are inflexible and actually work against thoughtful management.[d]

---

[d]For example, more than one state official has told us that they meet the comprehensive planning requirements for Title IV-C either by simply copying down passages of the federal regulations, by committing the state to what they are sure can be accomplished, or, indeed, to what has already been done.

In summary, these are examples of federal policies that shift federal attention from the change product to the change process and from the symptoms of disappointing student outcomes to a primary cause—inadequate institutional capacity. This policy perspective recognizes that change of the kinds that might enhance student performance has less to do with so-called better technologies than with the way the educational products are used and the climate for change in the system. It acknowledges that school improvement is a very difficult and demanding task, but one that in the final analysis must be accomplished by local personnel. However, this policy perspective also assumes that there is presently insufficient knowledge or resources (personal and fiscal) at the local level to bring about improvement without outside help. In most school districts, the talent and energy (and funds) that could be applied to investigating ways to strengthen the system are devoted to "running to stay in place" and maintaining the system as it is in the face of external pressures and ad hoc contingencies.

NOTES

1. *Federal Programs Supporting Educational Change: The Findings in Review,* R-1589/4-HEW (Santa Monica, Calif.: The Rand Corporation, April 1975).

2. See for example, J.A. Emrick et al. *Evaluation of the National Diffusion Network,* Vol. I (Menlo Park: Stanford Research Institute, 1977).

3. R-1589/4, op. cit.

4. *Federal Programs Supporting Educational Change: Factors Affecting Implementation and Continuation,* R-1589/7-HEW (Santa Monica, Calif.: The Rand Corporation, April 1977).

5. R-1589/4, op. cit.

6. R-1589/4, op. cit.; R-1589/7, op. cit.

7. R-1589/4 op. cit.; also *Federal Programs Supporting Educational Change: The Process of Change,* R-1589/3-HEW (Santa Monica, Calif.: The Rand Corporation, April 1975).

8. R-1589/3, op. cit., R-1589/4, op. cit.

9. R-1589/7, op. cit.

10. Ibid.

11. R-1589/7, op. cit.

12. *Adaptation With and Without Change: Maintenance Development and Decay of School Districts,* R-2010-HEW (Santa Monica, Calif.: The Rand Corporation, forthcoming).

Chapter Eight

Federal Education Goals and Policy Instruments: An Assessment of the "Strings" Attached to Categorical Grants in Education

Stephen M. Barro

The federal government participates in elementary and secondary education primarily by making categorical grants to state and local education agencies. The grant legislation and the accompanying administrative regulations specify, often in great detail, how federal funds are to be used. Most of the federal money is earmarked for specific target groups of pupils—principally the economically or educationally disadvantaged, the non-English speaking, and the handicapped. Some federal funds are earmarked also, or instead, for instruction in particular subject areas (such as reading or vocational education), for support of certain educational processes (such as individualized instruction), and for the purchase of certain resources (such as audiovisual materials or the services of teaching aides).

For a number of reasons, which will be discussed, it cannot be taken for granted that the federal money will automatically be used for the designated purposes or on behalf of the intended beneficiaries. Local school districts and state agencies have both the opportunity and the motivation to substitute federal funds for other revenue that would otherwise have been devoted to the federally aided activities or to divert federal funds to their own preferred uses. There is ample evidence that such diversion has been common under the existing categorical programs. Having recognized this problem, Congress and the federal agencies that administer the grants have inserted provisions into the laws and regulations that can be interpreted as control mechanisms for ensuring that grant recipients allocate their resources in a manner consistent with federal objectives.

Control provisions range from the stipulation that federal aid shall "supplement, not supplant," state and local funds, to requirements that grantees submit reports and keep auditable records, to prescriptions of expenditure patterns that grantees must demonstrate or service standards that they must satisfy to qualify for federal aid. Many such devices are used in different combinations in the various education grant programs. The question of which control mechanisms, or "strings," are effective and desirable comes up repeatedly in debates about the design of grant programs. It is a general, perennial issue—one that pertains to the whole array of intergovernmental aid programs of the federal government, not only to grant programs in education.

This chapter assesses the compatibility of the control provisions of existing federal education grant programs with the stated (or commonly understood) program goals. It approaches the issue of compatibility both in terms of sufficiency and necessity. For example, are the control provisions in current laws *capable* of bringing about the federally desired patterns of resource allocation and resource use at the state and local levels? Are the existing strings *needed*, or do they constitute pointless administrative burdens? To make the discussion concrete, these questions are asked in connection with a few of the larger categorical grant programs, selected to provide coverage of the major allocative devices currently in use in education. Conclusions from these specific cases are then used to address the following issues pertaining to grant program design in the future:

- How can existing grant mechanisms be strengthened? Where they are inadequate, what additional instruments can be introduced in their place to accomplish the federal goals?
- Which grant provisions could be eliminated or made less burdensome without jeopardizing the achievement of allocative goals?
- Given the types of policy instruments currently available, or likely to be politically feasible to incorporate into grant legislation in the future, what kinds of federal goals can be accomplished in elementary and secondary education?

To focus attention on the central issue, the scope of the chapter has been kept deliberately narrow in the following respects: First, a sharp distinction is drawn between allocative goals of the federal programs and substantive educational goals. Only the former are considered here. The significance of the distinction is brought out in the following section. Second, the discussion excludes any consideration of goals pertaining to the distribution of funds among states and localities and the grant provisions affecting distributional outcomes (i.e., distribution formulas and rules governing project selection). The distributional aspects of federal education programs have been analyzed extensively elsewhere. The separation between distributional and resource allocation considerations is somewhat artificial because some provisions of grant programs, such as requirements that grantees "match" federal funds, affect both kinds of outcomes. Where that occurs, only the resource allocation or resource use implications are dealt with. Third, objectives other than the control of resource allocation that may be served by provisions of the grant laws and regulations are referred to only in passing. For instance, certain planning and reporting requirements of federal education programs and certain procedural specifications, such as requirements for community involvement in decisionmaking, may be desirable for legal and political reasons or to facilitate program implementation at the local level. The relationships between grant provisions and goals of that kind are not examined in this chapter. Finally, the chapter deals only incidentally with the nongrant methods by which the federal government influences state and local school systems—notably, in recent years, through the enforcement of federal civil rights legislation and court orders. These federal activities are referred to only insofar as they are related to the aid programs, as, for example, where service requirements laid down by the courts may complement, or substitute for, service standards incorporated into grant legislation.

The remainder of the chapter consists of three sections. The section that immediately follows examines the allocative goals of the federal grant programs. The central issue in that discussion is the criteria for allocative success: What outcomes would we have to observe to conclude that the federal grant programs are having their intended effects? The following section considers, in light of those criteria, whether the various provisions used in the major, current federal programs are sufficient, either as currently implemented or as they could potentially be implemented, to stimulate the desired patterns of state and local resource use. This discussion concentrates on three large programs—compensatory education programs funded under the Elementary and Secondary Education Act (ESEA) Title I, grants to states for education of the handicapped, and aid for vocational education. The final section offers some general conclusions about the compatibility of federal grant instruments and education goals and applies the conclusions to several specific policy proposals. These include proposals for grant consolidation, for simplifying programs by eliminating unnecessary strings, and for using new types of grant provisions or new combinations of existing provisions to improve the allocation of federal funds. Also discussed are the potential consequences of new approaches to federal education aid that seem to be developing—notably, the practice of linking resource allocation standards to federal categorical grants.

ALLOCATIVE GOALS OF THE EDUCATION
GRANT PROGRAMS

The point that the main instrument available to the federal government is the intergovernmental grant is central in thinking about the goals of federal efforts in education. It has become so customary to speak of the federal compensatory education program, the federal Headstart program, and so forth, that one tends to forget that there are no federal programs in the sense of federal institutions or federal personnel providing services to children.[a] Instead, the programs consist of federal-to-state and federal-to-local transfers of funds, accompanied by more or less strict constraints on the behavior of the grant recipients. Nearly all the services that federal funds are intended to support must be delivered by local schools systems.[b] In addition, state governments play major roles as financial intermediaries and as the authorities directly responsible for overseeing federally funded activities in the local districts. This means that the federal funding agency is usually two steps removed from the operating level. With this institutional structure, the behavior of the state and local agencies is obviously crucial to the success of the grant-funded programs. Therefore, no matter what the ultimate educational goals of the federal programs may be, their immediate, concrete objectives must be to induce the state and local grant recipients to use their funds in a manner consistent with the federal purpose.

The Distinction Between Educational and Allocative Goals

The intergovernmental character of the federal programs has sometimes been neglected in evaluating the effects of federal education expenditures. This neglect takes the form of a failure to distinguish between educational outcome goals and resource allocation goals of the federal programs and to apply appropriately the evaluation criteria that correspond to each. Educational outcome goals are usually stated in terms of observable kinds of pupil behavior—achievement test scores, for example, or other measures of proximate or long-run accomplishment, such as earnings or career success. Resource allocation goals must be described in terms of desired patterns of resource use within school systems. Some hypothetical examples of allocation goals include the following:

- To direct 50 percent greater instructional resources to the education of each disadvantaged child than to each "regular" child
- To increase the amount of resources per pupil devoted to reading by 20 percent over the amount that would have been allocated from state and local funds
- To induce districts to employ qualified special education teachers in the ratio of one to every ten educable mentally retarded children

---

[a]There are a few examples of direct federal provision of services. The government operates certain special education institutions, such as the Gallaudet College for the deaf. These account for a negligible fraction of federal educational outlays.

[b]State agencies perform some educational services directly, notably for the handicapped. In addition, some services are provided by counties and other intermediate units. Several of the major federal grant programs make explicit provision for the support of state and intermediate operating units. Nevertheless, the great bulk of federal aid money is spent on services provided by local school districts. This chapter pertains mainly to federal aid that is expended at the local level, but much of the discussion applies equally well to activities of the intermediate agencies.

- To provide diagnostic-prescriptive reading services for each child whose reading ability is one year or more behind grade level

To some educators and evaluators it may seem like a pointless diversion to focus on these input-oriented and process-oriented goals, rather than on educational outcomes. What sense does it make, they might ask, to say that a grant program is supposedly working or successful unless it can be shown that there has been some improvement in relevant dimensions of pupil performance? However, the point is not that allocative goals are of greater or even equal importance, but that separate information about the allocative effects of the federal grants is needed for intelligent policymaking.

The best-designed educational treatment can have no beneficial effect unless the means are available to ensure its implementation at the local level. Under our federal system, these means consist mainly of the provisions of aid legislation that direct resources to the intended places, pupils, and activities. The problem of designing a grant system that channels resources to the right uses is separate, in most respects, from the problem of identifying educationally desirable uses of funds or of designing educational interventions that work. Therefore, separate information on allocative outcomes is needed to evaluate the performance of the grant system as distinguished from the substantive educational programs.

Moreover, findings about achievement of the educational performance goals cannot be interpreted properly without information on the allocative effects of the federal grant programs. To illustrate with an extreme case, a finding of "no significant effect" on pupil performance would be entirely reasonable if it were discovered in analyzing the allocative effects of a federal grant program that the resources earmarked for special services to certain pupils were actually being diverted to other uses or substituted for state or local revenue. Without information on allocative outcomes, the lack of a performance effect might be interpreted incorrectly as evidence of poor design of the educational intervention itself or of poor pedagogical performance at the local level.

The question of the effectiveness of grant instruments in accomplishing allocative goals should be viewed as complementary to the question of the effectiveness of educational treatments in accomplishing pupil performance goals. Ultimately, the educational outcome criterion is more fundamental, but it is a criterion that can sensibly be applied only to the performance of the whole federal-state-local public education system and not just to its federal component. The resource allocation criterion, on the other hand, applies specifically to the federal intergovernmental grant system. It is the appropriate criterion to use in deciding whether the federal categorical aid programs are appropriately designed and administered and whether the grant provisions are being adequately enforced. From the standpoint of the members of Congress and the staff members of the Department of Health, Education, and Welfare (HEW) who are interested in developing education programs that work, the allocative issue has two logical claims to priority. First, the federal government can accomplish little by prescribing how services should be provided, or to whom, unless a system exists that can channel school resources to the designated children and the designated uses. Second, federal officials, being two steps removed from the operating level, can contribute far more effectively to the development of the grant mechanisms than the educational treatments themselves. The grant control issue deserves more attention than it has generally received in the educational evaluation and policy analysis literature.

Types of Allocative Goals

It is not always possible to obtain general agreement on what the allocative goals are of a particular federal education program. The goals may be very different to each of the groups who participated in creating a program, to the federal agencies that administer it, and to the state and local agencies that are called upon to implement the program and actually deliver services to children. For instance, it has been observed that the compensatory education programs funded under ESEA Title I were viewed by some as instruments for helping poor children with special educational needs, by others as devices for channeling extra funds to hard-pressed central city school districts, and by still others as a "foot in the door" for general large-scale federal financing of elementary and secondary education.[1] Moreover, program goals need not be constant. A program may be seen in a different light once it is in place than before it was enacted into law. The client and service-provider groups that come into being when a large program is created may redefine and reshape the program in their own interests. Nevertheless, the question of purpose cannot be avoided. It is central to any attempt to evaluate programs or to relate means to ends. Fortunately, for the limited purposes of this chapter, it is not necessary to deal with the problems that arise in trying to formulate goal statements for specific programs. All that is necessary is to identify the *generic* allocative goals that the main federal grant programs seek to achieve. Reasonable agreement can be obtained on this even though there may be controversy about the degree to which each generic goal applies or ought to apply to the individual programs.

It appears possible to subsume the allocative goals of past and current education grant programs under the following five headings:

1. *Allocation to Target Groups.* The principal stated purpose of many of the largest federal education programs is to provide additional services or resources—more than would have been provided in the absence of federal involvement—for the education of certain special categories of pupils. The main target groups of the current grant programs include the economically or educationally disadvantaged (ESEA Title I, Headstart, Follow Through), the non-English speaking (bilingual education), and pupils with mental and physical handicaps (various programs of aid for the handicapped, plus earmarking of

portions of vocational education, Headstart, and other funds for education of the handicapped).

2. *Allocation to Specified Educational Services.* Some federal programs are aimed at providing additional instruction in specified subjects or additional supporting services of specified kinds. The main areas of instruction that have been singled out for federal attention over the years include vocational training (vocational education grants to states), reading (Right to Read, plus major shares of compensatory education funds), and science, mathematics, and foreign languages (the National Defense Education Act). Federal funds have also been earmarked for noninstructional services such as guidance and counseling.

3. *Allocation to Specified Resource Categories.* A few programs provide support for acquisition of specified kinds of resources (objects of expenditure) rather than for specific pupils or services. The main current examples are grants for school libraries and instructional resources and for media and resource services for the handicapped. Federal support for the training of teachers and other educational personnel is closely related to this goal, but it is not considered here because those grants do not provide direct support for the operations of state and local education agencies.

4. *Allocation to Specified Processes.* Other federal programs are intended to induce adoption and implementation of designated methods, curricula, and organizational structures. This goal characterizes the federal programs that are aimed at affecting educational techniques and technologies rather than resource allocations per se. It applies primarily to grants for innovation and demonstration efforts. Until recently, the main such program was ESEA Title III, which has now been folded into a consolidated program of "support and innovation" grants. Other programs with strong process orientations include Right to Read, Follow Through, and parts of the programs for support of the disadvantaged and handicapped.

5. *General Support.* The least restrictive goal of federal aid is to provide general operating funds to financially hard-pressed school systems. The only major current federal education program explicitly intended to provide general purpose aid is the impact aid program (School Assistance in Federally Affected Areas, or SAFA). However, the issue of broader gauge general purpose aid has been debated in the past and will undoubtedly come up again. As also has already been noted, some people view categorical grants as de facto general aid, which means that the general support goal must be viewed as at least potentially cutting across all federal education programs.

The first three goals may be thought of as the pure allocative or resource targeting goals of the federal programs. The three are not mutually exclusive. Federal grant funds may be simultaneously earmarked for a particular type of pupil, a subject of instruction, and a category of resources—for example, a program to support employment of specialists to provide reading instruction to disadvantaged elementary school pupils. The fourth goal is different in that it is oriented toward the educational process or the method of resource use. This raises special problems for the design of federal grant programs, which can be touched on only very lightly in this chapter. The general support goal is included for completeness, but it is not discussed further because it is not a resource allocation goal in the sense that term is used in this chapter. General aid proposals need to be considered in relation to broad issues of school finance, which are beyond the scope of this analysis. However, the possibility of state and local conversion of federal funds into general purpose aid is discussed because it is at the heart of our concern over the adequacy of federal controls.

Congruence and Conflict Between Federal and State-Local Goals

An important issue in assessing the adequacy of grant instruments is the degree to which the goals of the federal grantors of aid and those of the state and local grantees diverge or coincide. Obviously, if goals coincided completely, there would be no difficulty in having federally funded programs carried out according to the wishes of their designers. The issue of adequacy of control would be of no concern. We could focus our attention on ridding the education grant system of unnecessary requirements and "red tape." On the other hand, if goals do not coincide the question of the sufficiency of grant instruments becomes salient. Can the various control mechanisms of the grant programs ensure that states and local school systems will use federal money as Congress and the administering agencies intend even though the aid recipients, if left to their own devices, would prefer to put that money to different uses?

Precisely what does it mean to say that federal and state-local goals are in agreement? A rigorous behavioral definition is that goals coincide if, and only if, state and local education agencies would allocate their resources in exactly the same manner in response to a fully enforced categorical federal grant and in response to the same dollar amount of completely unrestricted general purpose federal aid. For instance, suppose that the $2 billion ESEA Title I program were suddenly eliminated and in its place were put an equally large program of general federal aid, distributed in the same amounts to the same districts. If local agencies continued to spend the whole $2 billion for compensatory education even though under no compulsion to do so and if they diverted no funds to other activities or used none to supplant local funds, then it would be reasonable to say that the local authorities assign the same priority to compensatory education as does the federal government. No one has claimed that federal and state-local preferences coincide so completely. To believe that they do is to disregard a substantial body of evidence on how states and districts allocate their own funds, how they use incremental dollars when they become available, and how they respond to outside aid.

The history of compensatory education provides one body of relevant information. When ESEA was first enacted, it was evident that the states did not share the federal government's view of the urgency of special aid for the disadvantaged. Only three states operated their own compensatory programs in 1965.[2] There was very little extra state or local money for the education of poor or minority children. If anything, these children tended to receive lower than average amounts of available district funds rather than extra, compensatory services.[3] Not surprisingly, it was found in the early years of the program that significant amounts of Title I money were being converted into general district resources or being substituted for local funds allotted to Title I schools.[4] This motivated the development of comparability requirements, which stipulate that eligible schools must receive their federal Title I money *in addition to* amounts of local support that are "comparable" to those allocated to non-Title I schools.[c] Even after the installation of comparability provisions, however, it was found that gaps in their enforcement permitted funds to be diverted from the target pupils and designated uses to other activities of the local districts.[5] Thus, there is continuing concern that states and local districts do not share the high federal priority attached to special funding for education of the disadvantaged. State and local attitudes toward compensatory education do appear to have become more favorable over time. Nevertheless, it remains unlikely that anything like the full amount now earmarked for compensatory programs under ESEA Title I would be allocated to that purpose by the states if the federal funds were converted into general aid.

More general evidence on this issue comes from the large body of empirical work on determinants of local school spending and the impact on that spending of state and federal aid. Nearly all such studies have found that a large fraction of external aid tends to be substituted for the local district's own revenue.[6] Thus, only a portion of the grant money (most estimates are in the range from one-third to two-thirds) translates into net local expenditure for *any* purpose. Most expenditure determinants studies have not directly addressed the question of additivity of the federal categorical grant funds. One recent study that did examine this issue reported that approximately two-thirds of Title I funds translate into additional local spending.[7] However, this refers to additional spending for all purposes and not necessarily for the compensatory education programs for which Title I funds are intended. There have been no statistical studies of the impact of grants on spending for the designated educational activity as opposed to other categories of expenditure of the districts.

There is also a small body of literature on the allocation of resources

---

[c]The comparability requirements were introduced into the Title I regulations in 1970 and written into the law in 1972. The details of the comparability rule are described and the effectiveness of the rule is evaluated in the following section.

among individual schools and among categories of children within districts. These studies show that local decisionmakers tend to favor majority pupils, defined either in terms of race or of income.[8] Especially germane are the studies conducted in connection with equal protection lawsuits, such as *Hobson v. Hansen,* which specifically address the question of resource inequality between rich and poor and between black and white schools.[9]

A final type of relevant evidence is the survey study reported by Callahan and Wilken of expenditure priorities as seen by state school officials.[10] The results show that low priority is assigned to incremental funding for the disadvantaged as compared either with funding for regular programs for majority pupils or funding for other special groups. This reinforces the belief that state and local officials, if left to their own devices, would tend to reduce special funding for compensatory-type activities in favor of other types of local school spending.

The evidence that federal and state-local goals diverge is more clear-cut in the area of education for the disadvantaged and in the closely related area of bilingual education than in other areas. The reason is that federal financing is dominant in the compensatory and bilingual fields, and the contrast between strong federal commitments and weaker state-local commitments is apparent. In two other fields where the federal government is heavily involved, education for the handicapped and vocational education, the relative priorities of the different levels of government are more difficult to compare. State and local financial contributions in both areas are many times greater than federal contributions (the federal government provides only about 14 percent of the financial support for each field, according to recent estimates.[11] Nevertheless, recent federal policy appears to be aimed at stimulating the state-local sector to still greater efforts. The new Education for All Handicapped Children Act (PL 94-142) establishes standards for state and local service provision that if fully implemented and enforced would probably require a sharp increase in nonfederal support for handicapped children.[12] This can be taken as evidence that from the federal perspective the state-local priority assigned to education of the handicapped is still not high enough. For most other programs, it is difficult to say anything about relative priorities because data are lacking and expenditure studies have not been undertaken. For instance, although instruction in reading is of great federal interest, it is impossible to assemble data on the resources devoted to reading by state and local education agencies or to determine how outlays for reading have responded to federal stimuli.[13]

Evolution of State and Local Goals in
Response to Federal Programs

One possibility that complicates the issue of congruence or conflict of goals is that state and local priorities in education may be shaped by the federal programs themselves. It appears that in at least some areas, state and local goals resemble federal goals much more closely now than they did before the federal programs were initiated. Again, ESEA Title I provides the best example. In contrast to the situation that prevailed ten years ago, when almost no special funding was available at the state level for disadvantaged pupils, many state governments now earmark significant sums of their own funds for such pupils over and above the amounts received from Title I and other federal programs. According to the U.S. Office of Education's (USOE) 1975-76 survey of state school finance systems, fourteen states operate explicit compensatory education programs with expenditures totaling $240 million.[14] In addition, even larger sums are now allocated for disadvantaged children under school finance plans that give extra weight to the poor or educationally disadvantaged in distributing state aid to local school districts.[15] Some local school systems also earmark resources of their own for extra services for children with special educational needs. A typical method of doing this is to establish staff allocation formulas that allow higher teacher-pupil ratios in schools with large concentrations of disadvantaged children. Unfortunately, there are no data from which to determine how important such arrangements are on a national basis. Regardless of the figures, however, it seems extremely likely, although probably impossible to prove, that the federal initiative under Title I and the consequent implementation of compensatory programs around the country led states to value compensatory education more highly than they would have otherwise.

Vocational education seems to provide another example of state and local officials responding to federal leadership. The federal government has played a pioneering role in the development and diffusion of vocational education ever since enactment of the Smith-Hughes Act in 1917. Throughout the postwar years, however, state and local outlays for vocational programs have grown more rapidly than federal outlays and many times more rapidly than would have been required to satisfy the expenditure matching requirements of federal law.[16] Although it is impossible to demonstrate causality in any rigorous manner, it is likely that, at least in the early years of the program, the federal presence helped to establish a higher priority for vocational education programs among state and local officials than those programs would otherwise have enjoyed.

It is not necessary to be an idealist to appreciate the potential effect of federal categorical programs on the funding priorities of state and local education agencies. To say that state and local preferences have come to resemble the federal preferences more closely does not mean that officials have "seen the light" or even that anyone's tastes have changed. A more down-to-earth explanation of the observed changes in allocative behavior is that implementation of major federal categorical programs creates client and provider interest groups and state and local bureaurcracies, all of which generate political support for the programs. That is, an indirect effect of federal funding may be to shift the balance of political forces within state and local jurisdictions so that more internal funds are allocated to federal aided activities. One feature of federal grant programs that may exert special influence of this kind is the practice of setting aside a fraction of grant funds for support of the state offices that administer federally funded programs.[d] In all the major federally aided areas—compensatory and vocational education and education of handicapped—earmarked federal funding provides the main sustenance for state-level, program-oriented bureaucracies. These offices may constitute effective internal lobbies in favor of the federal priority programs and may have significant impact on allocative outcomes. This phenomenon cannot be analyzed within the scope of this chapter, but it warrants special attention in future studies of grant program designs.

Targeting of Funds, Additivity, and Goal Achievement

Assuming that the goals of the federal categorical programs are to direct additional funds to target pupils, activities, or categories of school inputs, what are the appropriate measures of goal attainment? What allocative behavior must we be able to observe or would we want to observe in principle, to assure ourselves that the federal grants are being used as intended? The essential step in thinking about these questions is to focus on the *net economic impact* of the grants. What counts is the difference between the total amount expended for the grant-aided activity and the amount that would otherwise have been expended in the absence of the grant. If that difference is equal to (or greater than) the amount of the grant, it can be concluded that the grant funds have been used for the intended purpose (this criterion must be modified if there are matching grants, as is explained below). If the difference is smaller than the amount of the grant, funds have been at least partially substituted or diverted to other uses. To determine how thoroughly the uses of federal funds are being controlled, therefore, is to determine the degree to which they are *additive* to funds otherwise available for the designated purposes.

The proposition that additivity is the appropriate resource allocation criterion squares with the mandate of most education grant legislation that federal funds "supplement, not supplant," state and local funds available for the federally assisted program. Recent grant legislation has even made it explicit that supplantation is to be judged by comparing actual program outlays with amounts that would otherwise have been expended in the absence of the grant.[17] The statutes and regulations do not specify precisely how "amounts that would otherwise have been expended" should be determined. However, certain provisions of grant legislation can be interpreted as attempts to make the concept

---

[d]Under ESEA Title I, 1 percent of each state's entitlement is set aside for state administration; under the Education for All Handicapped Children Act, the administrative set-aside is 5 percent of the amount earmarked for the state (which is distinct from the amount earmarked for distribution to local districts); under the vocational education act, funding of state administrative activities is authorized but no specific set-aside percentage is established.

operational. For instance, most major education grant programs include the requirement that grantees not reduce their own financial support for the federally assisted activity (maintenance of effort requirements).[e] In addition, the standard requirement that federally funded and locally funded activities must be kept separate (the noncommingling requirement) can be interpreted as an attempt to ensure that federal money pays for "extra" services over and above those that would otherwise have been provided.

There is an essential distinction between the additivity criterion of allocative impact and an alternative criterion that is strongly entrenched in the language of grant legislation—namely, that the federal funds themselves must be "used for" the federally designated purpose. To make the latter criterion operational, elaborate requirements have been promulgated for record-keeping and accounting to make it possible for auditors to trace through or track federal grant funds to their final uses. The strictures against commingling, referred to above, serve to ensure that there is a clear audit trail. Because fiscal substitution is possible, however, success in tracking grant funds to the proper final uses does not guarantee that the grants have had the desired allocative effects. A grant may be used entirely correctly in the legal and accounting senses; yet to the extent that state or local funds are displaced and put to other uses, the net economic impact of the grant will be less than the nominal effect recorded on the books. In general, the criterion of additivity and the criterion of proper use of funds (in the accounting sense) are not equivalent. The latter is far less restrictive. Only where the possibility of supplanting local funds does not exist (e.g., because the grant-aided activity is 100 percent federally funded) does allocation to the proper end use guarantee the additivity of federal aid.[f]

Parenthetically, it should be noted that there are cases in which full compliance with the terms of a grant may mean something other than 100 percent additivity. If there are matching requirements, more than one incremental dollar might have to be expended by the grantee for each dollar received in federal aid.[g] More than 100 percent additivity would also be expected where states or districts must comply with some minimum requirement in order to be eligible for federal funds. This might be necessary, for example, to satisfy the comparability requirements of ESEA Title I or the

---

[e]The requirement that grantees maintain their own contributions is not logically equivalent to nonsupplantation because it is possible that in the absence of the federal aid the grantee would have raised or lowered its own support for the program.

[f]There seems to be very few instances in which some opportunity for supplanting does not exist. Even when the federal government undertakes to pay 100 percent of the cost of special services for designated pupils, the question remains of whether the grantee is able to divert funds that would have been used to provide regular services to the same pupils. Perhaps the only cases of assured additivity are those in which the beneficiaries of federal aid would not have been served at all in the absence of the grant.

[g]Whether a matching grant calls forth additional spending by the grantee depends on the level at which the grantee was already supporting the aided program. The possibility of more than 100 percent additivity exists only where the initial level of non-federal support for the program is too low to satisfy the matching requirement.

service standards of the Education for All Handicapped Children Act. The new legislation for the handicapped establishes a special rule under which something less than 100 percent additivity may be required. It explicitly allows grant recipients to use federal aid to supplant local funds if the requirement to provide appropriate services to all handicapped children has been satisfied throughout a state.[18] The implications of the provisions mentioned here are discussed later in this chapter.

THE ADEQUACY OF EXISTING CONTROL INSTRUMENTS

The difficulties that the federal government faces in attempting to achieve its allocative goals are inherent in the federal-state-local structure of support for public education. For federal purposes to be accomplished, local authorities must direct funds over and above those that would otherwise have been allocated to the educational activities specified in federal grant legislation. However, the amount of funds that "would otherwise have been allocated" is a hypothetical construct. It cannot be measured or observed. This means that either local compliance or the lack of it cannot be established in any simple or straightforward manner. Indirect, inferential methods are needed to determine whether federal grants are having the intended additive effects on federal priority programs. Moreover, the means available to grant administrators in HEW to ensure state and local compliance are sharply limited. Federal officials have neither the authority nor the resources to exert comprehensive control over local allocations of funds. They cannot command that so much be spent for compensatory education, so much for the handicapped, or so much for instruction in reading. Instead, they must rely on relatively narrow and indirect control instruments to induce the desired allocative behavior and to prevent aid recipients from supplanting their own funds and diverting the freed resources to their own preferred uses. In this section, the main provisions of the major education grant programs that are intended to exert this type of control are discussed and evaluated.

Formulation of the "Adequacy of Control" Issue

To formulate the control issue precisely, consider each federal grant to be made up of two parts—a transfer of funds from federal to local (or state) government and a set of conditions, or "strings," specifying how resources are to be used at the local level. In the absence of any constraints, it may be presumed that the local recipients would use the federal funds just as they would use their own tax receipts or any other local revenue. That is, they would allocate the funds in accordance with their own goals and priorities, which in general would not coincide with federal preferences. If federal funds were made available with no conditions at all (e.g., an unrestricted federal block grant for elementary and secondary education), it is likely that only a fraction of the aid would be expended for the present federal priority activities. The key question, then is what is the effect of appending the constraints. Do the strings shift the pattern of fund use from that preferred by the local district to a pattern more consistent with federal goals? If so, to what degree?

In general, the effectiveness of strings in producing the desired allocative outcomes depends on three factors: (1) the degree to which federal and local goals agree or diverge; (2) the pattern of resource allocation that exists at the local level independent of the federal grant—in particular, the availability of nonfederal resources for the purposes that the federal grant is intended to promote; and (3) the characteristics of the strings themselves and the means of their enforcement. The effectiveness of a grant control mechanisms cannot be assessed without taking into account the context in which it is to be applied. One should not expect to find that a particular mechanism, such as a comparability requirement, always is or is not an effective device for directing resources to desired uses. Whether the mechanism is effective will usually depend on the treatment already being accorded by local authorities to the type of educational activity or type of pupil for which the federal funds are earmarked. Nevertheless, it is meaningful to discuss the *potential* effects on resource allocations of each type of control instrument, provided that it is recognized that actual and potential effects differ. By demonstrating that a particular device is effective only under special circumstances, it may be possible to show that its effectiveness in the real world is likely to be low.

It is also important to distinguish between the effects that a federal program requirement could have if it were fully enforced and the effects that it is likely to have under an enforcement policy in real life. This chapter deals mainly with issues of grant design rather than enforcement policy, and the latter is referred to only peripherally. It should be kept in mind that even the tightest strings are likely to be nonbinding where either the administrative resources or the political will to enforce them is lacking.

In the remainder of this section, the effectiveness of grant control provisions is discussed from two points of view. First, there is a brief review of the main devices that are currently used to control resource allocations under the major federal education grant programs. As part of this review, there are comments on the potential effectiveness of each device and on the circumstances under which that potential is likely to be realized. Second, to pursue the same question in a more concrete manner, the discussion is shifted to a consideration of the provisions of some specific education grant programs. The following three programs and selected grant provisions have been chosen to represent the major approaches currently used to target federal educational resources: (1) the comparability requirement and related provisions of federal compensatory programs funded under ESEA Title I; (2) the matching and maintenance of effort requirements incorporated into the program of grants to states for vocational education; and (3) the service requirements and the principle of payment for excess costs that are included in the Education for All Handicapped Children Act of 1975.

Types of Control Instruments and Their Potential Effects

Most provisions of federal education grant programs, other than those that specify the level of funding and the distribution of funds among states and localities, can be interpreted as devices for controlling the grantees' behavior. The devices that pertain primarily to resource allocation and resource use can be grouped under the following four headings:

1. Statements of permitted uses of funds and of the responsibilities of grantees
2. Quantitative constraints on resource allocation
3. Requirements for record-keeping and reporting
4. Incentive and penalty mechanisms

In addition, there are three other categories of grant provisions that are not examined in this chapter because they do not pertain primarily to resource allocation. However, these categories should be acknowledged because of their significance for intergovernmental relations in education. These are provisions aimed at securing the rights of individuals affected by the federal programs (nondiscrimination requirements, due process stipulations, rules for access to information, etc.); provisions aimed primarily at influencing the organizational framework and procedures for decisionmaking at the local or state levels (mandated advisory councils, requirements for parent involvement, etc.): and requirements for evaluation of the educational effects of federally supported programs. Although some of these provisions probably influence allocative outcomes, an examination of their effects is beyond the scope of this analysis. The following discussion briefly explains and assesses the specific devices that fall into the four categories of resource allocation control instruments listed above.

Statements of Intended Uses of Funds and Responsibilities of Grantees

Two methods are used in combination to define permitted and prohibited uses of federal funds under the education grant programs. The first method is to specify in the grant legislation or the accompanying regulations how funds are to be applied. For example, ESEA Title I specifies that funds are to be used for "the excess costs of programs and projects. . .which are designed to meet the special educational needs of educationally deprived children in school attendance areas having high concentrations of children from low income families. . . ."[19] Additional language in the act and especially in the regulations defines the terms in this statement of purpose and places limits on what grantees can purchase with Title I funds.[20] The second method is to require the grantee (this may be the local education angency or the state or both) to submit detailed plans specifying how grant funds will be used. Such plans, which must conform to general federal guidelines and to the statements of purpose in the law, normally describe the educational treatments to be offered and the organizational structure for the federally funded program in addition to providing information on what the federal funds will buy. The major categorical grant programs for compensatory education, vocational education, and education of the handicapped all impose requirements for submission of plans upon the states or the local grantees.[21]

Where state and local agencies both participate in operating federally funded programs, it is necessary to have language in the law that defines the obligations of each level of government. Typically, the responsibility for ensuring the correct use of funds is imposed upon both levels of government—that is, the local agency is responsible for using funds correctly and the state agency is responsible for enforcing correct performance at the local level.[22] In effect, the state is expected to function as an agent of the federal government for the purpose of monitoring and enforcing compliance with federal law. The practice of relying on states to supervise the use of federal resources instead of on direct federal supervision raises serious questions about federal enforcement policy, which, unfortunately, cannot be dealt with in this chapter.

Is the earmarking of federal money effective? Does the insertion of a statement in the law that federal grant funds are "to be used for" some specified activity make the net impact of the grant any different from that of unrestricted aid? Assuming that the standard auditing and accounting requirements are imposed (see below), the answer is "yes, under certain special conditions." The conditions are, first, that the federally supported activity must be recognizably different from other activities of the local school system and, second, that it must be an activity that the locality would not have undertaken in the absence of the federal grant.[h] Where these conditions are met, opportunities for the substitution of federal money for local money do not exist; correct use of federal funds (in the accounting sense) become synonymous with additivity. The cases that most nearly fit this description are those in which grant funds are earmarked for pupils not previously served (e.g., preschool pupils or certain categories of the handicapped) or in which new types of educational services are provided.[i] Some federally funded demonstration programs and innovation projects may also fit this category. However, only a minor fraction

---

[h]Strictly speaking, partial additivity is assured if the amount of the federal grant is greater than the amount that would otherwise have been expended for the designated activity out of nonfederal funds.

[i]Even where federal funds are earmarked for a new activity—for example, a type of instruction not previously provided—opportunities for substitution still exist. State and local funds may be shifted away from the regular instructional activities that were foremerly provided for the children receiving the new service. Opportunities for substitution are truly minimal only where no services at all would have been provided for target group children, as, for example, preschool children receiving services under Headstart.

of federal grant money is allocated for educational programs of these kinds. More commonly, federal funds are earmarked for activities that are also supported by state and local revenue or that are indistinguishable from nominally separate activities that receive such support. Where the federally funded program is not unique in the sense defined above opportunities for fiscal substitution exist. Therefore, earmarking alone is insufficient to ensure the additivity of federal funds. Note, especially, that earmarking of grant money for the benefit of a certain target group, such as the disadvantaged, is insufficient to ensure that the grant will translate into incremental services for that group. The reason is that the use of federal funds for the target group does not preclude shifting of nongrant funds from that group to other pupils. Categorical labeling alone is therefore an inadequate control strategy for the programs that account for the bulk of federal education outlays.

Quantitative Constraints on Resource Allocation

The next step beyond earmarking is to impose constraints on resource allocation patterns at the local level—not just on the application of federal funds. There are approximately a half dozen types of provisions now in use in education grant programs that can be interpreted as devices for promoting the additive use of federal funds for the stated purposes. The following comments pertain mainly to these constraints as they currently exist. Discussion of possible variants and new forms of constraints is reserved for later.

The Nonsupplantation Rule. The standard provision that grants "supplement, not supplant," local funds that would otherwise have been expended is included under this heading because it has the *form* of an expenditure constraint—that is, it seems to set a floor under total spending for federally aided activities. However, since the amount that "would otherwise have been expended" usually cannot be ascertained, by itself the nonsupplantation rule is not an effective constraint. It is probably more appropriately thought of as a goal statement. However, this characterization does not necessarily apply to the more specific rules that have been developed in some programs as means of operationalizing the nonsupplanting concept.

Limitation to Excess Costs. This provision, which is included in programs for the disadvantaged and handicapped, states that federal funds shall be used only to pay for costs of the federally assisted programs that are in excess of the costs of "regular" programs of the local agencies.[23] The provision applies especially to pupil-targeted programs, the costs of which can be contrasted to costs of services for regular pupils outside the target group. If fully complied with, the excess cost rule would force expenditures for the designated pupils or activities to exceed regular expenditures by the amount of the federal grant. However, this outcome is necessarily synonymous with additivity only where no nonfederal funds are available to meet the excess costs of the program in question. Moreover, serious technical problems arise in attempting to measure excess costs. Those problems are discussed in connection with federal aid for the handicapped later in this section.

Maintenance of Effort. A common provision of federal education grant programs is that grantees (states or localities or both) continue to allocate at least as much of their own money (either total or per pupil) to the federally assisted activity as they allocated in some specified base period. Such provisions appear in the compensatory education, vocational education, and handicapped legislation.[24] (For ESEA Title I, however, the requirement pertains to the level of support for all education activities instead of only for compensatory education.)[25] The maintenance of effort requirements can be interpreted as attempts to give some operational content to the stricture to supplement, not supplant, and, therefore, as devices aimed directly at promoting additivity of federal funds. The potential effectiveness of these provisions is limited because they set the required local expenditure floor equal to prior-year expenditures and not to expenditures that would have been made in the current year in the absence of federal aid. This constraint is likely to be nonbinding when the aided program is growing, when program costs are increasing, or when federal aid makes up only a minor fraction of program expenditures.[j] Some potentially more effective variations of the maintenance of effort requirement are discussed in the concluding section.

Comparability. The comparability principle was developed specifically to control the allocation of compensatory education funds under ESEA Title I. It has not yet been implemented in other programs. Implications of the specific Title I provisions and comparability definitions are discussed later in this section. The general comparability principle is that the nonfederal resources devoted to the education of children who are the targets of a federal categorical program should not be less than the resources allocated to other children served by the local agency. A comparability requirement encompasses the excess cost rule defined above, but it goes one step further. It requires that the nonfederal resource base for target and nontarget pupils be equalized. If target pupils

---

[j]When the federally assisted program is growing, the maintenance of effort requirement is automatically satisfied. It is possible, nevertheless, that federal grant funds or increments therein substitute for increments in nonfederal funds that would otherwise have been forthcoming. If the costs of the federally assisted program are increasing, it is possible for a locality to cut back on the real resources it devotes to the program while still maintaining its dollar contribution. When the federal contribution to a program is small compared to the state-local contribution, the normal year-to-year increase in state-local funding is likely to be of the same order of magnitude as the *total* federal contribution. That makes it easy to substitute federal for state-local funds merely by adjusting the size of the state-local increment as needed to accomplish the substitution.

are initially receiving less state and local funds than nontarget pupils, the imbalance must be rectified as a condition for federal aid. Under some conditions, this may constitute a requirement for more than 100 percent additivity of federal funds. However, where the target group pupils receive special state or local support, a comparability rule alone cannot guarantee that federal money will not be used to supplant these extra nonfederal funds. Therefore, imposition and enforcement of a comparability requirement may have a weak or a strong influence on the net fiscal impact of a grant, depending on the budgetary choices that have been made at the local level.

Matching Requirements. A common requirement of federal grant programs in fields other than education is that the grantee "match" the federal contribution with nonfederal funds. Among the major education programs, only aid for vocational education has a matching provision.[26] Its characteristics are discussed below. In general, a matching provision imposes the constraint that the total resources devoted to a federally assisted program must be equal to at least a specified multiple of the amount of the federal grant. If the prescribed matching ratio is one to one, for example, the grantee must be able to show that at least twice the amount of the federal grant is being spent for the designated activity. By requiring local matching, the federal government may be able to exert leverage over considerably more funds than it expends for grants. However, the effectiveness of matching depends on the availability of local support for the aided activity. If the grantee would have provided funds in any event equal to or greater than those required by the matching formula, then the matching requirement has a zero net effect. There are forms of matching used in noneducational programs of the federal government and in state grant-in-aid programs that may have more powerful effects than the method currently used in vocational education. Several possibilities are discussed later.

Expenditure or Service Standards. An approach that has not yet been used in elementary and secondary education but that could be foreshadowed by recent legislation (see the discussion of the Education for All Handicapped Children Act below) is to impose quantitative expenditure or resource allocation standards as a condition of eligibility for federal grants. Such standards could take any of the following forms:

- Total expenditure per target group pupil must be at least X dollars per year.
- Expenditure per target group pupil must be at least P percent greater than expenditure per regular pupil.
- The teacher-pupil (or total staff-pupil ratio) must be at least Y for target group pupils.
- The teacher-pupil or staff-pupil ratio must be at least Z percent greater for target group pupils than for regular pupils.

There is a precedent for absolute staffing standards in the regulations governing federally assisted child-care programs, which receive funds under the Social Security Act.[27] There are also models for relative expenditure standards in some of the newly reformed state school finance systems, which establish differential expenditure ratios for various categories of exceptional pupils.[k] Despite these precedents, the introduction of such standards into the major pupil-targeted grant programs would represent a basic change in the federal role in education. The implications of the standard-setting approach are discussed below in connection with federal aid to the handicapped as well as in the section of this chapter that discusses policy implications.

Record-Keeping and Reporting

All enforcement of the resource allocation provisions of grants is contingent upon the availability of data on resource use at the local level. Requirements for maintenance of auditable accounting data are included in all the categorical grant programs. The possibilities of enforcing compliance depend critically on the comprehensiveness of the required data, on the level of detail at which information is collected, and on the categories that are used to classify local educational expenditures. It is useful to distinguish among three levels of data collection and three corresponding levels of enforcement capability.

Level 1—Federal Fund Accounting. The record-keeping requirement that is most commonly found in grant legislation, but which has the least usefulness for monitoring compliance, is that grantees must maintain accounting records of how they expended federal funds. The premise underlying this requirement is that certain eductional resources used by a local educational agency (i.e., certain staff members, certain items of equipment, and certain facilities) can be identified as having been purchased or hired with federal funds. Consequently, records showing how those resources have been used within the school system can establish that federal funds have been used for legitimate purposes. The philosophy of this accounting approach is conveyed most clearly by the strictures in the grant laws against "commingling" of federal funds with state or local funds—requirements that are supposed to have the effect of "preventing Federal funds from losing their separate identity."[28] The weakness of the approach is that the process of labeling resources as "federally funded" takes no account of whether the same or equivalent resources would have been acquired by school systems in the absence of the federal grant. For example, that ten teachers are designated "Title I teachers" does not imply that ten additional teachers have been employed by the school system because of the availability of Title I funds. The records that purport to show how grant funds are used do

---

[k]Some state plans stipulate that expenditures for designated categories of pupils shall be equal to or greater than specified multiples of the expenditure for "regular" pupils. See note 56.

not establish that the earmarked resources are *incremental*—that they have been purchased by the grantee in addition to the resources that would otherwise have been acquired with nongrant funds. Therefore, by themselves the federal fund accounts are of little use in determining the net resource impact of federal aid.

Level 2—Records Pertaining to Specific Allocative Constraints. In addition to the standard requirement for federal fund accounting, some grant programs require granteees to maintain records that will permit monitoring of state and local compliance with the quantitative resource allocation constraints discussed above. For example, the vocational education regulations require that accounting records be kept of the uses of local matching money as well as federal grant money, and the Title I regulations establish a special data reporting system for demonstrating local compliance with the program's comparability provisions.[29] But not all allocative constraints are supported by reporting systems. The technical problems of measuring the excess cost of a program have not been solved, for example. Therefore, the excess cost provisions of the handicapped legislation are not backed up by a special reporting system in the same sense as are the comparability provisions of Title I.[30]

The usefulness of these special reporting requirements depends entirely on the effectiveness of the allocative constraints that they are designed to support. Under the circumstances in which matching requirements, comparability rules, and maintenance of effort provisions are effective, the corresponding record-keeping provisions help to promote the additivity of federal funds.

Level 3—Comprehensive Accounting for Local Resource Use. Wherever there are opportunities for substantial substitution of federal funds for state or local funds, accounting data of the kinds mentioned above will not be sufficient to establish the degree to which federal funds have been used additively. To analyze the net economic impact of federal grants, it would be necessary to have data showing the total resources and funds, regardless of source, used for each of the federally aided activities and for other activities of the school systems. For instance, to investigate the allocative effects of federal aid for the handicapped, we would need to know about all the resources that a school system devotes to the education of handicapped pupils regardless of whether the resources are said to be purchased with federal, state, or local funds. In addition, to determine compliance with excess cost provisions, we would need similar information about the resources allocated to other pupils in the district and in the individual schools. The level of detail of the resource and cost records would have to correspond with the level at which programs are differentiated within the school system. That is, if handicapped children are served in special classes, the data system would have to be designed to record resource and cost information at the classroom level; if handicapped children are served primarily in regular classes, but with certain special supplementary services, then pupil-based accounting systems would be needed to record the costs. None of the current federal grant programs calls for such detailed or comprehensive accounting. However, certain provisions of the new Education for All Handicapped Children Act may represent moves in this direction.

No set of accounting records can be used by itself to show that federal grant funds have been expended additively for the designated activity. The reason is that accounting data do not indicate what resources would otherwise have been available. An adequate accounting system is a necessary, but not sufficient, condition for the control of grant funds. Even with adequate data, the task remains of inferring what states and localities would have done in the absence of federal aid. But without adequate data, any tightening up of resource allocation constraints would be largely symbolic because the means of verifying compliance would not exist.

Programs Plans and Reports. A final point about record-keeping and reporting concerns the utility of federal requirements for collection and submission of nonaccounting data—specifically, reports on planned and actual resource use in federally assisted programs. As was noted earlier, most federal programs require the preparation of local and state plans or both as a condition of eligibility for aid. Most also require reports on program activities and accomplishments. Potentially, these documents could provide valuable data for determining whether resources are being used properly. This potential is often not realized because (1) descriptions of planned and actual programs do not contain quantitative information about resource use, such as numbers of hours during which children are in contact with specified types of instructional personnel; (2) information about resource use is not reported in standard forms by different grantees; and (3) data are rarely included that would permit comparisons of the resources provided to children who are served and not served by the federal program. If the planning and reporting requirements were modified to emphasize the collection of data needed for comparative cost analysis, the ability of state and federal grant administrators to determine the effects of their programs would be considerably enhanced.

Incentive and Penalty Mechanisms

The degree of state and local compliance with grant provisions is likely to depend on the perceived consequences of noncompliance. Some grantees, to be sure, will comply voluntarily because "it's the law," because they share the federal goals, or, perhaps, because members of target groups are able to assert their claims to federal funds. Others are unlikely to comply without strong incentives to do so, especially if they do not share the federal perception of educational priorities or if they disagree with the specified means of achieving educational goals. Recognizing the need for an enforcement mechanism, Congress has prescribed sanctions for state or local agencies that violate grant program provisions.

The sanctions in the federal education programs have three salient characteristics.[31] One is that they are exclusively negative. Penalties are prescribed for grantees who fail to comply with their assurances to HEW or who expend funds improperly. No rewards are provided for compliance or good performance. The principal penalties allowed for by the law and regulations are withholding or suspension funds and the requirement to refund to the federal government funds that were expended illegitimately. The second characteristic is that withholding is generally "all or nothing" in nature. Graduated withholding, scaled to the seriousness of the offense, is not now provided for. The third characteristic (one that reflects the nature of the HEW bureaucracy rather than the design of the programs) is that the sanctions have rarely been invoked. The probability of recouping improper expenditures is small, and the probability that withholding will actually be imposed is miniscule.[32] Therefore, in effect, the present system is one of voluntary compliance.

There have been proposals for changing all the above-mentioned characteristics of the sanction provisions.[33] To make the enforcement system less negative, it has been suggested that there should be incentive bonuses for states and districts that demonstrate compliance. In addition, grantees could be rewarded by being relieved of certain program strings as they passed specified compliance thresholds. The all or nothing aspects of the sanctions could be modified by linking the size of a penalty or reward to the percentage of funds misused or some other measure of the extent of misallocation. Enforcement might be more feasible politically if positive incentives were available and if penalties could be varied to suit the offense.

The issues of sanctions and enforcement policy are complicated. Legal and political considerations are involved as well as issues of grant program design. A major study of the present system and possible alternatives has been conducted within HEW.[34] Therefore, no attempt will be made to pursue the general issue any further in this chapter. Only occasional reference to penalties or incentives is made in the following discussions of the compensatory, vocational, and handicapped education programs.

ESEA Title I: The Uses and Limits of the Comparability Approach

The principal targeting problem in connection with federal compensatory programs is to get extra resources to the disadvantaged pupils whom the program is intended to serve. A source of some confusion is that there is a distinction between economically disadvantaged pupils, who are counted for the purpose of determining the interstate, intercounty, and interdistrict distribution of funds, and educationally deprived pupils, for whom compensatory services are to be provided at the school level. The inherent difficulty of defining the latter group would make it hard to determine, even with the most sophisticated pupil-by-pupil record-keeping, precisely how well the distribution of compensatory funds is correlated with the distribution of special educational needs. For the present purpose, we neglect these definitional problems and consider the more clear-cut issue of whether the provisions of the Title I program would be adequate for directing federal funds to members of a well-defined stratum of disadvantaged pupils.

The Title I legislation contains many of the quantitative resource allocation constraints described above. It stipulates that federal aid shall supplement, not supplant, local or state funding; that grant funds shall be used only to pay the excess costs of Title I programs and not for general aid; that the local grantees shall be required to maintain their levels of fiscal effort; and that non-federal resources shall be "equitably provided" to schools with and without Title I programs.[35] The most important constraint, however, and the one that is most thoroughly backed up by reporting and monitoring systems, is that

> State and local funds will be used in the district of such [local] agency to provide services in [Title I] project areas which, taken as a whole, are at least comparable to services being provided in areas in such district which are not receiving funds under this title.[36]

This comparability requirement, which was developed in response to evidence of the misuse of Title I funds in the early years of the program, represents the most serious effort by a federal education agency to ensure that grant funds are used for the benefit of the designated target pupils.

To understand the implications of the comparability requirement, it is necessary to consider another basic feature of the Title I program—the designation of certain schools within districts as "Title I schools" eligible for programs and funds. Although the Title I grants are earmarked for educationally deprived children, local authorities are not permitted to distribute the funds to serve those children wherever they may be located. Instead the funds must be allocated to schools that have certain concentrations of low-income pupils.[37] There are several reasons for this approach, some of which have little to do with controlling local uses of funds. One is the theory that a concentration of such pupils represents a special problem in itself, that is, a larger problem than would be represented by the same number of pupils if dispersed throughout the system. Another is that it is more efficient to organize a special compensatory program if there is a certain minimum number of pupils to serve. The reason that is most pertinent here, however, is that the school is the smallest organizational unit for which it is convenient to keep records of expenditures and resources. In this respect, the Title I legislation is eminently practical. If the law had called for allocation of extra resources directly to individual disadvantaged pupils throughout the system, the allocative outcomes would be almost impossible to monitor without an elaborate system for recording the hourly activities of individual pupils.

Because the comparability rules and other quantitative resource allocation constraints and reporting requirements stop at the school-building level, the degree of control that can be exerted upon the use of Title I funds within schools is limited. Although the regulations specify that Title I services may be provided only to target group children and not to other pupils in the same schools, the absence of requirements for reporting the costs incurred for Title I and non-Title I pupils within each school leaves USOE without effective tools for monitoring and enforcement.[38] Thus, some resources are likely to be diverted away from the target pupils. Another implication of the strategy of designating Title I schools is that some members of the eligible stratum of pupils are not served at all because they attend other schools in the district. The emphasis on school-level resource allocation represents a tradeoff. On the one hand, it makes monitoring of comparability feasible with a relatively low-cost data system; on the other hand, it reduces the precision with which resources can be directed to low-income or educationally disadvantaged pupils.

The Title I regulations define specific comparability standards and verification procedures. First, they stipulate that certain pupil and resource data must be reported for each Title I school and for all other schools of corresponding grade levels in a district. Next they establish the following two tests for determining that services supported by state and local funds in the Title I and non-Title I schools are comparable:

1. The number of children enrolled per instructional staff member. . .for each public school serving a Title I project area is not more than 105 percent of the average number of children per instructional staff member in all other public schools in the applicant's district; and
2. The annual expenditure per child [for salaries of instructional staff members]. . .in each public school serving a Title I project area is not less than 95 percent of such expenditure per child in all other public schools in the applicant's district.[39]

Note that these standards leave some leeway for districts to support regular schools more generously than Title I schools. Since the comparability rules pertain only to instructional staff ratios, salaries, and materials they do not constrain the distribution of funds for school operation and maintenance and supporting services (however, these are constrained in some respects by the "equitably provided" rule). In addition, "salaries of instructional staff" is defined to exclude salary increments based on length of service.[40] This means that a district can assign its less experienced teachers to Title I schools without violating the comparability standard. Moreover, the use of the expenditure standard of 95 percent, rather than 100 percent is more significant than it may seem. It could allow a substantial fraction of Title I funds—on the order of 20 percent—to be used to provide resource to Title I schools that other schools receive from nonfederal funds.[1] The main issue that concerns us here, however, is not the presence of loopholes in the present regulations, but rather how the comparability principle works in general as a device for directing resources to the right places.

Under the circumstances that existed when the federal compensatory education program came into being, a comparability requirement would have been potentially a very strong device for ensuring that the target schools received extra resources commensurate with the full amount of the federal grant. The key circumstances were that there was virtually no state or local money earmarked for compensatory education and that many schools with large concentrations of target pupils were initially receiving fewer resources than other schools in their districts. The significance of the first point—that the federal government had the field almost to itself—is that there were no significant opportunities for fiscal substitution within the compensatory education program. There were no state and local funds to displace. This eliminated the need to determine what compensatory education services would have been provided in the absence of Title I grants and reduced the compliance problem to ensuring that Title I schools received the appropriate base program. The significance of the second point—that some Title I schools were not receiving their fair share of regular district resources—is that there was a possibility that the target school would benefit by more than 100 percent of the amount of the federal grant. That is, in order to be eligible for funds, a district would first have to raise the resource levels in target schools to satisfy the comparability requirements, and then the full amount of Federal aid would be made available to conduct special compensatory programs. In reality, comparability guidelines have not been strongly enforced.[41] This factor in combination with the built-in loopholes of the system almost certainly has resulted in much less than 100 percent targeting of federal Title I funds, but there is no way to quantify the actual targeting ratio.

Circumstances have now changed in compensatory education. Many states have developed their own programs, and substantial amounts of non-federal money have become available. Although the main effect of this is to increase total financial support for compensatory education, another effect is to reduce the power of the comparability approach to ensure that future increases

---

[1]To illustrate, suppose that "regular" outlays per pupil in a district are $1,000 and that the Title I program provides an additional $250 per target pupil in compensatory funds (an amount consistent with Title I guidelines concerning concentration of funds). The 95 percent comparability requirement implies that state and local funds could be as low as $950 per pupil in Title I schools. Therefore, as much as $50 per pupil of Title I money, or 20 percent of the grant, could be used merely to bring the resources in Title I schools up to the $1,000 per pupil provided to the other schools of the system.

in Title I funding will be additive to the resources that would otherwise have been allocated to the Title I schools. The reason is that comparability only require Title I funds to be additive to the regular, or base program, resources to which each target school is entitled, but not necessarily to the state or local compensatory education funds that would have been allocated to those schools in the absence of Title I funds. Therefore, in the absence of other constraints, it would be possible for districts to substitute Title I funds (or, especially, increments therein) for the nonfederal compensatory funds that would otherwise have been distributed to the target schools. Therefore, we have a seemingly paradoxical result. An instrument that is effective in controlling the use of funds when federal and state-local priorities diverge becomes less effective as the federal goals are internalized by the state and local agencies.

Other provisions of ESEA Title I limit the substitution opportunities that districts would otherwise enjoy under the comparability approach. The "equitably provided" rule has been interpreted by USOE as a constraint on the division of state and local compensatory education funds between the Title I and non-Title I schools (each group taken as a whole). The rule to supplement, not supplant, funds can be used to limit the ability of local districts to reduce the allocations of nonfederal copensatory funds to Title I schools when additional Title I funds become available.[42] Nevertheless, these provisions do not restore the potential for ensuring full additivity that existed when there were no nonfederal compensatory funds, nor do they alter the conclusions about the effectiveness of the comparability approach itself.

A factor that complicates the assessment of the comparability approach in Title I is that there is now great diversity among states in the degree to which state and local education agencies have provided for compensatory education. Several states operate sizable programs of their own, some of which contain more precise and detailed targeting provisions than the federal program. Other states have not even gotten started in the field. The comparability rule is not equally effective or useful in these different environments. Where state and local interest in compensatory education is minimal, rigorous enforcement of comparability standards may be the best way to ensure that extra services are provided to target pupils. Where compensatory education has become a jointly funded federal and state-local activity, the same approach no longer serves to ensure that increments in federal funds will not displace state and local resources. Alternative control mechanisms are necessary to ensure additivity. One such alternative (or supplement to comparability) is the combination of provisions mentioned above. However, other approaches not now used in compensatory education, such as the imposition of matching requirements or establishment of relative expenditure standards, are potentially stronger instruments for directing resources into compensatory education. A final point is that in one respect the present comparability rule may deter mobilization of state and local resources for the disadvantaged. Until recently, the comparability requirements would actually have prevented states and localities from extending any Title I-type services to disadvantaged pupils attending non-Title I schools until all Title I schools had been served.[m] The current regulations establish an exemption to the comparability rules that permit such services to be offered under certain conditions. Nevertheless, localities are still not free to deploy their combined federal, state, and local compensatory education resources according to their perceptions of educational needs, even where there is no question that federal target-group children are receiving compensatory services at least equal in value to what they would have received under the Title I program alone.[43] An important unresolved issue is whether grant provisions can be written that vary the constraints according to the stage of development reached in each state and locality.

Vocational Education: Matching and Maintenance of Effort

The resource allocation goals of the federal vocational education program are different from those of the compensatory education program in several fundamental respects. First, there is no well-defined target group for vocational programs, identifiable by such characteristics as family income or level of educational achievement. Second, although there is the usual provision to supplement, not supplant funds nothing in the law requires that children served by federally aided vocational programs receive more resources than children not in the program. Third, there are no distinct federally funded vocational projects analogous to the Title I projects; instead federal funds are to be used, together with state and local funds, according to approved program plans. Federal vocational aid is supposed to "encourage" and "subsidize" state and local efforts and to act as a "catalyst" for state and local programs—terms that suggest a goal of stimulating nonfederal expenditures. These objectives are reflected in the two major constraints on resource allocation that appear in the vocational program: (1) the requirement that federal funds must be matched by funds from state and local sources; (2) the condition that the grantees must maintain the levels of their own financial contributions to vocational education programs.

Vocational education is unique among the large HEW education grant programs in mandating state-local matching of federal funds. The legislation requires that states and localities provide 50 percent of the funding for programs conducted under approved state plans, with the exception of certain special activities for which the federal government will pay 100 percent.[44]

---

[m]The effect of spending extra state and local money for compensatory services in non-Title I schools would be to make the state-local allocation to those schools higher than the allocation to the Title I schools, thereby violating comparability. It would have been possible to allocate such funds to non-Title I schools if equivalent additional funds were allocated to the Title I schools in addition to funds provided by the federal program.

Matching funds are subject to the same use restrictions and reporting requirements as the federal grant funds. The matching requirements apply only on a statewide basis; the regulations specify that matching is not required for each local district or each vocational education activity.[45]

Theoretically, there are conditions under which matching provisions would have a stimulative effect on spending by the state and local aid recipients. However, only a cursory look at the grant and expenditure figures for vocational education is needed to establish that these conditions do not apply. The key points are that the vocational matching grants are closed-ended—that is, there is a ceiling on the amount to which each state is entitled beyond which the federal government does not match additional state effort, and that substantially more is spent on vocational education by state and local agencies than is required to satisfy the matching requirements. In fiscal year 1974, for example, federal outlays for vocational education were approximately $468 million. State and local outlays in the same year were $2,966 million—many times the amount required to match federal funding at the stipulated ratio of one to one. Every state spends considerably more for vocational programs than is required by federal law.[46] Because of this overmatching, an increment in federal aid calls forth no necessary state-local response. There is already enough state and local money in the system to match an increase of several hundred percent in federal aid. In terms of the impact of additional federal aid on nonfederal contributions to vocational education, there might just as well be no matching requirement.

If the federal program were open-ended—that is, if the federal government offered to pay a fixed fraction of the level of vocational spending chosen by each state—then it is possible that federal aid would have a stimulative effect. Each incremental dollar of state-local outlay would earn a certain fraction of a dollar in federal vocational subsidies. Looking at it another way, the state would be able to obtain a dollar's worth of vocational education resources at a discount price. If the federal government offered to subsidize, say, 25 percent of the program's cost, then each dollar of vocational spending would cost state and local agencies only 75 cents. This effective reduction in the price of vocational education services could stimulate a greater contribution to the program from state and local sources than would otherwise be forthcoming.[n] However, at the current level of funding, the federal government finances only about one-sixth of the cost of vocational education. It is not clear that open-ended matching at a ratio of one to five would provide a significant fiscal incentive to state and local agencies. A shift to open-ended matching

---

[n] Whether a matching grant would stimulate greater state and local effort for the aided program depends on the price elasticity of demand for vocational education in each state. No empirical studies seem to have been conducted of price elasticities for individual educational programs. Consistent elasticity estimates have not yet been obtained even for education services in general.

would also have major and not necessarily desirable distributional repercussions.°

Other variations on the matching theme are possible. A method used in some state school finance plans and some noneducational grant programs of the federal government is *variable matching,* in which the matching rate varies from one grantee to another on the basis of "ability to pay."[47] Another approach would be to match only *increments* in state-local vocational education outlays or to match the portion of state-local spending that is in excess of a specified minimum standard. A number of designs merit attention, not only as methods of funding vocational education, but also as alternative approaches to supporting other federal education programs. All such alternatives involve trade-offs between fiscal goals, such as additivity and stimulation, and distributional objectives. In addition, the level of federal funding imposes a constraint on what can be accomplished. Where the federal contribution is small relative to total support for the program, it is difficult to create a financial incentive strong enough to make a difference. Where the matching requirement is strong enough to matter, the grantee may choose not to participate rather than to make the required fiscal effort. A fine line must be drawn to make the matching formula both effective and acceptable.

The "maintenance of effort" provision sets a floor under state and local spending for vocational education. It stipulates that

> No payments shall be made. . .unless the Commissioner finds, in the case of a local educational agency, that the combined fiscal effort per student or the aggregate expenditures of that agency and the State with respect to the provision of vocational education by that agency for the fiscal year preceding the fiscal year for which the determination was made was not less than such combined fiscal effort per student or the aggregate expenditures for that purpose for the second preceding fiscal year or, in the case of a State, that the fiscal effort per student or the aggregate expenditures of that state for vocational education in that State for the fiscal year preceding the year for which the determination was made was not less than such fiscal effort per student or the aggregate expenditures for vocational education for the second preceding fiscal year.[48]

This is a dual requirement in two senses. First, it applies separately to vocational

---

°Under an open-ended matching program, the amount of federal vocational education money flowing to each state would depend on the willingness and ability of the state government and the local districts in the state to support vocational programs with their own resources. Neither ability nor willingness are necessarily correlated with measures of the need for vocational education services. If no adjustments were made for differences in ability to pay, the likely outcome would be a distribution of aid funds skewed in favor of the wealthier states and districts.

outlays by the local districts and the states. Second, it applies either to total or per pupil expenditure (whichever constraint is the least restrictive).

There are certain conditions under which a constraint of this kind could have a binding effect on a state or a local district and could force it to spend more on vocational education than it might otherwise prefer, but those conditions are rarely likely to be met. Under normal circumstances, year-to-year cost inflation provides some leeway for real program reduction, if that is the intent of the state or locality, without violating the maintenance of effort constraint. For instance, if the cost of vocational education were to increase by 8 percent from one year to the next, a school system would be able to cut back on program resources by 5 percent while showing an expenditure increase of 3 percent. This would constitute increased effort according to the definition in the law. Moreover, the act provides for an exemption from the requirement in the event of "special circumstances," such as tax base reduction, that might pose fiscal obstacles to local compliance. Only a district determined to cut back sharply on its vocational programs would be likely to find its freedom restricted by the law.

It does not follow that no maintenance of effort requirement can be effective. If the requirement were framed in terms of real per pupil spending, for example, it would set a more meaningful floor under state and local contributions in some places. However, in fields where state and local support for a program is growing, the possibilities are more limited. Maintenance of effort provisions are intrinsically static. They cannot prevent increments in federal funds from displacing increments in local funds that would otherwise have been forthcoming.

In sum, it seems unlikely that the matching and maintenace of effort provisions, when combined, produce allocations to vocational education that are significantly different from the allocations that would result from an equal amount of general purpose aid to the same local agencies. The matching requirement does not compel any state to spend more for vocational education than it voluntarily chooses to spend, as is evidenced by universal overmatching. The maintenance of effort provision establishes an expenditure floor that is likely to affect very few jurisdictions. State and local officials are free to substitute federal vocational aid funds for funds that would otherwise have been provided from nonfederal sources with little fear of violating the terms of their grants.

Education of the Handicapped: Service
Standards and Excess Costs

The federal program of aid for education of the handicapped is now undergoing a complete transformation. The principal financial aid mechanisms of the Education of the Handicapped Act were superseded in November 1975 by the new Education for All Handicapped Children Act (PL 94-142). Beginning in fiscal year 1978, states and localities will receive their funds under a new formula and will be subject to an array of constraints in the new law. Since the main funding provisions of PL 94-142 are yet to be implemented, any analysis of what they will mean in practice is necessarily speculative. Nevertheless, certain features of the act have such large potential implications that they must be accorded a central place in a discussion of the system of federal categorical grants in education.

Under the old law, the federal government imposed only minimal constraints on the uses of grants for education of the handicapped. Each state was required to submit a plan for approval by the Commissioner of Education indicating how the federal funds were to be used. The law contained the usual exhortation that federal money not be used to supplant state and local funds. The program regulations included an unusually feeble maintenance of effort provision.[49] Federal funds for the main program of grants to states, which amounted to approximately $200 million in fiscal year 1976, constituted only about 5 percent of total extra funding for special education from federal, state, and local sources.[50] The combination of a low federal funding ratio with weak constraints meant that states were under little federal compulsion to make any fiscal provisions for education of the handicapped that they would not have made by themselves.[51]

The new Education for All Handicapped Children Act represents a potentially radical shift in the federal approach to categorical aid. The authorized increase in funding levels is itself dramatic. If the program is fully funded, grants to states would increase according to a prescribed schedule from $387 million in fiscal year 1978 to more than $3 billion in fiscal year 1982. Moreover, these figures would be adjusted upward each year at a rate equal to the national average rate of increase in per pupil expenditure for all elementary and secondary schooling.[52] Even more significant in the long run are the conditions attached to the grant program. Potentially the most important of these is the imposition of a universal service requirement or service standard. According to the act, each state must undertake to provide "a free appropriate public education" (by September 1, 1978) to all handicapped children between three and eighteen years old in order to be eligible for federal funds. In addition, PL 94-142 contains the following stipulations concerning resource allocation and resource use:[53]

- Federal funds shall supplement, not supplant, state and local funds, except that this requirement may be waived if all handicapped children in the state are receiving a "free appropriate education."
- Federal and state funds shall not be commingled.
- Federal funds "shall be used to pay only the excess costs directly attributable to the education of handicapped children."
- "State and local funds will be used. . .to provide services in program areas which, taken as a whole, are at least comparable to services being provided

in areas of such jurisdiction which are not receiving funds under this part."

- Special education shall be provided to all children in the "least restrictive" environment.
- The local education agency will establish an "individual education program" for each handicapped child.

In addition, the proposed regulations call for reporting of all federal, state, and local funds used for education of the handicapped—that is, something akin to the "level 3" reporting system referred to earlier.[54] Several of these provisions merit attention, notably the excess cost provision, the provisions pertaining to educational processes, and the reporting requirement.

The full impact of the requirement to serve all handicapped children "appropriately" is hard to assess in advance. The concept of an appropriate public education for a handicapped child has not yet been given an operational definition, much less quantified.[55] There is still uncertainty about how USOE will interpret and administer the requirement that all children be served. However, the potential impact of the provision is very great. The service requirement may represent, in embryonic form, a resource allocation control mechanism more powerful than all the comparability rules, matching provisions, and maintenance of effort requirements that have been used to date in federal education programs.

The key to this potential impact is quantification. If the federal government were eventually to establish quantitative standards for an appropriate education, defined in terms of total spending or total resource inputs per handicapped pupil, determination of the portion of school budgets pertaining to the handicapped will have become a federal responsibility. The states and localities would be required to match the federal aid funds by putting up the difference between the cost of the specified appropriate programs and the amount of the federal grant. Use might also be made of the principle of comparability in the following modified form. Instead of defining service standards in absolute terms, USOE might borrow a leaf from recent school finance reform efforts and formulate its standards as relative expenditure ratios. Thus, for example, mentally retarded pupils might have to receive 2.0 times the resources of regular pupils, physically handicapped pupils 1.5 times the regular allotments, and so forth.[56] In order to be eligible for grants, local districts would have to demonstrate that target pupils were receiving resources comparable to the specified multiples of resources for regular pupils. Any of these devices would give federal policymakers great leverage over resource allocation at the local level. There is no existing device that provides a comparable degree of control.

Of course, none of these scenarios may develop. It is possible that USOE will interpret the service standards in the same laissez-faire spirit as numerous requirements for certifications and plans are interpreted now. In the proposed regulations for PL 94-142, the concept of appropriate services is left nonquantitative and subject to definition by each state. However, if the experience in Title I is any guide, questions will arise over whether adequate services are being provided to the target group and whether state and local behavior complies with the federal law. There may be lawsuits claiming that the requirement has not been met by particular states or localities. In Title I, these developments eventually led to the quantitative comparability requirements. It would not be at all surprising if there were similar outcomes in education for the handicapped.

The allocative impact of quantitative service standards would vary greatly from one state to another. The critical factor is the initial gap between actual statewide provision for the handicapped and the goal of an appropriate education for all handicapped children. Where the gap is small, the new law will exert relatively little leverage over intrastate allocations of funds. In fact, a state that has satisfied the service standards on its own could be rewarded with general purpose federal aid under the provision permitting a waiver of the non-supplanting requirement. Where the gap is large, the state may be forced to raise new funds for the handicapped from its own (and local) sources that are equal to several times the amount of its grant under PL 94-142. It has been estimated that approximately $9 billion in state and local funds would have to be raised nationally to finance special education at prevailing levels of service for all handicapped children (assuming full funding of PL 94-142).[57] To construct estimates for individual states, it would be necessary to have quantitative definitions of the standards as well as better data than now exist about numbers of handicapped children and current levels of service.

It has been suggested that the high costs of compliance might lead states with large service gaps to opt out of the program. In its proposed regulations, USOE has taken the position that many of the provision of PL 94-142 reiterate basic rights of handicapped children as specifically set forth in Section 504 of the Rehabilitation Act of 1973.[58] Therefore, even if a state elects not to apply for grants under PL 94-142, it would still be required to satisfy the requirements covered by Section 504 so long as it receives any other federal assistance. This does not necessarily mean that the specific provisions of PL 94-142, or any quantitative service standards that might be adopted in the future, would automatically apply to states or localities that chose not to participate in the program. It will probably be impossible to clarify the legal issue completely until specific standards are set and the courts decide whether they are synonymous with or in excess of basic civil rights guarantees.

The roles of the excess cost, comparability, and supplement, not supplant, provisions of PL 94-142 will depend on what is done to implement the universal service requirement. If the federal government controls the total resources that are provided to handicapped children, efforts to enforce the other provisions might then become redundant. That is, if handicapped children were receiving the appropriate levels of service, it would make little difference how the federal funds themselves were being used. But if service standards are left nonquantitative or if their definitions are left to the states, a system for monitoring excess costs and ensuring nonsupplanting could have an important role.

By itself, an excess cost (or comparability) requirement cannot ensure that federal aid will translate into incremental services for handicapped children. The reason is that the federal government would finance only a fraction of the excess costs of special education even if PL 94-142 were fully funded, and there is nothing to prevent the substitution of federal funds for some of the state and local money that would otherwise have been earmarked for the handicapped. Enforcement of the excess cost rule can guarantee only that resources commensurate with the federal grants will be provided to handicapped pupils. That is a relatively insignificant accomplishment since most states already do considerably more in their special education programs.

An excess cost rule in combination with other constraints could be more effective. One possibility would be to require grantees to maintain their own levels of support (preferably, defined in terms of real resources) for the excess costs of special education programs. Another possibility would be to require state or local matching of the federal contribution to excess costs, perhaps with a system of variable matching rates to enhance interstate equity. Outcomes under the latter approach could be similar to those produced by a system of expenditure standards.

The effectiveness of a control system based on excess cost would depend on how excess cost is defined and on the type of data collection system that is established to record the costs of special and regular education. The excess cost concept is well established in the special education field, and it figures in several state laws pertaining to aid for education of the handicapped.[59] Nevertheless, the problem of determining how much of the cost of special education is truly incremental to the cost of regular education has not been fully solved, either at a conceptual or practical level. The measurement difficulties have grown more severe as the practice has taken hold of integrating handicapped children into regular classes to the greatest extent possible. These difficulties will become even more serious when school districts implement the individualized education programs that are mandated by PL 94-142. The definition of excess cost in the proposed regulations is not helpful because it presupposes that a clean distinction can be made between costs of regular instruction programs and costs of programs for handicapped children.[60] A much more detailed definition, linked to a specific accounting system, will have to be developed if the excess cost provision is to exert any influence on resource allocation at the local level.

It is instructive to compare the excess cost provision in PL 94-142 with the comparability requirement of ESEA Title I.[61] Both are aimed at ensuring that federal funds provide resources to target-group pupils that are in excess of those provided to regular pupils. However, the Title I rule applies at the school-building level. To implement it, one requires a system for reporting expenditures and staffing ratios in each school. In contrast, the excess cost provision of PL 94-142 seems to apply to the classroom level (assuming that there are distinct special education classes) or even to the individual pupil (assuming that handicapped pupils are integrated into regular classrooms). On its face, monitoring and enforcement of such a provision would seem to require a data collection system far more detailed and costly to operate than any developed or even suggested for other categorical programs.

There may be omens for the future in the provisions of PL 94-142 that mandate specific approaches to instruction of the handicapped. The act requires states to assure that

> . . .to the maximum extent appropriate, handicapped children. . .are educated with children who are not handicapped, and that special classes, separate schooling, or other removal of handicapped children from the regular educational environment occurs only when the nature or severity of the handicap is such that education in regular classes with the use of supplementary aids and services cannot be achieved satisfactorily. . . .[62]

In addition, a local agency must provide assurance that it

> . . .will establish or revise. . .an individualized educational program for each handicapped child at the beginning of each school year and will then review and, if appropriate revise, its provisions periodically, but not less than annually.[63]

The proposed regulations soften the impact of these provisions somewhat by leaving it to the states to determine specific criteria for implementing the "least restrictive environment" rule and by stipulating that the individualized educational plan is not a binding contract between the school district and the handicapped pupil or the parents. Nevertheless, these two provisions are striking examples of the use of federal funding as a lever to compel adoption of particular educational processes as well as particular patterns of resource allocation.

A final noteworthy feature of the Education for All Handicapped Children Act is that it takes some initial steps away from the time-honored but unfruitful concept of tracking federal funds to their final uses. This departure from the traditional approach is more implicit than explicit in the language of the law. PL 94-142 does contain the conventional noncommingling language. The critical difference is that the act separates the service requirements from the federal funding. There is no pretense that the federal money will pay for the mandated services, nor even that federal funds plus required local matching funds will pay the bill. Rather, the wording of the act suggests a kind of contractual arrangement. That is the federal government will supply a certain amount of funding if the states and localities in return undertake to provide certain services to members of the target group. The key requirement is that the services be provided, not that the federal funds themselves be spent in a particular manner. The new spirit of this legislation is demonstrated by the provision that explicitly allows federal funds to displace state and local resources once the service requirements have been met thoughout a state. This is indicative of the shift of attention from the proper use of earmarked funds to a new focus on service delivery.

The possibility of formalizing these quid pro quo or contractual relationships in the intergovernmental grant programs merits further exploration. Many of the grant applications, plans, and certifications required by current laws and regulations have the form of contractual commitments, but so far they have not had the substance. A shift in emphasis from the federal funds themselves to the services that state and local agencies have undertaken to provide may make the commitments more enforceable and may contribute to more concrete understandings about the behavior that is expected in return for federal aid.

CONCLUSIONS AND POLICY IMPLICATIONS

The Effectiveness of Existing Control Provisions

At the beginning of this chapter, the issue of whether the control provisions of the education grant programs are necessary or sufficient to accomplish the stated allocative goals was raised. In the preceding section, these questions were addressed, first, by commenting on the potential effectiveness of each major type of control provision and, second, by examining the specific provisions and combinations of provisions that appear in the programs of aid for compensatory education, vocational education, and education for the handicapped. The main conclusions emerging from this two-pronged analysis follow.

Conditions Under Which Strings Are Likely to be Effective

The main constraints on resource allocation found in the current education grant programs are inherently capable of ensuring that federal funds are used as intended only under certain special conditions. Specifically, the net impact of federal categorical funds on the target pupils or target activity is likely to be greatest (assuming that the provisions of the law are enforced) under the following conditions:

1. *When the federally funded activity is new and different from*

other activities supported by the local district. If federal funds are earmarked for a new type of educational service or for pupils previously not served, it is relatively easy to control the use of funds. Under these circumstances, normal accounting and auditing procedures may be sufficient to ensure that the earmarking provisions of the grants are observed. If the purpose of a new federal program is to direct extra resources to target pupils who were previously receiving only regular or less than regular services, enforcement of excess cost or comparability provisions may be sufficient to ensure compliance. The likelihood of obtaining the desired allocative effect diminishes where federal money is provided for activities indistinguishable from those supported with nonfederal funds.

2. *When federal funding is large compared to state and local resources devoted to the federally assisted program.* Where the federal government undertakes to pay either 100 percent of the costs of a particular service or 100 percent of the excess cost of special services for certain children, conditions are favorable for achieving the intended resource impact. As the proportion of federal funding declines, it becomes increasingly difficult to be sure that federal funds are having the intended net effect on the target activity. Where the federal government finances only a minor fraction of a program, it is very easy for state or local agencies to substitute federal money for nonfederal funds that would otherwise have been made available, and the bulk of the federal grant may be converted to general aid.

3. *Where the aided program is operated by distinct organizational units of the grant-receiving agency.* It is easiest to ensure the proper use of federal funds when the federally aided activities are organizationally segregated, and it becomes increasingly difficult to obtain the desired net impact the more closely the aided activities are tied in with normal activities of the schools. Specifically, targeting of resources is easiest where the federal program is conducted by separate organizational entities, as in Headstart; it is relatively easy where the target unit is the school building, as in Title I; and it becomes very difficult where funds are earmarked for particular groups or especially for individuals within schools, as in vocational and handicapped programs and at the subschool level in Title I.

4. *Where federal funds are earmarked for categories of pupils or activities for which accounting records are normally kept, or for which such records could be kept at reasonable cost.* It is relatively easy to control the use of funds earmarked for objects of expenditure, such as salaries of instructional aides of purchases of equipment, because such categories appear in standard accounting systems. It is more difficult to control the use of funds earmarked for a subject of instruction, such as reading, because accounting by subject category is not a common practice.[64] Some target groups are normally represented in accounting systems while others are not. Allocations for handicapped children

generally show up in special education categories of school district budgets; allocations for the disadvantaged usually do not receive comparable treatment.P

Effectiveness of Control Instruments as They Are Currently Applied

Although the major control provisions of the existing programs would be at least partially effective under certain conditions, for the most part, those are not the conditions under which the provisions are applied. Moreover, the conditions under which the commonly used constraints would work well occur relatively infrequently and usually only in the early stages of a program. The following are more specific conclusions about particular control mechanisms:

1. *Maintenance of effort.* The requirement that grantees maintain their existing levels of fiscal effort is unlikely to be effective in the form in which it appears in current education grant legislation. If levels of state and local support were static and if costs were constant, such provisions might prevent substitution of federal aid for state and local funds. In fact, however, state and local money has been flowing into the areas where federal funds are concentrated, and costs (input prices) have been rising rapidly. Therefore, grantees can easily cut back on the real resources that they provide to a federally assisted activity without violating the maintenance of effort constraint.

2. *Limitation to excess costs.* The stipulation that federal funds must be used only to pay the excess costs of a program is capable of ensuring that federal aid is additive for the specified purpose when only federal money is available to pay for excess costs and when accounting systems either exist or can be installed to permit measurement of excess costs. In the area where the excess cost concept is best entrenched—education of the handicapped—state and local funds pay for a much larger fraction of the excess costs of special education programs than do federal funds. The excess cost provision does not prevent federal aid from supplanting this nonfederal support. In addition, accounting systems are insufficiently developed to ensure that the excess costs of programs for target group children are as large as claimed by the grantees.

3. *Comparability.* The comments about the excess cost rule also apply to comparability. The comparability requirement, as introduced in the ESEA Title I program, is potentially effective for ensuring that federal funds

---

PIt should be no more difficult to identify the costs of special services provided to the disadvantaged than it is to determine the costs of special education for the handicapped. The latter is simpler only where the handicapped are educated in special schools or separate special education classes. If anything, the practice of mainstreaming should make it more difficult to determine the costs of serving handicapped children. A possible reason for reporting costs of special education, but not compensatory education, in school budgets is the historical one that the former was accepted as a distinct but normal district activity, to be funded with a mix of local, state, and federal money, while the latter came into being only recently, and then as a program supported entirely with outside funds.

provide extra services for target group pupils when no significant amount of state and local money is available for the same purpose. The comparability requirement becomes weaker in established, ongoing programs where federal, state, and local funds in combination provide services for a target group. This is because some federal funds may replace some state and local funds that would have been allocated to the federally assisted activity (compensatory education, in the case of Title I) if there had been less federal aid. In the specific case of the Title I program, the ability of local districts to substitute federal funds for state and local compensatory education funds is limited by USOE rules based on the "equitably provided" provision.[65] However, this does not alter the conclusion that the comparability approach itself loses some of its effectiveness as federal funding ceases to dominate the financing of the assisted program.

    4. *Matching requirements.* The requirement that state and local agencies must match federal grant funds probably has a near-zero effect on resource allocations in the one major area where it is now used—vocational education. Federal funding makes up such a small fraction of total support for vocational programs that the matching requirement is satisfied automatically. As additional federal funds become available, grantees could easily substitute them for their own funds without violating the matching provision. Thus far, matching requirements have not been imposed where they might be effective, namely, where federal funding is dominant and the federal government wants to encourage larger state and local contributions, as in compensatory and bilingual education, for example.

Lack of Control Where There Is Only Fractional Federal Funding

    None of the currently used grant provisions or combinations of provisions has the power to ensure the additivity of federal funds where federal aid constitutes only a fraction of the total support for a program. Once the grantees have had a chance to adjust to the infusion of aid, such funds are likely to be effectively transformed into general purpose revenue of the local school districts. This is especially true of annual increments in the federal funds earmarked for established programs that receive the bulk of their support from nonfederal sources.

    This conclusion applies specifically to federal support for vocational education and education of the handicapped (prior to implementation of PL 94-142). The federal government finances only a small fraction of outlays in both fields. State and local officials are able to take account of the availability of federal money in making their own funding decisions. There is little about these nominally categorical grants except, perhaps, the force of moral suasion that would lead the recipients to fund vocational programs and programs for the handicapped at a level higher than they would have chosen, given the same amounts of unrestricted aid.

The strategy of imposing quantitative expenditure or service requirements on grantees, which may emerge from the qualitative service requirements established by PL 94-142, could give the federal government greater
leverage in areas where federal funds provide only a fraction of program support. The possibilities of this standard-setting approach are discussed below.

The Weakness of the Fund-Tracking Approach

Some of the accounting provisions that seem to be intended to control uses of resources are of little value for that purpose. Prominent among these
are the provisions designed to permit tracking of federal funds to their final uses.
These include the requirements that grantees not commingle federal with state
and local funds, that they report planned and actual uses of federal funds, and
that they keep records showing which specific staff members are supposedly
paid with federal money. There is a large element of ritual to such provisions.
Under most circumstances, labeling of some school personnel or some items of
equipment as "federally funded" is an arbitrary exercise. Such labeling does not
imply that those particular staff members would not have been employed were it
not for federal aid. Nor does anyone assume that it does. Therefore, very little
can be learned from the resulting reports and accounting records about the
net resource impacts of federal grants.

If the process were costless, these fund-tracking requirements would
be of little concern. However, several kinds of costs, both tangible and intangible, may be incurred. First, there is the administrative time and energy
consumed in recording purported uses of federal money. Second, it is possible
that resources devoted to federal funds accounting are at the expense of forms
of record-keeping that would be more useful, namely, maintenance of accounts
on the *total* resources devoted to the federally assisted activities. Third, local
efforts to keep federal and nonfederal resources separate so that accurate accounts can be kept may interfere with the efficient organization of services. Adherence to the letter of noncommingling provisions might even make it necessary in some instances to organize parallel federally funded and nonfederally
funded projects in a district to provide similar services to similar types of target
pupils. There appears to be an opportunity to reduce administrative burdens
and, at the same time, to eliminate some nonfunctional restrictions on local
resource allocation by deleting accounting requirements that cannot in principle
serve the purpose of controlling federal funds.

One cautionary note—some of the provisions referred to here may be
useful for purposes other than the control of local resource allocation. For instance, certain planning and reporting requirements may make positive contributions to program governance and the program implementation process. Formal-
isms like noncommingling may also be useful for political and legal purposes
even though they do not reflect the realities of resource use at the local level.⁹

---

⁹One legal reason for maintaining separate account of the purported uses of
federal funds is that nonpublic, including church-related, schools are entitled to shares of

These functions, as well as the control functions, should be taken into account in deciding whether the provisions are worth preserving.

Policy Implications

The foregoing findings are relevant to several perennial issues in the education grants field and to other issues of grant program design that may become salient in the future. The concluding part of this chapter summarizes the implications under five headings: (1) strengthening existing control provisions, (2) grant simplification, (3) grant consolidation and block grants, (4) life-cycle and geographic variation, and (5) the standard-setting approach.

Strengthening Existing Control Provisions

On the basis of the foregoing analysis, it appears that there are a number of things that could be done to improve the effectiveness of the control instruments that already are in the federal arsenal. These are outlined very briefly below because they have already been mentioned in this section as well as the preceding section.

One approach is to correct what seem to be mismatches between programs and strings. Certain control instruments are ineffective where they are now used, but they could influence patterns of resource allocation if applied to other programs. The prime example is the use of matching provisions. Currently, federal law requires matching only in vocational education. The amount of state and local money going into that area is so much greater than the amount required to match federal aid that is virtually certain that the matching requirement has no effect. Meanwhile, there are other programs, such as compensatory and bilingual education, in which the federal financial contribution is dominant and in which it would be a major achievement to draw in significantly more state and local funds. By appending matching requirements to those programs it might be possible to stimulate more state and local financial participation, especially in parts of the country where such participation has been minimal, and to discourage substitution of incremental federal funds for such state and local funds as have already been made available.

A second approach is to modify some of the existing instruments in ways that would make them more effective. The most obvious candidates for modification are the maintenance of effort requirements. By restating those constraints in terms of real (i.e., cost-adjusted) per pupil outlays, rather than nominal dollar amounts, it might be possible to establish meaningful floors for state and local support. Another possibility is to replace the present maintenance of effort provisions with requirements that grantees match the rate of growth

---

the federal money. A political reason is that the various groups and areas within a school district that have claims to categorical funds need some basis for determining whether they are receiving their proper shares. However, maintenance of separate accounts provides only the illusion of being able to protect one's fair share because the accounting data provide no information on what funds would have been available in the absence of federal aid.

in federal funds. This would make sense where federal support for a program is increasing and where it is the federal intent that state and local support should keep pace. There are also several ways in which matching requirements could be modified to increase their stimulative effects. One possibility, referred to earlier, is to make matching grants open-ended, so that each increment in state and local spending earns an increment in federal aid. A second possibility is to match only the portion of state and local funding that pays for the excess costs of a program or only the portion of per pupil expenditure that exceeds some specified base level. Either option would make the matching provision of the vocational education program more meaningful than it is at present. The same options would also be applicable to ESEA Title I and other target group programs. Yet another approach would be to create a hybrid of the matching and comparability principles by establishing comparability ratios in excess of 100 percent. For example, federal grants could be contingent on state and local allocations of, say, 10 or 20 percent greater instructional staff resources to target group children than to regular pupils. By using appropriate combinations of the devices suggested here, plus those already in use in the categorical programs, it would be possible to extend the range of conditions over which federal grant funds are likely to have their intended effects on resource allocation patterns within the districts.

Grant Simplification

State and local officials have campaigned for years to reduce the number of strings in federal grant programs, to simplify the program requirements, and to cut down on required reporting and other paperwork. Some of this can be dismissed as pleading for further weakening of already weak constraints on the use of federal funds, or ultimately, for the transformation of categorical grants into unrestricted general aid. Some of it, however, represents a legitimate complaint against grant requirements that are costly, time-consuming, and of little value for accomplishing federal goals. For reasons explained earlier, some record-keeping and reporting requirements of the education grant programs do little to encourage proper targeting of federal funds. There appear to be opportunities for cutting down paperwork while obtaining more useful information at the same time on resource use at the local level than is currently collected.

The goals of grant simplification and better targeting of resources would both be advanced by a shift away from emphasis on tracking federal funds and toward surveillance of the total resources available for national priority programs. In compensatory education, for example, this would mean less concentration on how Title I funds are spent and more concentration on the amounts and kinds of extra resources that school systems provide to their educationally deprived children. The accounting requirements would be simpler because it would not be necessary to go through the labeling exercise to create separate federal funds accounts. The ability to target resources would be enhanced because more information would be available on the resources that are actually reaching target group children. This information would be especially useful—in fact, necessary—in conjunction with a standard-setting approach to federal assistance, as discussed below. The type of record-keeping referred to here seems to be required by PL 94-142 for activities related to the handicapped (although it is not yet known what level of detail will be required). It would be valuable to have the same information on the full range of federally aided education activities.

Grant Consolidation and Block Grants

During the last few years there have been repeated administration proposals for consolidation of categorical grants into a general block grant for education.[r] The proponents of consolidation have argued that block grants would free the states and districts from unwarranted administrative burdens of the present categorical system and would permit federal funds to be used more efficiently and flexibly under varying local conditions. The opponents have contended that consolidation would mean the abandonment of national priorities in education and, in particular, that federal funds would be diverted away from the federally designated target groups. Compromises have been proposed that would consolidate most federal funds while retaining certain control provisions of the major categorical programs.[s]

Evidence that existing grant provisions are too weak to accomplish federal allocative goals can be interpreted either as an argument in favor of consolidation and block grants or as an argument for tighter constraints and more rigorous enforcement of the targeting provisions. Where one comes out in this debate depends on one's judgments about three factors: (1) the way in which state and local agencies are likely to behave toward the categorically assisted activities and target groups if constraints are relaxed; (2) the feasibility of developing and implementing more effective control instruments; and (3) the importance of achieving the allocative goals of the categorical program or, more

---

[r]In 1971, and again in 1973, the Nixon Administration introduced the Better Schools Act. As originally conceived, this legislation would have consolidated some thirty categorical programs into a single "special revenue-sharing" program for education. Subsequently, it was modified to retain the identities of five categories of education aid. The Ford Administration proposal (H.R. 12196) was introduced in 1976. It would have established a broad block grant for education while retaining certain constraints on amounts to be allocated to major target groups.

[s]Under the Ford Administration proposal, the block grants to states would have been subject to the condition that at least 75 percent of the grant funds must be spent for the educationally disadvantaged and handicapped. In addition, states would have been required to maintain the previously established shares of support for vocational programs. Another compromise proposal was introduced by Senators Domenici and Bellmon in 1976. This would have retained the existing funding formulas, allowed individual states to decide whether to administer the combined categorical grant funds as a block grant, and preserved the identity of three broad categories of education aid.

pragmatically, the magnitude of the economic and political costs that one is willing to incur in order to achieve those goals.

There is very little direct empirical evidence on how state and local agencies would behave if the existing categorical grants were replaced by block grants. However, certain conjectures can be offered about the major programs. Based on existing patterns of spending for compensatory education and on the historical data on compliance with targeting restrictions in ESEA Title I, it appears likely that fewer resources would be available for programs for the disadvantaged if the present restrictions were relaxed. In contrast, present levels of support for vocational education programs and programs for the handicapped have been determined primarily by forces other than federal grants. It is unlikely that support for those programs would be substantially reduced if categorical support were eliminated.[t] However, this does not mean that the service levels envisioned under PL 94–142 would be attained in the absence of federal funding and federal program constraints. In sum, even though the existing control mechanisms are weak in many respects, there would probably be some significant reallocations both among and away from national priority activities if the existing constraints were removed.

As to the feasibility of strengthening control over categorical grants, it does appear that more effective constraints than the present ones are technically feasible to incorporate into categorical grant programs. Several options were outlined above, and others are presented below in the discussion of the standard-setting approach. The real questions concern costs and political acceptability. Just in terms of administrative costs, it would probably not be rational to develop strong control mechanisms for small programs. The record-keeping, auditing, and monitoring activities needed to control a $50 million grant program may not be substantially smaller than those needed to ensure compliance with the provisions of a $1 billion program. Therefore, the option of strong controls realistically applies primarily to a handful of programs in, say, the $250 million and upward range. The other critical issue is whether there is political support for imposing severe constraints on states and school districts and then for enforcing the law. It has been observed that Congress is willing in principle to specify tight constraints for resource use and to establish sanctions for violators, but it is much less willing to countenance withholding of funds or imposition of financial penalties in actual cases.[66] There are also significant variations among programs. In aid for education of the handicapped, for example, support was successfully mobilized at the national level for legislation

---

[t]As explained earlier, existing levels of support for the handicapped and vocational programs have been established in the presence of nonbinding federal constraints and relatively small amounts of federal aid. In contrast, compensatory programs receive heavy federal funding, but the existing constraints and enforcement mechanisms are only partially effective in ensuring the proper targeting of the funds. If the existing strings were removed, therefore, it is likely that there would be shifts to funds from the compensatory programs to both the handicapped and vocational areas and to general support of programs for "majority" pupils.

that imposes strong financial and programmatic constraints on the states and districts. Comparable support does not appear to be present for a stronger federal role in determining the magnitude of state and local effort for the disadvantaged or for other categories of aid beneficiaries.

The importance of accomplishing allocative goals is, of course, a political value judgment. The only contributions that analysis can make is to point out the degree to which goals are or are not being achieved with current policies and to clarify the costs of achieving more thoroughgoing compliance. It appears that a case can now be made for moving simultaneously in two directions within the education grant system. On one hand, there are programs that probably are not succeeding in channeling extra resources to the designated pupils or educational services and that are either too small to justify strong control measures or insufficiently popular to make strong controls politically feasible. There is a good case for consolidation of such programs or for their merger into educational block grants. On the other hand, there are some larger programs whose allocative goals are also not being fully met but for which stronger targeting of funds may be feasible, especially if coupled with measures that simplify and reduce the burdens of the overall grant system. It would be reasonable to distinguish between the two categories, to develop appropriate control instruments for programs whose goals are taken seriously, and to move toward general purpose funding to replace categorical programs whose objectives are less highly valued or more difficult to attain.

Life-Cycle And Geographic Variation

An important implication of this analysis is that both the need to control resource use and the difficulty of controlling resource use vary over the life-cycle of a federal program and among states and localities at any given time. The strings that work to ensure nonsupplantation of federal funds when a program is new and mainly federally supported weaken once state and local funds have been drawn in and federal funding has become less dominant. At the same time, the need to constrain resource use may be less once federal goals have been assimilated at the local level. However, the stituation is more complicated than that because state and local reactions to federal categorical grants vary geographically and evolve in different places at different rates.

The concept has not yet taken hold of modifying the terms of grants in response to the behavior of the grantees. The aforementioned findings about the conditions under which various strings are likely to be effective suggest that such a policy may be both feasible and desirable. In the Title I program, for example, some of the constraints that were applicable when the federal government funded nearly 100 percent of compensatory education are not the appropriate ones to apply to states that have large compensatory programs of their own. It may be desirable to replace them with provisions that draw in nonfederal funds and expand the program's coverage, such as matching requirements and service standards. The same point applies to other programs. There is an unfortunate, if understandable, tendency to retain grant provisions forever once they have been enacted into law. A policy of periodic review and updating would represent an advance in the state of the art of grant program administration.

Recently, there has been some discussion of possibilities for differentiated treatment of states and districts that have developed their programs to different degrees. Two approaches have been suggested. According to the discretionary approach, an appropriate official (e.g., the Commissioner of Education) would be empowered to rule that a grantee has met certain standards of program participation or compliance and to waive certain program requirements. According to the automatic triggering approach, a grantee that meets certain objective performance requirements (e.g., pertaining to levels of funding or numbers of pupils served) would be automatically relieved of certain constraints. There have already been a few significant but small-scale departures from the practice of imposing uniform conditions on all grantees. An example is the provision of the impact aid program that permits a state to treat federal impact aid funds differently, depending on whether the state school finance plan meets a specified equalization standard.[u] However, the concept has not yet been generalized, and further development of methods for according differentiated treatment is needed.

The Standard-Setting Approach

The incorporation into PL 94-142 of the requirement that states provide a "free appropriate" education to all handicapped children could represent the first step toward a new and more powerful form of federal control over the allocation of educational resources. How the new handicapped law will evolve is uncertain, but the possibilities are evident. When and if an appropriate education is quantified, the federal government will have become involved in setting standards for the resources or dollars to be devoted to the education of particular types of pupils. Once established, there is no reason to expect that role to be limited to education of the handicapped. The logic of standard setting applied at least as well to pupils who are educationally disadvantaged and to other federally designated target groups as to those with physical or mental exceptions. Therefore, it is important to consider what standard setting could mean to the whole system of federal education grant programs.

---

[u]Normally, a state is not permitted to take account of local receipts of federal impact aid funds in computing the amount of state aid that local districts are entitled to under state-funding formulas. However, the current regulations permit an exception in the case of a state that has achieved a certain degree of interdistrict fiscal equalization in its own school finance system. Such a state is permitted to count federal impact aid as part of the local resources available to each district and to reduce the state contribution accordingly.

One implication of the standard-setting approach is that it would greatly strengthen the ability of the grant-administering agencies to guarantee that target group children actually receive the extra services intended by Congress. Standards could take the form of floors under absolute or relative levels of per pupil spending or under instructional staff ratios or other measures of resource input. Appropriately designed standards would be more effective than the maintenance of effort, excess cost, comparability, and matching requirements now in use. They would impose direct constraints (lower bounds) on the portions of school district budgets earmarked for the education of handicapped, disadvantaged, and other target group children. Moreover, standards would be easier to enforce than the present types of grant constraints. Proper record-keeping and auditing would still be necessary, but the relevant records would show amounts of resources allocated to different pupils and programs at the local level. There would be no need to waste energy tracing federal money through state and local accounting systems.

Grantees that voluntarily meet the federal standards with their own funds would be less constrained by expenditure or service standards than by the present requirements. They would be free to use their federal grants as general aid. In this respect, the standard-setting approach provides a reward for performance. The loss of additivity that this suggests is probably more apparent than real because no existing grant provisions impose effective constraints on grantees who contribute significant amounts of their own funds to the federally assisted programs.

An attractive feature of the standard-setting approach is that it is consistent with grant simplification and consolidation. If expenditure or service standards were established for federally aided programs, it would be possible to do away with some of the present constraints, record-keeping requirements, and monitoring procedures without sacrificing control over the use of federal funds. In particular, grant consolidation could be accomplished without diverting resources from the disadvantaged or handicapped if standards were set up for services to be provided to these groups. The combination of an education block grant and a set of service standards is potentially a more effective instrument for directing resources to priority areas than is the existing system of categorical grants. This point is significant politically. Those inclined to oppose standard setting as an extension of federal control of education might be willing to accept it as part of a thoroughgoing consolidation proposal. Those who think that the simplification and consolidation of grants mean abandonment of national goals in education might view the matter differently if standards were set for federal priority programs. Thus, the standard-setting approach could become the key to resolving long-standing controversies about the design of grant programs and the proper role of the federal government in education.

NOTES

1. For discussion of these differing perceptions of Title I goals, see Milbrey W. McLaughlin, *Evaluation and Reform: The Elementary and Secondary Education Act of 1965, Title I* (Santa Monica, Calif.: The Rand Corporation, R-1292-RC, January 1974), ch. 1; and Stephen H. Bailey and Edith K. Mosher, *ESEA: The Office of Education Administers a Law* (Syracuse, N.Y.: Syracuse University Press, 1968).

2. McLaughlin, op. cit., p. 8

3. The evidence on intradistrict inequality (as well as interdistrict and interstate inequality) is summarized in Christopher Jencks et al., *Inequality: A Reassessment of the Effect of Family and Schooling in America* (New York: Basic Books, 1972), ch. 2.

4. Among the studies that have documented the misuse of Title I money in the early years of the program are Washington Research Project and NAACP Legal Defense and Educational Fund, *Title I of ESEA: Is It Helping Poor Children?* (Washington, D.C., 1969); and Michael J. Wargo et al., *ESEA Title I: A Reanalysis and Synthesis of Evaluation Data from Fiscal Year 1965 through 1970* (Palo Alto, Calif.: American Institutes for Research, 1972).

5. For summaries of the evidence on noncompliance with comparability and other targeting provisions of the Title I program, see G. Hendrickson, *A Decade of Title I: From Problems to Progress* (Washington, D.C.: Office of the Assistant Secretary for Planning and Evaluation, Department of Health, Education, and Welfare, June 1976), draft; and Elizabeth J. Demarest, *The HEW Sanction Study: Enforcement Policy in Title I ESEA: Analysis and Recommendations* (Washington, D.C.: Office of the Assistant Secretary for Education, Department of Health, Education, and Welfare, January 1977).

6. For a summary of the empirical evidence on substitution of grant funds for the grantee's own revenue, See Stephen M. Barro, "The Impact of Intergovernmental Aid on Public School Spending," Ph.D. dissertation, Stanford University, May 1974, pp. 59–66.

7. Martin Feldstein, "The Effect of a Differential Add-on Grant: Title I and Local Educational Spending," Report to the Compensatory Education Division, National Institute of Education, 1977.

8. Selected studies include John D. Owen, "The Distribution of Educational Resources in Large American Cities," *Journal of Human Resources,* 7 (Winter 1972), pp. 171–190; Jesse Burkhead et al., *Input and Output in Large City High Schools* (Syracuse, N.Y.: Syracuse University Press, 1967); Martin T. Katzman, "Distribution and Production in a Big City Elementary School System," *Yale Economic Essays, 24* (Spring 1968); and Allan S. Mandel, *Resource Distribution Inside School Districts,* (Lexington, Mass.: Lexington Books, Additional references may be found in the Mandel book and in Jencks, op. cit.

9. In *Hobson* v. *Hansen,* plaintiffs contended that the resource allocation pattern within the Washington D.C. School System discriminated systematically against poor and minority pupils. The court found for the plaintiffs and the D.C. schools have operated under a court-ordered equalization

plan since 1971. Among the studies stimulated by the case are Stephen Michaelson, "For the Plaintiffs—Equal School Resource Allocation," *Journal of Human Resources*, 7 (Summer 1972), pp. 283–306; Dave M. O'Neill, Burton Gray, and Stanley Horowitz, "For the Defendants—Educational Equality and Expenditure Equalization Orders," ibid., pp. 307–325; and Herbert S. Winokur, Jr., "Expenditure Equalization in the Washington, D.C. Elementary Schools," *Public Policy*, 24 (Summer 1976), pp. 309–335.

10. National Conference of State Legislatures, press release summarizing the results of a survey of state education committee chairmen, August 31, 1976.

11. The estimate for programs of education for the handicapped is from William H. Wilken and David O. Porter, *State Aid for Special Education: Who Benefits?* (Washington, D.C.: National Foundation for the Improvement of Education and National Conference of State Legislatures, May 1976), Table I–12. The estimate for vocational education is from U.S. Senate, Commitee on Labor and Public Welfare, *Report on the Education Amendments of 1976* (Report 94-882), May 14, 1976, p: 46.

12. Wilken and Porter, op. cit., estimate that it would cost two or three times the amount now spent for special education to serve all handicapped children, and that two-thirds of the needed amount would have to come from state and local sources even if PL 94–142 were fully funded (p. I-44 and Table I-27). The authors do not specify the assumptions about levels of per-pupil services that underlie these expenditure estimates.

13. Conventional school district accounting systems report expenditures by function (instruction, administration, operation and maintenance, etc.) and by object of expenditure (teachers' salaries, equipment, etc.). Cost and expenditure data are rarely collected by program or subject of instruction. A major thrust of proposals for the introduction of program budgeting systems into local school districts is to obtain such data (see, e.g., S.A. Haggart et al., *Program Budgeting for School District Planning*, (Englewood Cliffs, N.J.: Educational Technology Publications, 1972). A major obstacle to collection of data by subject of instruction is that it would be necessary to record the time allocated by pupils to each subject. Depending on how instruction was organized in a particular system, this might require classroom-based or even pupil-based systems of time and cost accounting.

14. Esther O. Tron, *Public School Finance Programs, 1975-1976* (Washington, D.C.: Office of Education, 1976), Table 3.

15. For example, the school finance formula in New York State allows 25 percent greater weight for "special educational needs pupils" in computing each district's state aid entitlement; the Pennsylvania formula allocated $117 million (in 1975-76) under a system of additional payments for children from low-income families. The details of these and other provisions may be found in the individual state descriptions in Tron, op. cit.

16. In fiscal year 1965, state and local outlays for vocational education were only about twice as large as federal outlays. By 1974 they were six times as large. The historical data are summarized in U.S. Senate, Committe on Labor and Public Welfare, *Report on the Education Amendments of 1976*, op. cit., p. 46.

17. For instance, section 106(a) (b) of the recently amended Vocational Education Act specifies that "Federal funds made available under this Act will be so used as to supplement, and to the extent practicable, increase the amount of State and local funds *that would in the absence of such Federal funds* be made available for the uses specified in the Act, and in no case supplant such State or local funds" (emphasis added). U.S. House of Representatives, *Conference Report to Accompany S. 2657* (Education Amendments of 1976), Report 94-1701, September 27, 1976, p. 106.

18. PL 94-142, Sec. 613(a) (9). The license to supplant is not automatic. According to the law, the Commissioner of Education may wave the non-supplantation requirement if he concurs with the evidence provided by the state that all handicapped children are being appropriately served.

19. ESEA Title I, Sec. 141(a) (1).

20. There are detailed regulations defining the schools in which Title I funds may be spent and the children who are eligible for Title I services. In addition, there are rules defining permitted expenditures for staff salaries, employment of instructional aides, and for the purchase of equipment. The most recent versions of these rules appear in parts 116 and 116a of Title 45 of the *Code of Federal Regulations* (hereafter referred to as 45 CFR) published in the *Federal Register,* September 28, 1976.

21. The planning requirements differ in form from one program to another. Under the Vocational Education Act, a state is required to submit a five-year statewide plan plus annual "program plans and accountability reports" (*Conference Report to Accompany S. 2657,* op. cit., pp. 106-111). Under PL 94-142, each state applying for aid is required to submit a statewide plan for serving the handicapped, and each locality applying for aid (to the state) is required to submit an application setting forth its plans for serving handicapped children. The plans for vocational education and education of the handicapped are subject to approval of the Commissioner of Education. Under Title I, localities are required to submit applications to their state agencies setting forth their plans for serving educationally deprived children, but there is no requirement for federal approval of a general statewide plan.

22. Under PL 94-142, for example, the obligations of the state agency are set forth in Section 613 and the obligations of the local agency, some of which are expressed in precisely the same language as the state requirements, are set forth separately in Section 614. A feature of particular interest is that responsibility for adhering to the "supplement, not supplant," rule is assigned to both the state and local grantees.

23. The excess cost provision appears in Section 614(a) (2) (B) of PL 94-142 and implementing regulations appear in "Proposed Rules, Education of Handicapped Children and Incentive Grants Program," *Federal Register,* December 30, 1976, Sec. 121a.82. The reference to excess costs in ESEA Title I appears in Sec. 141(a) (1) of the act, but it has not yet been reflected in regulations separate from those pertaining to comparability.

24. The maintenance of effort provision concerning vocational education appears in Sec. 112 of the Vocational Education Act (in *Conference Report to Accompany S. 2657,* op. cit., pp. 114-115). The provision concerning

compensatory education appears in Sec. 143(c) (2) of ESEA Title I. The provision concerning education of the handicapped does not appear in the language of the Education for All Handicapped Children Act, but the "supplement, not supplant," language of the act has been interpreted in the proposed regulations to be equivalent to maintenance of effort (see "Proposed Rules," op. cit., comment following Sec. 121a.109).

25. The requirement refers to "fiscal effort. . .for the provision of free public education," which the regulations define as current expenditure per pupil by a school district less funds derived from federal programs (45 CFR, Sec. 116.19).

26. There are a number of matching provisions, or the equivalent, in other federal programs, but they generally apply only to small, special purpose funds. For example, the Education for All Handicapped Children Act provides that federal funds used by a state to provide direct services or support services must be matched from funds other than federal funds (PL 94–142, Sec. 611 [c] [2] [b]).

27. The Federal Interagency Day Care Requirements adopted pursuant to the Economic Opportunity Act (1967 and 1972 amendments) establish maximum child-staff ratios for programs funded under Title XX of the Social Security Act. However, the 1976 amendments to Title XX have permitted some postponement of the implementation of these standards.

28. This language appears, for example, in the regulations pertaining to vocational programs for the disadvantaged (45 CFR, Sec. 102.67). The regulation goes on to state that separate bank accounts for federal funds are unnecessary "so long as accounting methods will be established which assure that expenditures of such funds can be separately identified from other expenditures."

29. The data reporting requirements are itemized in 45 CFR, Sec. 116a. 26(b).

30. The Title I regulations establish requirements for keeping special school-by-school records on numbers of Title I and non-Title I pupils, instructional staff, and staff salaries. Logically, similar categories of data, but at the classroom or pupil level rather than the school level, would be needed to determine the excess costs of programs for the handicapped. No such requirements are established by the PL 94–142 regulations. Instead, only general guidelines for computing excess costs are provided. See note 60.

31. The comments in this paragraph are based on two recent studies of HEW compliance and enforcement mechanisms—Demarest, op. cit., and Hendrickson, op. cit.

32. According to USOE data cited in Demarest (op. cit., p. 19), $259 million in Title I expenditures have been questioned or recommended for refund by the HEW audit agency since the beginning of the program. Of that amount, USOE has requested reimbursement of approximately $12 million and actually collected only about $1 million.

33. Alternative approaches to sanctions are suggested in the two studies cited in note 31.

34. The Demarest study, op. cit., is one element of a department-

wide study within HEW of the sanctions attached to federal grant programs. The other major education program covered by the effort is vocational education (grants to states under Part B of the Vocational Education Act).

35. For detailed explanations of all those provisions, see S.M. Barro, "ESEA Title I: Resource Allocation Issues and Alternatives" (Washington, D.C.: Office of the Assistant Secretary for Education, Department of Health, Education, and Welfare, August 1977), draft.

36. ESEA Title I, Sec. 141(a) (3).

37. Detailed rules for identifying eligible attendance areas and schools are prescribed in 45 CFR, Sec. 116a.20.

38. Local applicants for Title I project funds are required to certify, among other things, that "expenditures for the project. . .are proposed for use solely to meet the special educational needs of educationally deprived children"; that "the project has not been designed to meet. . .the general needs of schools or of the student body at large in a school or of a specified grade in school"; and that "any services or resources provided under Title I will be offered to only those children who have been selected to participate in the project in accordance with [the needs assessment procedure prescribed in the regulations]" (45 CFR, Sec. 116a.22). Nevertheless, there is no requirement for a system of within school cost accounting that would make it possible to determine compliance with these requirements other than on an ad hoc basis.

39. 45 CFR, Sec. 116a.26(e) (1-2). There is also a requirement that each district must establish policies for ensuring that instructional materials are distributed among schools on a comparable basis.

40. 45 CFR, Sec. 116a.26(b) (3).

41. For a detailed discussion of enforcement policies and practices in Title I, see Demarest, op. cit.

42. The effects of these provisions are analyzed in S.M. Barro, "ESEA Title I: Resource Allocation Issues and Alternatives," op. cit.

43. The exemption from the comparability computation applies to "State and local funds expended for state and local programs similar to programs provided under Title I for educationally deprived children." However, to be eligible for the exemption, the program must have certain specified characteristics and be evaluated as a distinct compensatory program. In addition, the local educational agency must be "separately accountable" to the state for any funds expended for such a program (45 CFR, Sec. 126.a27 [j] [5]).

44. The main program category for which the federal government pays 100 percent of the cost is vocational education for the disadvantaged (45 CFR, Sec. 102.132).

45. 45 CFR, Sec. 102.133(b).

46. State-by-state data on the proportion of vocational education outlays from federal sources are presented in U.S. Senate, Committee on Labor and Public Welfare, *Report on the Education Amendments of 1976,* op. cit., p. 47. In fiscal year 1973, no state contributed less than twice as much from its own sources as it received in federal aid. Nationwide, $5.29 of state and local money was expended for vocational education for every dollar in federal funds.

47. The methods of distributing state education aid to school

districts, known as "percentage equalization" and "district power equalization," are based on the variable matching principle. They are designed to allocate aid according to the fiscal effort exerted by the grantee (defined as the ratio of the grantee's contribution to its fiscal capacity), but not according to wealth or ability to pay. For descriptions of such formulas, see Stephen M. Barro, "Alternative Post-*Serrano* Systems and Their Expenditure Implications," in J. Pincus, ed., *School Finance in Transition* (Cambridge, Mass.: Ballinger Publishing Company, 1974).

48. Vocational Education Act, Sec. 112 (in *Conference Report to Accompany S. 2657*, op. cit., pp. 114-115.)

49. The regulations pertaining to the now superseded Education of the Handicapped Act provided, under the heading "maintenance of level of support," that a state educational agency in developing its policies and procedures for administering the program shall "take into consideration" the state and local resources provided for the education of handicapped children in the current year, as compared with the resources provided in the two most recent fiscal years. No requirement to actually maintain the level of state or local effort was prescribed (45 CFR, Sec. 121a.13).

50. According to Wilken and Porter, op. cit., state and local government outlays for education of the handicapped were on the order of $4.7 billion in 1976) (p. I-2). The $200 million program of aid to states provides less than 5 percent of this amount. However, other federal programs bring the federal funding ratio up to the 14 percent figure cited earlier.

51. Although the federal grant programs are not the force that has caused the recent rapid rise in state spending for special education, it is not correct to say that states have assigned the current high priority to the handicapped voluntarily. A major factor has been a series of court decisions mandating equal educational opportunity for the handicapped. The principle cases are *Pennsylvania Association for Retarded Children* v. *Pennsylvania* and *Mills* v. *Board of Education*. These cases are discussed in Betsy Levin, "The Courts as Educational Policymakers and their Impact on Federal Programs," R-2224-HEW (Washington, D.C.: The Rand Corporation, August 1977).

52. The act provides that each state shall receive an amount equal to the number of handicapped children who are receiving special education services multiplied by a specified percentage of the average per pupil expenditure for elementary and secondary education in the United States. The specified percentage rises from 5 percent in fiscal year 1978 to 40 percent in fiscal year 1982. If states serve all their handicapped children (up to the maximum permitted limit of 12 percent of the school-age population), carrying out the aid computation at current levels of national per pupil expenditure would yield the expenditure figures cited in the text. Any increase in per pupil spending between now and 1982 would result in higher expenditures. Of course, such amounts may not be appropriated, in which case the law provides for ratable reduction of each state's entitlement (PL 94-142, Sec. 611).

53. PL 94-142, Secs. 612, 613, 614.

54. Under the "evaluation" section of the act, the commissioner of education is directed to collect data on "the amount of Federal, State, and local

expenditures in each State specifically available for special education and related services" and also to collect related personnel data (PL 94–142, Sec. 618).

55. The recently issued proposed regulations for PL 94–142 leave the definition of an appropriate education up to each state except for the requirement that certain age groups be covered and that there be individualized programs of instruction. See Sec. 121.a.4 of the Proposed Rules" and the preceding discussion, which addresses questions pertaining to the definition of "appropriate."

56. The leading examples of such "pupil-weighting" schemes are the school finance reform plans recently adopted in Florida and New Mexico. The former, for example, recognizes twenty-six special programs, each with its own cost factor. There are cost ratios of 2.3 for educable mentally retarded, 3.5 for physically handicapped, and so on. For details, see the individual state program descriptions in Tron, op. cit.

57. Wilken and Porter, op. cit. (see note 12).

58. The USOE view on the issues, "Is [PL 94–142] basically a civil rights law?" and "Does a state have to meet the requirements of the Act if the State elects not to receive a grant?" is presented at some length in the "Proposed Rules," op. cit., p. 56967.

59. For an exposition and illustrations of the excess cost concept, see R.A. Rossmiller, J.A. Hale, and L. Frohreich, *Educational Programs for Exceptional Children: Resource Configurations and Costs* (Madison, Wis: National Educational Finance Project Study No. 2, University of Wisconsin, 1970). A more general discussion of costs of educating the handicapped appears in Joseph J. Marinelli, "Financing the Education of Handicapped Children, 1976), pp. 164–173 in F.J. Weintraub et al., Public Policy and the Education of Exceptional Children (Reston, Va.: The Council for Exceptional Children, 1976), pp. 164–173.

60. The requirement to compute excess costs is set forth in Sec. 121a.82 of the "Proposed Rules," op. cit. According to the definitions provided in this section, costs of regular education are to be determined by subtracting from the total expenditures of the local agency the amounts expended for various special programs, including programs for handicapped children. The question is not faced of whether existing accounting systems provide a meaningful way of separating costs of such programs from other costs of education.

61. It might seem more natural to compare the excess cost provision in PL 94–142 with the provision of the same name in ESEA Title I and to do the same with the comparability provisions in the two laws. At present, however, detailed regulations have been established for implementing only one of the two provisions in each law. In the case of ESEA Title I, it is the comparability provision, and in the case of PL 94–142, it is the excess cost provision. Interestingly, the Proposed Rules for PL 94–142 make no attempt to establish an operational definition for comparability (Sec. 121a.110). It is unlikely that any meaningful definition could be established in the absence of pupil-level accounting data.

62. PL 94–142, Sec. 612(5). A discussion of the meaning of the requirement that children be educated in the "least restrictive environment" appears in the "Proposed Rules," op. cit., p. 56972.

63. PL 94–142, Sec. 614(a) (5). The requirement for individualized instruction is discussed in the "Proposed Rules," op. cit., p. 56970.

64. To assemble cost data by subject of instruction, it would be necessary to keep records at the classroom level or, where there are individualized programs of instruction, at the individual pupil level, of the instructional time devoted to each subject. These records are not maintained under conventional accounting systems, but such record-keeping has been called for in the program-budgeting literature—see, e.g., Haggart et. al., op. cit.

65. For an analysis of the "equitably provided" rule, see S.M. Barro, "ESEA Title I: Resource Allocation Issues and Alternatives," op. cit.

66. Demarest, op. cit., p. 15.

Index

About the Contributors

Stephen M. Barro, formerly Senior Economist with The Rand Corporation, is a consultant in Washington, D.C.

Paul Berman is a Senior Social Scientist, The Rand Corporation.

Lawrence L. Brown is a Program Analyst with the Assistant Secretary for Planning and Evaluation, DHEW

John J. Callahan is Director of the State-Federal Relations Office, National Conference of State Legislatures

Stephen J. Carroll is a Senior Economist with The Rand Corporation

Alan L. Ginsburg is a Senior Economist with the Assistant Secretary for Planning and Evaluation, DHEW

Robert J. Goettel is Professor of Educational Policy and Administration, State University of New York (Albany)

Betsy Levin is Professor of Law, Duke University

Milbrey Wallin McLaughlin is a Senior Social Scientist, The Rand Corporation

Michael Timpane, formerly Director of Rand's Center for Educational Finance and Governance, is now Deputy Director of the National Institute of Education, DHEW

Mary Vogel, formerly with The Rand Corporation, is now a doctoral student at Harvard University

William H. Wilken is Director of the Legislator's Education Action Project, National Conference of State Legislatures

Rand Educational Policy Studies

PUBLISHED

Averch, Harvey A., Stephen J. Carroll, Theodore S. Donaldson, Herbert J. Kiesling, and John Pincus. *How Effective Is Schooling? A Critical Review of Research.* Englewood Cliffs, New Jersey: Educational Technology Publications, 1974.

Carpenter-Huffman, P., G.R. Hall, G.C. Sumner. *Change in Education: Insights from Performance Contracting.* Cambridge, Mass.: Ballinger Publishing Company, 1974.

McLaughlin, Milbrey Wallin, *Evaluation and Reform: The Elementary and Secondary Education Act of 1965, Title I.* Cambridge, Mass.: Ballinger Publishing Company, 1975.

Pincus, John (Ed.) *School Finance in Transition: The Courts and Educational Reform.* Cambridge, Mass.: Ballinger Publishing Company, 1974.

Timpane, Michael, (Ed.) *The Federal Interest in Financing Schooling.* Cambridge, Mass.: Ballinger Publishing Company, 1978.

OTHER RAND BOOKS IN EDUCATION

Bruno, James E., (Ed.) *Emerging Issues in Education: Policy Implications for the Schools.* Lexington, Mass.: D.C. Heath and Company, 1972.

Coleman, James S. and Nancy L. Karweit. *Information Systems and Performance Measures in Schools.* Englewood Cliffs, New Jersey: Educational Technology Publications, 1972.

Haggart, Sue A. (Ed.) *Program Budgeting for School District Planning.* Englewood Cliffs, New Jersey: Educational Technology Publications, 1972.

Levien, Roger E. *The Emerging Technology: Instructional Uses of The Computer in Higher Education.* New York: McGraw-Hill Book Company, 1972.

LB
2825
.S9
1976

Date Due

APR 0 7 2010			